All Under
Heaven

To Peter

Merry Christmas 2003

Linda and Archie.

Frontispiece The Island Pagoda, 1873.

Photograph by John Thomson. Reproduced courtesy of the National Museum of Photography, Film & Television, Bradford.

RAYNE KRUGER

All Under Heaven

A COMPLETE HISTORY
OF CHINA

WILEY

Published in the UK in 2003 by John Wiley & Sons Ltd, The Atrium, Southern Gate,
Chichester, West Sussex PO19 8SQ, England
Telephone   (+44) 1243 779777

Email (for orders and customer service enquiries): cs-books@wiley.co.uk
Visit our Home Page on www.wileyeurope.com or www.wiley.com

Other Wiley Editorial Offices

John Wiley & Sons Inc., 111 River Street, Hoboken, NJ 07030, USA

Jossey-Bass, 989 Market Street, San Francisco, CA 94103-1741, USA

Wiley-VCH Verlag GmbH, Boschstr. 12, D-69469 Weinheim, Germany

John Wiley & Sons Australia Ltd, 33 Park Road, Milton, Queensland 4064, Australia

John Wiley & Sons (Asia) Pte Ltd, 2 Clementi Loop #02-01, Jin Xing Distripark, Singapore
129809

John Wiley & Sons Canada Ltd, 22 Worcester Road, Etobicoke, Ontario, Canada M9W 1LI

British Library Cataloguing in Publication Data

A catalogue record for this book is available from the British Library

ISBN 0-470-86533-4

Typeset in $10\frac{1}{2}/13\frac{1}{2}$pt Photina by Mathematical Composition Setters Ltd, Salisbury,
Wiltshire.
Printed and bound in Great Britain by T.J. International Ltd, Padstow, Cornwall.
This book is printed on acid-free paper responsibly manufactured from sustainable
forestry in which at least two trees are planted for each one used for paper production.

Contents

Rayne Kruger died on 21 December 2002 shortly after completing this work.

Preface

*T*his book has drawn on the work of a legion of Sinologists. While expressing my admiration and gratitude to each of them, I should perhaps single out Joseph Needham's *Science and Civilization in China* and *The Cambridge History of China*, both immense works into which the reader intent on further knowledge might profitably delve. Like a good Confucian spouse my wife, Prue Leith, has sustained me through the long, long march; I honour her and our daughter Li Da and son Daniel, to all of whom this book is dedicated.

I thank the eminent Oxford Sinologist Anthony Hyder for cleansing the MS of at least some inaccuracies, and would note only that I have used the old rather than new method of translating Chinese names throughout.

Rayne Kruger
Cotswolds,
July, 2001

Books by the same author

Novels
    Tanker
    Young Villain with Wings
    The Spectacle
    My Name is Celia
    The Even Keel
    Ferguson

History
    Goodbye Dolly Gray
    The Devil's Discus

About the author

*R*ayne Kruger was born in South Africa. He began his working life on a Johannesburg goldmine, then became a lawyer, and was a broadcaster and touring actor before migrating to England in 1947. He joined the Overseas Service of the BBC and left to write a number of well-received novels. He then turned to history (1959) and published *Goodbye Dolly Gray*, the story of the Boer War, which has remained in print these forty-odd years since. After a controversial book about the death of the last King of Thailand, he founded a successful property group, and partnered his wife, Prue Leith, in her catering group. While researching his Thailand book he could find no readily accessible history of China and so determined to write one – a task that off and on preoccupied him for over twenty years

CHAPTER ONE

Ape-men to the Shang
(700,000 – 1750 BC)

C hina is the size of a continent – marginally smaller than Europe and larger than the United States. The north is brown, being semi-arid with hot summers and cold winters that bring snow. The south is green, rainy, subtropical and though cold in winter seldom sees snow. Three great west-to-east river systems mark this division together with a central area: in the north, the Yellow River (which has dozens of times changed its course to the sea); in the centre, the Yangtze; and in the south, the Pearl (west).* Its scenery encompasses hill and mountain ranges, deserts and fertile sandy plains, forests and jungles and gorges and countless streams and lakes. In this land ancestral apes, ancestral humans, and modern man, with much evidence of continuity between them, have laid their bones for two million years. Indeed, finds in south China in 1983 have been claimed by some scientists to place our first ancestors there, not in Africa, about ten million years ago.

When it comes to recounting a history of China, two contradictory tendencies catch attention. On the one hand, no people have been more assiduous in recording their history than the Chinese, whose first accounts were set down in the final millennium BC and punctiliously updated in dynasty after

---

* In this narrative, the area northwards of just south of the Yellow River will generally be referred to as 'the north' and the area south of it as 'the south'.

dynasty. On the other hand, efforts to resurrect the remotest times have not been helped by a peasant tradition of using ground-up fossil-bones – called Dragon Bones – for curing any malady you can think of, dragons being considered beneficent. The practice did no harm, which, as a Scots scientist remarked, is more than can be said for many drugs in the British Pharmacopoeia; but it has meant the consignment of priceless information to the stomachs of the credulous.

Current theories have it that the earth emerged out of chaos 4,600 million years ago, that the diminutive shrew-like creatures from whom we descend were hunting insects in the trees sixty million years ago, and that ape and man diverged over ten million years ago. By such reckoning modern man who appeared perhaps over a hundred thousand years or so ago is mint-new.

Before the 1983 finds, ancestral apes were thought to have spread from Africa to Java and thence to China. They evolved into early but true humans, *Homo erectus*, who have left indications of their existence in south and north-central China from about 700,000 BC. There followed a steady evolutionary development into beings of whom the most famous representative is named Peking Man after his occupation of a cave near what became Peking (Beijing) – in fact about twenty-five miles westward of it in hills at a place called Chou-k'ou-tien. By his time – starting about 400,000 BC – mankind was becoming divided into its five basic racial groupings, of which one, the Mongoloids, are believed to have given Peking Man his genes.

His brain size of over 1,000 cubic centimetres approached modern man's 1,350, but he was not very prepossessing. Standing about five feet high, with a low, beetling brow and receding chin, no doubt bloodied and stinking, he had but a three in a hundred chance of reaching the age of fifty. He ate mostly deer, but also leopard, bear, sabre-toothed tiger, hyena, elephant, rhino, camel, water-buffalo, boar and horse; his diet included wild fruit and nuts; and he consumed the flesh, brains and marrow of his fellow humans whom he killed by blows to the skull. He cooked his food, for he was one of the world's first makers and users of fire; and he collected brightly coloured pebbles, perhaps for the pleasure of their sparkle in the light of his fire, suggesting a dawning aesthetic sensibility. He left a multitude of Old Stone Age tools.

In the course of his 200,000-year occupation of his cave – has any habitation ever provided a continuous home for so long? – he and his fellow cavemen elsewhere in China made significant evolutionary advances. These culminated, as his immediate successor, in modern man, *Homo sapiens* ('wise man' – perhaps done into Latin to fend off mockery). It is interesting that Neanderthal Man, the precursor of *Homo sapiens* in Europe, seemingly never appeared in China, suggesting that those scientists are right who believe he was in an evolutionary cul-de-sac and not on the road to modern man. Interesting also is the fact that Peking Man and his descendants carried the seeds not only of the Mongoloid sub-races to be called Chinese but of most Far Eastern races, of the Eskimos, and of the American Indians.

While the ascent of man in China first reached the *Homo sapiens* stage in a sprinkling of places in the north and south of the country, from about 50,000 BC people with diversified cultures were living all over it. Their most famous brethren left their remains, dated about 18,000 BC, in the same hills at Chou-k'ou-tien once occupied by Peking Man, but in a higher cave, hence called the Upper Cave.

They belonged to the worldwide culture of the Late Stone and Mesolithic Ages. It was a culture tirelessly inventive in consolidating the triumph of *Homo sapiens* in evolution's survival stakes. While the last Ice Age neared an end, men and women reached their full prowess as hunters and gatherers. Those in the Upper Cave preyed on tigers, leopards, boars and wolves in the nearby woods, deer and gazelle in the nearby steppes, and huge fish in nearby lakes. For these purposes they used not only stone but also bone, shell and wood to make shafted spears, harpoons with detachable heads, bows and arrows, and specialized tools with finely polished blades. They built temporary summer shelters away from their winter cave. They plied eye needles to hemstitch leather for clothes and containers. They perfected the felling axe; devised pick and adze, and, as big game diminished, made traps for smaller animals together with nets and hooks for fishing, which led them to chip out canoes and start adding the waters to their domain.

Theirs was probably a communal clan society with membership through the mother, since the status of father doubtless did not exist until the unobvious connection between copulation and pregnancy was realized. It has been deducted that they had totems, taboos, initiation and other rituals, respect for the dead, fear of spirits, belief in a Fertility or Mother Goddess and similar features still surviving among primitive people. Only late in the day did warfare seem to start: after all, the hunting grounds were large and the entire world population would not have crowded a modern city. People moved about in small groups, such as the one that left their relics in the Western Hills near Peking.

In the aftermath of the last Ice Age which ended in about 10,000 BC, the earth's climatic and geophysical conditions made possible man's first steps from survival towards civilization. By about 8000 BC people in the Tigris – Euphrates area of the Middle East had began to farm. They sowed the soil and domesticated animals. And they began to make pottery, from which later generations would derive immeasurable technological progress. Above all, these developments, producing surpluses and leisure, led to the building of towns and cities, for all that this would mean to science, commerce, the arts and politics.

In post-glacial China, which was warmer and more moist than today, the agricultural revolution occurred later. If an area to the north is considered, from about a hundred and fifty miles west of where the river Wei flows into the Yellow, to some hundreds of miles downstream of the latter, and a couple of hundred miles on either side, we are looking at the anteroom of Chinese civilization. Here, in the fertile plains and valleys, people who had achieved the final refinements of Stone Age tool-making developed a number of farming communities in the millennium before 5000 BC.

Unlike their fellows in the south who also made pottery but continued to live in caves, they built small houses, usually round but sometimes rectangular, six – nine feet in diameter with plastered floors usually sunk below ground level, and they had storage pits for their grain which they processed with pestles and mortars. They made spears, harpoons, arrows, hoes, chisels and sickles; their remains include bone net-knitting needles, hairpins, and turquoise ornaments. In kilns heated up to nine hundred degrees Celsius they wrought coarse pottery, mostly red or brown without much decoration, in the form of jars and bowls. They chiefly domesticated pigs and dogs, and also for their food – as well as for material and medicine – they could experiment with the cultivation of a variety of indigenous plants, which included two kinds of millet, artichokes, soybean, garlic, mallow, onion and cabbage, and also peaches, plums, apricots, persimmons and mulberries, not to mention cannabis. (In the south, the earth offered a different but as wide a range that included rice, taro, yam, red beans and spinach and also oranges, kumquats, loquats, lychees, olives – and tea.)

The first clear delineation of this farming culture by about 5000 BC comes to us through the discovery of what is called, after its village of origin hard by the Yellow River, the Yang-shao Culture. It was not exclusive to the middle Yellow River basin where the Wei and Fen rivers converge with the Yellow – for example, it arose also, with regional variations, quite extensively further west, to the north-east, along the coast, and up the Yangtze. In various phases it lasted for nearly two thousand years and basically shaped Chinese civilization.

Much hunting and fishing still went on, and the gathering of seeds from chestnut, hazelnut and pine trees in the then abundant woods. But essentially these were farming com-munities cultivating, like their forebears, millet (some of it processed into flour) in the north, rice in the south, and vegetables; and they kept mainly domesticated dogs and pigs but also cattle, sheep and goats. They raised silkworms, adumbrating the product which above all others would distinguish the Chinese. Their technique of crop cultivation was slash-and-burn, and they shifted their settlements from time to time to let harvested areas lie fallow.

These settlements were large, sixteen miles in extent. They could have as many as a hundred houses grouped round a centre, with a surrounding ditch beyond which were placed the cemetery on one side (for adults, laid out on their backs; children were buried in rows between the houses) and kilns for pottery-making on the other. Animal pens and storage pits were clustered in the middle. The houses had fire-hardened floors set below ground level, with wattle-and-daub walls and thatched roofs on wooden posts; all had a hearth. They were arranged in groups, with sometimes in front of each a larger house with internal partitions, and sometimes there was a central longhouse over sixty-five feet long and twenty-five feet wide. The organization of these settlements has suggested to experts the existence of a clan system that would persist into the fabric of the future state. Another foretaste was their pottery: made on a turntable, some of it was quite beautiful, with cord, mat and basketwork impressions or polished red and black designs, but most significant were incised symbols in which some authorities see the source of Chinese writing.

In the millennium following 4000 BC the Yang-shao Culture and its affiliates in various regions interacted with each other – a nation-building process had begun – and by the millennium-end a higher culture had been progressed to. Its most famous manifestation is called the Lungshan Culture, situated in a wide area of the middle Yellow River valley but also along the Yangtze River and down the coast. Houses now tended to be rectangular, sometimes raised on a platform, but the most distinguishing feature of the villages was the surrounding wall. The Chinese had begun making themselves the greatest wall-builders on earth. At one site, for example, the twenty-foot high thirty-foot wide wall enclosed a rectangle with sides about four hundred yards long: starting with a ditch over forty feet wide and five feet deep, the builders spread a layer of loess – the area's dry yellow earth borne by winds from the far northern deserts – and tamped it down; added another layer, tamped it down; and so on upwards, with each layer marginally narrower so that the wall gradually sloped inward for stability.

Such walls suggest a defensive purpose, just as the finds of quantities of arrows, spears and suchlike suggest periodic warfare: indeed at one site the remains have been found of people scalped or decapitated. More elaborate burials, often furnished with articles of use or adornment, suggest increasing religiosity, as does the manufacture of ritual vessels among the more advanced pottery, which was wheel-turned and hard-fired. (This hard-firing also accounts for the first objects of metal – copper alloys, even bronze.) Of interest also in the Lungshan Culture was the first use of scapulamancy, the birth of the oracle-bone practice whereby animals' shoulder blades were burned to produce cracks which could be divined as communications of the gods – gods malign and benign who, wherever else they may exist, have been lodged in the Chinese mind, or at least in the simpler minds, right up to the present day: not a clutch of gods as in ancient religions like the Greeks', nor a single god as in Christendom and Islam, but hordes.

The period, then, of China's history called the Yang-shao and Lungshan Cultures, that is, from about 5000 BC to 2000 BC, saw an important transformation: an increasing difference among the populace in wealth and political power, increasing ritual (and remember that ritual in conduct has been one of the most enduring characteristics of Chinese society), increasing violence in both internal and external relations, increasing movement of goods and ideas between the various centres, the beginning of metallurgy and, at the end of the period, the beginning of the art and glory of writing. We have reached Chinese civilization.

Writing took thousands of years to develop, from the first signs imprinted on 5000 BC pottery to true writing on bamboo and boards before about 2200 BC. That is the century when, tradition has it, the first dynasty was established. Experts now generally accept that this, called the Hsia, is a fact. Scores of little 'states' were in being and it is probable that the Hsia were the strongest and most advanced, with perhaps one of their capitals on the River Lo not far from its confluence with the Yellow River and in the same broad area of the Yang-shao and Lungshan Cultures. Here have been found the vestiges of two grand palaces, one almost square with sides of three hundred and fifty feet. Stone, shell and bone still provided the implements for agriculture, but also in use were bronze vessels and weapons, as well as a wide range of pottery and lacquer.

China was not of course alone in its accelerated progress between the third and second millennium BC. The period was also marked by the development of fully stable urban societies in pioneering Mesopotamia and the Levant, Anatolia, Iran and Central Asia, by the blooming of the Indus Valley, by the first pyramid-building as dynasties arose in Egypt, and by the arrival of the early Greeks in the Peloponnese. And here we may pause to look back on the outline these pages have presented: across untold millions of years ape-man in China evolved into man and then modern man, who from being a cave-dwelling hunter went on to participate in the three great developments that have shaped our world – first the practice of farming, begun in the Middle East before about 8000 BC and leading to the founding of villages and towns; next, the deployment of metallurgy, again first discovered in the Middle East where doubtless a potter, perhaps before the third millennium, observed the effect of the heat in his kiln on copper and other minerals; and third, recording and communicating by writing – perhaps started in the third millennium BC, by priests keeping tally of tributes in the temples of Sumer. The Chinese, particularly in their core area around where the Yellow River having flowed south down the eastern side of its great loop proceeded to the sea, echoed these developments with some distinctive features of their own, such as silk production. But were the developments indeed an echo of what happened in the West or were they spontaneous? The answer to this question, long the subject of fervent debate, lies in the further question of how could communication have occurred over so vast and forbidding a terrain – thousands of miles of huge mountain ranges and immense deserts?

As to farming, the cultivation of crops in the fertile loess terraces along the Yellow River could have been learnt from Nature herself who spreads seed and grows it; while penning-in amenable animals must have seemed an obvious surer provider than the chase. Writing had a long period of local gestation, not suggestive of any external influence. This leaves the issue of metallurgy. The smelting of copper ore has been dated beginning in China by the third millennium BC. The areas where it was first practised had ample ores of their own, and while the Egyptians took a thousand years to learn how to make bronze by using the copper they worked, the Chinese, because their ores were frequently mixed – tin often appeared even in copper – very early (about 2200 BC) stumbled on the copper – tin process to produce bronze as the fortuitous consequence of smelting.

At all events, by 2200 BC, shrouded in the mists of time, the first dynasty of paramount rulers emerged, the Hsia Dynasty, of which only myth and legend offered a glimpse long before archaeology afforded hesitant confirmation.

These myths and legends describe a rather different cosmic genesis from the one in the Bible or for that matter the one in these pages. Some remarkably adumbrate modern theory: from a Great Beginning of total emptiness came primal matter and vital forces, 'that which was clear and light' drifting upwards to become heaven while the earth solidified; 'then, without being created, things came into existence … but all became different, being divided into diverse species of fish, birds, beasts … and man was born out of non-being to assume form in being'. Another account, also eschewing the Western notion of a Creator, is more picturesque. In the beginning, it says, the universe was an egg. It split open and the upper half became the sky, the lower the earth, while from it emerged ancestral man. Upon his death 18,000 years later he split into parts: his head formed the sun and moon, his blood the rivers and seas, his hair the forests, his sweat the rain, his breath the wind, and finally his fleas became the ancestors of mankind. For 216,000 years twelve Emperors of Heaven ruled the universe. They were followed by three sovereigns with human heads and snake-like bodies. They gave way to a series of earthly emperors, of whom the last five were recognized by China's first historian writing in the century before Christ. The foremost was called Huang-ti, the Yellow Emperor, said to have ascended the throne in 2698 BC and to have had a notoriously ugly wife named Mo-mu: he is regarded as the founder-hero of China; and besides defeating encroaching barbarians and securing supremacy of 'the land within the passes' – the middle Yellow River below the surrounding hills and mountains – he introduced the institution of government, while his chief minister devised written signs.

The benevolent reign of the Yellow Emperor was a Golden Age when all men were pure of heart and they prospered amid increasing civilization. His successors, whose reigns were likewise marked by universal accord, initiated astronomical observation, the calendar, and flood control. Each of these rulers were chosen not by birth but merit. Thus it is told of one that seeking a successor he was advised of a humble bachelor named Shun: 'He is the son of a blind man. His father is stupid, his mother is deceitful, his half-brother is arrogant. Yet he has been able to live in harmony with them and be splendidly filial. He has controlled himself and not come to wickedness.' On the strength of this encomium the Emperor decided to give Shun two of his daughters in marriage and then observe his behaviour. The test was a success. 'Come you, Shun,' the Emperor said, 'in the affairs on which you have been consulted, I have examined your words. They have been accomplished and capable of yielding fine results for three years. Do you ascend the imperial throne.' Shun demurred because he thought his virtue inferior to the task but he finally accepted the Emperor's abdication.

Shun, known as Emperor Yü, it is who is credited with founding the Hsia Dynasty of seventeen kings, hence his regal title, Virtuous Founder of Dynasty. The last of his line, five hundred years later, was a very different man, being a cruel and wicked tyrant, labelled Degenerate Terminator of Destiny upon being justly overthrown to give way to the first dynasty that stands clear and certain in the full light of history – the Shang Dynasty, dating from about 1750 BC.

CHAPTER TWO

The Shang
(?1523 – ?1027 BC)

While we are about to follow the fortunes of the Shang, it should be noted that other, probably comparable, dynamic societies arose in different parts of China, and more will doubtless be disclosed by the onward march of archaeology. Strong differences existed among them all, but also an essential unity. It is, however, the well-documented Shang that we follow because they provide the golden thread by which historians trace Chinese civilization.

Breaking out from their tribal lands on the western outskirts of the Hsia, the Shang moved their capital about for a century or more until shortly before 1400 BC when their King, the able P'an Keng, selected a site for the Great City Shang. It was near modern Anyang, a little north of the Yellow River, midway between the eastward bend and the sea, and about four hundred miles south-west of today's Peking. The place P'an Ken chose was protected on three sides by a river, and on the fourth side he had a massive wall built with a double gate capped by a tower.

The acres of rich loess outside the city were irrigated and intensively cultivated for crops, the land being tilled by hand, the farmer using a forked spade. Cattle, sheep and goats grazed on pastureland; grain-fed dogs supplemented Shang diets, and both oxen and water-buffalo were kept as beasts of burden and cart-pullers.

Within the city walls, houses arose for the increasing multitude. Their superiors' rectangular dwellings were on projecting platforms made of beaten-down earth, so hard that the rains of three thousand years have not crumbled them; on these, inset from the edges, pared pillars from the wooded mountains seventeen miles away were placed, and light rafters set upon them to support matting which was plastered over to complete the gabled roofs. The pillars were carved and decorated, and rooms demarcated by screens. (The principle of a pillar-supported gable roof and raised rectangular terrace would be applied by the Greeks many centuries later.) For the less privileged and for storage the beehive structures of previous ages were made, sunk sometimes as deep as seven feet. Around the grander establishments were walls, creating courtyards, especially the grandest of all, the King's palace whose buildings were dispersed over sixteen acres: within, a wealth of interior embellishment with murals of red, white and black designs, fine carvings, and inlays of mother-of-pearl and of ivory from the tusks of wild boars.

Near the palace the artisan quarter shaped, carved, forged, turned and spun innumerable artefacts. In the teeming alleys stone-workers made marble bracelets, jade rings, figurines of creatures and men, and everyday articles like knives and dishes which carried echoes of the Stone Age. Workers in bone, including tortoiseshell, wrought objects ranging from elaborately carved ladles to hairpins with cock's-head shaped ends, often polished to a mirror sheen and precisely drilled. Metal-workers included goldsmiths; shell-workers turned out ornaments and toothed tools; there were workers in jade and lacquer. Textilers and furriers produced tailored garments with sleeves and buttons. They could call on the silk industry, observed thus by an ancient poet:

> With the spring days comes the warmth,
> And the oriole sings its song.
> Young women lift their baskets deep
> And go down the narrow paths,
> Searching for the tender leaves of the mulberry ...

In the silkworm month they strip the leaves off the mulberry,
Taking axe and hatchet
To those that are too high ...
In the seventh month the shrike is heard;
In the eighth month they begin spinning,
Making dark fabrics and yellow.

Though much of the work carried out in the artisan quarter was a matter of craft, like the carpenters' production of shafts for weapons and tools, boats, and chariots, much had the quality of art. Potters, for example, while turning out by hand or wheel grey or reddish-patterned utensils for cooking, eating and washing, also produced fine white unglazed porcelain-like articles for solemn rites or best, and numerous figurines and models ranging from the grotesque to the beautiful. Indeed some of the work ranked with that of the greatest art of the Shang's contemporary Minoan, Babylonian, Egyptian and Indus civilizations. This is true of, for example, their superb marble sculpture which was mostly black but sometimes white and more massive than anything achieved by their successors – whole oxen bigger than life, and dragons with horns a foot long, presented non-naturalistically and hence somewhat alien to Western eyes. But the Shang's greatest glory was their bronzes.

Although weapons, tools and ornaments were cast, scarcity of metal confined most articles to ritual vessels for religious ceremonial. The best of them, that eminent authority H. G. Creel has written,

> are almost undoubtedly the finest things of their sort in the world; in fact they are probably the most exquisite objects which men have ever created from metal, regardless of time or place.

Their distinguishing feature is their intricate maze of grooved lines, some of them a quarter of an inch in relief, to create patterns and formalize real and imaginary creatures, particularly what is called an ogre mask, *t'ao-t'ieh* – a kind of geometrically rendered animal's face divided in two, each side forming part of the outline of other animals, so that the ear, for example, might be a dragon's body which in turn forms part of a bird. Among the vessels were ceremonial drinking cups a foot high and three-legged containers, of which one for pouring libations was called chüeh, perhaps after a bird whose cry supposedly meant, *Temperance! Temperance! Enough! Enough!*

The Shang bronze workers invented bellows to bring the heat in their furnaces to the desired level for smelting copper (eighty-three per cent) and tin (seventeen per cent). First a mould was made of wax, which was then painted, layer upon layer to reproduce the tiniest tracery, with watery clay until thick enough to be baked strong, when the wax would melt and drain away. After the bronze poured over it had cooled, the clay was broken off, leaving the article ready for polishing and, often, painting-in of the grooves. Easy though it may sound, technically it has never been bettered, even with every twenty-first century aid.

One authority on Chinese art cared so little for bronzes that he would as soon, he said, decorate his home with an old stove. They are in fact for the Westerner an acquired taste. As Creel has written, 'Only gradually does one come to realise that these animals and designs which seem grotesque to us had a very definite meaning ... As one sees more and the designs become familiar, he begins to appreciate the surpassing skill.'

The costliness of bronze vessels made them a valuable form of capital when the method of exchange was mainly barter. Cowrie shells, threaded together in strings of ten, provided a rudimentary currency, but the mouth of the Yellow River, five hundred miles away, was the only source. Goods like grain and silk were therefore used but, while communities were still largely self-sufficient, trade had scarcely begun.

The best bronzes in the Great City Shang were buried with the dead, especially the royal dead. An enormous cemetery lay a mile to the north. Bodies were wrapped in matting, and what a man took with him to the afterlife depended on his importance: it might merely be an axe and a few pottery pieces, but for a King it could be a veritable treasure of marvellous white pottery, huge marble sculptures, bronze vessels two feet high, helmets by the hundred.

To accommodate everything for a royal burial the Shang dug out a pit that could have swallowed a modern five-storey block of thirty flats. Over most of the bottom, reached by a staircase down each side, they built a pavilion ten feet high with wonderfully carved and decorated walls. Into this went the corpse and its attendant riches – and also over a hundred corpses of the sacrificed royal wives and household staff. Layers of earth were then thrown down and pounded hard to fill the whole pit.

People were sacrificed for many religious services besides funerals, since most of the world then and later (the Greeks and Romans, for example) believed it pleased the gods. The Shang's victims were decapitated and their heads usually buried in groups of ten or multiples of ten – once, three hundred altogether – suggesting a nascent awareness of the decimal system. They were slaves or prisoners of war, often captured by expeditions sent out for the purpose.

The gods propitiated were the quintessential spirits of the mountains, of the streams, the winds, the clouds, lightning, heavenly bodies, and most importantly that giver of crops, the earth. They had nothing to do with morality, being neither good nor bad; to be placated they required nothing more than sacrifices. There was some belief in a supreme god who through the female earth-spirit procreated all plants and animals; others accorded him parity of rank with the other gods. Called Ti or Shang-ti, Lord-on-High, he was to endure through history and be mistaken by Westerners for an oriental version of their own God. If he started as the apotheosis of the Shang's ancestral King he provides a bridge between the Nature gods and their peers, the spirits of the dead. While Chinese philosophers and artists, no less than the peasantry, have never ceased their dialogue with Nature, believing that harmony between them is the key to universal wellbeing, the practice of ancestor worship has endured to this century. Of it Sir Leonard Woolley has written, 'The simple Shang belief that men lived after death and became sources of guidance and protection for their descendants and proper objects of worship satisfied a natural craving in man and did more than anything else to form the ideal of Chinese civilization.'

The emergence of Ti and Jehova at the opposite ends of Asia was coincidental. At about the time of the earliest Shang Kings, Abraham and his family were wandering the wilderness where the writ of the Moon God and other deities of their native Sumerian religion did not run because there were no temples to worship them in. Abraham was therefore confined to the worship of the one god who went everywhere a Sumerian went, namely his family god. Thus the family god of Abraham, of Isaac, and of Jacob evolved in importance to the omnipotent Jehova. While he was not an ancestral god as perhaps Ti was, and achieved an awesome status Ti did not, the link between family and deity is a curious link also between East and West.

The Shang believed that a man's breath was his spirit (Latin *spiritus* = breath) which rose heavenward when he died and then, possessed of nameless powers, could make or mar family fortunes. If it was the King's spirit the whole nation's welfare was involved. If a spirit was not succoured by sacrifices it wandered hungry in a miserable limbo for ever: to avoid this terrible fate and ensure his own familial wellbeing a man had both to maintain sacrifices and try to beget children who would in due course do likewise for him. Family loyalties and reverence for the family elders has in consequence of ancestor-worship been a major factor in Chinese lives.

The need to offer sacrificial food to the spirits was logical, since, although a man's spirit parted from his body at death, it was still essentially him, as the living knew from seeing him in their dreams. The spirit took the essence of the food which could thus remain for consumption by the worshipper – a practical arrangement not too distant from Christian communion. For the spirits of kings the sustenance offered could be massive – three hundred cattle and a hundred sheep, for example – and besides food the sacrifice could be of valuable objects, like jade, and chariots, and even a troop of horses complete with fine bridles. There was frequent pouring of libations, making the crops for beer-manufacture highly important.

Shang beliefs and practice in relation to sacrifices varied widely. Priests or shamans might officiate, or the family head, while in the Great City Shang the King himself might address the gods in the ancestral temple which was a lofty, ninety-foot-long building constructed with the help of elephant labour. The task was not for the ignorant. To begin with you had to be literate: you wrote your message out and burnt it so that the words could be borne heavenward. If you were addressing an ancestral spirit you respectfully avoided naming him, referring instead to his relationship with you and the week-day of his death: Grandfather Tuesday, Great-aunt Friday. You might be seeking advice about the sacrifice required, or expressing gratitude, or asking questions that ranged from the trivial ('Will next week be lucky?' – the answer determining your proposed activities) to grave matters of military strategy.

The answer was obtained by the method of bone divination used by earlier people. Pieces of bone, particularly the foot-long carapaces of a breed of tortoise peculiar to the Shang, were polished to a mirror sheen after the creature had been solemnly smeared with the blood of an ox and sacrificed, and then an oval depression about an inch long was gouged out and a heated point held to the underside: this caused a pattern of cracks for oracular interpretation. Often the original question was scratched on for record purposes before the bone was filed away – archives that would astonish posterity: Western scholars doubted whether Shang civilization ever existed outside of legend, until nineteenth century AD farmers began ploughing up these oracle bones.

The fact that the exact date might be vital for an oracular prognostication was one of the reasons for the need of a calendar. The Hsia may have had one; the Shang certainly did, and very accurate. From astronomical observation they calculated the lunar month to be 29.5305106 days long (the modern astronomer says 29.530585) and the year 265.25 days.

The year started in the spring (but the first month was moved about to mark the start of a new reign), and consisted of twelve months each of twenty-nine or thirty days; seven months were tagged on across a cycle of nineteen years to take up the additional days of the year, which disturbed the Shang no more than we are by leap years and by calling the ninth to twelfth months by names that mean respectively seventh to tenth. The reconciling of the lunar and solar years has ever been a nice problem, and the fact is that the Shang's solution preceded the Greeks by a thousand years. In short, the Shang calendar was framed with a scientific accuracy which, says Woolley, 'neither Babylon nor Egypt could rival'.

Their writing calls for a brief explanation. In Mesopotamia where writing was first invented the Sumerian language consisted basically of one-syllable words. The pictures of two or more of them could be joined to make a different and if necessary abstract word, as say 'claptrap' if the drawing of hands applauding were added to a drawing of a trap. Homonyms followed the rebus to depict monosyllabic words that could not themselves be drawn – for example, drawings of a yew tree and an animal paw for 'you pour'. By further and increasingly subtle means the Sumerians, highly stylizing their pictures in cuneiform writing, developed a complete system. In the fullness of time and by constant abbreviation this evolved through the Phoenicians in the last millennium BC into the alphabetical system with whose gift the writer in English has potentially limitless power of expression through the deployment of a mere twenty-six letters.

The Chinese, also with a monosyllabic language and also beginning with pictures, followed much the same course but never arrived at an alphabet. Instead of composing their words by a selection from twenty-six characters, they depict every word by its own character. Hence modern Chinese has over 70,000 characters, of which 7,500 are in daily use, grown from 2,500 used by the Shang.

The latter's use of them may be illustrated by the sentence, quoted by Creel, 'The servant saw birds coming from the eastern woods collect above the house.' 'Servant' was depicted by an oriental eye on end, this being an abbreviation for 'head', since captives were described as so-many head, and captives often became slaves and then servants; 'saw' was drawn as a man dominated by an eye looking to the left; a variety of grain whose name sounded like 'come' followed; the drawing of a bird (the plural being plain from the sense) was clear enough; for 'from' the drawing of a nose is thought to have been derived from the Chinese habit of pointing to their nose when alluding to themselves; a circle designated as the sun by a line for the horizon through it and rising behind a tree conveyed 'east'; two trees complete with roots conveyed 'woods'; for 'collect' a bird perched on a tree was a simplification for a number of birds coming together; 'above' was illustrated by a short line above a longer, just as a short line below a longer meant 'below'; and finally the outline of a house completed the sentence. Perhaps the most sexist use of drawings was that of a pair of women to mean 'quarrel'.

In the course of time, simple pictograms like these became immensely stylized, so that the beautiful flowing Chinese script bears but vestigial remains of its origins; although derived from drawing, calligraphy has always been an art allied to painting. The brush developed as the writing instrument, possibly on silk, certainly on strips of wood or bamboo which, for a book, were strung together like a miniature picket fence. No Shang literature has survived except, apart from the oracle bones, in echoes caught by the poetry of the next dynasty. As for the writers, we have only a clue in the aristocracy's archery contests for which, to keep the score by dropping bamboo tallies into a bowl, the most intelligent servants were appointed, and it is they who were perhaps the first oracle bone diviners and then scribes – progenitors of that unique class, the scholars, of whom more later.

These archery contests provided both recreation – followed by heavy convivial drinking – and the martial education essential for the Kingdom's survival. The bow was the most powerful weapon in the Chinese armoury and remained so for all the centuries until guns arrived. Gracefully shaped like Cupid's, and known to us as the reflex or Tartar's bow, it had a pull of one hundred and sixty pounds, discharging bamboo-shaped feathered arrows with a violence greater than that of the English long-bow nearly three thousand years later.

Similarly, hunting, which still provided the Shang with a large part of their food, was essentially an opportunity for military manoeuvres. In these the chariots were the most spectacular arm (as they were in the Middle East from about 1600 BC). They had two spoked wheels, at first pulled by two matched horses harnessed to a pole, later four. The bronze work on car and harness was superb. The crew consisted of a driver, an archer, and a spearman carrying an eighteen-foot lance, so that when the chariots were drawn up in a row the enemy confronted a thicket of pikes. They may be imagined in action under the sun: the flashing metalwork, the red knee-covers and gold-coloured slippers of the charioteers, the bowmen with thimbles and armlets as they fired in unison while the drums sounded at the command of the aristocrats wearing plumed bronze helmets extending over the napes of their necks.

Besides bows and spears the army used sling-shot, and for in-fighting a battle-axe and a dagger with its blade at right-angles to the handle. In the average expeditionary force of about five thousand, most of the troops were infantry, drawn from the peasantry who downed tools for the occasion. There was also an element of slaves but the Shang were unusual in the ancient world in not on the whole being slave-owning.

The whole tenor of their society suggests indeed a strong moral code and social enlightenment. For example, women were respected: they were not made to work the fields but brought their men food there; departed queens as well as kings were sacrificed to; kings rarely had more than one or two wives; and servants led tolerable lives, often holding positions of increasing trust and being sent as emissaries to other tribes, since the King could not always rely on relatives whom family taboo prevented him punishing.

These trusted servants were gradually to evolve into ministers; but government was still a fairly uncomplicated business, its vital purpose being to maintain the integrity of the Kingdom. The King achieved this by a system of aristocratic fiefdoms. In the capital knights were enfeoffed; outside, barons; further away, counts; on the borders, marquises, each entrusted with administration of his area and service to the King. While the Turkic-Mongol horsemen of the steppes far to the north had begun the raids that would affright China for ages to come, for the moment their threat was distant and instead they were a fruitful source of ideas – they may have introduced the chariot, and horse-breeding, and shamanistic magic together with star-worship. But everywhere across the vast subcontinent pressures of ambition and economic necessity were producing regional powers or city-states at various stages of development, posing a constant threat to the Shang.

The King's assertion of direct control was restricted to the short distance his chariots could travel without attenuated lines of communication or natural barriers. Therefore he relied much on vassal chieftains bound by solemn treaties entered into by each party wiping his lips with the blood of a sacrificial animal, with whose corpse a copy of the treaty was buried to invoke the spirits' wrath upon him who broke it. Besides, the Shang's outstanding civilization and military strength meant that their King's ancestral spirits gave his nation a menacing superiority. He also deployed diplomacy, like making lavish gifts (fine bronzes, strings of cowries, lacquered bows) to successful commanders and loyal vassals, and arranging expedient marriages. The mustering of an army derived from the 'well-field' system.

This was the system of land allocation. In the broad plains of northern China the fiefdoms were square in shape, their boundaries marked by piled earth and trees. Within them square areas of land were divided into 'wells' of nine sections, each perhaps upwards of twenty acres and worked by a family except for the ninth which was communally worked for the benefit of the local lord. For administration, four wells constituted a 'town', four towns a 'ch'iu', four ch'ius a county, and four counties a district. Every ch'iu and county had to provide the sovereign with a certain number of chariots, horses, cattle and armed men. (Weights and measures were similarly based on units of four. Thus there were sixteen ounces to a catty or 1.3 English pounds, which holds to this day, although decimal counting followed in the next dynasty.)

The Shang line was carried from brother to brother or to a son when no brother remained. Of the reign of the thirtieth King, starting shortly after 1100 BC, tradition paints a picture that was more vivid than true but which was believed for countless generations. It depicts a powerful man with keen eyes and acute hearing, clever and eloquent but cruel and lustful. Once, charged by an older relative with governing badly, he retorted, 'Men say you're a sage. It's said that a sage has seven openings to his heart. Let me see for myself.' Thereupon the man was killed and his heart torn out for the King's inspection. Tradition also has him indulging the vicious propensities of the second of his two wives; at her whim naked youths and girls chased each other in orgiastic display in a wine-filled pool and among trees hung with viands.

At this time there lived in the basin of the Wei River a tribal chief his people called the Accomplished King. The tribe was the Chou,* a name that was to be conjured with alongside that of their contemporaries, the Greeks, who were busy gutting the Aegean civilization, and whose first barbarous appearance gave, like the Chou's, no hint of the intellectual explosion to follow.

Where now wheatfields mark the site, the Chou capital stood near the modern city of Sian, three hundred miles across rivers and mountains from the Great City Shang. By force the tribe had established leadership over all other tribes in the Wei Valley. The

---

*The spelling of proper names adopted by most Sinologists for a century and more before 1968 was subjected to a new Official Standardization in that year. The present work follows the old system.

23

Accomplished King, son of a Shang princess whom his father had been given to secure his vassaldom, extended the conquests and at last set his sights on the distant palaces and riches of the Shang themselves. Undaunted by the distance, the obstacles, and the fact of a mighty Shang army, he planned his campaign. He died before he could undertake it, leaving his son, Wu, to do so. Called by his people the Martial King, Wu spent nine years preparing his army and forming a federation of tribes sworn to his cause. His first move across the Yellow River was checked, but two years later, in about 1050 BC, he struck when the Shang King's strength was sapped by insurrection to the east. Tradition speaks of the Martial King's 50,000 men being pitted against 700,000 Shang, which is less likely than the solid fact that a single day's decisive battle broke the Shang.

Their King fled the field: in his palace he put on his most sumptuous clothes, decked himself with jewels, then entering his favourite pavilion set it alight. As he died in the flames his two wives hanged themselves. When Wu arrived he shot three arrows into the charred corpse and cut off the heads of the three dead to display them on his banner.

The rude chiefs who had helped him bring their adventure to this breathless pass were all for gorging themselves on loot and returning to their fastnesses. But the Martial King silenced them. There would, he declared, be universal obedience to his rule, from 'the corners of the sea and the sunrising'.

CHAPTER THREE

The Western Chou
(?1027 – 771 BC)

A s the end of the second millennium BC approached, two thousand years of the epochal Bronze Age had laid the foundations of mankind's civilization. It had built its monuments – the cities of the Tigris – Euphrates, Nile, Indus and Yellow Rivers. It had brought the Minoan, Phoenician, Babylonian and Hittite states into being, and Moses out of Egypt; raised up the Assyrian host; prepared the Aegean shores whence classical Greece would spring; and generally confronted the Indo-European people, mysteriously erupting into the Middle East and Europe, with the opportunities of the impending Iron Age.

Upon the conquest of the Shang the Chou period was to last eight hundred years but only for the first three hundred did the Chou kings have, first, real and, then, diminishing authority: the former phase is named the Early or Western Chou, which now calls for description.

As the Chou forces moved due eastward and north- and south-eastward, they occupied both virgin soil and conquered hunting-fields as well as farmland. At first, ownership was tribal, but this gave way to individual ownership by the emergent class of aristocrats who were the King's relatives, allied leaders, and local chiefs, including such of the Shang who surrendered quickly enough. As the new State became ever bigger than the old, soon embracing almost all north-east China from beyond the Yangtze River to the deserts, with roads few and poor, the countryside hostile, and the distant Chou capital lacking administrative machinery able to govern so extensive a territory, a more thorough-going feudal system than that of the Shang developed, akin to what was to prevail in medieval Europe more than ten centuries hence. The newly occupied and conquered lands were enfeoffed to the aristocrats who gave fealty to the King, rendering service and revenue to him.

He invested them, and appointed officials to senior positions, at impressive ceremonies. First, he took his seat facing south in the central hall of his ancestral temple; then the investee, ushered in by the Minister of Sacrifices, stood facing him. The King declared his intention to invest, told the investee what was expected of him in the exercise of his ownership and administration, announced what gifts were to be given him, and instructed the Historiographer to confer the order, which the Historiographer did by handing out the document containing the order of investment. The investee thanked and praised the King, made obeisance twice – that is, knocked his head on the ground – and withdrew. The gifts he received varied with rank, ranging from millet wine for the lowest – ninth – to bronze vessels, slaves, horses, chariots, weapons, jade objects, cattle, red shoes, cloth and shell. The more important recipients often had bronze vessels made with an inscription to commemorate the event, and those that survived have become a valuable source-material for historians. Feudal lords also received a jade sceptre – shorter than the royal sceptre – which they had to have in hand whenever they met the King.

In moulding the new state the influence of one man would place him among the giants of Chinese history. When the Martial King died, soon after the conquest, his minor son succeeded to a turbulent inheritance – incomplete, unconsolidated and liable to disintegrate. At this moment the Martial King's brother, the Duke of Chou, made himself Regent, and by the force of his character and intellect as much as by ruthless military prowess and skilful persuasion, he imposed the King's peace and authority.

At the outset he had to put down a Shang rebellion fuelled by his own brother who suspected him of excessive ambition. Mustering the reluctant Chou leaders he fought for three years to destroy Shang power for ever. Then he removed the flower of their nobility and artisans to south of the Yellow River. There he set them to work on a new city which was more central than the existing Chou capital in their distant homeland. Approval of the site by the gods was obtained by divination, and when the ground had been marked out these gods were ceremonially sacrificed to. (Animals were the victims. Human sacrifice was countenanced less and less.)

The religion of the Shang was but little changed by the Chou, except that the latter had acquired from the nomads north of them notions of star-worship that made Heaven the supreme god; and this belief was grafted on to the Shang's belief in Ti as the supreme god, making Ti and Heaven synonymous, and having an earthly delegate, namely, the King, who hence came to be called the Son of Heaven. The concept of 'Heaven' was as extra-ordinarily nebulous as the West's Almighty was to be. It was at the same time a *place* – home, for example, of the ancestral spirits in which the Chou also believed – a cosmic moral *force* directed at maintaining the harmony of the spheres and of Nature, and a *being* with intelligence and will impartially guiding the destinies of men. In true feudal style Heaven enfeoffed a hierarchy of subordinate Nature gods, of which the God of the Earth and the God of Grains were the most important and not neglected in the sacrifices.

Then the Duke of Chou convened at the site of the city-to-be a mighty assembly of Chou leaders and the unfortunate Shang. He enunciated a doctrine that for thousands of years would dominate Chinese political thought. It was that the King's appointment was by the 'Mandate of Heaven'. This mandate was achieved because of the virtue of the appointed person: let him not rule virtuously and the mandate would be withdrawn.

Though arms might be seen as the instrument of overthrow, what underlay it was the withdrawal of the Mandate of Heaven. Therefore, he said, 'may the King now urgently pay careful attention to his virtue. Look at his ancient predecessors, the Lords of Hsia: Heaven indulged them and cherished and protected them, but they came to lose their mandate.' Likewise, he said, 'there are many former wise Shang Kings in Heaven, but in the end good men lived in misery.' Consequently, 'August Heaven, the Lord-on-High, has changed his principal son and the great state Shang's mandate.'

In asserting his royal nephew's lineage from the ancient Hsia Dynasty the Duke thus sought to validate the new house's legitimacy, and in citing the will of Heaven as having caused the Shang's decline he diplomatically gave them a face-saver. (He also, incidentally, permitted their royal line to continue nominally so that essential ancestral sacrifices could be maintained. But in reaction to alleged Shang decadence he introduced liquor prohibition, with draconian penalties for any breach.) He concluded by declaring the purpose of the new city to be at the hub of the Chou Kingdom and urged the King, having made the great city, 'he shall from here be a counterpart to August Heaven. He shall carefully sacrifice to the upper and lower spirits, and from here centrally govern.'

At this place, called Loyang (north of Lo', a tributary of the Yellow River; about ten miles from the modern city of that name), a great city did indeed arise. The inner walls enclosed an area of nine square miles, the outer about ten times that area. Within were palaces, pleasure gardens, hunting parks, the treasury, granaries, a shrine for the God of Earth and another for the God of Grains, houses of ministers and officials, hostels for visiting envoys, all surrounded by the people's houses, artisans' quarters, and markets close to the city gates, the outer of which had moats and ponds beyond them spanned by movable bridges. Both the inner and outer gates, constantly guarded, could be raised or lowered and were always lowered at night, throughout which guards beat the watches through the city. Duties had to be paid on merchandise passing through them – payment being in goods or cowries or bronze-shells.

When the young Son of Heaven came of age, the Duke of Chou confirmed his adherence to principle by gracefully giving up power. However, his royal nephew abjured his advice to rule from Loyang and in ill-omened practice rarely went there.

The Chou absorbed the culture of the vanquished, adopting its laws, its clothing, its language, its morals, and also its crafts, although the Chou bronzes, despite being made mainly by Shang artisans, were strangely inferior to their predecessors. As noted, the Chou also adopted Shang religious beliefs, though importing the idea of Heaven, as well as the magic-practice of shamanism and the building of tumuli above tombs. Shang-ti, the Lord-on-High, or Heaven, had little contact with people's lives and was sacrificed to only by the King. More relevant to the individual were the Gods of Earth and of Grains at whose shrines sacrificial ceremonies were periodically carried out – as, for example, for the God of Earth at the annual grand spring festival, when colourful robes were worn, music was played, and elaborate ritual was observed. The King and aristocracy had, besides, ancestral temples – a 'great temple' which was dedicated to all ancestors, and a 'special temple' which was dedicated to one particular ancestor and was destroyed after a number of generations. For all the people there were gods of the sun, moon, and stars who controlled snow, frost, wind and rain; and gods of mountains and streams who directed floods, drought and plagues. Ceremonies involving one or other of these gods were held as occasion required – sickness, before and after battle, flood, fire, the eclipse of the sun, and so forth. Sacrifices were of animals, silk and jade, all usually destroyed in the process. At the royal court four groups of officials dealt with religious affairs, headed respectively by the Grand Officer of Prayer, the Grand Officer of Ceremonies, the Grand Diviner and the Grand Historiographer.

The society that developed in the early centuries of the Chou dynasty had the King at its apex. His state was divided up into dukedoms, each virtually a state within the state, with its walled capital and subordinate fiefdoms owned by noble houses whose incumbents were called *ta-fu*. Ducal and noble houses appointed managing Fief Administrators; other ministerial appointments were an officer of Prayers, a Historiographer, a Director of Commerce and a Minister of War, while the Household Manager was akin to a prime minister, given on his appointment an estate he had to relinquish when he left office.

For the aristocracy the most important things in life were sacrificial ceremonies and warfare. The specialist in war, called *shih* – later the term for a scholar – was carefully trained. Sons of the King, of feudal lords and *ta-fu* were taught archery, charioteering, the use of shields and spears, dancing, music, ritual, and poems learnt to music. Like the knight of medieval Europe, the ideal warrior was supposed to be not only skilled in arms but loyal, to regard honour above safety and duty above life, and to be undaunted by adversity. Before he took command of a chariot in preparation for battle, his driver was appointed by divination. Often if the warrior were killed in action eulogies would be composed to laud him.

The nobility became known as the Hundred Names, since only they had proper names. Beneath were the great mass of people – the 'black haired ones'. The majority of them were serfs who worked the land – parcelled out in areas measured by the flight of an arrow – paid tribute, served in the army when required, and provided such labour as their lord demanded of them. They were not likely to ignore such demands since he had powers of life and death over them and could buy, sell, mortgage or donate them. Some, however, could become independent farmers, which was the only respect that they differed from the class beneath them, slaves. These were prisoners of war or convicts, and a feudal household could own as many as ten thousand of them producing food, clothing, salt, chariots, weapons, and musical and ritual implements for their masters. All a slave's family were slaves, and the status was inherited. Manumission was rare.

For serf or slave, existence could be hard. A peasant's life is thus described in a folk-poem: month 1, gets agricultural implements; 2, begins ploughing and his wife takes his meals to the field where he works under the superintendence of a foreman, while his daughter goes along the paths between the fields with a basket to gather mulberry leaves for feeding silkworms. Warfare presumably occupies much of the ensuing five months because the poem continues at month 8 when the harvesting is begun while the daughter reels off silk which is dyed black, yellow or red for her lord's clothing; 10, rice is cropped and wine made, and, the harvest completed, the peasants go to the lord's house to make thatch and rope; thanksgiving ceremonies and convivial parties are held, lambs are cooked, and all go to the lord to present wine and shout, 'Long life!'; 11, fox-hunting to provide the lord's fur; and in month 12 there is military training, and the peasants present fattened pigs to their lord and chop and store ice for him. This hard life could be made worse if a lord's conduct were callous, and it indeed often was, with consequent revolts, of which there were many as the sixth century BC advanced.

By then Chou history had entered a new phase. For what had happened as the years progressed was that the dukedoms had increasingly evolved into fully-fledged states of their own. The barons waxed fat on the settled conditions, became absorbed in local problems, and could call up strong loyal armies, and the comradeship forged in the fires of conquest receded into the past. In short, they became ever more independent of the King, to whom in their rendering of military service and revenue they grew increasingly reluctant.

In this situation, when individual ambition could readily be inflamed to internecine dispute, all depended on the abilities of the King to maintain the unity of the Kingdom and defend it against external attack. But the hereditary system is a lottery of the womb, and while good, strong and able kings checked the slide to disintegration, the bad, weak and foolish ones hastened it. And here the wisdom of the great Duke of Chou could be appreciated, for by continuing to rule from their original western capital instead of Loyang they were out of touch with their barons and too close to the hostile barbarian tribes that pressed down on them from the north.

These people were nomads. They pressed upon the Chou homeland in the Wei Valley from the mountainous surrounds, but essentially they were part of that complex of races associated with the steppes. Little in the whole panoply of history so fascinates the mind, or so confuses it, as the story of the Central Asian nomads. Under various names, mostly Huns and Mongols, having opted out of the confining if civilizing influence of the settled way of life offered by the onset of farming, they travelled wherever the need for grazing their herds took them. They learnt a complete mastery of horsemanship, and the flying hooves of their ponies seemed to loose a wildness of spirit that drove them ruthlessly onwards. For untold centuries, even to modern times, their hordes periodically raised their savage banners from the shores of the Pacific to the towns of Hungary; they threatened Rome; under Attila their thrust to the Baltic was what probably drove the English tribe to migrate to the island which for a large part bears their name. Certain of them – confederations of clans, riding fast with the joy of slaughter and loot their only aim – have left in the names of their Khans, like Genghis and Tamerlane, bitter memories; and across their mighty theatre of mountains, plains, inland seas, forest margins, oases and deserts, where the extremes of neither heat nor cold could repress their terrifying energies, the names of great states which they made and unmade are not less familiar than cities like Bokhara and golden Samarkand which came to stand at the rough divide of the eastern and western elements of their world. But generally it was a world so lacking definition, its peoples so constantly changing their groupings and leadership, and much of their origins and activity so obscure, that detailed knowledge requires very devout scholarship indeed.

Here, for the present, it is enough to note that the mountain shepherds and steppe nomads beginning to disturb the Chou

Kingdom were Huns – of Mongolian, Turkic and Tibetan stock – ethnically related to the Chinese which many of them would in fact become and with whom their discourse in terms of war, culture and trade is to a degree maintained to the present day. Lured by easy booty, or finding their pastures occupied by Chou settlements from which they had then to get winter feed at often extortionate rates, they made constant raids. These should have been no more than the buzzing of flies around the head of the Chou giant, but for the King to mount punitive expeditions depended on his barons' support; and this as we have observed was a waning resource, especially after about 878 BC when a man called Li ascended the throne.

His greed and cruelty aroused criticism, which he dealt with by ordering a shaman to point out the leading critics, whom he then murdered. Many barons protested by not making their periodic visits to court for government business and paying fealty. The incensed Li so increased his oppressive measures that he ignited a revolt that drove him into exile in 841 BC.

His heir the Crown Prince took refuge in the chief minister's house. A mob surrounded it, demanding the Prince. The feudal code of chivalry made this impossible for the chief minister so he gave his own son (who happily escaped). The government continued under a regency during what is called the General Harmony era.

When Li died fourteen years later the Crown Prince succeeded. Popular belief attached prophetic significance to what boys sang and one day he heard some of them singing

A basketry quiver and wild mulberry bow
Will for sure mean the end of Chou.

On hearing that at that moment a man and woman were selling those very articles in the city, Li was so alarmed that he ordered the arrest and execution of the two vendors, who, however, contrived to get away. As they fled they heard the cries of a baby girl abandoned at the roadside and paused to rescue her.

A most strange legend was to grow about her origins. It was said that the wicked King Li had opened a coffer kept secure since the Hsia Dynasty when a cloth had been put in it after being spat upon by two royal ghosts who had appeared before the reigning monarch in the guise of dragons. Upon Li's opening the coffer, the spittle flowed from the cloth and turned into a small reptile. A little girl chanced upon it in the harem and on reaching puberty she became pregnant, subsequently abandoning the baby rescued by the fleeing street vendors.

The legend served the purpose of explaining the malign influence of the woman the baby grew into. She became the favourite concubine of a successor to Li, King Yu, and dominated him with her capricious will. To amuse her he caused the beacons to be lit that signalled invasion, and it indeed made her laugh to see the barons arrive pell-mell with their armies on a wild-goose chase. The gratified Yu kept repeating the trick until the barons took no notice of the beacons. When he conferred honours on her that properly belonged to his wife, the Queen, the latter's outraged father formed an alliance that included some of the barbarian tribes and in 771 BC attacked Yu's western capital. Too late the barons discovered that this time the flaring beacons were for real, and all that a group of them – led by the Duke of the small neighbouring fiefdom of Ch'in – could do was to rescue a royal prince from the doomed city.

They made their way with all haste eastwards while the barbarians were in full cry across most of the Chou's western dominions. Reaching Loyang safely the loyal barons installed the royal prince as King; and ruling at last from the capital the great Duke of Chou had intended, he ushered in the period called Eastern Chou, better known in its first phase as the era of Spring and Autumn.

CHAPTER FOUR

The Eastern Chou (771–476 BC) – I

For the royal house it was wholly autumn, if not winter. Its temporal authority almost gone, its only real function was religious, since to procure the gods' beneficence for the nation nobody but the Son of Heaven could perform the necessary sacrifices and ceremonies – such, for instance, as the symbolic act of ploughing and its accompanying rites at the year's beginning to insure against crop failure. While he exercised the office of supreme pontiff his barons contended among themselves for political and economic power.

As they did so, they did not stop short of incest, sexual abduction, corruption and every kind of depravity. They intrigued, sprang murderous plots, bribed, betrayed and waged war to reduce weaker neighbours to vassalage and extend their lands northward, westward, and southward across the Yangtze, in the process creating almost sovereign states within the state.

Technically the state had no meaning, since the King had the Mandate of Heaven to rule all the earth under it. For the Chou what defined their kingdom was their civilization: people who did not fully embrace it were barbarians. Even that once small fiefdom of Ch'in – whose ruler had led the rescue of the royal line and which had subsequently gone on to reconquer the invaded lands – did not rise above the description of semi-barbarous. The only civilized principalities – so-called states – in the midst of the Spring and Autumn period were those in the basin of the Yellow River where the cultures and dynasties of the past had taken root in the rich loess. Collectively they were called Chung-kuo, the Middle Kingdom. (Later, China itself tended to be called this, unsurprisingly of a country that regarded itself as the centre of the universe – All Under Heaven – and the sole repository of civilization; and so the Chinese name their land to this day.)

There were about eleven states in the Middle Kingdom and about fourteen outside it; but of these twenty-five nearly half were dependencies of their more powerful neighbours in endless paroxysms of ambition. It was an activity often interrupted by the need for unity in the face of barbarian invasion. Without an authoritative King, someone strong enough had to lead. Hence, from about 685 BC, a series of 'Dictators' arose. Entitled Hegemon to preserve the fiction of subordination to the King, each was the most powerful baron of his time, not only directing military campaigns but arbitrating between his peers, forming alliances to check excessive aggression, receiving revenues previously paid to the King, and exercising power almost as absolute as his had been. By such means was a semblance of State cohesion preserved for most of the Spring and Autumn period.

Despite all its immorality and turbulence it was a period of great progress. For one thing, the Age of Iron had arrived – true, six or more centuries after its inception in the Hittite realm, but thereupon the Chinese far outstripped the West in iron technology. The iron-masters of the Middle East were few and jealous of their secret – the introduction of charcoal to carbonize the molten iron ore – and this may explain the tardy communication of the discovery eastwards; but more mystifying is how the Chinese, having perfected in their pottery-making powerful bellows that enabled them to achieve the temperatures needed to produce cast iron, as distinct from the West's wrought iron, and then going on to make steel, kept their knowledge to themselves until the Bessemer process was reinvented in England two thousand years later. Not only could the West solely make wrought iron, but even that was in quantities of less than thirty pounds a time, against Chinese cast-iron in half-ton lots. Wrought iron can only be laboriously hammered into sheets, while the Chinese metal could be cast: cheap and plentiful, it was used to make cooking pots and pans, weaponry, farm equipment, harnesses for horses and cattle. It was also turned into plough-shares, for the plough had now arrived.

The spread of iron technology among the states conduced to their independent economies. The richest was the state of Ch'i which, besides its revenue from the iron ore shipped from the south, supplied most of the east of the country with salt, obtained by evaporating sea water and ordained by the duke to be a state monopoly. Differences in wealth between the states were matched by many others which the traveller would have encountered: local dialects, varying weights and measures, and even the widths of the roads. But even more might he have been struck by the essential unity of this civilization, because it stemmed always from its past and like a tree never cut down or withered but with only a branch lopped off here or there grew ever stronger.

At its root was filial piety, nourished by ancestor-worship. Society and religion, man and god, came together in the family unit, made by sacrifice and ritual an unending estate of the living and the dead. That unit usually comprised several generations living in the same household over which the older parents, first the man then his widow, wielded absolute power, and they received in return unquestioning devotion:

O my father who begat me!
O my mother who nourished me!
You indulged me; you fed me;
You held me up; you supported me;
You looked after me; you never left me;
Out and in you bore me in your arms;
If I could return your kindness
It would be like that of Heaven, illimitable.

One had to be ready to die for one's brother and to avenge him if he were harmed. Among the aristocracy this could result, while the power struggle raged between and often within the states, in the wiping out of all the relatives of a murdered man, even if he had been executed for treason, lest the relatives tried to exact revenge; but among all classes punishment for a crime was often visited on the wrongdoer's family to underline the doctrine of collective familial responsibility. A family's goods were likewise held in common, although the head of it could dispose of anything much as he pleased, and instead of following normal procedure by appointing his principal wife's eldest son as his heir he might choose someone else, including even the son of a favourite concubine.

This possibility offered a concubine, who was usually but her master's plaything recruited from the servants, one of the few ways to higher honours and privileges within the family. Well above her ranked the principal wife and then there were the secondary wives of her master's class whom she could thus seldom aspire to join. The great increase in concubinage and polygamy reflected both the swelling wealth of the Chou and their attitude of male dominance compared with the more matriarchally inclined Shang. A well-off household would have a veritable harem, leading to its custodians emerging as a new class, the eunuchs, who were to play an extraordinary role in Chinese history.

The status of women differed little from serfdom, from which they could liberate themselves only by great sex-appeal, character, or age, or else guile and wickedness – of which one of many examples was that of a woman who framed the heir to her husband the duke on a charge of intending to poison him, thus discrediting the accused man so that her own son could succeed. The fact is that women's status made inevitable the intrigues that blighted dynasties right down the ages. And inevitably men, having mainly themselves to blame, expostulated: in the words of a poet,

Disorder does not come down from Heaven –
It is produced by women.

Moralists delighted in tales of the catastrophes brought down on prominent men by their women, like those who ended the Hsia and Shang dynasties. Of a man executed as the result of his wife's betrayal of a secret they commented: 'He told his wife; indeed he deserved to die.'

The inferior status of women is well illustrated by some verses written about a King which could broadly be applied to the upper, if not most, ranks of society:

Sons shall be born to him –
They will be put to sleep on couches;
They will be clothed in robes;
They will have sceptres to play with;
Their cry will be loud.
Daughters shall be born to him –
They will be put to sleep on the ground;
They will be clothed with wrappers;
They will have tiles to play with;
It will be theirs to do neither wrong nor good.

From her childhood she was prepared for her expected destiny of marriage. Helping about the house, she learnt weaving, dressmaking and cookery. And she participated in the uniquely Chinese feminine activity of silk-culture. Tradition holds that the idea of making silk cloth occurred to the chief concubine of the Legendary Yellow Emperor as she watched a silkworm spin its thread. Certainly the industry was very old, pre-dating the Shang, and it was becoming increasingly important for clothing the upper classes and its use in barter or tribute. While gold has long spread its glitter over the West, in China silk became the stuff of avarice and poetry. The West would not even set eyes on the material until late in the last millennium BC, and not learn how to manufacture it for many centuries after that, making this one of the best kept technological secrets in history, jealously guarded by the Chinese who executed anyone trying to smuggle a silkworm out of the country. But for our young woman it was quite matter of fact. She knew that for the silk to be unwound in the necessary continuous thread from the cocoon spun by the caterpillar, the chrysalis that would otherwise rupture the cocoon to emerge as a moth had to be killed; she knew that the caterpillar had to be fed an unvarying diet of mulberry leaves; and much else besides, which doubtless she thought less about than learning to read and write, which too were among her domestic pursuits.

She could hope for marriage when she reached about seventeen. It would be arranged between her parents and those of the prospective husband, usually a youth of about twenty and possessed – if we are talking of the upper class which alone had surnames – of a different surname. There must, however, have been occasions such as visits to the temples or at picnics in the spring when her heart might have led her into the anguishes and pleasures of secret assignations.

> Oh, you with the blue collar,
> Always and ever I long for you.
> Even though I do not come to you,
> You might surely come?
>
> Here by the wall-gate
> I pace to and fro.
> One day when I do not see you
> Is like three months.

Like all the verse quoted in this chapter, these lines come from the *Book of Odes* (or Poetry – *Shih-ching*), one of the great bequests of antiquity to the world's literature. It has about three hundred poems, lyrical and liturgical (for singing or reciting at ceremonies), of unknown authorship, since much of it belonged to folklore. It was collected in the period we have reached, about 600 BC, and forms part of the Classics which became the most potent force in Chinese civilization for thousands of years, and to which we shall return.

Among its many love songs, and by way of contrast with the reticence of the young man with the blue collar, it reveals the impetuosity of a certain Mr Chung:

> I pray you, Mr Chung,
> Do not come leaping into my garden;
> Do not break my sandal trees.
> Do I care for them?
> But I dread the talk of people.
> You, Mr Chung, are to be loved,
> But the talk of people
> Is also to be feared.

How much to be feared is clear from the judgement which has a familiar ring:

> Ah! thou, young lady,
> Seek no licentious pleasure with a gentleman.
> When a man indulges in such pleasures,
> Something may still be said for him;
> When a lady does so,
> Nothing can be said to her.

This is from a long poem put in the mouth of a woman who eloped in defiance of her family and the world. The years brought disillusionment:

> I was to grow old with you –
> Old, you give me cause for sad repining ...
> In the pleasant time of my girlhood, with
>   my hair simply gathered in a knot,
> Harmoniously we talked and laughed.
> Clearly we were sworn to good faith,
> And I did not think that faith would be broken.
> I did not think that faith would be broken –
> And now, it is ended.

But what of her for whom no Mr Chung leapt the garden wall or who tempted her into elopement?

> Dropping are the fruits from the plum tree:
> There are only seven-tenths of them left.

For the gentleman who seeks one
Now is the fortunate time!

If happily the time did prove to be fortunate, tradition prescribed that there should be brought to her father at his ancestral temple a wild goose sent by her suitor's father to symbolize a proposal of marriage. If father agreed, the spirits were divined for their views and, if favourable, for appointing the time. On the auspicious day the bridegroom set out in his carriage for the bride's home. She waited with her duenna and perhaps her younger sister or other relatives to fill the role of secondary wives – a King might have nine such adherents from noble families. After the exchange of ceremonial greetings, the woman climbed into the bride's carriage whose driving seat was occupied by the bridegroom while he drove for three revolutions of its wheels, whereupon he returned to his own carriage and, followed by that of the bride, journeyed home. Here they all ceremoniously feasted and then the couple retired to the nuptial chamber. This did not conclude the matter, for next day the bride had to provide her parents-in-law with a ceremonial meal and afterwards partake of one provided by them, and even if she acquitted herself without disaster she was still on three months' probation, during which she might be sent away as unsatisfactory. If all went well she was accepted as truly wed, presented to her husband's ancestors, and henceforward participated in the family sacrifices and ritual. Her husband's family was now as much hers as if she had been born into it, and she owed her in-laws the complete obedience of their own children.

She had, however, preserves of her own, especially if she were the principal wife with sometimes even the power of life and death over her servants. True, she had to be retiring if visitors called, even staying behind a screen if her husband were a lord receiving important people; but they often brought her gifts as tokens of respect. And her status was secure so long as she was obedient to her in-laws, fertile and faithful, and did not steal or talk too much ('A woman with a long tongue', says the *Book of Odes*, 'is a stepping stone to disorder'). A breach of these rules risked divorce – her husband simply sent her packing. But he could not do that if she had no parental home to go to, or if she had proved her piety by wearing mourning during three years for one of her in-laws, or if he had been poor when they married and had since become rich. For her part she was tied to him for life, and a widow's remarriage was frowned upon.

Her chief purpose was to produce male children who would in due course maintain the ancestral sacrifices. Nevertheless, whether one of her sons became the heir depended largely on her hold on her husband: he might trust her completely, constantly seek her advice, even leave her in charge of a whole state during his absence on campaign, but she was born to the risk at the heart of the heart:

> You feast with your new wife.
> And think me not worth being with ...
> You disdain my virtues –
> A pedlar's wares that do not sell ...
> You do not think of former days,
> And are only angry with me.

If she were actually maltreated her only recourse was her parental family. An anecdote describes a young man who married, he told a friend, for the sole purpose of getting up in the world; he so ill-used his wife that she complained to her brother, who promptly strung the husband up on the branch of a tree, and the friend passing by scorned his pleas for release, saying, 'You said you wanted to get up in the world, and now you have.'

But, however a woman fared for most of her life, all came right with old age. The elderly of either sex enjoyed universal privilege and reverence, and if her husband predeceased her the change in status from her former inferiority was even greater, for she acquired an awesome authority. The old women of China have exercised an influence, if not a tyranny, rarely matched in the

West. The consequence could be grievous but also absurd, as the Swedish scientist Anderson found early in the twentieth century when he was on the trail of Peking Man: he was stopped from digging out a fossil deposit by an old woman who, outraged at the threatened disturbance of ancient spirits, sat on the hole and refused to budge and the public's hostility to anyone trying to disregard an old woman's will compelled Anderson to quit the scene. An illustrative case at a loftier social level is recorded of the Spring and Autumn period itself. A senior official gave a dinner at which he served a very small turtle, whereupon the chief guest declared, 'Gentlemen, let us wait for this turtle to grow up before we eat it,' and stalked out. So angered was the host's mother by her son's parsimony that she drove him from his own house and only let him back five days later when the highest woman in the state, the duke's wife, interceded.

The primary factor in the kind of life any woman led – her standard of dress, comfort, education, influence on affairs at large – was the class to which she belonged. The Chou of the Spring and Autumn period continued the class structure of the Eastern Chou. At the bottom were slaves, though probably fewer of them than elsewhere in the ancient world, and next the peasantry, the great mass of people who manned the armies and whose forced labour provided the food and the physical props for their states – irrigation-works, roads (many tree-lined), temples, buildings of every kind and considerable walls along frontiers.

These serfs were tied to their feudal lords and if the latter over-taxed or oppressed them they could only rebel at the risk of almost certain death, or run away to wherever rumour spoke of better conditions:

> Big rat, big rat,
> Do not eat my millet!
> Three years I have served you,
> But you will not care for me.
> I am going to leave you

And go to that happy land,
Happy land, happy land,
Where I will find my place.

They had no education and were intensely superstitious. Their chief release from toil were the great seasonal festivals when religious solemnity could give way to bacchanalian rites in which the countryside's youths and maidens met. Closer to them than, as a rule, to their superiors, were the benign and malign spirits in all the elemental forces of Nature, in the seasons, in the earth and sky, at every crossroad, in all the dominant features of the landscape like mountains and rivers (the Yellow River's spirit had particular influence on warfare: the supplicant hoping for victory threw into the water whatever of his valued possessions were asked of him in his dreams). To a greater extent than their superiors the peasantry took to shamanism, a kind of Nature-worship practised in northern Eurasia from ancient times. Its chief practitioner, the shaman, was given to trances, claims of prophecy and exorcism, frenzied dancing, weird dressing-up, and rain-making. Little regarded by the upper classes who condemned his intimacy with the spirits as an impropriety like fawning on one's betters, he only very occasionally reached any prominence in government, but he – or she, since shamanism provided women with a rare opportunity for a professional career – enjoyed great respect among the masses.

Above the peasants was a miscellaneous class including domestic servants, sailors, miners, even robbers, and artisans; also pedlars, many of whom were now progressing into merchants who, while having to wear distinguishing clothes and holding no rank, could wax rich on trade, particularly in textiles and food. An expanding network of roads and rest-houses built for officials and envoys facilitated the merchant's travel all over China, an opportunity not missed to gather commercial, political and military intelligence for his state. At the state's frontiers he paid tariffs: over-supply had debased the cowrie currency and replaced it with copper or other metal. There was a unit of weight, about half a pound, but by 600 BC the idea of coinage, just taking on in the Near East, was still a century away.

The predominant class remained the aristocracy. Directly or through patronage they carried Chinese civilization forward, so to them we must now turn.

CHAPTER FIVE

The Eastern Chou
(771–476 BC) – II

*T*he aristocracy at the top of the Chou's fundamentally two-class society was itself stratified. The King stood over all, but more in name than fact, and indeed many dukes were openly calling themselves king of their state. The Chou Kingdom had thus become a centralized state in name only, unlike its massive contemporary Persian (Achaemenid) empire in which the satraps of the constituent provinces and countries were directly responsible to the capital.

Beneath the Chou dukes were three senior grades – marquis, count and baron. Among the remaining six grades was a lesser nobility of knights, ministers and, increasingly, scholars. Importance was determined by land-owning. The duke's state was divided and subdivided into estates held by the descending grades, each as fief of his superior to whom tribute and service were rendered, and the holder of an estate wielded absolute power over its occupants.

They had little protection from the law, which was of the sketchiest kind. Until this century the Chinese, like the British, never had a written constitution; but unlike the British, and indeed like the Chou's contemporary Assyrians, Persians and Israelites, who were all voluminous written lawgivers, the Chou set store mainly by custom, unwritten precedent, and man's sense of justice. When in 536 BC a minister of one of the states drafted a criminal code, another official protested heatedly that kings of old relied on their example of righteousness, on moral instruction, and on appointing virtuous administrators; and while they might have decreed punishments 'to awe people from excess', they did not attempt precise statutes because 'when people know what the exact laws are they do not stand in awe of their superiors. And they come to have a contentious spirit, and make their appeal to verbal technicalities.'

What laws did exist mainly concerned military discipline and crime. The former were against looting, for example, or breaking ranks for personal pursuits, and a charioteer might forfeit his life for so much as driving out of line; while the criminal laws visited dire punishment on the guilty – from death (by a variety of means including boiling) to fines, and in between could be branding, castration, and the cutting-off of nose, ears, toes, or feet. But all this was for the masses and very much at the discretion of the accused's master. Among the aristocracy no writ of law ran at all, although if a wrongdoer's superior were sufficiently strong he might exact punishments that included execution, confiscation of possessions, and reduction to commoner status.

In civil litigation, which could only be between equals since no one had any rights against a superior, and in criminal cases the law seems wholly to have been the presiding person's interpretation of custom. Many offences were dealt with within the family or clan, and all jurisdiction was so local that the magistracy usually knew the parties intimately and was sensitive to the feelings of the community. Warming though it may be to contemplate a legal system that was without lawyers or that put justice before law, it was not without corruption (the gift of a beautiful girl, for example) and placed the unprivileged at the mercy of the privileged. Thus a duke receiving bad news which he did not want spread by the seven people with him, cut their throats; another, a collector of swords, tested them on his subjects; another posted himself in a tower to shoot up passers-by for the fun of it; another tried out suspect food on his servant; and another killed his cook whose meal displeased him. All this was done with impunity; but that it was recorded suggests that such aristocratic behaviour was not the norm.

In truth, the Chou aristocrat had much to recommend him. Usually born to silk he could, however, rise on merit. So long as political unrest, military activity or personal ambition did not beset him, he embraced the riches of life with a cultivated mind. He could read, write, aptly quote poetry illumined for him by his appreciation of Nature's beauty, dress well in robes of silk or fur, adorn his pleasure parks with pretty pavilions, and display polished manners. He observed the highly elaborate etiquette enjoined by certain texts which were later put together under the title, *The Ritual*, minutely detailing the rules of behaviour by the different grades of aristocracy. These included the ceremony of donning the cap that marked an aristocrat's coming of age; social and diplomatic visits; major or minor archery contests; and marriages, mourning, burial, sacrifice, and endlessly so on. Behind such rules lay a profound concept of patterns that governed the inner harmony of the individual, of society, and indeed the whole Natural Order of the universe.

This did not inhibit a zest for pleasure. He loved sport: pitch-post, which was the game of tossing arrows into a pot, is thought by some scholars to have been the forerunner of games like dice, cards and chess (though the Egyptians were playing a form of draughts before 3000 BC), hunting and charioteering; and cock-fighting. But most enthusiastically the Chou perpetuated their predecessors' archery contests. The only formal schools in existence were archery schools. Contests were held at every opportunity, the participants shooting in teams so that no individual could lose face by personal defeat – indeed a very superior aristocrat might find his miss recorded as a hit. Much feasting and drinking was done in the process, and music was played – if an archer did not shoot in time to it he had his shot disallowed.

Music indeed, whether for purpose of ceremony or pleasure, occupied a prominent part in an aristocrat's life. Most probably he played an instrument himself, such as the classical 'lute', a kind of zither. He either maintained or could summon professional musicians. They were usually blind, held official rank, and enjoyed great respect. At every sort of function they were in attendance as quartets who also sang, or in groups of reed-organists, or as whole orchestras which played chiming stones (suspended pairs of L-shaped stones), wind and silk-stringed instruments, large and small drums, and bells. The latter – developed, perhaps, from the rounded grain-scoop – were hung in a row in a frame, and being made with the utmost truth of tone were used to tune all the other pieces. A remarkably advanced twelve-note scale had been evolved. None of the music played has survived but many of the lyrics are preserved in the *Book of Odes*. One such depicts a fairly lowly musical fellow in the person of the court jester:

> Easy and casual! Easy and casual!
> I'm ready to perform ten thousand dances ...
> With my large figure
> I dance in the ducal courtyard ...
> In my left hand I grasp a flute;
> In my right hand I hold a pheasant's feather.
> I'm red as if I were rouged.
> The Duke rewards me with a cup of liquor.

A great many cups of liquor had long since drowned the death-threatening prohibition decreed by the great Duke of Chou during the Chou conquest. Wassailing lubricated companionship.

> And shall a man
> Not seek to have his friends?

asked the poet. At informal meetings or formal banquets, at sport or prayer, liquor was seldom absent. Often it was only fruit juice or low-alcoholic grain-juice, but a heady millet beer could sometimes have deplorable consequences.

> When the guests first approach the mats,
> They take their places on left and right
>   in an orderly manner ...

All harmonious are they and reverent.
Before they have drunk too much
Their deportment is carefully observant of
　proportion;
But when they have drunk too much …
They shout and they brawl;
They disorder the dishes;
They keep dancing in a fantastic manner.
Being drunk
They become insensible of their errors.
With their caps on one side and like to
　fall off,
They keep dancing and will not stop.
If when they'd drunk to the full they went out,
Both they and their host would be happy;
But remaining after they are drunk
Is what is called doing injury to virtue.
Drinking is a good institution
Only when there is good deportment in it.

They were considerable and discriminating eaters. A duke's chef ranked as an important state official and the development of his art is reflected in the distinctive place Chinese cooking holds among the world's cuisines. Apart from particular delicacies like bears' paws, the dishes comprising a dinner menu in the year 600 BC might have been composed from the following:

Soup	– beef, mutton, pork or vegetable.
Fish	– sturgeon, bream, carp or mudfish; or turtle.
Meat	– boiled or sliced mutton or beef; minced beef; roast pork with gravy and mustard; dog; tripe and cheek; plain or spiced dry meats; deer- elk- or snail-stew; or hare.
Birds	– pheasant or quail.
Vegetables	– celery, mustard, bamboo sprouts, duckweed, pondweed, taro or beans; or fern (two types).

They were fond of pickling – snails, mallows, leeks, leek-flowers, rush roots, melon – and salting, and they were liberal with relishes and sauces. For dessert they could choose from peaches, plums, tomatoes, wild grapes, oranges, melons and Chinese dates (fruit of the jujube tree). A surprising fact about Chinese diet is that, despite not only keeping milk-producing animals from times immemorial but also having close contact with milk-drinking people, they never until the advent of ice-cream in the twentieth century consumed dairy products, to which they are constitutionally allergic.

At every meal, food and drink were offered in sacrifice to the spirits. This was not equivalent to the West's grace-saying, since the pious were not expressing thanks but keeping their ancestors well-fed. As time passed and a spirit became accustomed to his condition he needed a smaller amount, but always, not only at meals but on every occasion of any moment, respect and filial devotion were essential because of the formidable powers of the spirits of the dead. They could take possession of individuals, appear as ghosts or in various disguises, influence events to reward or punish their descendants; and if by lack of sacrifices doomed to hungry wandering, they might vent their misery in acts of arbitrary vindictiveness. Being possessed of such powers they were a strong deterrent against evildoing or plotting rebellion, since this might bring death on the culprit's family as well as himself and thus deprive his own spirit of sacrifices. Ancestral spirits could also, however, be useful allies; their mere reputation could make an ambitious duke think twice about attacking a neighbour weak in arms but strong in ancestry. The tiny eastern state of Lu, for example, is said to have survived among the far stronger surrounding principalities because its founding ancestral spirit was that of the great Duke of Chou.

At home, religious observances were in the charge of the head of the family. In a temple, this was the responsibility of the senior aristocrat of the area, since it was the temple of his ancestors. In the highest temple, to the King's and hence the nation's ancestors, the King himself officiated. The officials and servants who assisted were the nearest approach the Chou had to a priesthood, for they looked after the fabric, were versed in ritual, and composed prayers.

Praying seems to have been less a matter of routine than need. The most frequent prayer besought the boon of old age – because of the pre-eminent place the aged held in the family and society. A rich man might inscribe a special prayer on a bronze vessel whose costliness the most froward spirit could scarcely disregard, but usually the Shang method sufficed, of burning a letter for the smoke to carry the message aloft. There seems to have been some ambiguity by now about where the spirits lived. Heaven, where they had been supposed to reside, was increasingly thought of as Shang-ti – Lord-on-High – the primary force keeping the universe in harmony, while the spirits had their abode in a place beneath the earth called the Yellow Springs.

If a reply were sought from the spirit, the art of divining was needed. Even the essential prerequisite of a sacrifice could not be made without the spirit's approval of the proposed article or animal being first obtained. Some contemporary Western civilizations such as the Etruscans, from whom the Romans were to learn, used animal entrails, but the Chou followed the Shang's employment of bone, particularly tortoiseshell. They varied this method with others, of which the most important involved the milfoil plant. For generations a work called the *Book of Changes* (*I-ching*) detailed arrangements of differing lengths of milfoil stalks from which the initiated could interpret the will of the spirits and foretell the future. No one now understands this book, the oldest in Chinese literature; it seems merely a cabalistic manual for sorcerers. Yet for ages it was to evoke profound and subtle commentaries by great thinkers. One must remember that until only a few centuries ago gobbledegook and science were indivisible. Pythagoras could be helping to lay the foundations of Western science while proclaiming the mystical qualities of beans.

The principal place outside the house for the invocation of spirits was the ancestral temple where their names were inscribed on wooden tablets, before each of which a mat and armrest were kept ready. The ancestral temple was the most important place in every community, and those of the dukes and the King the most important in the states and the Kingdom respectively. In these temples business with gods and men came equally. There were transacted the highest affairs of government, including the nomination of an heir, the promulgation of decrees, appointment to office, taking title to conquered territory, making diplomatic exchanges, even the holding of official banquets; and thence armies marched on campaign, carrying some of the wooden tablets that they would return with in victory or defeat. Thus scarcely anything of moment was done without involving the spirits. From reverence for them evolved the minutiae of temple ritual which was reflected in the elaborate ceremonial of the aristocratic class.

The subject of ritual reaches to the core of Chinese civilization, and in so far as sanctions to procure ethical or moral behaviour are concerned, marks it off from any other. The sanctions applied by the West have been a mixture of religion, law and public opinion, but religion came late as a sanction because at first it only obliged people to perform the prescribed rites, for only these and not virtue had anything to do with propitiating the gods – hardly surprising if morality is considered as simply defining how people can best live together in society. The change to the belief that the gods required more than mere religious observances lay perhaps in their personification as perceived by so many civilizations, from the Etruscan, Persian, Assyrian, Hebrew, Phoenician and Egyptian to Greek: they were perceived, mystically and transcendentally, as men or man writ large. With this process of personification went incidental beliefs – that, for example, the riddle of the Beginning is explained by the creation of the universe by a god who begat himself; that the god has a moral code (thus the Hebrew prophets were insisting that Jehova was supremely a just god but the Greek gods were quite immoral); that according to an individual's compliance with this code is he rewarded or punished; and that the purpose of life is to serve the god. From that assumption of a superfather concerned with his children's behaviour flowed the sanction of divine retribution. The idea might never have taken root, when all too often wickedness appears to prosper, but for the remarkable further idea of immortality which comforted the individual with the prospect of getting his just desserts in the next world if not in this. The great Hebrew Prophets, contemporaries of the Eastern Chou, were only now urging this belief as they sought to shift the emphasis from ritual to ethics. Nevertheless, ritual has ever retained its primacy as an expression of religious faith, demanding a whole class of professional priests to supervise it.

The educated China of 600 BC held with little of this. The immortality it believed in lacked paradisaical reward or hellish punishment – suffering, yes, but only if sacrifices were not maintained. Ti, the supreme deity, was no cosmic manufacturer, no lord chief justice, no author of moral codes, and the only concern with virtue was that it was the prerequisite of divinely appointed kingship – virtue not as supposedly defined by the word of a god but as understood by every man. Though the Nature spirits, so rampant among the peasantry, were vaguely personified – no doubt by analogy with the ancestral spirits – Chinese thought was increasingly turning to *forces*, which were not the regimented good and evil demons lately depicted to the Persians by Zoroaster, but more like that of, say, gravity or magnetism. These operated according to their particular character, not to divine statutes (to which we still defer by misnaming scientific hypotheses 'laws'), and the supreme primordial force kept the universe together by maintaining order, a pattern not fixed but constantly changing and evolving as the diverse forces interacted to produce a harmony or balance in and between all things; the universe was a whole and its harmony the harmony of its parts, and man among his fellows was as much of its parts as the sun in the sky.

Morality, then, simply belonged to the natural order. Good behaviour was consistent with the harmonizing of human society in tune with the heavenly spheres; bad behaviour was a dissonance and counter to the general wellbeing. A vague inclination to give morality a religious sanction may be thought of in the Chinese passion for precedent, which made any deviation from an ancestor's conduct or opinions dangerously likely to be construed as disrespect, but the efforts of some thinkers to urge that virtue in itself pleased one's ancestors made little progress. If, however, religious belief's sole expression was in ritual, the latter never became as prolix as, say, Indian brahminism, or needed a professional priest class to conduct it.

Instead the Chou civilization bred a related but quite different class of men. They were the products of a time which, when the first simple era of military occupation had given way to the internal complexities of far-flung government and the external intricacies of power struggles, required that rulers lean more and more on learned men for administration and advice. These men were heirs to a tradition begun largely by servants and slaves of the Shang, and carried on by the descendants of their masters – for the humbled former aristocracy were among the teachers of the Chou ardently embracing the conquered civilization. Thus emerged a highly educated class to provide an unrivalled civil service and superb thinkers and artists. These men who were the font and conduit of Chinese intellectual attainment are known as the Scholars.

Although he was usually born into the upper classes, a scholar might with exceptional ability and luck rise to it through his learning. What he believed essential to an informed mind was an education neither technical nor vocational but in the humanities. A typical curriculum, proposed for the schooling of a duke's heir shortly before 600 BC, comprised history, poetry, music, literature, state documents, ceremonial and etiquette; and the values to be derived from these and applied in every office from chief minister to household tutor were integrity, loyalty, and concern for the common weal.

He it largely was who preserved or composed much of the monumental works called the 'Five Classics'. They are the earliest writings known since the Shang tortoiseshell inscriptions and are the ground-texts of Chinese culture. Their vast influence resembles that of the Bible in the West, woven into the very fabric of national being. There are no accounts of divine revelation, to which the Orient was not privy, but the resemblance applies to the variety of content, ranging through history, real and imaginary, songs and stories, and political, ethical and religious expression. And their authorship and authenticity have been as much puzzled and argued over.

Of the Five, reference has already been made to three – the *Book of Odes*, *The Ritual* and the *Book of Changes*. The other two are histories. The earliest, *Shu-ching*, is called the *Book of History* but also *Book of Documents* because it is a collection of state announcements, speeches (like the great Duke of Chou's address at the founding of Loyang), reports, and so forth, all probably reliable about the Western Chou but fanciful or mere propaganda about the preceding Shang and Hsia dynasties. The last classic is the *Spring and Autumn Annals* (*Ch'un-ch'iu*), somewhat later than the rest: although it is the chronicle of only one of the states, from 722 to 481 BC, its name is given to the whole of the period under review.

With these books was opened the gate to literature. Science too was much advanced, because even if the scholar hardly distinguished in kind between the divining milfoil stalk and the solstices and equinoxes, Chinese technological progress matched that of the other major contemporary civilizations. Doubtless it was an alliance of scholar and artisan that had wrought the achievements already touched on, like musical instrument-making and salt and iron manufacture, irrigation, and now the invention of the foot-rule. It was calibrated in ten inches, which indicates a predilection, apparent since 1400 BC in Shang times, for a decimal system, used earlier and more consistently than anywhere else we know of. Some such system is of course essential to the development of mathematics and of precise measurement techniques.

However, it is in his role of teacher and civil servant that the scholar most contributed to his country's civilization. His greatest weapon in counselling a ruler was to cite ancestral precedent, which could never be disregarded; and if he invented it in order to turn a ruler away from an unwise policy, this was not really departing from the scholar's dearly held integrity but reasoning from moral arguments which it was inconceivable had not guided esteemed ancestors. Sometimes he could find no diplomatic way of persisting in advice contrary to a strong-willed ruler's wishes, in which event he risked both his office and his life, but this did not deter him, for he was prepared to die as an act of devotion to his ruler. This loyalty was inseparable from his integrity and concern for the common weal: he saw that if a ruler were unjust, cruel, oppressive or dissolute, bad consequences could flow – rebellion, unsettled economy, the flight of refugees who could strengthen an ambitious rival state; besides, such behaviour was not only unbecoming in an educated man, and a prince at that, but an impiety to his ancestors.

During the unremitting power struggle of the Spring and Autumn era, amid the internal upheavals, cruelty, treachery and corruption, the scholar in his role of official played a part for good and ill, not least in his influence on the overlords who filled the vacuum left by the King's enfeeblement. Thus, Kuan Chung, first minister to the very first Hegemon, the Duke of the state of Ch'in, proved the efficacy of his kind when, perceiving how the King's pleas for resistance to the barbarian invasion went unheeded, he persuaded the Duke to give up land conquered from surrounding states, thereby making friends of them and freeing his armies with their cooperation to repulse the barbarians.

From this time in 679 BC for the next two centuries a succession of overlords prevailed to keep the country precariously together. None of the contending states pushed victory to the point of total conquest. But in 479 the dam waters burst, as the semi-barbarous state of Ch'u in the Yangtze valley completely overwhelmed a smaller neighbour and so began the two centuries-long, huge and bloody struggle called the period of the Warring States. It was for the mastery of all China – the body of China, that is, for its soul was to be won by a man who by a curious coincidence died obscurely in that very year of 479 BC. Destined to influence probably a greater proportion of mankind and for longer than any man who has ever lived, he was called K'ung Fu-tzu, Master K'ung, which the West has Latinized into Confucius.

CHAPTER SIX

From Confucius
to Empire - I

T he choice of BC/AD to distinguish the so-called ancient and
modern worlds has created the impression of a wall, in the
gloom beyond which only a shadowy kind of semi-man existed
until, in AD 1, he emerged fully fledged into the sunlight. It
denies him his essential continuity. One has only to read the
literature of the Greeks, the poetry or letters of the Egyptians,
say, or of the Assyrians, much less of the Chou, to be aware that
a man's a man for a' that. A Babylonian magicked into the
twenty-first century might well be staggered by the sight of an
aeroplane, a television or a computer, but put him through a
contemporary schooling and he would be quite capable of
understanding and using them. The complexities of our
emotions and the structure of our minds have probably not
changed since before the Stone Age; but if, in creating the
concept of ancient and modern, we have to select a dividing line
in human thought we could well look at the hundred years
between the mid-sixth and mid-fifth centuries BC. In 558 BC
Zoroaster began his prophetic work that would produce the
religion of Persia; in the succeeding decades the Deutero-Isaiah
Hebrew prophets were at work in exile in Babylon; in 520 the
traditional founder of Taoism, Lao-tzu, whose beliefs would be
in contrast to those of Confucius, died; so in 486 did Siddhartha
Gautama, founder of Buddhism; Confucius' death in 479
preceded by ten years the birth of Socrates, thirty-eight years

before Plato's. Thus, in such a brief period were conceived and cradled many of the metaphysical/ philosophical/religious and political ideas that, with Christianity and Islam arriving respectively a half-millennium and a millennium later, became the stuff of civilized mankind.

The second son of an unknown family, Confucius was born in about 551 BC into that petty aristocratic class to which minor knights, scholars and civil servants belonged, the *shih* – a stalwart class of gentry with often the blood but seldom the perquisites of nobility, given to public service and with values the modern world might call bourgeois. His birthplace was in the small town of Tsou, which has long disappeared, near modern Ch'ü-Fu in present Shantung province, but which was then the state of Lu, tiniest of all the principalities in the Chou Kingdom but with the immense cachet of having been founded by the immortal culture hero, the Duke of Chou, whose ideas were to be the predominant influence on those of Confucius.

The affairs of the state in which he grew up mirrored, in the corruption, treachery, and ruthless aristocratic power-seeking that prevailed in the Spring and Autumn period, those of the Kingdom, even though its provenance saved it from being gobbled up by its more powerful neighbours, who invaded only about once a decade. The prime cause of its sickness was the ambitious rivalry of three families descended from a duke who had ruled the state in the previous century. They were called Eldest, Third and Youngest (*Chi*). When Eldest was passed over for the succession to his father he tried to murder the heir but was prevented by Chi whose clan then predominated, although all three sons steadily usurped the ducal power; indeed, shortly before Confucius' birth the 'Three Families' relegated only ceremonial duties to the reigning duke, whose situation was therefore analogous to his King's.

Confucius must have received from his parents – for only in the great households did scholar-officials give part of their time to tutoring – an education in reading, writing, music and archery. When he was fifteen the Chi family extended its authority over a full half of the state, confining the other families to a quarter each and confirming ducal impotence, but he had scant hope of a position in any of their courts. It seems – for details of his life are largely matters of surmise – that at some stage he made his way closer to the centre of activity – if not the capital, then one of the fortified towns on which the Three Families were respectively based, where he found work as a clerk.

His first jobs were keeping store accounts and checking livestock quality. These were scarcely taxing but books fed his developing mind, hard though they were to come by when they were still in the form of bamboo strips laced together by horizontal cords, with many scattered in separate parts that would only later be consolidated. What he learnt of the lives and beliefs of past scholars, and of his state's highly principled founder, together with the indoctrination of his own *shih* class's values – these were influences of one kind. Another was the scepticism shared by an increasing number of intellectuals, about the practical efficacy of religion. A powerful ancestor palpably did not prevent great families falling into disgrace and poverty, however rich and pious their ritual sacrifices; nor did princely spirits avail a man weak in military strength; and solemn treaties made under the aegis of heavenly hosts were broken with impunity by the party with the stronger earthly army. This scepticism encouraged rational judgement on the conditions about him which were causing indignity and grief on every side; a sensitive and thoughtful young mind could not be indifferent to them. He seems to have known neither dire need nor personal violence which might have made him countenance extremes of action or revolt, which, with one late exception, he never did. Instead he developed both a passionate concern for the masses and a balanced view of how their welfare might be transformed. Above all perhaps his experience confronted him with the affront of privilege.

His inability to curry favour, intrigue, double-talk or smooth-talk could not have helped him in his career. That he was shy, even tongue-tied, can be deduced from his dislike of oratory: 'Stray far from clever talkers,' he was to say; 'language should be such as fully to convey one's meaning, but no more.' And if he was sensitive about his lowly origins he could not but be aware of his intellectual superiority over those whom mere birth had called to rank above him. But to his bosses he must have seemed stiff-necked, a bit of a pedant, and awkwardly censorious, which for a man lacking a suitable pedigree was not conducive to worldly success.

He married, and had at least one child, a son, of whom it is only known that Confucius considered him a disappointment; and his wife appears simply as a fact, immured in the silence of the ages. His home, then, is unlikely to have compensated for the unrewarding years but provided a spur to his scholarship. This he advanced in the context of his fellow-feeling for the toiling, deprived masses, not learning for learning's sake but as a man might study the plough, to till the ground. 'To study,' he once said, 'and when occasion arises to put what one has learnt into practice – is that not deeply satisfying?'

The greater part of his life lacked any such occasion or satisfaction but he endured it with an unquenchable optimism, a dry humour embarrassing to solemn commentators who came after him, and an intense capacity for friendship. About his thirtieth year there gathered about him a group of young men mostly of no better family and younger than he, which perhaps made him less shy and encouraged him to open up about the conclusions he had reached. For from this time we know something of the trend of his ideas. They were never to be systemized or even recorded in his own lifetime but have to be sought in the old literature – his purported sayings called the *Analects*, the book of Mencius, born in the next century, and a history of Lu in Confucius' lifetime, and later writings added to the tangle of legend.

The friends were enthralled by the power and erudition of his mind, and the magnetism of his gentle but firm character. They called him their Master. This word, like the efforts in later ages to sanctify him, is misleading about a man who believed in pleasure as an essential ingredient in the balanced person and balanced society which above all else he advocated. He loved sports like fishing and archery, delighted in music, with gusto joined in informal singsongs; and high spirits as much as earnest conversation marked their meetings.

But the times were remorselessly challenging. Tidings arrived from the great southern state of Wu about the fate of its duke. Invited to a banquet by an ambitious relative he was wary and posted soldiers all the way from his palace to the banqueting hall, and at the entrance, where they made every waiter entering with food strip naked before changing his clothes and crawling forward on his knees; but one of the servants had a dagger concealed in the fish he carried, and pulling it out thrust it into the duke, even if, says the chronicler, 'at the same moment did two swords meet in his breast'. In Confucius' own state of Lu when he was thirty-four, the nominal duke tried to regain his proper power by attacking the head of the Chi family but the Three Families closed rank and drove him into exile. They then resumed their perpetual intrigue, influenced by jealousy of the Chi or by any convenient issue from gambling to women. The masses were driven to even greater lengths to provide for the extravagant luxury of their leaders whose ministers were the instruments of deceit, violence and corruption.

Events like these confirmed Confucius in the convictions which he propounded to his young friends. There was, he insisted, a fundamental defect in the system: it was carried on for the sake of those who governed. Hence the appalling struggles for power and the exactions made on the people. If instead it were carried on *for the governed*, if moreover it were carried on by the most virtuous men available regardless of birth, and finally if this virtue were supplemented by training in the skills of government, then the state would prosper, the people cheerfully bear its misfortunes because they would share in its good fortunes, would gladly support it, would flock to it without conquest, and war and injustice would end. He believed that social advancement needed cooperative effort, and that, justly dealt with, men by their very nature would give that effort. The West's ideas about Original Sin, and men's need for 'redemption' which is only possible through submission to a divine agency, would have been alien to Confucius' thinking, because he believed that people are born potentially virtuous – that is, considerate, honest, reasonable and benevolent – and a soundly run society would realize this potential. All depended on the quality of the leaders.

This quality was an ethical standard of the highest order. Confucius' proposition that government of the people should be for the people was to help mould Western democracy; but while he also held that government should be by the people, in the sense that it should be chosen from all the people, he would have been puzzled by our method of selection. He would have asked how the ballot box could possibly identify the most virtuous and trained – in a word, fitting – men to run the country. The prime need was a virtuous leader who would surround himself with virtuous, able ministers who in turn would similarly select – since an essential element in virtue was a readiness to recognize that same quality in other people – the officers of state below them, and so on through every rank of government. What he visualized was a self-perpetuating meritocracy, its total emphasis on the character of the individual. He put forward ideas but not rules, for he would have nothing relieve a man of his duty to think for and be true to himself.

There was beginning to grow in his time a belief that a Golden Age had once existed when all rulers were noble and all their subjects happy. So emerged the cultural heroes like the Yellow Emperor referred to earlier. Many civilizations retain similar wistful dreams of their lost Eden. But while Confucius admitted to 'believing in and loving the ancients' he did not share this belief, though his ideas might have stimulated it. What he did believe was that there had been a loss of nobility in China's ruling class, but he was thinking of a time no further back then than that of the leaders of the Chou Conquest, the Martial King and his son the great Duke of Chou, especially the latter who had expounded the notion of a Heavenly Mandate and of the need for humanity and justice in any authority's dealings with the people.

Confucius laid no claim to originality – 'a transmitter and not a maker', he described himself. Thus he thought only of a feudal society – the only kind he knew: an enlargement of the family and, like it, only successful on the basis of reciprocal responsibilities, however subordinate some members might be to others. But his ideas of how that society should be governed included the revolutionary proposal of throwing open the ruling class to anyone of merit; making the only privilege that of serving the people; the novel introduction of systematic training; and all on the basis of every individual being the object of respect and concern.

He inspired his friends to want to help produce the reformed world he pointed to, and in preparation for this work to advance their education to his exacting standards. So it was that he began to teach them. What he taught was the syllabus he believed essential for every candidate for government office. Some of the subjects were technical, like government documents and protocol and rules; some were practical, like ceremonial procedures and music; and some the liberal arts like history, literature and philosophy, which he considered his tools for character training.

As he increasingly devoted himself to regular classes he gave up his job and lived on whatever payment in cash or kind his students could afford, even if it was only a lump of dry meat, for he turned no one away except a fool or an idler. He differed from anyone who had taught before by being not only a professional teacher, the first in China, but one to whom anyone of whatsoever birth could come and be educated on principles other than those sustaining the existing pattern of society. Yet he saw himself not as a teacher but a man preparing for a great task. He had a messianic conviction that he would be called upon to put into practice the reforms he preached. His students were his potential lieutenants to help achieve the task when the call came.

Although the followers of Confucian ideas in later ages were so scholarly that the word Confucian became synonymous with literati, Confucius himself was only interested in books as sources of practical knowledge and character-training. He said of his most-used book, the *Book of Odes*, that it would 'stimulate your emotions, help you to be more observant, enlarge your sympathies, and moderate your resentment of injustices'; besides it gave practical information like the names of flora and fauna, guidance in one's conduct, and worldly experience. He sought to develop his students' critical faculty, exhorting them to watch and listen but to suspend judgement on what was doubtful, and he was hard on students who in copying out a text guessed at what was not clear instead of leaving blanks.

More than any man in China he established the august authority of the teacher, which is ironical since he made clear his own fallibility, readily admitted ignorance, and rejected any claim to a monopoly of the truth. If he thought a student was right, he said so; if wrong, he reasoned with him, and if he failed to persuade he dropped the matter. He never hectored or bullied ('A man who covers his inner weakness with a harsh and overbearing manner is no better than a thief,' he said). He perceived all knowledge as tentative and all reasoning a frail barque on an ocean of uncertainty. This approach to the truth, viewing every conclusion as a hypothesis which might be disproved, embodies what we now call the scientific method, which also is ironic because he had little regard for science: for him the proper study of mankind was man, not the stars. Asked about virtue, he answered, 'It is to love man.' Asked about knowledge, he answered, 'It is to know man.'

He excluded archery and charioteering from his curriculum because they belonged to a military aristocracy, but seeking to build on tradition – for he was the quietest revolutionary who ever lived – he did adopt such aristocratic beliefs and practices as served his purpose. Their addiction to what was called *li* is a particular example. The word originally meant a vessel used for making sacrifice, in time the whole ritual of sacrifice. We have seen how ceremonial distinguished little between the living and the dead, making temples the centre of affairs both religious and secular, and spirits and men coexistent. Sacred vessels were also used for feasting one's friends; ceremonies for a living king differed little from those for the corpse of one – thus, an ambassador returning from a mission for his ruler who had meanwhile died would make his report to the bier. In time *li* became a matter of everyday as well as religious conduct, tending to formalize manners and etiquette, not only between man and god but man and man.

The subject was of absorbing interest to Confucius, not only because learning to behave with the correctness of a high dignitary was relevant to his own ambition of participating in government, but because he sought to shape into potential ministers people not always conditioned by an aristocratic upbringing. Also, he endowed *li* with greater importance than a prescription of when one must bow or where to seat one's most honoured guest (on the left; in later China it was changed to the right). He saw it as comprehending the totality of man as a social being: 'Behave in all your dealings,' he told his students, 'as if you are receiving an honoured guest; and if you are placed in charge of others, discharge the trust as if you were assisting at a great sacrifice.'

Since manners could be mere show or even conceal indifference or ill-intent, these were not true *li*. He would have nothing of mere correct behaviour unsupported by sincerity. He said: 'It is *li*, they say; it is *li*. Does *li* mean no more than a display of jade and silk?' It meant vastly more, from the highest dictates of courage to simple good sense – as when the hemp cap required by *li* to be worn at sacrifices became very expensive he did not baulk at wearing the more economical silk cap. But traditional *li* was not lightly to be departed from: before having an audience of a ruler people should not fail to bow at the outer steps before entering, since he insisted on respect for a ruler, a true respect which meant that a subject should speak his mind honestly even at the risk of his life. The keynotes of *li* were restraint in one's actions, moderation in one's judgement, respect for others, dignity in the face of adversity, never losing one's good manners or parading one's wealth or knowledge. Confucius said that a certain person knew well how to maintain a friendship because, however long the acquaintance, he was still always respectful. He saw the relevance of *li* to his concept of education thus: 'If a man's natural qualities exceed his training he is uncultivated; if his training exceeds his natural qualities he is little more than an educated lackey.' Hence it was only when qualities and training harmoniously complement each other that we have a man qualified to belong to the governing class. *Li* was at once an important subject in training a public man how to behave and both a discipline and expression of character in knitting together the attributes needed for government.

In its insistence on decorum, *li* has had a profound influence throughout Chinese history. It has been called the principle that has been the objective of Chinese national life, its cultivation distinguishing the Chinese from the barbarian and the beast. If its tendency to repress radicalism and to respect an authority no longer meriting respect accounts for the periodic outbursts of excessive violence, as if a lid has been too long kept on, this is misleading about the Confucian concept. To him *li* embraced an utter integrity, a passionate striving after wisdom, and an undaunted belief in the qualities all men rate highest, like courage, and justice, and compassion.

Related to *li* and like it an aristocratic addiction which Confucius adopted for his own purposes, was music. With us the subject ranks as a polite art in education. It was not so in the classical world either of Greece or China. When more than fifty years after Confucius' death Plato wrote that 'musical training is a more potent instrument than any other because rhythm and harmony find their way into the inward places of the soul', he expressed the Master's views precisely. The orderliness of rhythm and the harmonious relationship of sounds translated what Confucius meant about *li* as the art of living in society. Not only did they have this inward connection but in their outward manifestation of instrument-playing on the one hand and ceremonial on the other they were also closely related because the one usually accompanied the other. Music was also important to young men aspiring to a ruling class much given to playing and listening to it. Confucius himself played a kind of lute and sang. Tradition has it that he arranged the *Book of Odes* which is really a book of songs to long-lost music, but we have no evidence that he himself taught music, which he possibly left to a specialist tutor while he kept impressing its importance upon his students: their character, he said, should be 'stimulated by poetry, established by the study of *li*, and then finished by the study of music.'

We must turn now to how he taught, who his students were, and what fate had in store for his remaining years.

CHAPTER SEVEN

From Confucius to Empire – II

Confucius taught in an easy-going but disciplined fashion, largely by the tutorial method. He was not above losing his temper and giving a student a whack on the shanks, but these were rare occasions for a man who tried hard to live up to his belief in complete self-control. His relations with his students were marked by the psychological insight of a great teacher.

Tzu-lu, for example, a bluff, prudish, humourless, impetuous fellow with a soldier's rectitude and fidelity, was gently teased. Towards Jan Ch'iu, highly able, smooth, ambitious and a political opportunist unlikely to be killed in a lost cause, Confucius was apt to be curt but he never abandoned him. Sometimes he took sly digs at Tzu-Kung, who was to achieve much popularity without compromising Confucius' principles, a relaxed and urbane man destined to be a distinguished diplomatist and political adviser, and a philosopher in his own right who yet made considerable wealth: after the Master he stood first in rank among Confucius' followers. By contrast, Yen Hui was perhaps the poorest of the students, who was to die young and without achievement: him Confucius treated as his own son.

These were among the very few names preserved by history. Each starting as a student was to follow Confucius as a disciple to the end. From first to last there were perhaps only two or three dozen of them – estimates vary from a score to several thousand, perhaps because of confusion over the difference between disciples and students, since presumably there were many young men who studied for his prescribed three-year course and then went their way.

He made clear to prospective students that he was not there to teach them how to get rich. He did not believe even that a man's aim should be to become well-known – but to become worthy of being well-known. Nor that a man's aim should be to seek office – but to qualify himself to hold office if he were to be privileged with it. His rigorous principles and training thus ensured that however ill-connected a student might be he emerged uniquely qualified for posts in government. Yet Confucius himself, though never relinquishing his own hopes of high office, went unregarded through the years of state graft and avarice. And then suddenly, when he was already nearly fifty, everything was thrown in the balance by a convulsion in his state of Lu.

It was not unusual in the prevailing conditions for subordinate officials to take leaves out of their superior's book: sometimes a man appointed governor of a town closed its gates and made it his personal property, or, if it was on a border, joined it to the neighbouring state for higher favours. Now, in about 505 BC, a subordinate went even further. One Yang Hu attacked the head of the ruling Chi family to which he was chief officer, imprisoned him and forced him to vest Yang with his authority, which Yang then compelled the heads of the other two families to affirm by solemn covenant, so that he alone, above any of them or the nominal Duke, governed all Lu. By force or guile he tried to recruit supporters. Thus he won over the governor of Chi's home town, a man of scruple, by persuading him that the object of the *coup* was to restore the legitimate authority of the Duke. On this basis the governor invited Confucius to join the revolt by taking office in his administration. Confucius had never approved of the Three Families' morals, or of their usurpation of ducal authority, so this first taste of government ever offered him must have been tempting with the thought that it might provide a start to his helping to regenerate all China. But it was a wistful thought, of a man conscious of age overtaking him, and he rejected the offer as Yang Hu's true intent became palpable when he tried to kill the heads of all three families. Discovered at the last moment and compelled to flee to neighbouring Ch'i, Yang tried in vain to drum up an invasion, and the Chi family securely renewed its sway.

But it had learnt the need for able officials who would not turn traitor. Confucius graduates began to come into their own. The important posts they were given included the highly influential one of steward to the Chi family. Yet Confucius himself was offered nothing, even though the son of the Chi family became something of a patron. When his friends were embarrassed at receiving office while their Master was passed over he tried to reassure them: a man could make sufficient contribution to government, he said, by being a good citizen.

His inability to toady for office is illustrated by his exchanges with the Chi son. When the latter gave him a gift of medicine which anyone else in Confucius' inferior position would have accepted with gratitude he declined even to taste it: 'Not knowing what it is, I daren't.' When the Chi son asked his advice on curbing an outbreak of stealing, Confucius replied, 'If *you*, sir, had no improper desires, people would not steal if you paid them to.' This principle, that virtuous government breeds a virtuous people, accorded with Confucius' intense belief in the power of example. It could not have appealed to the Chi son who, when his half-brother mysteriously died and he succeeded to the head of the family, showed himself as ready as his forebears to wage war and keep the Duke powerless, though the chronicles credit him with considerable administrative ability.

But Confucius compelled too much respect to be shut out indefinitely. Presently he was offered office as no less than a Councillor of State. At last the way seemed open to his being heard where it mattered, where his years of thought might be translated into positive action that might help usher in a new golden age. He accepted with his accustomed modesty, and at court comported himself with formal respect towards senior officials while, as he told his friends, he 'followed after' the lowest grades. He spoke more truly than he knew, for in his unworldliness he did not detect how he had merely been fobbed off with a high-sounding title. When one of his disciples who was in the government arrived late for an appointment with him and made the excuse of having been detained by an affair of state, a puzzled Confucius retorted that the affair could not have been important or he himself would have been consulted. The truth dawned slowly, but when it did he reacted with hard resolve: he would leave Lu. Somewhere in the length of China he would surely find a prince ready to listen to him and give substance to his dream. Gathering a small band of followers about him he set off from his native state in about the year 497 BC.

They went west to the neighbouring state of Wei. In the century before, its capital had been so rigorously besieged that the inhabitants were reduced to eating each other's children, but the experience had wrought no lasting moral improvement by the time Confucius arrived, when the duke's wife was said to be her own brother's mistress and dabbling in politics. Nevertheless she and her husband gave Confucius flattering attention and probably a stipend – but no offer of office, and after several years he moved south.

There, in the state of Sung, one of his disciples was a son of the leading family. His elder brother was the Duke's favourite despite being an arrogant extortionist so detested by senior officials that one of them beat him up and all verged on rebellion. The young brother, likewise despising the ducal favourite, now feared that his family might take revenge on Confucius for 'corrupting' him. Confucius scorned his fears: 'If you look into your own heart and find nothing wrong, you have nothing to worry about and no one to fear.' His equanimity was belied when the elder brother sprang an ambush to murder him, failing in the attempt but compelling Confucius and his band to hasten on. They made themselves so inconspicuous in clothes and manner that nobody recognized them, so they got no support and reached the safety of the next state weak from starvation.

They needed time to recoup here and in the small neighbouring principalities. One of these, Ch'en, epitomized the prevailing degeneracy, for its one-time duke and two of his ministers were all said to have been pleasured by the same mistress and even wore articles of her clothing in court; when another minister protested at their boasting about it he was murdered. Nor were the subjects in these principalities made any happier by the fact that the contending armies of the two great southern states of Wu and Ch'u made them their battleground. In the tempestuous atmosphere an itinerant teacher could scarcely have expected to be heard but in fact Confucius found a listener in a popular and successful Ch'u general called the Duke of Shê, which was an upgraded title since the proper Duke of the state called himself King in eloquent disregard of the once sacrosanct prerogatives of the Chou King, remote from these southern outposts of the then Chinese nation, where the people were still regarded as semi-barbarous.

The general entirely agreed with Confucius' idea that government should be governed by virtue and in the interests of the people. He strove after this in practice, and for a while doubtless gave Confucius hope that here at last would be the executant of his messianic mission. But the prospect vanished when, asked by the general whether a man's first duty was to the state or his family, Confucius answered, 'His family.' In thereby baring the essential difference between the authoritarian and liberal schools which have ever wrestled for the soul of mankind, Confucius appalled the general. He asked one of his disciples what sort of a man was this that he followed. When the disciple reported that he did not reply, the Master drily reproached him: 'Why didn't you tell him, "He is this sort of man: so intent on enlightening those eager for knowledge that he forgets to eat, and so happy in doing so that he forgets his sorrows and does not realize that old age is creeping up on him"?'

Fresh hope came in the form of an invitation to him to join the administration of a town in Ch'i, the rich northern neighbour of his native Lu. But again hope was to be deferred, for Ch'i was in the throes of civil war and the opponents of the town's governor had control of the Duke of Ch'i, obliging Confucius to decline to join a faction technically committing treason. His lack of progress is distinguished by nothing more than the stoicism with which he endured it. Only one moment of despair is recorded: 'Am I a bitter gourd, fit merely to be hung out of the way and never eaten?'

At all events the call from Ch'i seems to have turned his steps homeward, for he spent his sixty-seventh birthday in Lu's western neighbour, Wei, where he had started his odyssey. Since then the incestuous duchess had provoked much unrest. In particular her son, heir to the dukedom, had become (it is supposed) so disgusted with her conduct that he persuaded a minion to murder her, but the man's nerve failed him and she ran screaming to her husband, whereupon the son took refuge abroad. When the Duke later died, not the exile but *his* son was installed, provoking the exile to invade the state; at the time of Confucius' arrival he had seized one of its cities. The real power in Wei, however, lay with the young duke's chief minister, K'ung. He was ruthless and ambitious yet earned Confucius' praise for being 'diligent and fond of study, and not ashamed to ask questions of those below him'. Perhaps the praise was not entirely disinterested, for K'ung both gave him a stipend and sought his advice. The promise in this situation met what was now become a familiar fate. K'ung, wanting to make an example of the invading claimant and flouter of his will, asked Confucius how best to attack him. Confucius would have nothing to do with it. He prepared to leave Wei and sent for his carriage. K'ung apologized and begged him to reconsider. While Confucius hesitated, messengers arrived from Lu bearing presents in earnest of an invitation to take office there.

What had happened during the thirteen years while Confucius roamed the country was that the disciples he left behind had steadily grown in influence in the state and its ruling Chi family, and indeed one of them, Jan Ch'iu, had lately gained immense stature by leading the successful resistance to a Ch'i attempted invasion. Now they offered him honours and influence.

It would be satisfying to end this story here, with an old man's triumphant return home and his noble ideas put into practice. So it promised, for honoured he was on his arrival, probably given office, and sought out by leading men for his advice. But the little known for sure about his incumbency of office in the ensuing years is not lustrous, for his advice was seldom taken, as two examples show. When Jan came for his opinion about how best to impose more taxes Confucius urged on him that the people were already impoverished, yet the government went ahead regardless, with Jan in charge of collection, moving Confucius to rare anger: 'Jan is not a follower of mine,' he cried. 'Beat the drums, my children, and set upon him – I give you leave.' (But such bitterness was too uncharacteristic to last and Jan remained a follower.) The other example concerns a family who, given asylum in neighbouring Ch'i, crowned a record of treachery by killing the Duke there, whereupon Confucius urged an invasion – not for revenge on a troublesome neighbour but to remove tyranny and restore the legitimate dukedom: his pleas to the court, prepared for by traditional fasting, and bolstered with the argument that local hostility to the usurpers would assure the success of an expedition even from so small a state as Lu, persuaded the Duke; he had, however, in his impotence to defer to the Three Families, and they made no response. This effort by Confucius, the only one he ever made advocating war, was his last in public life – an old man's final spasm of frustration.

Tradition has it that he now turned his hand to literary work. Doubtless he collated manuscripts gathered on his travels, and though claims that he compiled all the Classics are probably excessive they may be right about his authorship of the *Spring and Autumn Annals* – a seemingly arid catalogue of historical events but to later scholars full of subtle nuances expressing Confucius' commentary – and his putting together the *Book of*

Odes. (Perhaps he was thus engaged one day at his house when a visitor of whom he disapproved was announced, seeking an interview: Confucius declared himself to be ill, but as the visitor went away Confucius played his lute and sang, as if to confess to the visitor that he had told a little white lie to avoid giving offence, since he once said, 'To conceal resentment and remain on friendly terms with those towards whom one feels it – I should be ashamed of such conduct.')

Mostly, however, he concentrated on his avocation of teaching, taking on a new generation of youths. Many of his earlier disciples had died. These included the bluff Tzu-lu who had gone into K'ung's service in Wei and, scorning a chance to escape during a rebellion, lost his life in trying to save his master. The news moved Confucius to grief more unrestrained than the death, also at this time, of his disappointing son; for he seems to have regarded his disciple Yen Hui as his real son and cried out at his death, 'Heaven is destroying me!'

He himself once fell so seriously ill that he lapsed into unconsciousness. His disciples could not bear the thought of his dying unrewarded by greatness, so they gathered about him in the clothes of ministers waiting upon an august statesman. When he came to he gently reprimanded them: 'By making this pretence of being my ministers when I have not any, whom do you think I deceive? Shall I deceive Heaven? And is it not better that I should die in the hands of you – my friends – than in the hands of ministers?'

In the year 479 BC he did indeed die. He was seventy-two. It is said that his disciples held vigil by his grave for three years, and one disciple for three years more. Theirs was the epitaph: 'From the birth of mankind until now, there has never been his equal.' Such was the mortal failure who would become an almost deified immortal to the Chinese people. But as yet his death was only something for the private grief of the few in the gathering chaos of the Chou Kingdom as the epoch of the Warring States, ushered in that same year by the state of Ch'u's conquest of its neighbour, began its violent course.

As has been noted, Confucius' travels among the states in the hope of gaining influence over their princes were not unusual occurrences during the Warring States period, since increasing population pressures, the endless fighting inside and between the states and with barbarians, unrest among the oppressed people, and the technological revolution caused by the arrival of iron, induced many feudal lords to seek the help of the scholar class as advisers and diplomats. There came into being whole schools of philosophy, the so-called One Hundred Schools, and the paradox is that while the bloody and tumultuous business continued of greater states gobbling up smaller ones between the sixth and third centuries BC, these schools represented the intellectual flower of ancient China.

The word 'Hundred' in the title reflects the Chinese addiction to extravagant numeration, for there were essentially six schools of importance. Besides the Confucians, there were the Logicians or School of Names, the Taoists, the Mohists, the Yin-Yang School, and the Legalists or School of Law. Many of the scholars attended academies, of which the most famous was the Academy of the Gate of Chi in the capital of the State of Ch'i. Founded by its ruler in about 318 BC (at about the time that Plato established his Academy in Athens), it welcomed thinkers from all over the country, provided them with board and maintenance, and awarded the most important the rank of Great Prefect.

They included the most illustrious living leaders of all six schools. Their trains of thought, including Confucianism, provide some insight into the intellectual Chinese mind of the second third of the last millennium BC.

The term *Logicians* is a translation of *ming-chia* which has also been translated as sophists or dialecticians, but as none is quite accurate recourse has been had to the School of Names, for it was with names that its followers, known as *pien-che* (debaters, disputers, arguers), concerned themselves. They conducted, as an early historian has written, 'minute examinations of trifling points in complicated and elaborate statements'. They set out, for example, to prove that a white horse is not a horse – because 'white horse' denotes both whiteness and a horse together, not either alone, so a white horse is not a horse any more than it is whiteness. Another line of reasoning involved the difference between 'universals' – names like whiteness and hardness which exist regardless of whether there are any hard or white objects – and 'actuals' like hard white objects; there was a famous proposition, 'the separateness of hardness and whiteness', the argument for which was that there are some objects which are white but not hard and some hard but not white. Universals lie beyond actual shapes and features, like Plato's 'Forms'. We can, however, say that all things are similar in that they are things, but are different when compared with each other – this was a famous 'argument for the unity of similarity and difference'. Some names are absolute, some relative: in the statement 'this table', the name 'table' is an absolute, descriptive of any table anywhere, but 'this' is relative as it relates to a particular table. Relativity is further demonstrated by the fact that the yesterday of today was the today of yesterday and the today of today will be the yesterday of tomorrow. Similarly; for example, destruction and construction are relative: if one makes a wooden table, from the point of view of the wood it is destruction while from that of the table it is construction. Perhaps not surprisingly many of the leading lights in the School of Names were lawyers – one, for example, framed the legal code for the State of Wei – but their analytical nit-picking ended in a clear social conclusion: because all things are relative and in a state of flux, all things are essentially one and should be loved without discrimination.

Taoism – just as Mencius (372–289 BC) in the century following Confucius' death became, after studying under Confucius' grandson, the foremost expounder of the Confucian philosophy, so was Taoism brought to full exposition after its originator Lao-tzu by Mencius' contemporary, Chuang-tzu. Taoism as a school of philosophy must be sharply distinguished from the religion of the same name. Philosophical Taoism concerns itself with *following* nature – thus death, for example, is accepted quite calmly as a natural consequence of life. The religious Taoist, on the other hand, *opposed* nature – techniques were sought, for example, to avoid death – and in this respect its spirit was that of science, so that much scientific advancement was to be owed to it.

The philosophical Taoists ridiculed Confucius for his efforts to save the world. The world, they believed, should be left to itself: they declared that if the world could be saved by their plucking a single hair from their body they would not do it. Their starting point was the preservation of self and the avoidance of injury, which could be achieved by one's escaping into the mountains and forests as a hermit. They extolled uselessness, citing the sacred oak because, its wood being good for nothing, it escaped the axe. Yet despite every care – avoiding doing either good or evil – the possibility of suffering remained, for 'the reason that I have great disaster is that I have a body. If there were no body, what disaster could there be?' So in its final development Taoism became mystical, seeking to see life and death, self and others, from a higher point of view: by emptying the mind of *all* knowledge, it aimed at transcending this world and reaching another in which self was abolished by being merged into the universe.

Although *Tao* is usually translated as 'The Way', its meaning to its devotees was as the originator of all things, the great uncarved block of the Non-Being from which Being came, and hence all beings and things. It is not itself a thing but universal and nameless, through which all named things come into being, and these obtain something from Tao called Te, meaning power or virtue, and is what the thing naturally is. Tao produces it; Te endows its nature. Man should always follow his Te, restricting his activities to what is necessary and natural to him – never overdoing it, taking simplicity as the guiding principle and contentment the aim; hence desire and knowledge, being corrosive of contentment, are to be avoided: 'When knowledge and intelligence appeared, Gross Artifice began.'

While agreeing with Confucius that the ruler should be a wise and virtuous man – in a word, a sage – Taoists saw a different role for him: far from enlightening his people, promoting justice and legislating for improvement, he should do nothing. The troubles of the world, Lao-tzu said, came not because things are not done but because too many things are done. 'Banish wisdom, discard knowledge, and the people will benefit a hundredfold. Banish do-gooding, and the people will be dutiful and compassionate. The more cunning craftsmen are, the more pernicious contrivances will appear. The more laws are promulgated, the more thieves and bandits there will be.' The sage should rule his people 'by emptying their minds, filling their bellies, weakening their wills, and toughening their sinews, ever making the people without knowledge and without desire.' All things came from Tao which itself does nothing 'yet there is nothing that is not done' – an example of the paradoxes in which Taoists delighted.

The *Mohist School* was very much more down to earth than the Taoists, more commonsensical than the School of Names, and at one with the Confucianists in being practical. The modern philosopher would have little difficulty accepting its tenets. It attempted to create a pure method of logic, encompassing deductive and inductive methods, classifications of knowledge, and dialectic. It foreshadowed Jeremy Bentham's 'principles of utility', believing like him that the aim of morality is the greatest good of the greatest number. Its criticisms of other schools reveal its simple clarity of thought. For instance, taking to task the Taoist teaching that learning is useless, it argued that as teaching and learning are related terms, once there is teaching there is learning, and if teaching is useful, learning cannot be useless. It took on the School of Names over, for instance, its insistence on the separateness of whiteness and hardness in the description, 'hard white stones', by pointing out that these qualities are not separate but simultaneously inhere in the stone. But, like the School of Names, if more positively and vigorously, Mohists espoused the doctrine of universal love – an all-embracing love of all men.

The *Yin-Yang School* had its origin in the practice of the occult arts, which were of six classes, such as astrology. Hereditary experts in these arts were attached to every aristocratic house of the early Chou, but as the feudal system disintegrated they scattered among the people. Occultism is a brand of magic but one strand of it desired to comprehend the natural forces shaping the universe. This strand, like the religious aspect of Taoism, encouraged scientific thought, just as alchemy did in the West's Middle Ages. Central to the school was the concept of *Wu-hsing*, the Five Elements. Starting as meaning actual water, fire, wood, metal and soil as the basic constituents of all matter, it developed into their being regarded as the abstract forces, Five Powers, that govern the universe which the school viewed as a mechanism in which the human and natural worlds inter-relate: if one part becomes out of order – as, for example, by a sovereign's bad conduct provoking the anger of Heaven – the whole gets out of harmony, resulting not least in abnormal phenomena. The school maintained that the Five Elements produce one another, and that the sequence of the seasons accords with this fact: wood, which dominates spring, produces fire which dominates summer, and so on. Likewise the succession of dynasties accords with the succession of the Elements, each of which has a colour, so that the legendary Yellow Emperor, for example, at his succession when soil was in the ascendancy assumed its colour, yellow (wood was green, metal white, fire red, water black). While the structure of the universe was explained by the Five Elements, its origin lay in Yin and Yang, the two primary forces by which all phenomena are produced. Yang represents masculinity, activity, heat, brightness, dryness, hardness, etc., while Yin represents femininity, passivity, cold, darkness, wetness, softness, etc. Everything that happens in the universe results from the play of these opposites.

From the Yin-Yang theories sprang that strange tome previously referred to, the *Book of Changes* with its appendices called Ten Wings. The book was derived from the ancient method of divination using milfoil sticks: represented by eight sets each of three short divided or undivided lines, they could be shuffled in sixty-four combinations known as hexagrams.

These, with the book's guidance, were believed to answer every question. An important idea in the Ten Wings is that the secrets of the universe could be disclosed by numbers, of which those in Yang are always odd and those in Yin even.

Of all the schools, while each has played a part in shaping Chinese thought and belief, that of the Confucians – in time called the Literati – has been the most profound. But the most immediate in its practical impact on history has still to be described, the *Legalists*. For as we shall see they greatly influenced the State of Ch'in which ended the Warring States period by conquering every other state, enabling its king in 221 BC to become First Emperor of the united country to which the West has given its name; and the imperial sway was exercised on Legalistic principles, progenitor of the totalitarianism that has blighted the twentieth century.

CHAPTER EIGHT

Ch'in into China

*T*he basic difference between the Legalists and all other schools of thinkers lay in the latter's harking back to what they believed were historical precedents, especially back to a Golden Age, which they sought to revive. The Legalists' attitude is exemplified by a story told by their foremost exponent, Han Fei-tzu, about a farmer ploughing his field when he saw a hare rush against the stem of a tree, break its neck and die; whereupon the man deserted his plough and stayed by the tree waiting for another hare to be caught: 'If you wish to rule the people of today by the methods of the early Kings, you do exactly as the man who waited by the tree.' The Legalists' revolutionary idea was that history is a process of change. The breakdown of feudalism had created new circumstances and methods of government must be changed to meet them.

These methods consisted of the state being run solely on the basis of punishment and reward. Unlike the Taoists the Legalists believed that man is born not innocent but evil, with only a tiny minority of people doing good of themselves, wherefore the ruler must govern with the full rigour of the law. He need not be wise or, as Confucius would have him, a virtuous example to his people. Indeed, he should be as the Taoists would have him, entirely inactive save, said the Legalists, for exercising the authority of rewards and punishment once he had appointed people to the offices of state. If they properly carried out the duties attaching to their posts they were to be rewarded; if not, punished. Thus incompetence could not long survive. The citizen for his part had to have no idealistic aspiration to virtuous behaviour; Confucian virtue had nothing to do with the state, and the citizen had only one overriding duty – to obey the law. It was to be mercilessly enforced and all men were to be equal before it. In this respect the Legalists followed the revolutionary Confucian principle of ignoring class distinction; but instead of trying to elevate the common people to a higher standard of conduct, the Legalists aimed to reduce the nobility to a lower standard by relying solely on rewards and punishment for everyone alike.

The better to explain the emergence of the Ch'in as the victor of the Warring States period and the unifiers of China in 221 BC, a glance at their history is needed. Legends place the tribal origins of the Ch'in in the third millennium BC, but with certainty the story starts in 897 BC when a petty chieftain and skilled horse-breeder was given by the Chou King a small territory to raise horses for the royal household. The chief's descendants were soon calling themselves dukes. It may be recalled that in 770 BC their then Duke helped rescue the Chou royal prince who went to the new (Eastern) Chou capital and was installed as King. He rewarded the Ch'in by making theirs a fully fledged principality which, like all the other principalities, evolved into states owing increasingly tenuous loyalty to the Chou Dynasty. Their lands on the Wei River west of its junction with the Yellow and the old Chou capital were protected by rivers and mountains, and from here in the succeeding centuries they waged wars against both the western and northern barbarian horsemen (Huns, variously called the Jung, the Hsiung-nu and the Hu) and their neighbours along the Yellow River, in the process steadily enlarging their territory.

Throughout their history up to the end of the Warring States period the Ch'in were regarded by other Chinese as semi-barbarians. They had many of the customs and beliefs of their barbarian neighbours, and their uncouthness was reflected in their alleged ignorance of traditional mores, relationships and virtuous conduct. Nevertheless they gradually adopted many of the institutions and cultural practices of the Chinese to the east of them. These included the important summer and winter festivals, and even human sacrifice when an important person died, which first happened upon a duke's death in 678 BC and sixty-six men accompanied him to the grave. The practice was officially forbidden in 384 BC, although they were occasional instances in China until as late as AD 1398. Another kind of sacrifice copied from their eastern neighbours was the giving of a Ch'in princess as wife to the god of the Yellow River: a beautiful girl was selected annually to be decked in wedding finery and set afloat on a raft looking like a marriage bed, which would presently sink with its occupant.

Feudalism within the State and with it the power of the aristocracy was gradually eroded by advancing government organization. Thus in the fifth century BC a land tax was introduced for peasants to pay in grain to the state instead of performing labour services for their overlord. But it was in the following century that the Ch'in were infused with a new dynamism that was to carry them to the climax of their story.

The descendant of a minor royal's concubine came from a neighbouring state in 361 BC to serve the Duke. He was a Legalist named Shang Yang; at his first interview the Duke fell asleep, but after several more encounters Shang won the Duke over. Later to be known as Lord Shang, he quite soon so gained in influence that over the next two decades he oversaw wide-ranging reforms based squarely on Legalist principles. His end came when the Duke's successor accused him of plotting rebellion, and upon his trying to flee he was slain and his corpse torn to pieces by chariots.

His reforms, however, endured. In 350 BC, the year that the Ch'in after establishing various capitals in the previous centuries finally settled on Hsien-yang, he divided the state into thirty-two counties, each administered by a centrally appointed non-hereditary magistrate in a further exclusion of the hereditary aristocracy's power. Similarly his abolition of the ancient well-field system and its service for overlords made possible the sale and purchase of farmland, to the encouragement of both landowning and recruitment of peasants from other states to a still quite small population. He added to the pool of agricultural land by eliminating the web of paths between the well-fields and by promoting the appropriation of wasteland. But above all he concentrated on the Legalist obsession with rewards and punishment in relation to the law. That no one should be in doubt about the ordinances he promulgated, he had copies posted up in the capital on specially erected pillars in front of the palace gates. He divided the population into groups of five or ten families, with each having responsibility for all its individuals. A biography attributed to Lord Shang says:

> Whoever did not denounce a culprit would be cut in two; whoever denounced a culprit would receive the same reward as he who decapitated an enemy; whoever concealed a culprit would receive the same punishment as he who surrendered to an enemy.

On the reward side of his Legalist measures he instituted a hierarchy of non-hereditary ranks awarded for meritorious conduct. Starting with military achievement – 'He who cuts off one head is given one degree of rank' – the ranks ranged from No. 1, the lowest ('Official Gentleman'), to No. 18. They carried exemptions, varying from labour services to taxes, as well as for some ranks the conferment of land or office. They constituted a further step in the down-sizing of the traditional aristocracy. What Lord Shang aimed at was a powerful centralized state based on a tightly controlled bureaucratic administration, an industrious peasantry, and a highly disciplined peasant army. These were the people's 'primary occupation'; the 'secondary occupation' of trading and manufacturing luxury goods was discouraged, and indeed the merchant class (with a notable exception – see below) was through much of Chinese history to be denied prominence. Finally, reflecting his espousal of efficient administration, he standardized weights and measures.

In 325 BC, a few years after Lord Shang's death, the Duke followed his peers in most of the other states by calling himself King – indicative of the dwindling importance of the Chou ruling house (which in fact the Ch'in was finally to abolish in 256 BC). A little later the office of Chancellor was instituted, divided between the Chancellor of the Left holding the highest position after the ruler, and the Chancellor of the Right, the second highest.

During a period of a hundred and thirty years the Ch'in were engaged in no fewer than fifteen major wars or campaigns, inflicting casualties of a million and a half, though the accuracy of the figure has been questioned. Everywhere the bloody struggles and merciless intrigue of the Warring States intensified. By about 250 BC conquest had reduced their former number of about twenty-four to a mere seven. The Ch'in therefore now contemplated six rivals beyond the Yellow River and south of the Yangtze.

In that year a remarkable man called Lü Pu-wei became their Chancellor. He was the richest merchant of his time and is the only merchant in Chinese history to rise so high. His adroit manoeuvres resulted finally in the ascent to the throne of a concubine's son named Cheng, then a boy but before long to begin ruling to some purpose. When he came of age in 238 BC, reacting to an affair between his mother and Lü (actually the resumption of an earlier affair of which, many believed, Cheng was the issue), he banished Lü who took poison and died. By then an even more remarkable man had appeared on the scene. This was Li Ssu, most notable of all Legalist statesmen. Arriving in 247 BC he was to achieve forty years of eminence, his offices including that of Chancellor of the Left.

The Ch'in's army, grown so ruthless in defeating the barbarians and others on their borders as to earn for its Kingdom the sobriquet 'the state of tigers and wolves', was a strictly disciplined fighting machine with much experience. Their homeland, girt by rivers and mountains, was almost impregnable. Their economy was flourishing – with commerce discouraged it was an agrarian economy sustained by the iron plough and ambitious canal and irrigation works. Their relative freedom from the cultural traditions of the other states, and their welcome to able men from other states, like Lord Shang and Lü Pu-wei and Li Ssu, readily allowed the continued introduction of radical innovations. These were effected by the promulgation of ordinances to give the state direction over every aspect of life, whether it concerned arable land, stables, parks, granaries, criminal acts or whatever. They were enforced by punishments that included execution, the cutting-off of the left foot or the nose, forced labour, fines or severe reprimands. Administrative efficiency was strictly enjoined on the bureaucracy: thus the instructions to officials included these:

> When a request is to be made about some matter, it must be done in writing. There can be no oral requesting or requesting through a third person.
> When documents are transcribed or received, the month, day and time of their sending and arrival must be recorded.

From the compilation of agricultural statistics to the specification for the quantity of seeds to be sown for different crops, little escaped attention. Yet the people seem not to have had any sense of oppression: they were, visitors reported, in awe of the officials, but the latter were conscientious 'without displaying partiality or forming cliques'.

This, then, was the highly organized state of Ch'in which in 230 BC launched its armies eastwards against one after another of the surviving six Warring States. Within a single decade it conquered the lot. Confucius' state of Lu had for some years been incorporated in a neighbour and now all the once formidable states of Chao, and Yen, and Ch'i, and Ch'u, and Han, and Wei all came under the heel of the Ch'in. And so China was unified under King Cheng, whose first act was to adopt the reign title of Shih-huang-ti, August First Emperor, in 221 BC.

His country extended for a thousand miles westward of the Pacific shore and from the deserts of the north to the lush lands south of the Yangtze. This was the core China which despite periodic fragmentation and with substantial accretions of territory has subsisted as a country and a nation these two and a quarter millennia – one of the major political entities on earth – while innumerable other imperial entities have risen and fallen.

The First Emperor moved swiftly to consolidate the unification. His chief architect was Li Ssu. The states formerly governed by rulers, aristocracy and officials, were divided into magisterial counties as Lord Shang had done within the Ch'in state, and the counties were grouped into thirty-six commanderies, each administered by a centrally appointed, non-hereditary triumvirate of civil governor, military commander, and imperial inspector who represented the Emperor. Through these commanderies and counties the central government could maintain close control to the furthest corners of the land. And just as after the Chou conquest the Duke of Chou had shepherded the defeated Shang aristocracy into his capital of Loyang, so were the rulers, aristocracy and officials of the former states shepherded into the Ch'in capital of Hsien-yang, where new palaces were built for them – 120,000 of them, it was said, though again the figure is likely to have been more metaphorical than actual – where they could be kept watch on lest any plotted rebellion.

That most unifying feature of Chinese life, their script, was standardized, for in later Chou times many divergences had arisen: Li Ssu simplified and rationalized what had been called the Large Seal script of the early Chou, replacing it with the Small Seal script which, further developed in the next dynasty, held sway until the present century. Thus while dozens of different dialects were spoken all over China, the written language was everywhere understood by the literate elite – rather like, at a simpler level, we understand road signs regardless of the language of the country they are in. The standardization of weights and measures imposed by Lord Shang was, along with most of his laws, extended to the whole country. The width of roads was added so that the wheels of vehicles could everywhere fit the cart ruts, which was vital for travel across deeply eroded roads, not least those in the friable loess soil northwards. And, so important to the economy, the metal currency was standardized. Although metal coins had been in use for perhaps a score of years, all sorts of objects were also employed for exchange – pearls, jade, tortoiseshell, cowrie shells, silver, tin – but now there were to be only two kinds of currency, namely, gold and bronze circular coin with a square central hole which, called cash, was to remain standard for millennia to come.

A huge building programme was undertaken. A series of broad tree-lined imperial highways radiated in all directions from the capital, most notably a five hundred-mile north–south road called the Straight Road. Altogether it is estimated that the Ch'in imperial highways cover 4,250 miles in length (Gibbon estimated the Roman road system, from Scotland to Jerusalem, at 3,740 miles). They lasted the best part of five centuries before the development of waterways hastened their decline. But by far the Ch'in's most famous building work was the Great Wall.

As noted before, the Chinese were great wall-builders. A number of walls already existed along some of the former states' northern frontiers to fend off the endless forays by the nomadic barbarians beyond. These were now incorporated in one continuous bulwark, over two thousand miles long, across mountains and semi-desert. The prodigious feat was accomplished in little over ten years under the leadership of the First Emperor's commander-in-chief, Meng T'ien, who was also responsible for the simultaneous building of the Straight Road. 300,000 men were employed, and the ever-lengthening lines of supply in a sparsely populated country could scarcely have called for less; in the intense cold of winter and heat of summer untold tens of thousands died.

Besides the building of palaces for many miles along the Wei River above and below the capital to house the displaced aristocracy, whose original buildings were said to have been meticulously copied, the First Emperor started the building of a huge new throne hall called the Nearby Palace; and he continued the work already started on his immense mausoleum which, when partly opened in the present century, was to astonish the world. The ancient records speak of 700,000 men being employed on palace and mausoleum, though again scholars query the figure.

With only a few years' pause after unification, the Ch'in military machine went into action again. Campaigns to the north, including what is now Inner Mongolia, and well to the south of the Yangtze, added new territory which was divided into three or four commanderies to add to the original thirty-six. To facilitate the transport of grain in support of the southern campaign, a three-mile canal was built across mountains to link a tributary of the Yangtze with one of the West River It has remained in use to this day as part of a system subsequently developed to a total of 1,250 miles, an unparalleled length of internal waterways.

Hundreds of thousands of people were despatched to colonize the newly won lands. Some were ordinary civilians, volunteers induced by the award of ten to twelve years' exemption from labour services or an advance of one degree in rank. Some went under duress, like convicts, or fugitives from military service, or (reflecting the prejudice against commerce) merchants, or bonded servants – sons of poor families made to work for creditor families and liable to enslavement if the bond were not repaid in three years. Others again were bureaucrats who had failed in their responsibilities and hence, on Legalist principles, were as liable to punishment as anyone else.

One of the most striking unifying events of the First Emperor's reign was the imperial processions he made through the length of his domain. Scarcely a year passed without Shih-huang-ti travelling for some months, in the first instance westward and after that eastward to the sea, whence he returned in a wide arc, making as many of his far-flung people as possible aware of their subservience to a single ruler.

In all this process of consolidating the unification – including the administrative arrangements; the universal application of the law; the standardization of weights and measures, road-widths, currency and the script; the building of roads, canals and walls; and the acquisition and colonization of more territory – the record of the First Emperor and his Chancellor is much to be admired. So too is there in their establishment of an Academy of Learning to which seventy scholars were attached, enjoying the prestige of the original Academy of the Gate of Chi in the previous century. But in 213 BC there occurred an episode the like of which has ever been the hallmark of the totalitarian.

That year, at a banquet in the imperial palace, many academicians rose to wish the Emperor long life. One of them also praised him for bringing peace and maintaining it by the replacement of the former aristocratic regimes with commanderies and counties. Thereupon another scholar spoke up. Although the Empire was governed on Legalist principles, Confucianism together with Taoism and the Yin-Yang theories had never lost a place in the intellectual climate, and this speaker spoke as a Confucian. Previous dynasties, he said, had lasted so long because the kings gave fiefs to their sons and meritorious officials, whereas while 'Your Majesty possesses all within the seas, yet his sons and younger brothers remain common men. Of affairs which, unless modelled on antiquity, can long endure I have not heard.'

Chancellor Li Ssu's response was devastating. 'There are some men of letters who do not model themselves on the present but study the past in order to criticize the present. They confuse and excite the ordinary people.' If this was not stopped, he added, 'the imperial power will decline above and partisanships will form below'.

And stopped, he was determined, it would be. An imperial decree ordered that while the historical records of the Ch'in themselves, the texts in the Academy of Learning, and works on medicine, divination, agriculture and forestry were exempt, all other historical records and writings of the various philosophical schools and all classical works, were to be brought to the commandery governors for burning; people so much as discussing the *Book of Odes* or the *Book of Documents* were to be executed and their bodies exposed to the public; not only those who 'use the past to criticize the present' but their relatives also were to be put to death; officials failing to report any violation of these regulations were to be considered equally guilty; and persons failing to burn the forbidden texts within thirty days would be tattooed and sent to do forced labour.

The loss to learning occasioned by this 'burning of the books', although its worst effects were widely circumvented, created in later Chinese scholars a profound revulsion against the Ch'in empire. Nor was the Emperor's posthumous reputation improved by his conduct after he fell under the influence of magicians, in particular one named Master Lu. The ideas of the Hundred Schools invariably affected the imperial mind for all that his government adhered so rigidly to Legalist principles. Thus on the stone tablets he caused to be set up at important places during his country-wide processions the inscriptions lauding his achievements often included Confucian sentiments, such as, 'His sagely wisdom is humane and righteous'. From the beginning of his reign he paid more than lip service to the theory of the Five Elements or Powers, maintaining that their succession gave his dynasty the power of water, with its appended colour black and its number 6, so that his clothing, pennons and flags were that colour, while the dimensions of official hats and chariots were measured in units of six and chariots were drawn by six horses. But most appealing to him of all was Taoism, whose vocabulary he also invoked in the inscription referred to above, with the line, 'He embodies the Way and practises its power'. What drew him, however, was less the philosophy of Taoism than its admixture of shamanism and sorcery which borrowed from the Five Elements' cosmologists' search for the elixir of immortality. A cult had developed, mainly along the east coast, whose followers believed that if found or created such an elixir would enable its partaker to live indefinitely on certain supernatural mountains situated on islands off the mainland.

Following his initial procession to the west the Emperor on his first visit to the east made his acquaintance with these magicians. One implored him for permission to undertake a sea-borne expedition to explore for three supernatural island-mountains said to be inhabited by immortals. The Emperor assented and sent several hundred boys and girls with the expedition, which was never seen again. On a later procession to the east he sent four magicians including Master Lu on voyages in search of the elixir. Upon the Emperor's return to his capital he was joined by Master Lu after voyages quite fruitless except for the revelation of a magic text which foretold that the barbarous Hu would destroy the Ch'in, whereupon the Emperor despatched his general Meng T'ien with a huge army to attack the Hu along the northern frontier. Master Lu was at it again a few years later when he advised that if the Emperor kept aloof from other people discovery of the elixir would be facilitated, upon which the Emperor ordered that two hundred and seventy palaces around his capital be linked by walled or covered roads so that he would not be seen when visiting; he condemned to death anyone disclosing his whereabouts, and indeed from then onwards no one knew his whereabouts.

Not long afterwards Master Lu and his fellows were overheard denigrating the Emperor and fell smartly out of favour. They fled but the Emperor visited the death penalty on four hundred and sixty scholars thought to have been associated with them. Such a dreadful deed has been doubted since apocryphal stories gather round most great historical figures. Another such is that when one of his processions was stopped at a mountain by a violent wind he was enraged by what he regarded as the malevolence of the god of the mountain, so he ordered three thousand convicts to strip it of trees and paint it red – the colour of convicts' clothing.

What is certain is that returning from a procession to the east in 210 BC he suddenly fell ill and died. He was forty-nine, having reigned for thirty-seven years, of which only for the last twelve had he been Emperor. But the imprint of his rule remained on the Chinese state for two thousand years and more.

His body was interred in the gigantic mausoleum which had been a-building since the start of tunnelling into Mount Li, thirty miles east of the capital, early in his reign. It was befittingly grandiose, being packed with rare objects and costly jewels, surrounded by underground rivers of mercury flowing to a sea, lined with bronze, its vaulted ceiling picturing the heavenly constellations and its floor marked out with the extent of his empire complete with palaces, mountains and rivers modelled in quicksand, while mechanical crossbows were arranged to fire at anyone trying to break in. Candles of walrus fat were calculated to stay alight for a very long time. Numerous concubines were immolated and the workers on the tomb were buried with him to preserve its secrets. So much is recorded by China's first great historian, but in 1974 a further and more astonishing dimension was added.

A chance dig in the loess soil a short distance from the tomb disclosed, at a depth of about twenty feet and over an area of more than three acres, an entire Ch'in military division made of terracotta. Some 7,500 life-size, realistically coloured soldiers were found in formation in passageways leading to the tomb. Visitors today speculate that the figures must have been modelled from life because the faces are all different, with individual expressions and variations in the way their hair is combed and whiskers trimmed. Their caps, belts, jackets, shoes, armour and weapons were seemingly meticulously reproduced. Some stand to attention and others kneel to fire crossbows; they are flanked by cavalry and charioteers driving chariots drawn by pottery horses. Since this army only occupies one of the four sides of the tomb, the possibility is that further digging will disclose a similar situation on the other sides, quadrupling the assembly of figures. But whether that happens or not, in the thirty-six years it took for the present known complex to be completed, many thousands not only of craftsmen and labourers, but of philosophers, diviners, sorcerers, civil servants and army officers must have been employed, coordinating their ideas and skills to create what would surely have ranked, had the West known of it, with the Seven Wonders of the Ancient World.

When the First Emperor died, his eldest son was with the great General Meng T'ien on the northern frontier. Accompanying the Emperor at the time were Li Ssu and the Emperor's favourite son Hu-hai, and also the first of a long line of eunuchs destined to cast a malign shadow over Chinese history. He was named Chao Kao, holder of the office of supervising the despatch of imperial letters and sealed orders. He persuaded the aged Li Ssu to support Hu-hai in a bid for the throne and to this end they withheld the late Emperor's letter calling on his eldest son to succeed him, replacing it with a false decree appointing Hu-hai and ordering the eldest son and Meng T'ien to commit suicide, which in due course they did. Thus at the age of twenty-one Hu-hai ascended the throne as Second Emperor.

His most distinguishing characteristic was his gullibility, making him easy meat for Chao Kao. The latter instigated him in 209 BC to make the laws harsher and to execute a number of his siblings. Later that year a man in charge of taking nine hundred convicts to a penitentiary was delayed by heavy rain and knowing that under the draconian laws the penalty for lateness was death, he determined on rebellion. It immediately kindled a fire which over several months resulted in the widespread killing of commandery governors. Several other men contended for leadership of the growing bands of rebels, among them a minor police officer called Liu Pang, a name fraught with destiny. Extensive fighting continued into 208 BC.

By now Chao Kao had schemed his way into complete power at court and he persuaded the young emperor to arrest Li Ssu. The glittering career of the great statesman culminated in mutilating punishments ended only in the marketplace of the capital where he was cut in two at the waist; his close relatives were also killed. Amid increasing disorder in the country, Chao Kao presented the Emperor with a deer, calling it a horse; when the assembled courtiers endorsed this description the Emperor, doubting his sanity, withdrew into seclusion. There before long Chao Kao's further machinations induced him to commit suicide. The eunuch replaced him with one of the First Emperor's grandsons, one Tzu-ying. The move served Chao ill, for upon calling at Tzu-ying's apartments he was stabbed to death.

A few months later, a rebel army under the police officer Liu Pang broke through a southern pass and advanced on the capital. Tzu-ying went out and surrendered to him, but early in 206 BC a rival rebel leader sacked the city – probably destroying more valuable texts than the notorious 'burning of the books' had done – and executed the hapless Tzu-ying. The mighty Ch'in power and empire were no more.

CHAPTER NINE

The Former Han – I: (206–141 BC)

The three years of insurgency that felled the Ch'in Dynasty exploded into nearly five years of bitter civil war. This ended in 202 BC when the forces of the one-time police officer Liu Pang surrounded those of his chief rival who committed suicide. Liu Pang was then enthroned as Emperor, progenitor of the dynasty called Han – a name which, synonymous over nearly four centuries with the heights of power and accomplishment, came to be applied to the ethnic Chinese as their own. The dynasty was in fact to be interrupted by an interregnum, the period prior to which is known as that of the Former or Western Han and the subsequent period the Later or Eastern Han.

The Emperor's reign-title was Kao-ti. He established his capital at Chang-an where the Ch'in imperial palace had been located a short distance from their now destroyed capital of Hsien-yang, north-west of modern Sian. In a fertile plain sheltered by mountains it lay hard by three rivers, the Yellow, the Wei and the Ching. The construction of imposing palaces and of the city walls began apace. Kao-ti's father refused to live in the splendours of the new imperial palace, so Kao-ti had an exact replica of their home village built to which he moved not only his father but his father's friends and even his cattle and poultry, housed in pens identical to their old.

Although the generality of Ch'in laws and government structures remained, much else was new. Most particularly the lesson of the recent years' turbulence was not lost and gradually the steel grip of Legalism was loosened. Slowly but steadily Confucianism with its emphasis on ethical conduct asserted itself: indeed, Kao-ti's first edict charged officials to use the law for instruction and edification, not an excuse for punishment. He tempered the severity of some of the Legalist laws and he proclaimed a general amnesty after demobilizing the army; he arranged relief for the war-ravaged populace, and decreed that uprooted citizens could return to their own hearths and recover lost farms. Scholars from Confucian' one-time state of Lu were brought in to wed Confucian ceremonial to that of the Ch'in at the Han court. Ch'in state religious observances, however, were continued by the worship of the Five Elements or Powers, with water and the colour black given the same prominence as before.

The Chancellor, or sometimes the Chancellors of the Left and Right, together with the Imperial Counsellor and the commander of the forces, were Kao-ti's chief advisers. Below these so-called three Dukes were nine ministers in charge of the various departments of state, namely:

Grand Rector – rites, medicine, schools.

Grand Master of Ceremonies – relations with the Kings (see below) and barbarians.

Constable of the Court – police and prisons.

Grand Director of Agriculture – taxes in kind and public finance.

Privy Treasurer – taxes for the private finance of the emperor; palace staff, library and archives; palace secretarial and eunuchs.

Constable of the Guards – palace police.

Commander of the Emperor's bodyguard; also supervisor of the gentlemen of the court.

Grand Coachman – stud farms, arsenals, palace horses and carriages.

Director of the Imperial Clan (chosen from the ruling house of Liu) – maintenance of royal premises.

Beneath these ministers in the second century BC was a host of officials in descending order of importance. But while family connection, patronage and wealth had determined entry into the civil service, Confucian influences were now asserted in a growing emphasis on moral standards and ability: in the year before he died, Kao-ti directed his provincial officials to send all the men they knew of merit and virtue to the Chancellor to give them posts that would properly deploy them.

Although the county divisions of the Ch'in were replaced by sub-prefectures, the system of their being grouped in commanderies directed by the central government was retained in the western half of the country. A governor rather than a triumvirate now administered a commandery and a sub-prefect a prefecture. They governed, oversaw agriculture, judged lawsuits, raised taxes that included a contribution to the central treasury, performed the required ceremonies for the official religion, raised and commanded troops, and superintended the schools maintained by the chief towns. The sub-prefectures were divided into districts of about five thousand families who maintained postal relay stations and police posts along the imperial highways. The districts again were divided into hamlets or communes of fifty to one hundred families: a local notable was responsible for assessing their poll and land taxes, for conscription, registering them for the census, land distribution and recording all transfers, and for their good behaviour. An elderly notable concerned himself with the morality of the families and directed his seniors' attention to pious sons, virtuous wives, and charitable persons. Another notable was the postmaster, responsible for policing and maintaining a stretch of road, and for ensuring the free passage of mail and traffic; he was also responsible for stabling, coach-horses and coaching inns for travellers. In time an inspectorate of twelve men was established, each charged with visiting a group of commanderies in the eighth month of the year to audit the accounts and check the administration of government and justice, so that a report could be presented at the capital on New Year's day. All officials, from the Three Dukes down, were paid partly in grain and partly in money.

The eastern half of the country presented a somewhat different picture, even though the commandery structure largely obtained. There leaders during the civil war and vestiges of the old aristocracy had proclaimed kingdoms in some of the territories of the former states. These men, initially ten in number, were now formally recognized by Kao-ti as kings on a feudal basis of fiefdom: they had to pay into the imperial coffer a share of the taxes they collected and annually attend court to pay homage to the Emperor. To counter any danger of a return to the Warring States period, the central government had 100,000 members of powerful families moved to the vicinity of the capital, and took various steps to control the kingdoms. Thus every opportunity given by death or other circumstance like rebellion was taken to replace a sitting king by a close relative of the Emperor; and, while the kingdoms were governed with all the apparatus of the central government, the latter increasingly directly appointed their leading officials. Moreover, of the two ranks of the peerage, the kings and marquises (standing above the eighteen ranks of honour created by Lord Shang), the marquises elevated by the Emperor on merit were many of them given chunks of the kingdoms to rule. In the course of time the kingdoms were more and more divided up or replaced by direct rule. They effectively became commanderies.

Distracted first by civil war and then the process of consolidation, the country was vulnerable to the ever-threatening aggression of the northern barbarians. The Hun tribes, called Hsiung-nu, roaming the lands above the petty kingdoms had a new leader who formed a formidable confederation which made punishing raids with hordes of horsemen turning in their saddles to fire their arrows backwards. In 200 BC, with 400,000 of his best cavalry, he contrived to ambush Kao-ti at the head of an army of 300,000, cutting off his group from supplies and reinforcements for seven days until Kao-ti managed to escape. The Emperor, lacking the means to maintain the Great Wall and its defences, decided that neither was he strong enough to mount any further offensive, since he lacked the horses essential for cavalry which had usurped chariots as the key arm in combat. He therefore embarked on a policy of appeasement. He sent a princess to marry the Hsiung-nu leader and agreed to make valuable gifts to him each year. But the peace that resulted was an uneasy one, interrupted by sporadic fighting. Kao-ti was sometimes himself on the battlefield and in 195 BC a stray arrow fatally wounded him.

There now appeared upon the stage the first of that cast of women which has played so tempestuous a role in Chinese history. Early in his career Kao-ti had taken to wife a member of a family called Lü in what is now Shantung province. Empress Lü bore a son, and although Kao-ti had favoured one of the seven other sons produced by various consorts, Empress Lü ensured that it was her son who succeeded. The standard histories of the period depict her as wanton and cruel: she had the late Emperor's favoured son poisoned and his mother murdered as a dire warning to her own son not to cross her; and she had three other of Kao-ti's sons murdered lest they tried to thwart her.

The new Emperor, aged only fifteen, was named Hui-ti. He died a mere eight years later. His reign is recalled first, for the establishment throughout the empire of shrines to Kao-ti's memory and, second, for an acceleration in the building of walls around the capital, Changan, and fortifying it. Periodic call-outs of labour brought tens of thousands of men and women to the task. Eventually a wall with a base over fifty feet wide and tapering to about forty feet at a height of over twenty-six feet extended for three-and-a-half miles around the city. Hui-ti's reign also saw a further softening of the draconian Legalist laws and a lifting of the ban on the literature involved in the Ch'in's 'burning of the books' – the so-called 'fires of Ch'in'.

Upon Hui-ti's death two puppet emperors only three years apart and both in their infancy were appointed, enabling Empress Lü to assume the regency of the empire. She issued edicts under the imperial seal, that jade symbol of power inscribed with words personal to the Emperor, and strenuously promoted the interest of her own family. Four Lü relatives were made kings, six were given marquisates, and others were appointed generals. She could not, however, prevent further damaging incursions by the Hsiung-nu who on one occasion took off two thousand prisoners.

She died in 180 BC after appointing one kinsman Chancellor and another commander of the army. The Lü family was emboldened to attempt the elimination of the imperial house of Liu but were themselves eliminated by a coalition of kings descended from their Liu forebear, Kao-ti. His oldest surviving son was chosen to be Emperor under the name Wen-ti. The choice derived from his high sense of duty and nobility of character which he shared with his mother who thus did not threaten to be another Empress Lü.

Wen-ti's reign was distinguished by the frugality of his ways in contrast with the extravagance of his predecessor. After his death in 157 BC his son and successor, Ching-ti (157 – 141 BC), likewise kept a tight rein on expenditure. Their reigns were periods of stability and, while holding increasingly Confucian ethical and humane tenets, were marked by an almost Taoist minimalizing of imperial intervention in government. This was balanced and made possible by two outstanding ministers, Chia I and Ch'ao Ts'o.

Legend has made of Chia I a paragon of a statesman, too little appreciated in his own lifetime. His compositions in prose and verse were highly regarded, including a famous essay detailing how the failures of Legalism were largely explained by the absence of Confucian principles. Rising only to a senior counsellorship at court he thought himself a failure and committed suicide at the age of thirty-three. Ch'ao-Ts'o, on the other hand, rose to be one of the Three Dukes as imperial

Counsellor, but his life too was to end sadly, with execution as the result of his rivals' machinations.

Both men gave similar advice to the Emperor. They advised, for example, against oppressive policies. Thus the two Emperors between them granted some eight general amnesties for people under sentence for crime; severe punishments involving mutilation such as castration and amputation of the feet were abolished, and there were six national bestowals of orders of honour to mark imperial occasions. The land tax was halved – even, for some years, suspended – yet imperial thriftiness resulted in enormous stocks of coin and grain being accumulated by the end of the two reigns. Coins, incidentally, by now consisted of the standard-shaped, hole-in-the-middle 'cash' made of alloy of copper and tin and weighing a little over five grams; a string of threaded cash was made up of a thousand coins, and ten rolls were worth a gold ingot of about 244 grams. The Ch'in monopoly of coining had been abolished, and the freedom to coin caused counterfeiting to become a widespread problem, as did the melting down of coins to sell their metal content.

While the accumulation of wealth by the Emperors was unostentatious, that of many merchants was not, for ever since the Ch'in the merchant class had burgeoned, for all that it was looked down upon. It consisted of shopkeepers, entrepreneurs who developed iron and cinnabar mines, salt merchants, cattle-breeders, landowners and usurers. They traded in bamboo, timber, grain, gemstones, leather, livestock, cloves, precious metals, silk fabrics and a host of other commodities. Some were immensely rich with as many as a thousand slaves. Laws passed to downgrade them by the imposition of higher taxes and barring their descendants from office were scarcely more effective than those forbidding their wearing silk or riding on horseback, so that in a petition to court Ch'ao Ts'o observed that they bought up land, dressed in silk, ate only meat and the best cereals, rode fine horses and carriages, and consorted with the aristocracy. They were a threat to the small farmer who was cheated when he sold his produce, had to overpay for essentials like salt and iron tools, and in times of drought or flood ran into debt that compelled him to sell his land at perhaps half its value and become his creditor's tenant, sometimes having to sell his children and even his grandchildren. But measures to check the merchant class seemingly continued to have little effect.

Ever since the Warring States period iron, animal-drawn ploughs had greatly increased agricultural productivity; moreover, the amount of farmland had been and was still being vastly incremented through massive irrigation and flood-control works, including the first measures to master the flooding of the lower Yellow River. But, although by such means hundreds of thousands of acres of new land became available, much of it was acquired by wealthy merchants, and life for the peasantry who formed the overwhelming majority of the population was no easier than it had ever been. Working their small fields – a typical family of five had about eleven acres to live off – Ch'ao ts'o said in his petition,

in spring they are exposed to the biting wind and dust; in summer they are subjected to the burning sun; in autumn numbed by the rains, and they shiver in the ice and cold of winter. They have not a single day of rest in the whole year.

Apart from the depredations of merchants, and frequent natural disasters like drought and flood, they were prey to the exactions of universal statutory service. All men between twenty-three and fifty-six had to spend two years in the army and were liable to recall in an emergency; and they had to spend a month per year in labour gangs at the direction of local officials. They might have to transport produce from field to state granary and from granary to central depots for use in times of drought; they might have to help build roads and bridges or in the upkeep of waterways; they might have to work on imperial palaces and tombs. In some circumstances it might be possible, though not by the average peasant, to avoid the corvée by paying others or by virtue of rank. One's order of honour was very important, not only in this respect but in many others, such as entanglements with the law when one's rank might bring mitigation of punishment. Thus at the top end of the scale a member of the upper class convicted of a serious crime might suffer only dismissal, exclusion from office, or exile in which his family and friends might have to join him, although even then it was sometimes possible to escape by paying a ransom to the treasury. For most people, however, transgressions against the law had severe consequences.

A new criminal code in 200 BC had enlarged the Ch'in code. A range of crimes brought death – including parricide, incest, rebellion, disobedience to the Emperor or denigrating him or using witchcraft against him, or fraudulently misrepresenting the number of enemy heads captured in battle. To harmonize with the cycles of nature to which it was believed humans were subject, executions had to take place in autumn and winter, seasons of decline and death, for if carried out in spring – season of pardons and mercy – natural disaster might result. A condemned person was either beheaded or cut in two at the waist by a hinged blade: this happened in market places or at gates in the town walls, where the corpse was exposed to further view. The severest punishment included extermination also of the guilty man's family – parents, paternal grandparents, wife, children and grandchildren – but sometimes he was instead reduced to slavery, the severest punishment after the death penalty.

Mutilation as a punishment had largely been replaced by strokes with the bastinado. This was often part of a sentence of forced labour, the most common penalty, for while heavy fines could be imposed instead, the Western idea of languishing in unproductive and expensive prisons was unknown except for accused persons awaiting trial. Forced labour was for up to five years, during which convicts had shaven heads and sometimes leg irons and an iron collar. Women might have to mill and sift grain but men toiled at public works like fortifications or dykes on the Yellow River, or served as soldiers. Together with slaves they constituted a large part of the workforce available for big government projects and were hence important to the Han economy.

Justice was administered locally, by the sub-prefect and his officials. A person accused of a crime was arrested, imprisoned (often in chains), and interrogated under torture, usually the beating of his soles, buttocks or thighs. Witnesses were similarly arrested, imprisoned and interrogated. All questions and answers were written down in an official document which was then read to the accused in confirmation. Difficult judicial questions might go to the Office of Censorship at the capital for a ruling, and it was this office that received the regional inspectors' annual reports on any irregularities in the commanderies. A convicted person had little hope of an appeal, his hopes of freedom or mitigation resting on his rank or the coincidence of an imperial amnesty.

The class structure remained unchanged except that mobility between the classes had become commonplace. At the top was the ruling class including scholars and artists; next, the peasantry; and below them the merchants, the artisans and the slaves. Many of the artisans were in fact slaves but in any event were little regarded. Nevertheless it was they who carried on the artistry which is evidenced by the Shang bronzes and has ever been a shining ingredient of Chinese genius. In jade, stone, bronze, lacquer or textiles they adorned the palaces and prepared the posthumous equipment, and embellished the mausoleums, of their rulers. They were prominent too in the manufacture of iron tools, weapons, and domestic articles.

The latter are well displayed in three aristocratic tombs opened up during the 1970s in the region of Changsha, a city just south of the Yangtze. The burial places, situated at the bottom of shafts over fifty feet deep beneath mounds nearly two hundred feet high, also provide an insight into many aspects of Chinese life in the second century before Christ.

One of the tombs contained over a thousand everyday articles, for people believed that upon their death while one of their souls, called *hun*, began the perilous journey to the abode of the Immortals on Mount Kunlun in north-west China, the other one, called *po*, descended to the Yellow Springs in the bowels of the earth; but in order to remain with the body for as long as possible so as not to affright the descendants in the form of a ghost, it had to be given offerings by way of burial goods and sacrifices. It was assumed that everything the deceased required in life would similarly be needed in death: hence the plethora of goods provided.

They included clothes and clay versions of cash; bronze, lacquer and earthenware vessels and baskets; gold and jewels, lacquered cosmetic boxes with combs, hairpieces, head ornaments, mirrors, board games and weapons; figurines of musicians and actual musical instruments such as bamboo mouth-organs over two feet long and seven-stringed zithers; materials illustrative of Han weaving and dyeing techniques such as silk taffetas, embroidered silk and gauzes in every variety of colour, most vividly in figured silk wonderfully patterned with curvilinear geometric, dragon or bird motifs; writing implements, and books written on silk or wood, providing a fine conspectus of an educated man's library – the Classics, works on philosophy, medicine, astronomy; even such subjects as horse-physiognomy, law, meteorology and cartography which also embraced actual topographical, military and town maps. The most beautiful adornment of each coffin itself was the silk banner placed over it after being carried aloft in the funeral procession: this funeral practice of a banner bearing the deceased's name has continued to the present day, but the specimens recovered from the tombs contain the earliest examples of Chinese painting and are masterpieces at that. Their themes relate to religious belief – the deceased's journey to the next world, the ascent to immortality, and so forth.

Furniture was not forgotten. There were mats, daises, arm-rests, chests, tables and screens. The Chinese did not use seats but knelt on their heels on mats – a posture that travelled via Korea to Japan – although upper-class homes also used a low wooden movable couch as a seat or bed. The latter was for most people an earthen, brick-faced dais covered with mats, blankets, or skins, and heated through pipes from a hearth within or without the house. Low, wooden, painted screens stopped draughts and afforded some privacy. The rich had fine hangings and paintings in silk on their walls. The tables in use were small, round or rectangular, and at mealtimes were usually carried in from the kitchen already laid with dishes, chopsticks, a spoon, a cup with a handle for drinking alcohol, and a goblet for water. The tableware of the rich was in lacquered wood, black inside and red outside with painted decoration. Trays were likewise except that for princes they were of gilt bronze, silver or gold. Large wine jars were of bronze while cooking and storage vessels were of stoneware or earthenware. For the less well-off, wood, bamboo and pottery dishes sufficed. Lacquer was in fact more expensive than bronze.

Food containers existed in a broad range of materials and designs which could provide for the wide variety of menus enjoyed by the Han and of which many specimens were found in the tombs. Food was preserved by salting, sun-drying, smoking, and pickling in vinegar. It was cooked by roasting, blanching, boiling, frying, braising and steaming – in short, by every twenty-first century means except microwaving. An authority on the period lists the main ingredients available to the Han cook:

Cereals: rice, wheat, barley, millet.

Vegetables: hemp-seed, soya, kidney beans, mustard-seed, rape, bamboo shoots, lotus roots, taro, chives, lentils, ginger, melons, gourd, mallow, shallots, garlic, knot-grass, sow-thistle.

Fruit: pears, jujubes, plums, peaches, arbutus berries, oranges, persimmons, water-chestnuts.

Meat: beef, mutton, pork, sucking pig, dog, horse, hare, venison, boar, chicken, pheasant, wild goose, duck, quail, sparrow.

Fish: various carp, bream, perch.

Seasoning and condiments: salt, sugar, honey, soya sauce, salt bean sauce, leaven, vinegar, cinnamon, galingale, ginger.

Beverages: rice, wheat and millet alcohol, fruit juice.

Dishes were essentially traditional, the basic one being a liquid stew with cereals, meat and vegetables. Various kinds of millet and rice were favoured, in the north and south respectively. Cakes were of rice flour until later when wheat flour was used and noodles and steamed bread were introduced. Dried foods were the staple of travellers and soldiers on service.

The Changsha tombs thus revealed how cultivated a life was led, at least by the well-off in the reigns of Wen-ti and Ching-ti (180–141 BC). They were as civilized as any people in the world, including their contemporaries in Greece and Rome. They inhabited a state where by now the foundations of efficient government were firmly established, together with the principles of administration and precedents for the treatment individuals might expect from officials. But while peace within the state was well established, despite occasional rebellions by one or other of the petty kingdoms, resulting ultimately in their all being broken up, the threat from the northern barbarians was always present. From eastern Mongolia to the Caucasus there now existed in effect a nomadic empire bestriding China's northern marches. The conciliatory policy initiated by the first Han Emperor was only partially successful: damaging raids occurred every few years, and indeed during Wen-ti's reign 100,000 horsemen came through his western passes and down the Wei valley to less than a hundred miles from his capital, Changan, before he could beat them off with a force that included a thousand chariots. The peace that was then concluded was repeatedly breached, notwithstanding the Han's increasing payments of tribute in silks, alcohol and food, and the usual giving of princesses in marriage. But a system of beacons and look-outs brought some relief for a time.

Nine years before Ching-ti died he nominated a six-year-old son as heir apparent. Wu-ti was thus fifteen when he began a reign that would last fifty-four years and make him the most renowned of Han emperors.

CHAPTER TEN

The Former Han – II: Wu-ti (141–87 BC)

*U*pon Wu-ti's ascent of the throne in 141 BC his capital Changan was one of the largest cities in the world. He made it a showcase of the dynasty's splendour. Nearly four miles square, in each side of its rectangular and moated surrounding wall were three gateways, with three lanes twenty-six feet wide which could enable twelve vehicles abreast to reach the straight three-laned avenues (the middle being solely for the Emperor) that intersected the city.

Five immense palace complexes occupied much of the area. One of these had forty buildings linked by raised, roofed passageways, and included an audience hall nearly five hundred feet long and almost as high, built on a terrace reached by a flight of steps and a ramp for the imperial carriage. This complex housed the Emperor and Empress, the court ladies, libraries, the arsenal and ancestral temples. Other complexes housed the Dowager Empress or served as government offices. Great figures and bells were placed at the entrance to the principal palaces, which were brick-walled between wooden frames, often three storeys high with a central section and two symmetrical wings, on rammed-earth terraces and roofed with tiles decorated at the eaves. There were many pavilion towers, one reportedly over three hundred and fifty feet high. Inside the palaces beams and columns were of scented or painted wood; the column bases were of jade, the floors of polished stone, and the walls faced with wood or adorned with paintings or silk hangings. Great frescos on palace and ancestral hall walls drew on mythical and naturalist subjects, made the more vivid by the invention of aerial perspective which solved the perspective problem that Western artists would struggle with centuries later.

The north-west corner of Changan, not far from one of the nearby rivers, had two very large markets. Here every kind of trade was carried on, public entertainers beguiled spectators, scholars sought work, people strolled about, and friends fore-gathered. Apart from the palace complexes, the city was divided into walled districts, each of about a hundred houses reached by lanes from a single gate which was kept closed at night or in emergency. Laid parallel to the roadways, a system of earthenware drains criss-crossed the city to carry waste into the canals linked to the rivers.

The city extended well beyond its perimeter wall to residential and commercial areas lived in by rich merchants and aristocrats seeking relief from the noise and congestion of the metropolis. But more striking outside the city was its hundred-kilometre Shang-lin park and hunting reserve. Here were leisure grounds and nature reserves containing every species of plant and animal* in the known world. By its lakes and in wooded mountains the Emperor had his pleasure pavilions. There was a pool large enough for a naval display, with a huge stone monster whose mechanical wings moved in the wind. And it afforded space and opportunity for military parades and aristocratic sports conducted in the guise of great hunts, marked by carnage and brutality which did not go unremarked by the poets and artists of the time. The park had existed during the Ch'in period but Wu-ti altered and enlarged it. When he proposed even further enlargement one of his counsellors objected: jade, gold, copper,

---

* The strange deer called *milu* came to be added. Described as having the hooves of a cow, a camel's neck and a stag's horns, fewer than thirty remained when the international force sent to quell the Boxers in 1900 finished them off to have venison for dinner.

iron, camphor, exotic woods and other valuable commodities were all found in the region and provided craftsmen with their raw materials: it was rich in millet, pear-trees, chestnuts, mulberries, hemp and bamboo; the soil was fertile and the rivers and lakes teemed with fish: to deprive people who depended on this abundance, destroying their tombs and houses in the process, would deny the state resources and harm both agriculture and the silk industry – and all to breed deer, increase the space for foxes and hares, and provide dens for tigers and wolves!

Wu-ti rejected the protest and he could not be gainsaid. Surrounded by an aura of mystery and sanctity he lived in his court, withdrawn from the world except for important audiences, councils, ceremonies and excursions to make sacrifice. His personal name was taboo; only he could wear certain kinds of clothing and jewellery, or ride in certain kinds of carriage, all specially designed for him. Described as living 'in the splendour of a majesty that cut him off from the commerce of man', he was surrounded by his ladies, his eunuchs and his 'faithful' – relatives of the Empress, a few favourites, personal friends and catamites, for the Han emperors were bisexual and many of them, like the Roman emperors, pederasts.

Yet his government was extraordinarily active by comparison with the Taoist-like, hands-off style of its predecessors, most notably in economic development and territorial expansion. The latter is related to the toils of one of the greatest travellers of antiquity, one Chang Ch'ien. A minister in the government, he set out to the north-west with a hundred-man mission in 138 BC, charged with reaching Bactria and there concluding with a powerful tribe an alliance against the Hsiung-nu who had driven it west some years before.

Along the way, however, the Hsiung-nu seized him and kept him prisoner for *ten years* before he contrived to escape and, undaunted, continue his journey. He reached Ferghana, north of modern Afghanistan and the best part of 2,500 miles from Changan. That distance was as the crow flew but he had to traverse desert, mountains, valleys and rivers. He was now within the eastern extremity of the Parthian (successor to the Persian) empire, from which he is said to have introduced wine-making into China following his introduction of the cultivated grape and also the walnut. At last he reached Bactria, from which the Greek influence established by Alexander the Great had but a few decades since been lost. After all his travail his overtures for an alliance were rejected. Turning for home he was again caught by the Hsiung-nu, but during the upheaval of a new Khan's appointment a year later he once more escaped and safely reached Changan in 126 BC. He had failed in his mission but he had opened Chinese eyes to a wider world, and his reports on the trade and political opportunities offered by Central Asia dramatically influenced Chinese thinking.

Already a massive thrust in the direction he pioneered was under way, for the policy of appeasing the Huns was abandoned at the Han court in favour of aggression. Four generals, leading armies of ten thousand men each, fought campaigns over a period of eight years that drove the Hsiung-nu out of the northern and north-western marches, including the whole of the Ordos within the great loop of the Yellow River, which was settled with 100,000 Han colonists. The Hsiung-nu were obliged to move their headquarters a long way north, and some of their chieftains actually came over to the Han. The Great Wall was not only repaired but extended westwards to enclose areas newly established as commanderies. Regular inspections, routine signals and patrols, and insistence on precise timing for all operations ensured a professional maintenance of the new fortifications which ended at the so-called Jade Gate near Tun-huang. They not only formed a shield against barbarian raids but kept in would-be absconders from justice or those avoiding tax or military obligations. Also they protected merchants and their caravans as far as the Taklamakan desert, which with the Tarim Basin formed the heart of Central Asia at the edge of the Persian and Roman worlds.

Routes westward along the northern and southern perimeters of the Taklamakan desert formed the Silk Roads, initiated during the Han dynasty by intrepid merchants and travellers. Defying the terrifying natural barriers and barbarian molestation alike, they had contrived with intermediaries to get precious goods to as far as Constantinople since 200 BC. These goods were spices, gemstones and, above all, silk, the secret of the manufacture of which the Chinese kept from the West for so many centuries.

While the extended fortifications and victories over the Hsiung-nu protected the caravans up to the western outposts of the country, as the merchants went on they were vulnerable to attack or deprivations of water and supplies by the numerous tribal kingdoms dominating the oases around the desert. At some time between 122 and 115 BC the indomitable Chang Ch'ien set out again, this time to seek friendships with these kingdoms that would be denied the Hsiung-nu. His efforts helped bring about a regular intercourse with no fewer than thirty-six small 'states', earning him ennoblement as a marquis. Legend has him seeking the source of the Yellow River and sailing upon the bosom of the Milky Way, but the reality of his work was a complex system of relationships with local rulers, some becoming subordinate to the Emperor, others remaining independent but kept under control by such means as the exchange of hostages.

The Han's westward advance was capped by a three-year campaign that reached almost as far from the capital as Alexander, marching in the opposite direction two centuries earlier, had reached from Athens, and captured distant Ferghana whose donkeys and large, fine chargers, swift and tireless, were much coveted. But the great cost – fifty thousand out of the sixty thousand men who set out – did not quench Han military ambition. Their armies also marched south, far south, bringing tribal states as remote as modern Vietnam under their sway; and north-east, into Manchuria and Korea, whence Chinese influence was carried to Japan. The success of their armies was owed to the increased use of iron and steel weaponry, not least the long swords of the cavalry, for whom all the nation's stud farms were emptied, to the adoption of iron mail, to the extraordinary precision of the longbow with its bronze mechanism, and to outstanding generals.

Thus by the end of Wu-ti's reign in 87 BC the Han state comprised most of modern China. The Emperor ruled over a million and a quarter square miles divided into commanderies and petty kingdoms. The population, approaching fifty million, was for the greater part thinly spread over so vast an area; it was of diverse ethnicity and spoke many different languages, but upon being absorbed into Chinese culture became in Chinese eyes no longer barbarian but Chinese. And now in truth the country could be termed an empire, comparable in extent to the contemporary Roman Empire.

Such a huge expansion demanded a similarly extended bureaucracy to administer it. Not long after Wu-ti's enthronement he decreed the establishment of official posts for academicians versed in the Five Classics; and the study of these Classics and Confucianism became the basis of all training for and promotion in the civil service, a process that was intensified when a quota was ordered of fifty pupils to study under the academicians, adumbrating the examination system that was to follow.

An official's equipment consisted of a writing brush, an ink slab, a knife and a seal. Drawing up reports, recording statistical and other data, copying imperial edicts, and so forth, he wrote on narrow strips of wood bound by hemp tapes; or for special documents, such as copies of certain literary texts, or for map-making he used silk. The knife was for erasing errors or scraping wooden strips clean for re-use. To close a document and authenticate it he pressed his seal into the small clay tablet by which the roll of strips was fastened. Some of the documents drawn up were passports or identity cards for presentation at points of control. Among them also were calendars distributed among the commanderies, especially after the method of counting the years was changed shortly before the opening of the last century BC: the old system of a series starting with the first complete year of an emperor's reign (Wu-ti 1, Wu-ti 2, etc.) gave way to a new name for each few years of a reign. These names, starting with The Grand Beginning, expressed attributes of character or aims of the dynasty, or they commemorated events. For example, the auspicious discovery of an ancient bronze tripod vessel gave rise to Very First Tripod as the reign title. Thus time was measured by event or idea, rather as if distance were measured not by milestones but place-names. (The Han's contemporaries, the Romans, were naming the years after their consuls.) Finally, all officials were subject to the scrutiny of the board of commandery inspectors which was thus continued, though with the addition of a thirteenth member and an increase in the area on which each had to report.

The military campaigns and consequent augmentation of the apparatus of government were not cheap. Nor, by eschewing the thrifty ways of his forebears, did Wu-ti help the economy: to the embellishment of his capital he added extravagant ceremonial and hospitality for visiting dignitaries; not least of those he wished to dazzle with the might and wealth of the Han empire were the princes and chieftains from whom he sought alliance or fealty. Hence the mountain of cash and grain reserves bequeathed him were soon used up. His government had to set about raising extra revenue.

New taxes were levied on market transactions – the first whisperings of Purchase or Value Added Tax – on vehicles and on property. The poll tax on minors aged three to fourteen was raised. A new copper coin of 3.2 grams became, and was for centuries to remain, legal tender; and in 103 BC private minting was banned in favour of newly founded government mints. After an intense debate that would be echoed in the West in the twentieth century between protagonists of nationalization and privatization, steps were taken after 120 BC to nationalize not only iron mining but the manufacture and distribution of iron goods, and all salt production, whether from the sea or deep wells in the interior. Salt sales were similarly brought under state control. No fewer than eighty-two commissioners, notably including a famous ironmaster and a salt magnate, were appointed to give effect to these measure.

The process did not stop there. The commissioners had also to superintend agriculture and to impose a tax on its products. The state ordained a monopoly of alcoholic production, and created agencies to stabilize commodity prices and coordinate transport. Immense efforts by way of dykes and dredging were made to aid transport and irrigation. More commissioners were appointed to supervise agricultural settlements in the newly won western lands, to which three million colonists are said to have been removed in the course of the reign. And the government ordered that annually ten large caravans manned by several hundred people were to set out from Changan to trade with the far west.

Amid all the military, administrative and economic activity in the Empire, Wu-ti's reign saw distinguished achievement in poetry, the art of history, the crafts, and philosophy.

Among a number of outstanding poets, the one appointed to the Emperor was Ssu-ma Hsiang-ju, born in 179 BC of a well-to-do family in what is now Szechwan province. He first came under the patronage of one of the petty kings round whom were gathered a group of brilliant scholars and poets; but upon the death of his patron and the ruin of his family's fortunes he returned to his native region. There he fell in love with the daughter of a rich contractor who frowned on her entanglement with an impoverished poet, so they eloped. To support themselves they ran a drinking booth in the market-place. Happily the wealthy parent relented and gave his daughter her inheritance, permitting Ssu-ma to resume his literary career. He developed a form of prose-poetry or rhymed description called *fu* which had been devised as long ago as the Warring States period but which Ssu-ma raised to new heights. A *fu* he wrote came to the Emperor's attention: he called Ssu-ma to his court, where he spent the remaining twenty-one years of his life. The *fu* flowered in diverse long pieces, ranging from moralizing to pure entertainment, pleasing by their rich language and beauty of style; and from criticism (derived from the techniques of rhetoric) to personal declamations, such as grief at a cruel fate or cruel society. Satire was often employed, and almost always an intoxication with words was evident, most intensely in fanciful accounts of heavenly journeys. The genre was fashionable, not only in Ssu-ma Hsiang-ju's time but for many centuries after.

From 140 to 110 BC another Ssu-ma, Ssu-ma T'an, filled the office of Chief Astrologer to the Emperor, a title less impressive than the job, which involved concern with the calendars and stars; he ranked next to soothsayers and was regarded with amusement by the Emperor who supported him like a singer or actor. However, this was the begetter of the first great work of Chinese history, called the *Historical Records*. Having begun collecting material for it he bequeathed to his son, Ssu-ma Ch'ien, the task of carrying forward and completing a form of history-writing that would be standard for two thousand years. He travelled extensively and held a number of government jobs, but in 99 BC tragedy overtook him. In that year a general named Li Ling surrendered to a superior force of Hsiung-nu and chose not to return, since a general returning from a defeat was beheaded; but the family of an officer imprisoned by the enemy also risked execution, and indeed Li Ling's mother, wife and son were done to death despite a plea from Ssu-ma Ch'ien to the Emperor. For this intervention Ssu-ma Ch'ien was held to have deceived the Emperor and sentenced to the revived penalty of castration. He did not have the means or influence to escape the sentence. Nevertheless, having endured it he continued his historical work for reasons set out in a letter he wrote just before its completion and four years before his death at the age of forty-one in 86 BC:

I have wanted to examine everything that concerns heaven and man, to understand the evolution that has taken place from antiquity to the present day and make it the work of a single author. Before I had finished the draft this misfortune struck but I would have been sorry not to complete my task; that is why I have calmly suffered one of the most terrible of punishments. When I have finished this book I shall place it on the Famous Mountain [the palace archives] so that it may be passed to men able to understand it and so that it may find its way into the towns and great cities. Then I shall have washed away the shame of my old disgrace.

His seminal study of nearly three thousand years of Chinese history required over half a million words, scratched with a stylus on bamboo strips. Far from ever being turgid it is often charming, as when he reflects on one who lived four centuries before him:

While reading the works of Confucius, I have always fancied I could see the man as he was in life; and when I went to Shantung I actually beheld his carriage, his robes, and the material parts of his ceremonial usages. There were his descendants practising the old rites in their ancestral home, and I lingered on, unable to tear myself away. Many are the princes and prophets that the world has seen in its time, glorious in life, forgotten in death. But Confucius, though only a humble member of the cotton-clothed masses, remains among us after many generations. He is the model for such as would be wise. By all, from the Son of Heaven down to the meanest student, the supremacy of his principles is fully and freely admitted. He may indeed be pronounced the divinest of men.

In the realm of thought, the greatest philosopher of the age was Tung Chung-shu (179–104 BC). He was foremost in consolidating Confucianism as the orthodox belief of the Han dynasty, and among the first to propose the periodic Classics-based examinations held by the government simultaneously throughout the country, through which people of any rank could aspire to serve in government. More fully developed later, the system lasted until AD 1905.

Upon a foundation of Confucianism Tung Chung-shu sought to combine the Yin-Yang and Five Elements theories and provide both a justification for the political and social order of his time and an explanation of how the universe worked. So intent on his studies that he was said never for three years to have looked out on his garden, he produced a book called *Luxuriant Dew from the Spring and Autumn Annals*, drawing for its authority on the *Spring and Autumn Annals*, whose authorship like all the Classics was ascribed to Confucius. When he came to teach in the Academy (the 'Grand School'), he is said to have expounded from behind a curtain, his disciples then transmitting what he said from one to another, to a remote distance.

Conspicuous in his beliefs was the concept of Heaven. It is not easy to grasp, being sometimes Nature, sometimes a benign but imperious force, and sometimes the divinity which presides over Nature. It is the first of the ten constituents of the universe, the others being Earth, Yin and Yang, the Five Elements (wood, fire, soil, metal and water) and finally man. Man is a replica of Heaven, both being pervaded by Yin and Yang. 'Heaven, Earth and Man are the original of all things': 'Heaven gives them birth, Earth gives them nourishment, and Man gives them perfection.' This perfection is culture and civilization, for which wise government should provide the necessary institutions aimed at the purpose of Heaven which is to make men good.

The basic stuff of man, Tung Chu-shu maintained, was neither evil as some philosophical schools held, nor good as Confucius' follower Mencius had proclaimed, but able to be good. To that end men must exercise the five Confucian virtues – human-heartedness, righteousness, *li* (proper rituals and conduct), wisdom and good faith, all of which, like the directions of the compass, have their correlations with the Five Elements (e.g. wisdom is correlated with water which is correlated with Earth). There are likewise five human relationships – sovereign and subject, father and son, husband and wife, elder and younger brother, friend and friend: in the duties each owes the other are the ethics of society.

In guiding men towards the good, rulers should govern on the Legalist principles of rewards and punishments. If the government behaves wrongly, such is the interdependence between Heaven and Man that unnatural phenomena will result – earthquakes, eclipses, droughts, floods. The sovereign, it had to be remembered, ruled by the Mandate of Heaven, and here Tung Chung-shu went somewhat over the top in asserting that when Heaven withdrew its Mandate from the Chou it conferred it on Confucius. But essentially behind his complex network of theories that linked together the seasons, the directions, colours, tastes, sounds, numbers, planets, dynasties, government and personal morality, lay the ancient Chinese belief of the oneness of man and Nature, and of forces whose interplay serves, if sovereign and man play their proper part, to promote the wellbeing, the harmony, of the universe.

While of such were the ideas of the intelligentsia, the great mass of people were content to believe in and worship their ancestral, and a host of other, spirits. For Wu-ti, however, although mindful of contemporary doctrines and true to his ancestor-worship, there was the need to maintain an emperor's association with the sacred powers in order to secure their blessing and protection for the nation. The Emperor did this by promoting, as only he personally could, the state cults and inaugurating some new ones. Thus he inherited the duty of worshipping at the shrine of the Five Powers, and he established cults to the Earth Queen and the Grand Unity, setting up the Office of Music to be responsible for the accompaniment to the services. His most spectacular act was a glittering ceremonial progress to the holy mountain of T'ai where he celebrated the triumph of his dynasty by sacrificing to Heaven and to Earth.

His real motive on this occasion, however, was a search for immortality: he was gripped by the same obsession which had so agitated the August First Emperor in the previous century.

Once again magicians of all kinds thronged the court. They offered to summon the Immortals from the Islands of the Blessed, to find the way to the paradise of the east, to foretell the hours of good and bad luck, to transmute cinnabar into gold, to restore one of the imperial consorts from the dead, to harness the Yellow River, and above all to find the elixir of life. In consequence many charlatans had honours heaped on them only to forfeit their heads when their wiles were uncovered, but Wu-ti never lost his credulity or longing for immortality.

The prevailing atmosphere of superstition at court stimulated the practice of black magic. Once, a palace woman was accused of using evil spells to restore a discarded empress to favour: she suffered execution, along with three hundred other people condemned by collective responsibility. And sorcery claimed the lives of many other aristocrats before the reign ended.

It was ending indeed amid a gathering crisis in the economy, amid national exhaustion after all the imperial expansion, and amid an increasing struggle for power between the families of Wu-ti's consorts. In 88 BC an assassin's attempt on his life failed, but the following year an illness succeeded and brought an unparalleled reign to a close. Only three days before, an imperial edict appointed as his heir, under the protection of a triumvirate, a seven-year-old son. Now on his father's death the boy was enthroned under the title of Chao-ti.

CHAPTER ELEVEN

The Former Han – III: (87 BC–AD 9)

C hao-ti, not quite eight years old when he succeeded to the throne in 87 BC, inherited a state economically straitened, exhausted and longing for peace after the sacrifices made under his father. These circumstances dominated government concern as the millennium approached its end, while around the throne itself a century of ceaseless intrigue, conspiracies, plots, killings and suicides sorely tried the benevolence of Heaven.

In 86 BC a commission went about the country to enquire into the sufferings of the people. Consequently the most grievously deprived received assistance. Then in 81 BC sixty Confucian scholars nominated by the provinces converged on the capital to report on the needs of the nation and to propose remedies. The vigorous debate that ensued has been immortalized by an account written some years later, entitled *Discourses on Salt and Iron*.

The title is misleadingly narrow, for verbal battle was joined across a broad terrain in which not only the specifics but the philosophy and practice of government, together with economics and foreign policy, all figured. At issue were the conflicting views of the so-called 'reformists' and the so-called 'modernists'. Both sides frequently called in aid, as the Chinese were wont to do, historical precedent: the shades of such as the Duke of Chou and Shang Yang were vividly present. If in the West the Bible is said to prove anything, history (or myth) fulfils the same function for the Chinese.

Both sides conceived of the universe as operating to the eternal rhythm of the Five Powers (Elements or Phases), but whereas the reformists saw the succession achieved by each Power growing out of its predecessor, the modernists believed that each Power overcame its predecessor. Their harder and less idealistic attitude was reflected in their addiction to Legalistic principles of government, which is to say the force of law, of reward and punishment; to state control of the economy through nationalization along with the promotion of trade, manufacture and transport; and, in foreign policy, to an offensive stance against the Hsiung-nu. These were the views of the Establishment, of which the reformists were fiercely critical.

They asserted that moral lessons and example were more valuable than punishment, the laws tending to treat the populace unjustly and stimulate widespread crime. The State monopolies and controls which the modernists claimed had brought profits into State hands and stabilized prices, had in the reformists' view produced shoddy goods on the one hand and on the other a yawning disparity between the poor and the rich – whose extravagance and luxury, apparent not least in the capital, affronted decency. They deplored the use of State labour in industrial activity, for above all they believed, like Lord Shang long before them, that concentration on agriculture not commerce would secure China's wellbeing – a view Cicero urged on the Roman Republic, and Jefferson on the infant USA eighteen hundred years later. On foreign policy they held that costly expansion had weakened the country without guaranteeing its safety. Reformist and modernist clashed too on the training of ministers and civil servants, for the modernist saw the practical needs of government and not theory as the desired curriculum, while the reformist insisted on the scrupulous application of the examination system with its basis of high moral tenets, for the bureaucracy had indeed grown bloated and corrupt.

The debate brought little immediate result but it signalled a change in political thinking. Subsequent years were marked by imperial decrees of an increasingly reformist colour. The new thinking was buttressed by untoward phenomena through which Heaven made known its response to earthly events. When the suspiciously early death of the Emperor Chao-ti occurred at the age of twenty-two in 74 BC, and the twenty-seven-day reign of one of Wu-ti's consorts' grandsons ended with his being deposed for lack of decorum, the new emperor, Hsüan-ti, gave due deference to these phenomena. Not all were adverse: the blessings of Heaven were detected in the roosting of beautiful birds at the palace, the fall of honeydew, and the sight of golden dragons – all events commemorated by reign titles. But portents such as poor harvests, earthquakes and untimely changes of climate were interpreted in imperial edicts to mean the displeasure of Heaven at harsh government policies. Hence reductions were ordained in court expenditure, salt prices, and taxation.

In foreign affairs the changed thinking brought a shying-away from aggression against the barbarians. Instead the idea arose of renewed settling of agricultural colonies in the western regions, consolidating friendly relations with the surrounding petty kingdoms so that they would not ally themselves with the Hsiung-nu themselves. In the process the institution of 'tribute' became firmly established. It encapsulated the Chinese attitude towards foreigners that has persisted to the present century.

It assumed that the Son of Heaven was dealing with inferiors – in short, vassals. Their leaders or their noble representatives were expected to attend the Han court at the great New Year's Day reception, bringing tributes and receiving in turn gifts from the Emperor. The 'vassals' had also to provide a princeling as a hostage at the imperial court, growing up at the Emperor's expense and imbibing a proper appreciation of Chinese civilization. They were bound to keep the peace, to which end the Han might grant a subsidy, and if the Han undertook a military campaign they had to contribute troops and forage. If the Son of Heaven sent orders to a vassal these were authenticated by the right-hand half of a bronze badge, usually bearing the figure of a tiger, which fitted into the left-hand half held by the vassal. Such orders were few, though, because China did not interfere in its vassals' internal affairs, even if imperial envoys constantly visited in order to keep the court informed, not least on trade opportunities.

China benefited by gaining a peace that lasted many years, and by commercial activity, but at enormous cost. The value of the annual tributes received was far less than that of imperial gifts, which included chariots, horses, gold, silk, and grain. And the vassals received frequent economic aid as well as the right to export to the Han. In short, the tribute system, supposedly expressive of the cultural and moral superiority of the Chinese, simply cloaked a massive hand-out to the barbarians to keep them quiet. It has been estimated that it absorbed seven per cent of the empire's total revenue, but who can say what savings in lives and property it bought.

The reign of Hsüan-ti is notable for a second significant gathering of scholars. Since Wu-ti's edict of 136 BC when he established an academy for the study of the Five Classics, making them the stuff of the developing examination system for the civil service, a number of texts had been much argued over. There were no authorized versions or agreed interpretations of what were becoming China's canonical scriptures, particularly as differently worded copies periodically turned up. The matter was of no mere academic importance but of vital practical consequence; from a golden past messages had been transmitted which had to be studied intently for the rules they contained, not only for personal conduct but the guidance of the sovereign. A number of extensive conferences culminated in the Emperor's call, in 51 BC, for a debate by all the country's best scholars at the Pavilion of the Stone Canal in the main palace. For no less than two years they discussed and worked on the various texts before publishing an official version and interpretation, to be taught henceforth at the Grand School and made compulsory for all government candidates, although alternative interpret-ations were not proscribed.

The dominant ideology continued to be that propounded by Tung Chung-shu (see previous chapter), and its mystic and cosmological aspects led to the development of a so-called apocryphal literature. This claimed to approach the Classics and especially the *Book of Changes* by way of a mixture of old non-Confucian beliefs, history, myth, and speculation on omens and numbers, in order to explain the universal; and it was widely read. A feature of the time also was the prevalence of occult and magical divinations; and the repercussive forces of Heaven, Earth and Man required much astronomical observation of the stars, the movements of the planets and their position relative to the twenty-eight constellations, the coronas around the sun and moon, eclipses, comets and meteorites. Thus arose the science of calamities comprising both celestial phenomena and earthly disasters like floods, droughts and locusts. Rival schools offered contradictory interpretations which political factions used to make points against each other – or to veil criticism of the Emperor:

> Since the accession of Your Majesty
> the sun and moon have lost their
> brightness; the stars no longer
> follow their normal courses;
> mountains collapse, springs overflow;
> the earth trembles; rocks crumble.
> It freezes the summer, and thunder
> rumbles in winter; in spring every-
> thing withers, and autumn everything
> is ablaze. Does Your Majesty think
> there is peace or trouble in the Empire?

The speaker concluded this extravagant exposition with the assertion that those responsible were among the Emperor's ministers, which so enraged them that they ensured he had his head chopped off. Nevertheless the interpretation of omens exerted a restraining influence on the Emperor who, had he known it, shared the prevailing belief in omens with his contemporary Romans.

With the accession of Yüan-ti in 49 BC the reformist tendency had gathered pace. Its proponents blamed the widespread onset of crime on the severity of punishments coupled with heavy taxes and corruption. In consequence, during the next forty years eighteen general amnesties were proclaimed, and a gentler approach countered the harshness of Legalistic measures: instructions were given to shorten judicial processes and mitigate punishments. The Emperor justified all this in three of his edicts by declaring that the was responding to the warnings of Heaven to correct the imbalance that his incompetence had caused in the cosmos.

The reformists scored much success in the curtailment of public expenditure, ushering in an era of austerity. The special establishments providing imperial carriages and horses, and the reservation of certain lakes and parklands, were suspended. Palace guards were reduced and officials ordered to cut their spending. Economies in state banquets and transport were introduced. Some of the games staged for entertainment were ended. A number of hunting lodges were closed, as were the factories that supplied the palaces with silk robes. Gradual reductions in the Bureau of Music were to culminate in its abolition in 7 BC when some 829 singers and instrumentalists became unemployed. The use of expensive fuel to force the growth of plants and vegetables out of season was stopped. But an effort to end the monopolies of salt and iron had to be given up after three years of heavy loss of revenue.

Religious observances, however, offered more scope. During the Emperor Yüan-ti's time, shrines for imperial ancestor worship in the provinces and capital numbered 343, requiring 25,000 sacrificial meals annually and employing over 60,000 guards, priests, cooks, musicians, people in charge of the sacrificial animals, and so forth. A shutting-down of over two hundred of them was ordered. While they were restored to invoke divine aid when Yüan-ti fell mortally ill, they were closed when they failed to save his life; and a temporary restoration occurred again for a period to help, vainly, to secure an heir for Ch'eng-ti who succeeded Yüan-ti in 33 BC; but overall a considerable saving was achieved. Within a year or two of Ch'eng-ti's accession a further heavy item of expenditure was reviewed. The traditional sites of imperial worship stood some distance from Changan, necessitating expensive progresses by the Emperor and involving the use of jade vessels and ornately decorated altars. Much of the cost of all this was saved by the erection of new temples to Heaven and Earth in Changan itself; earthenware replaced jade, while altars were quite plain. Efforts were made too to reduce the cost of imperial tombs which required not only jewellery, rich embellishments and supplies, but also whole estates to yield income for maintenance, and sometimes even the costly moving by force of large numbers of people to the area to provide the necessary services.

On the other hand, the economy was not helped by two adverse factors. One was a succession of natural disasters, such as the Yellow River floods of 30 BC which caused panic in the capital and needed five hundred boats to evacuate the inhabitants of threatened areas. That situation was eventually brought under control by conscripted labour toiling for thirty-six days to build a series of dykes that diverted the stream into auxiliary channels – completion of the feat being commemorated by the reign-title, 'Pacification of the River'.

The other adverse economic factor was an increasing difficulty in collecting taxes. Confucian officials betrayed their principles by such practices as forcing small farmers to pay taxes they themselves were meant to pay. Moreover, as senior civil servants and ministers acquired ever more land – frequently by exploiting lean years to buy cheaply from impoverished peasants – whenever they could they expunged their acquisitions from the tax registers.

The nobility, officials and rich merchants in fact accumulated land on a vast scale, securing an economic dominance over the peasantry that blighted the dynasty. Efforts to achieve a just redistribution were effectively thwarted by vested interests. The land was worked by salaried labour directed by the owner living on his estate or, if he was an official still in office, by tenants who shared the profits equally with him.

Slaves were rarely employed on the land, where abundant workers were available. Instead, those privately owned provided the domestic staff of a household, and in the great families they were also guards, armed militia, mounted escorts, acrobats and singers; beautiful young girls, trained for variety spectacles, frequently assuaged the sexual appetite of their masters or even became concubines. State-owned slaves worked on State undertakings, in forests, stud farms, arsenals and the imperial workshops; they were used too by the civil service as scribes, accountants, messengers and porters; and they served in the palaces. Altogether there were several hundred thousand privately and publicly owned slaves, or less than one per cent of the population. Those owned by the state were criminals sentenced to slavery; private owners got theirs by kidnapping or by purchase in times of distress when women and children were sold. Both also acquired slaves from Central Asia or the barbarian far south. All were generally well treated.

Slave-owning and land-ownership alike were aspects of the lavish lifestyle of the rich. They flaunted their wealth, riding abroad in their two-wheeled carriages wearing costly robes with deep cuffs and a coloured cloth around their heads, or strolling about the great gardens and artificial lakes laid out in their estates where they held horse-races or archery contests or ball games, and picnicked. Guests at their dazzling banquets were entertained by singers, musicians and dancers, strolling players from Central Asia, and wrestlers, acrobats and illusionists.

If they fell ill they were attended by Confucian scholars learned in the standard medical textbooks. These included the *Yellow Emperor's Inner Canon*, the *Divine Husbandman's Materia Medica* – both believed to comprise the wisdom of legendary sages and hence sacrosanct – the *Canon of Problems* and the

Treatise on Febrile Diseases, these two being regarded as human knowledge gained from experience. It has been asserted that Chinese medicine has not essentially changed since the composition of these books. In addition to the Confucian physicians, there were so-called hereditary doctors who served an apprenticeship with their fathers and sometimes acted as a family GP on an annual retainer. There was also an array of quacks, shamans and priests, and of old women who, despite being despised as ignorant and unscrupulous, often serviced gentlewomen's health-care needs and acted as wet-nurses and midwives.

While popular thought in pre-Han times had attributed sickness to evil spirits, it now – at least among the better-off – considered the causes to be social or supernatural, such as offending one's ancestors. For his part the professional physician perceived a disharmony within the body, and between the body, the environment and the universe – an imbalance between the body's vital energy, Yin-Yang, and the Five Powers. Medical belief thus derived from the philosophical and cosmological theories of the time. It was worked out in quite a complex understanding of anatomy, and in his approach to the patient to identify the specific disorder the doctor acted much as his modern counterparts: he examined the patient's case-history and environment and took his or her pulse. He then usually prescribed – and himself or a pharmacist made up – a combination in pill or powder form of a powerful 'principal' drug to break up the thickened blood, a 'leading' drug to reach the affected system, and auxiliary drugs to complement these or prevent side effects. The choice of drugs, all botanical or mineral-based, was huge.

Alternatively, or in addition, he might prescribe acupuncture or moxibustion, a technique of burning dried wormwood at points on the skin. Acupuncture, a practice which has spread all round the globe, likewise involved specified points on the skin, the totality of points being on fourteen invisible lines or meridians running the length of the body. The insertion of fine metal needles between half and several inches deep is calculated to remedy the imbalance of the energy flow causing the pain or disease. There are hundreds of these points along the meridians, each controlling certain physical conditions: and all were catalogued in the textbooks.

Doubtless the medical fraternity thrived on the maladies induced by the profligacy and decadence of the rich that frequently spilled over into debauchery. This deterioration in moral standards, a not-unfamiliar *fin de siècle* phenomenon, prevailed not least at the heart of the Empire, at the court of Ch'eng-ti who had been only nine years old when he succeeded Yüan-ti. As he grew older he gave way to indulgence in wine, women, and song; often he roamed his capital in disguise to pursue such pleasures as cockfighting.

It may be that the failure of his Empress to produce a son and heir turned his eyes towards a girl of lowly origins called Chao, whose skill as a musician and dancer had earned her the title of Flying Swallow. She and her sister gained the favours of the Emperor, and they then succeeded in having the Empress deposed on a charge of practising black magic. They too, however, failed to produce an heir; but when sons were born to the Emperor by a slave girl, he had them put to death lest their families threatened the position of the two sisters, who duly became Empresses.

Since the reign of Wu-ti the government of the Empire had gradually become invested in a secretariat, a cabinet, of favoured civilians and soldiers called the 'inner court' as distinct from the 'outer court' of Confucian officials who were sidetracked into administrative functions. In influence upon the government, eunuchs were rarely prominent in the Former Han dynasty, during which they staffed the state department of Palace Writers; but two men were an exception during the reigns of Ch'eng-ti's immediate predecessors. When a leading minister objected to their influence, their antagonism forced him to commit suicide. This was in 46 BC, the year Julius Caesar sailed down the Nile with Cleopatra. No other eunuchs of consequence followed and indeed early in Ch'eng-ti's reign the department of Palace Writers was abolished.

The inner court was headed by a powerful personage entitled Marshal of State. As Ch'eng-ti was only nine when he succeeded, a predominant role fell to Yüan-ti's widow. A member of the powerful Wang family, she was a redoubtable lady, the Dowager Empress. She caused the first appointee as Marshal of State to be her brother, and no less than four of her relations followed him. The last of them, however, was dismissed shortly after Ch'eng-ti died in 7 BC, when a grandson of one of Yüan-ti's consorts succeeded to the throne as Ai-ti, aged not quite eighteen.

The eclipse – momentary as it proved – of the Wang family heralded more intense manoeuvring than ever by rival families seeking imperial favour. To their dismay Ai-ti, despite having two empresses, turned his attention, which is to say his passion, to one even younger than himself, Tung Hsien, his catamite. In 2 BC Ai-ti actually appointed Tung Hsien Marshal of State and even talked of abdicating in his favour. But in 1 BC Ai-ti died, heirless, and the following day Tung was dismissed and degraded – invoking, at so grievous a loss of face, the custom of suicide.

These events brought a resurgence of Wang influence. The seniority of the Dowager Empress Wang, now the Grand Dowager Empress, enabled her to issue imperial edicts, and she immediately appointed her nephew, Wang Mang, as Marshal of State. Ai-ti's empresses were degraded, their tombs desecrated. And in succession to him an eight-year-old boy, son of one of Ch'eng-ti's half-brothers, was selected to reign as P'ing-ti.

With him but a child, authority rested firmly in the hands of the Empress Wang and her delegate Wang Mang. At first they sought to belie the prognostications which, ever since Ch'eng-ti's reign, had been interpreting various omens and natural disasters as foretelling the end of the Han Dynasty. An edict of 5 BC had announced that the new reign-title would be the Initiation of the Grand Beginning, and granted a general amnesty. To little profit, for before very long, shortly after marrying Wang

Mang's child daughter, P'ing-ti suddenly died, precipitating a dynastic crisis. His chancellor committed suicide. A one-year-old remote relation was made heir apparent and Wang Mang was first appointed Regent and then acting Emperor. A number of aristocrats reacted furiously, some accusing Wang Mang – against the probabilities – of having killed P'ing-ti. He soon put down the rebellions, and finding that the great majority of officials accepted him he was persuaded that the imperial house had lost all support. For several years he conducted a skilled campaign to gain public favour, especially by promoting a belief that he was descended from the legendary Yellow Emperor and next in line to found a dynasty – a proposition seemingly supported by a deluge of prodigies and auguries, including the alleged appearance of phoenixes and dragons. Early in AD 9 he struck. He declared the Han Dynasty defunct and ascended the throne himself as first of a dynasty called Hsin – New.

History did not in fact close its pages on the Han. The two hundred years of Liu Pang, the policeman who had seized power as Kao-ti, and of his descendants – a period known in retrospect as that of the Former Han – was punctuated, not extinguished, by Wang Mang's notable interregnum.

CHAPTER TWELVE

Interregnum (AD 9–25) and the Han revived – I

Only in the lifetime of his aunt and patron, the Grand Dowager Empress, did Wang's family become distinguished. She was the great-grand-daughter of a country gentleman in the north of what is now Shantung, and grand-daughter and daughter of minor officials. At the age of seventeen she entered the harem of the then Emperor, Hsüan-ti, and, subsequently becoming consort to his successor, Yüan-ti, bore a son who succeeded his father as Ch'eng-ti. It was in the latter's reign that his mother had her relatives appointed as five successive Marshals of State, culminating in Wang Mang.

Through his family's influence he had by that time held a number of prominent positions. They included some nominal military commands – among them, Colonel of Archers who Shoot by Sound – and several supernumerary posts as adviser to the Emperor – among them, Gentleman of the Yellow Gates. He had been ennobled as a marquis at the age of twenty-nine, and seventeen years later in AD 1 he received the new and grandiloquent title of Duke Giving Tranquillity to the Han.

It was not perhaps a tranquillity appreciated by the Han when within a decade he set himself on the imperial throne and set about ruling nearly sixty million people. He was fifty-four. Any attempt to describe what kind of man he was is bedevilled by a quirk of Chinese historiography. The authors of the official dynastic histories – starting with that of the Han and followed by twenty-three more right up to the twentieth century – were governed by the Mandate of Heaven doctrine. An emperor earned the Mandate by his merits, but if a man occupying the throne did not have those merits Heaven withdrew its Mandate. Because Wang Mang was, as we shall see, deposed after a relatively brief period, his loss of the Mandate could only have been for want of merit. Hence from Son of Heaven he was reduced to usurper and depicted as inept, devious, hypocritical and a megalomaniac. And since much importance was attached to a person's face as a mirror of his character (the assumption being that true Sons of Heaven had large noses and prominent foreheads), historians delighted in describing Wang Mang as having a big mouth, receding chin, bulging eyes and a loud coarse voice. What he in fact looked like is unknown, while his character must be deduced from his deeds.

There is no doubt that his education and extensive studying as a youth made him a convinced Confucian. There is no doubt also of the concern and care he showed for his relatives, his meticulous observance of the rules of proper conduct, and his giving away his wealth to others. The unusual breadth of his interests is evidenced by his administration during the boy Emperor P'ing-ti's brief reign: he wrought improvements to provincial schools while enlarging the Academy, had an important new road built through the mountains south of the Wei River, erected many great buildings and shrines, and in AD 5 he had called a massive conference to deliberate on a diversity of subjects ranging from pitchpipes and astronomy/astrology to divination and classical texts.

These last had come under renewed scrutiny because the so-called 'modern texts' approved by the great 51 BC conference in the Pavilion of the Stone Canal were criticized by the emerging so-called 'old text' school which wanted to revive neglected old-character commentaries descended from the Chou. The argument was led by the great scholar Liu Hsin who had continued his father's work of cataloguing the imperial library. He particularly deplored mystical theories and the manipulation of the Classics for prophecy and divination.

However, despite being a sponsor of Liu Hsin and himself a convinced Confucian, Wang Mang saw precisely in the area of prophecy and divination his way to the throne when P'ing-ti died. The Han dynasty was believed by many, including Liu Hsin, to have been ruled by the element fire, whose associated colour was red. P'ing-ti's death broached the notion that this element had been eliminated by the next in the cycle, soil. The colour associated with soil was yellow. Hence by claiming descent from the legendary Yellow Emperor Wang Mang endowed his aspirations with legitimacy. For three years following P'ing-ti's death he gained public and scholarly support, largely because of the appearance of hundreds of supposed prodigies and auguries pointing to the start of a new dynasty and good fortune. In truth, however, it was a false prospectus used to help bring Wang Mang the imperial seals, for the omens were many of them the products of adventurers turned forgers and deceivers for the occasion.

Unsuspecting that Heaven would not forgive him for the fraud, he started his reign with a rush of legislation. Four times he changed the coinage, debasing it with lighter weights at higher denominations, and counterfeiters who battened on the changes faced exile or death. The mass of the population, that is to say the peasants working the fields in their pyjama-like garments, were little concerned because they seldom used cash. While merchants and gentry could protect their capital by investment in land, the aristocracy were hard hit by being ordered to exchange all their gold for currency knives of gilt bronze, adding to the great reserves of gold in the imperial treasury – some of it from Siberia, but most from the West in payment for silk. A few years later gold was restored to circulation and the nobles ordered to exchange their knives for coins worth only the knives' weight in bronze. Thus the Han leading families were stripped of much of their wealth and soon afterwards they were deprived of their fiefs and marquisates. So were the seeds of discontent sown.

Wang Mang reorganized the bureaucracy and introduced new titles, as well as extensively renaming commanderies and counties. He enforced state monopolies in fermented liquor, salt, iron tools, coin-minting, and the income from mountains and marshes. He stabilized the prices of grain, cloth and silk by buying these goods when the prices were low, storing them in warehouses established in five major cities, and selling when prices were high. He levied a ten per cent tax on hunters, fishermen, sericulturists, artisans, professional people and merchants. And the salaries of officials were reduced in bad years in proportion to the harvest: doubtless they welcomed this as much as today's civil servants would welcome a salary-cut in proportion to a fall in the GNP.

Though sowing further seeds of discontent, all these measures had precedents in the Former Han period. So did the revival, in rather more wholesale fashion, of an attempt at land reform, for the scandalous accumulation of huge private estates had continued unabated. All able-bodied men were to receive an allotment of land, and families with more than a given holding had to distribute the excess among their land-poor relatives and neighbours. But the scheme proved to be unenforceable and was soon abandoned. Unprecedented, however, was Wang Mang's attempt to restrict slavery by prohibiting the buying and selling of slaves, but it was easily circumvented until it too had to be abandoned.

These attempts at reforms, with whose like the West would wrestle in future ages, at least bespoke a man of large and generous vision. He ruled directly, delegating little, and he closely monitored the performance of his officials. A stickler for royal integrity, he forced three of his sons, and a grandson and a nephew, to commit suicide for breaking the law. His wide-ranging curiosity was testified to by the intellectuals' conference he called in AD 5, and some years later he summoned a meeting of men with extraordinary skills suitable for warfare: it is recorded that one of them made two wings and flew, presumably from a tower, for several hundred double paces before falling, but the information is too scant to provide a credible page in aviation history. Before this, in AD 16, Wang Mang had ordered his grand physician to dissect an executed man to examine his viscera and arteries to find cures for diseases: not until 1315 did such an official dissection take place in Europe, by Mondino da' Luzzi at Bologna, for until then Western knowledge of anatomy was derived from the great Roman doctor Galen who dissected animals.

In foreign affairs he was resourceful and able. By force, or diplomacy backed by the threat of force, he ensured peace with very little interruption throughout the country and its borders. Once, faced with the threat of renewed hostility by the Hsiung-nu, he had one of their princes he held as hostage executed, in accordance with the hostage rules of the time.

Despite the seeds of discontent being scattered by his legislation, they were not to be germinated except by events beyond his control. Most by far of his officials supported him, and it is significant that, although even the great Wu-ti had been the target of a would-be assassin, no attempt was ever made on Wang Mang's life. His defeat, when it came, was essentially at the hands of Nature, or perhaps Heaven had not forgotten the means he had used to gain power.

The 'Pacification of the River' which Yüan-ti had commemorated as a reign title in 30 BC was cruelly mocked in about AD 4 by an immense flood. It poured across the southern half of the Great Plain in the east as the Yellow River divided into two. Having previously emptied into the sea to the north of present-day Shantung peninsula, it now thrust out another arm to the south of the peninsula. Seven years later there were more floods and another shifting of the river's course. For untold centuries the river had been silting up with the yellow loess which gave it its name, gradually raising the bed until the water level was above that of the surrounding countryside. Thus a bursting of the banks, which now occurred despite patchwork remedial works over the years, was bound to cause a huge inundation. The two calamities, the first compounded by the second, were far beyond Wang Mang's engineering resources to cope with. Those whom the floods did not drown fled to adjoining areas where there were not enough supplies for them. Famine spread and the peasants in hundreds of thousands left the Great Plain west of Shantung in a slow migration southwards, banding together to take food by force. In Shantung itself, overcrowded as it was by refugees, the two encircling arms of the Yellow River made escape precarious. The peasant bands grew into a large, if ill-organized, army which looted, killed and kidnapped its way through the peninsula. Wang Mang sent troops to quell them but they failed; four years later, in AD 22, the even larger army he sent was decisively defeated. To distinguish themselves from the government forces the peasants painted their eyebrows red and so became known as the Red Eyebrows.

Now was the time for the discontent caused by Wang Mang's legislation to take root. The gentry families in what is now southern Honan, with prominent among them the Liu family which had founded the Former Han Dynasty, joined with bands of peasants led by local chiefs from as far afield as the lower Yangtze to generate a violent uprising against Wang Mang, whose troops were again twice defeated in AD 23.

The various rebel leaders resolved to appoint a new emperor. They chose a member of the Liu family, a sixth generation descendant of Ching-ti. Entitled the Keng-shih Emperor – 'Emperor of the New Beginning' – he was the first emperor of the Later Han but, as events would prove, not the founder of its dynasty. His tenure was to be brief, this testimony of Heaven's dissatisfaction prompting historians' dismissal of him as a witless drunkard, which of course he was not. Indeed, the insurgent gentry and peasant chieftains consolidated the rebel movement around him and whole new Army of Han emerged to fight what had now become a civil war.

Wang Mang desperately mobilized a great army to set out from Loyang, the ancient capital, but after some initial success it was utterly defeated in July of AD 23. Disintegration began to crumble the Empire. The Han army advanced on the capital Changan. All the leading clans around the city led their followers into it in search of loot. They broke through one of the gates and, joined by people within, reached the main palace. A fierce day's fighting saw the imperial harem go up in flames. At dawn next day Wang Mang, exhausted and semiconscious, was carried by his men to the Terrace Bathed by Water, where in the late afternoon they were overwhelmed and killed; Wang Mang's head was cut off.

All his senior officials were dead, in battle or by suicide or execution. The Keng-shih Emperor, making Loyang his capital after the Han army captured it, at first held sway over nearly half the Empire. It was an empire in which a great convulsion of the population was under way, as millions of peasants migrated from the flooded north, particularly the Great Plain area, to the south.

The Keng-shih Emperor proceeded to make three bad mistakes. First, he sent a leading scion of his Liu family, Liu Hsiu, on a mission to restore tranquillity to the northern part of the Great Plain, enabling Liu Hsiu to develop an independent command. Second, when the Red Eyebrows advanced westward and, resting not far from Loyang, sent envoys to the Keng-shih Emperor, he antagonized them. And finally he moved his capital back to Changan, whose vulnerability Wang Mang had so tragically demonstrated.

The next year or so exposed the folly of these actions. Liu Hsiu defected from the Emperor and raised an army which advanced from the east. The Red Eyebrows moved against Changan. As they entered it, the Keng-shih Emperor took to his horse, but was captured. Abdicating did not save him, for having been ordered to herd horses in the open countryside he was there strangled. The Red Eyebrows sacked the city and terrorized the population.

Already, however, Liu Hsiu, with much-extended territory under his control, had proclaimed himself Son of Heaven. He ascended the throne (AD 25) as Kuang-wu-ti, founder of the Later Han dynasty. During the time that the Keng-shih Emperor was enduring his melancholy fate outside Changan, the new Emperor captured Loyang and made it his capital.

He faced eleven years of civil war. The great force of Red Eyebrows finally exhausted itself and surrendered to Kuang-wu-ti. He proceeded to overcome in turn uprisings in the Great Plain and Shantung, along the Yangtze and the Kansu corridor in the north-west. His most formidable opponent controlled a large swathe of territory adjoining the Yangtze gorges, below which he had a floating bridge built connected to fortifications on either side of the river: Kuang-wu-ti's army, deployed in boats to sail upstream with the wind, used torches to set light to the bridge, and then invaded the hostile territory to reach its leader's capital, where he died. Kuang-wu-ti was now undisputed monarch of all China and the dynasty of the Later Han firmly established.

When he made Loyang his capital, a thousand years had passed since its establishment by the great Duke of Chou after the conquest of the Shang. Less ostentatiously luxurious than Changan, it had an area of almost four square miles. It stood on the banks of encircling arms of a Yellow River tributary, bounded by high walls pierced by twelve gates. Within, it was laid out on a north–south axis, its streets forming a grid. The Northern Palace complex at one end and the Southern Palace at the other each covered about 125 acres and they were connected by an elevated covered avenue of three lanes, the central lane being for the Emperor. There were government offices, shrines, an arsenal, two gardens, thirty-two official inns which doubled as police posts, a market, and the homes of officials and nobles. One moat enabled shipping to bring in supplies; while from another, pumps and norias – a succession of buckets raised and lowered by a chain – provided water. Outside the walls, important buildings included the imperial observatory called the Spiritual Terrace, a cosmological temple called the Bright Hall, and the Academy, whose campus would eventually have

240 buildings with 1,850 rooms and an attendance of up to 30,000 students. An altar was there for the worship of Heaven and a host of divinities that included the Five Planets and the Twenty-eight Stations of the Moon; also there was an Altar of the Earth, numerous shrines, altars for ushering in the seasons, imperial parks and hunting preserves, the imperial tombs and funeral workshops, two more markets, and mansions of the rich. Altogether, Greater Loyang more than doubled the extent of the walled part, and with about half a million people was probably the most populous city on earth.

Of all the departments of the imperial palaces, the one that was to have the most potent influence on the course of events seems also the most unlikely. This was called the Lateral Courts – in short, the harem, kept by all emperors, even minors. In the course of the succeeding century its ladies came to number no fewer than six thousand. Once divided into fourteen ranks, these were reduced by Kuang-wu-ti to three – honourable lady, beautiful lady, and chosen lady. Selection for the harem took place every year in the eighth month. The girls had to be virgins from unimpeachable families and aged between thirteen and twenty by Chinese reckoning, which made a child one year old at birth and one year older on each subsequent New Year's Day. They were inspected by a senior counsellor, a eunuch harem assistant, and a physiognomist, who judged according to their beauty, complexion, hair, carriage, elegance, manners and respectability. A girl reaching the required standard would then be taken to the harem where after further tests she might be accepted or rejected. In fact intense political manoeuvring often determined selection, since it was always an honourable lady who became enthroned as Empress.

Seldom did love intrude, as suggested by the fact that eight of the eleven Later Han empresses were childless. The name of the game was power. An empress wielded immense influence, particularly as dowager empress after her husband's death, for usually her family gained the highest civil and military offices and thus often both dominated the government and determined the imperial succession, frequently by a minor through whom they could maintain their domination.

For this reason it has been said that the political history of the Later Han is essentially the history of its contending factions. There were four or five great regional families who, with their followers, strove for ascendancy. First one, then another gained it according to which provided the emperor's consort. But, if the position brought power, it also brought peril. For a supplanted consort family the consequences could be swift and brutal, including executions, exile, suicides, demotion and certainly temporary if not permanent eclipse. All this can be illustrated by a summary of the century and a half's politics following Kuang-wu-ti's ascent.

Kuang-wu-ti divorced his first Empress and she was exceptional in being allowed to live out her life peacefully. On his death a son by his second wife became Emperor as Ming-ti (AD 57–75) who, his wife being childless, appointed one of his sons by a concubine to be his heir. This son succeeded to the throne as Chang-ti (75–88) and when his Empress too had no sons, once more the son of a concubine was made heir apparent; but as the concubine – and her sister who was also in the harem – belonged to a clan antagonistic to the Empress's, she engineered the boy's downfall and the two sisters were put into prison where they drank poison and died. Later the elder of two other sisters in the harem produced a new heir apparent and again factional enmity brought death, to the sisters and their father, while their relatives were sent into exile. On Chang-ti's death his heir, entitled Ho-ti (88–106), was still a minor. In fact so many minors ascended the throne in the ensuing century that no fewer than seven regents were appointed. The first of these, a successful general, together with his three brothers committed suicide after a leading eunuch contrived a false accusation of plotting regicide. The same fate probably befell Ho-ti's first Empress after she was denounced for witchcraft. When Ho-ti died his successor Shang-ti was a child of three months who survived for only a few more months, to be followed on the throne by another minor, An-ti (106–125). When he grew up, his Empress being childless, he nominated his only son by an 'honourable lady' as his heir apparent, but his Empress had the honourable lady poisoned and the heir demoted and detained in the Northern Palace at Loyang. On An-ti's death the widowed Empress procured the throne for a minor, a grandson of Chang-ti, but he did not live out the year. In the midst of the Dowager Empress's deliberations on a successor the palace eunuchs took a hand. Binding themselves to each other by oaths to support An-ti's demoted and detained son, they set out one night and after a successful foray against opposing eunuchs freed An-ti's son and proclaimed him Emperor as Shun-ti (125–144). The Dowager Empress was stripped of her rank and a number of her faction executed or exiled to Vietnam. Shun-ti had an only son, by one of the honourable ladies, and though the boy became Emperor on his father's death he lived only a few months. Another of Chang-ti's descendants was then enthroned as Chih-ti at the age of seven, but he too only briefly survived, allegedly murdered in 145 by the Regent, a relative of Shun-ti's widow. Their faction had a great-grandson of Chang-ti succeed to the throne. Entitled Huan-ti (147–167) he was at the time two years short of being 'capped', which is to say reaching his majority at the age of sixteen. At seventeen he took as his consort a younger sister of the Dowager Empress. A decade later when both these women had died, he felt able to break the grip of their family, now led by the Regent, so he secretly colluded with eunuchs he could trust – for others were in the Regent's pay – to defend the palace while a thousand men surrounded the Regent's residence. Overwhelmed and dismissed, he forthwith killed his wife and himself: prominent relatives were publicly executed and his family never recovered its influence. Huan-ti took on a second consort, who lasted six years before being accused of black magic and drunkenness: she was sentenced to prison with orders to kill herself; her relatives were exiled or demoted, and thus another clan lost its influence. Huan-ti's third consort became the Dowager Empress when he died, and she appointed her father Regent, for since Huan-ti had no sons they ensured the succession by a twelve-year-old great-great-grandson of Chang-ti. He was entitled Ling-ti (168 – 189). Within a year his throne was rocked by a massive crisis.

CHAPTER THIRTEEN

The Han revived – II (25–220)

The eunuchs, recruited to look after the imperial harem, grew in numbers as the harem did. Their proximity to the throne inevitably resulted in their activities extending far beyond care of the honourable, beautiful and chosen ladies. The previous chapter showed a eunuch's hand behind the disgracing of Ho-ti's general-turned-regent in 92, and how the eunuchs both freed and enthroned Shun-ti in 128, and enabled Huan-ti to dislodge his Dowager Empress's family in 158; besides these there were many other occasions when they insinuated themselves into government affairs. They had been awarded noble titles and fiefs, and the right to pass these on to their adopted sons. By the time the twelve-year-old Ling-ti came to the throne they numbered no fewer than two thousand. Many had been castrated as boys for presentation to the palace; others had the operation – removal of the entire genitalia by one cut with a sharp knife – performed as adults in order to obtain an easy job in imperial employment. Hairless and, as a rule, haughty, suspicious, moody, greedy for luxuries, and gluttons, many were exceptionally able.

They were divided into ranks under a head eunuch and given to forming factions which contended for the favour of the Emperor, the Empress or the Dowager Empress. Ling-ti's predecessor Huan-ti had increasingly leant on his preferred eunuchs for advice, causing growing discontent among the civil bureaucracy which in any case despised them. With the advent of Ling-ti in 168 the eunuch issue became a burning one.

The Regent, named Tou Wu, father of the Dowager Empress, had a distinguished ally called Ch'en Fan, Grand Tutor to the Emperor. They discussed what to do about the ever-expanding tentacles of the eunuchs' influence. Ch'en Fan proposed nothing short of their total elimination and urged Tou Wu on more vigorously when an eclipse of the sun was interpreted as a bad omen. Memorials to the court calling for action against the eunuchs, on various grounds ranging from treachery to placing their clients in office all over the Empire, were rejected by the Dowager Empress who saw the eunuchs as the throne's vital bulwark against the bureaucracy, the army leaders, and the powerful families such as that of Tou Wu.

For some months the situation deepened into a crisis. Tou Wu and Ch'en Fan decided on a new tactic when an eminent fortune-teller, expert in astronomical portents, advised them that the planet Venus was behaving in a way 'not advantageous to ministers', which is to say the eunuchs. The two men reasoned that if leading eunuchs were indicted for specific crimes the Dowager Empress could hardly again frustrate them. A eunuch was tortured until he implicated his fellows. Thereupon a memorial to have a number of eunuchs arrested was taken into the palace by night for presentation at court next morning. But eunuchs secretly opened it and, shocked by the number of people named, seventeen of them swore an oath to kill Tou Wu.

They woke the young Emperor and hurried him to a safe part of the palace, where they gave him a sword and put at his side his former wet-nurse who had become a close confidante. Then they took the Dowager Empress by surprise, soon placing her in custody in the Southern Palace, and seized the imperial seals. These gave them the authority for, first, ordering soldiers to guard the palaces and, second, issuing an edict for Tou Wu's arrest.

Having been out for the night and hence unaware of its events until the edict was served on him, Tou Wu fled to his nephew who commanded one of the five regiments stationed at the capital. Meanwhile Ch'en Fan, also belatedly alerted to what had happened, hurried to the palace with some of his subordinates. Soldiers surrounded and overpowered him, then took him to prison where later in the day he was trampled to death. Tou Wu fared no better: when troops in his nephew's regiment began defecting in large numbers he killed himself. The rest of his family was killed, as were many key figures, sometimes with their families. Dismissals and banishments continued for some days and the record speaks of several hundred people forfeiting their lives.

Thus was another of the great families to influence events eclipsed. For the next twenty years the eunuchs were in complete ascendancy. They continued to be ennobled, and from AD 175 every department in the palace was headed by eunuchs, one of whom was even appointed commander-in-chief of the army. In what is known as the Great Proscription (169–184) all opposition to them was destroyed. Plots devised from time to time to control them failed. Their protégés, parents and brothers were given high appointments at the capital and in the countryside.

Indeed, high office in the civil service became not a matter of merit but of corruption. It could be bought for cash. The sales were negotiated in a building named the Western Quarter in the Western Garden, where what was called 'courtesy money' piled up by the million. While this process filled the upper echelons of government, the lower ranks were severely depleted by both the Great Proscription and exclusion rules which forbade appointments in the commandery of a man's birth or his wife's domicile. Since students of the university were not considered safe – in 172, following demonstrations, over a thousand of them were imprisoned by the eunuchs – a whole new university, the School at the Gate of the Vast Capital, was established and its candidates virtually guaranteed a job in the administration.

While the degradation of the civil service and the dominance of the eunuchs were two of the features that marked Ling-ti's reign, a third was the frequency of rebellions and border conflicts. These last were in fact a continuation of events going back to the reign of the Later Han dynasty's founder, Kuang-wu-ti. Constant raids on the northern countryside by tribes of the Hsiung-nu had prompted him to build additional walls, but the nomads went on roaming much of the north-west. And then the Hsiung-nu federation split up into a northern and southern section, upon which the latter was permitted to occupy, on a tributary basis, territory within the Great Wall – the Ordos region and adjoining parts of Shensi and Kansu.

A son of the southern Hsiung-nu's leader was kept as a hostage at the imperial court. Each year a new hostage was escorted south, meeting en route the previous hostage being returned to his father. Hsiung-nu envoys attended the New Year ceremonies at Loyang, going back with silk, brocade, gold and food as gifts from the Emperor to the Hsiung-nu's leader, his mother, principal wives, sons and high dignitaries. The system, however, lost its efficiency as rifts broke out between the Hsiung-nu and between them and the Chinese. The volatile situation worsened in Ling-ti's reign when elements of the Hsiung-nu entered southern Shensi.

Meanwhile China's Central Asian protectorate of the Western Regions, consisting of the oasis states along the silk routes, was given only spasmodic support against the northern Hsiung-nu and other tribes, and not long before Ling-ti's accession the imperial hold ended. A more direct threat came from proto-Tibetans called the Ch'iang who had been encroaching from due west and south-west since the time of Wang Mang. They constantly invaded the Wei valley and twice threatened the old capital, Changan.

The effect of all these conflicts was to denude the northern and western borders of Chinese peasants as they fled south. Together with the exodus southward which followed the great floods that undid Wang Mang, the migrations from north to south during the Later Han Dynasty accounted for eighteen million people. This vast movement profoundly affected the demography of China. The southern part of the country had hitherto been but sparsely populated, mainly by indigenous tribes collectively called the Man. As the Chinese from the north moved among them, penetrating deep along the valleys to appropriate the rich alluvial soil and establishing many new commanderies, the aboriginal people had either to acquiesce in becoming sinicized or take to the mountains as guerrillas. Conflicts were frequent, the Han court regarding non-compliant tribes as rebels: the Later Han experienced some fifty-three 'uprisings' in the area. Although all were put down, colonization largely collapsed until its revival centuries later.

The greatest of the many rebellions during Ling-ti's reign was by a movement known to history as the Yellow Turbans. While a variety of omens had not boded well for the dynasty – earthquakes, droughts, floods, locusts, caterpillars, epidemics and severe storms, prompting the court to proclaim amnesties and a rebate of taxes – the omens in 183 were good, for an excellent harvest followed the reported appearance of magic mushrooms and phoenixes. Nevertheless, in the following year the Yellow Turbans, so called because of their headwear, rose against the government in sixteen commanderies to the south, east and north-east of the capital.

They had started as a sect about a decade before on the north-eastern seaboard, under the leadership of one Chang Chüeh and his two brothers, who impressed the locals with miracle cures. At some point Chang Chüeh convinced himself that it was up to him to supplant the dynasty. He preached a doctrine derived from Taoism and Yin-Yang, and also the Five Elements, whence was derived the colour yellow, symbol for the element soil which would follow the element fire of the Han Dynasty. From Confucianism he drew on the principle of how the Mandate of Heaven may change, and the ideal of peace and equality, which inspired the title Chang Chüeh gave his movement, Way of the Great Peace.

So great was his success that by 184 he had several hundred thousand followers, who included some wealthy persons as well as poor peasants, and even many of the local officials and provincial elite. Their uprising was planned for 3rd April of that year, but when the plot was betrayed to the throne, Chang Chüeh struck in March. For ten months his people created mayhem, defeating commandery armies, capturing important cities, and kidnapping local rulers. A large army sent out by the government was needed finally to defeat them, leaving half a million dead, including the three brothers.

Other rebellions broke out elsewhere, their leaders sometimes calling themselves Sons of Heaven. To control the situation the court appointed generals as regional commissioners to take charge in troubled areas. They had full ministerial rank and wielded relatively independent powers. One of these men, named Tung Cho, advanced further from the west than his orders specified, pausing only eighty miles from Loyang.

At this juncture, on 13th May 189, the Emperor Ling-ti died – and with him, essentially, the Han Dynasty, although this was not at first manifest. His eldest son, aged thirteen, was enthroned as Liu Pien. His mother became Dowager Empress and Regent. She, her half-brother Ho Chin who was Grand Commandant, and the Grand Tutor who was a scion of the noble Yüan family, formed a ruling triumvirate. Liu Pien had an eight-year-old half-brother called Liu Hsieh and entitled Prince, the protégé of his grandmother and in the care of the eunuch commander-in-chief Chien Shih. All these people comprised the cast in the drama played out in the summer of 189.

Chien Shih tried to unite the eunuchs in a plot against Ho Chin with the object of replacing the emperor, Liu Pien, with his half-brother Prince Liu Hsieh. The plot, however, was leaked, bringing about Chien Shih's execution and the expulsion from her palace of his ally, Liu Hsieh's grandmother, who died a few months later from, it was said, fear and grief.

An army colonel, Yüan Shao – another member of the noble Yüan family – now took his place on the stage. He urged Ho Chin to eliminate the eunuchs, but the Dowager Empress refused. Yüan Shao then pressed a number of generals, including the insubordinate Tung Cho hovering eighty miles from Loyang, to send in memorials denouncing the eunuchs. Still the Dowager Empress held firm.

So matters stood until a day in September when Ho Chin appeared at the Dowager Empress's morning levee. Sight of him surprised and unnerved the eunuchs present, since he had declared himself to be unwell. They watched as he conferred with his royal half-sister and when told of the conversation by an informer who had eavesdropped they were shocked to hear that Ho Chin had asked for nothing less than the execution of them all. They did not hesitate. As Ho Chin left the palace they called him back on the pretext that the Dowager Empress had more to say to him. At the same time they gathered weapons and men behind the Dowager Empress's antechamber. When Ho Chin seated himself on the floor, there waiting to be called in, the chief eunuch stood in front of him and diverted his attention with a harangue which ended when a blow from behind removed Ho Chin's head.

Yüan Shao responded to the news by leading troops to the Northern Palace while his half-brother led troops to the Southern Palace. The latter's gate was set alight, smoking out the eunuchs who fled along the covered avenue to the Northern Palace with the Emperor, his half-brother the Prince, and also the Dowager Empress who, however, escaped in the melée. Within days, Yüan Shao's troops broke into the Northern Palace and killed every eunuch they could find, over two thousand of them. The chief eunuch had a brief escape, fleeing with the Emperor and the Prince towards the Yellow River, but, overtaken there, he leapt into the water and drowned. Thus did the eunuchs have their comeuppance.

Seeing from afar the capital alight, Tung Cho led his army in to seize the opportunity for loot. Then he set off to find the Emperor. The lad and his half-brother, following the chief eunuch's drowning, had wandered through the night on foot until they found an open cart in which they were riding when Tung Cho found them. He escorted them back to Loyang where he quickly asserted himself. First he browbeat Yüan Shao into quitting the capital for the east; next he forced the Dowager Empress to replace the Emperor, of whom he had formed a poor impression, with his princely half-brother, the child Liu Hsieh; and finally he had the Dowager Empress done to death.

Incensed by these actions, Yüan Shao and his half-brother, together with another colonel (and a fine poet) called Ts'ao Ts'ao, formed a coalition in the east to oust Tung Cho. In preparation for their attack Tung Cho sent the new Emperor and the court to the former capital of Changan. Thousands of people followed in a rabble that ravaged the countryside while harassed by Tung Cho's troops. Onslaughts by the eastern coalition presently forced Tung Cho himself, in 191, to leave Loyang which he put to the torch. He too went to Changan, where he was killed a year later.

Liu Hsieh now ruled as Emperor in little more than name. Chaos rent the Empire. Almost everywhere local warlords, rebels and independent officials vied for regional supremacy, and nowhere was there stability for more than a few months. Gradually the segmentation of the country into different power centres began to take shape.

For a while the oddest of these was an enclave a little to the south-west of Changan. A religious movement not unrelated to the Yellow Turbans ran it. Like them the movement owed much to Taoism and, called the Celestial Masters of the Five Bushels, it dreamed of a Great Peace. Its followers had each to pay five pecks of rice to their religious superiors, and they could supposedly be cured of any illness by publicly confessing their sins. The movement's political ideology was based on communal ownership of property, and it had a fully functioning administrative system. Even after it was suppressed in 215, it continued to attract adherents for the next two centuries.

Its suppression was by Ts'ao Ts'ao, one of the leaders of the eastern coalition against Tung Cho. By now the coalition had broken up in enmity between its leaders, with Ts'ao Ts'ao rapidly outstripping the others. When in 196 the Emperor, following his marriage the year before, decided to leave Changan where he had striven to keep the semblance of a court, and after a year's hazardous journey reached Loyang, Ts'ao Ts'ao used blandishments and threats to get him to move on to his own base city. Extending his grip on the north-east, in a great battle in 200 Ts'ao Ts'ao defeated Yüan Shao whose massacre of the eunuchs had initiated the years of tumult. Ts'ao Ts'ao then spread his power across the north-west until he held undisputed hegemony over all northern China except for the southern part of the West. This was under an intrepid soldier of fortune, Liu Pei, distant relation of the Han's founding family. Meanwhile China south of the Yangtze had come under the sway first of a brilliant warlord aged twenty-five, and then (on his death) of his brother, one Sun Ch'üan.

Ts'ao Ts'ao exercised his domination of the wretched Emperor by having the Empress deposed and her two sons killed, clearing the way for his own daughter to become Empress. If his death in 220 came as a relief to the Emperor Liu Hsieh, it was short-lived. Ts'ao Ts'ao's son Ts'ao P'i took over the many titles and offices his father had rewarded himself with, and then for many weeks, as prognosticators foretold an imminent change in Heaven's Mandate, he pressurized the Emperor into yielding his throne.

On 11th December 220 Liu Hsieh abdicated in favour of Ts'ao P'i who declared himself first Emperor of the Wei Dynasty. The four-hundred-year Han Dynasty was at an end. The Empire it had governed was split in three – the north under Ts'ao P'i, the south-west under Liu Pei, who laid tenuous claim to the Han name, and the south under Sun Ch'üan. Each claimed Heaven's Mandate and entitled himself Emperor. And so began the sixty-year period called the Three Kingdoms, initiating three hundred and sixty years of Chinese disunity, sometimes called China's Dark Ages.

That the Han Dynasty had been a mighty one can scarcely be disputed, propelling China as it did to ranking with the Roman Empire. Indeed, two of its contributions to world civilization exceed in importance anything provided by the Romans. One was the compass; the other, paper.

The compass was a by-product of geomancy. Of all the numerous forms of divination on which the Chinese so heavily depended in all their affairs, geomancy was most firmly rooted. It rested on the belief in a cosmic breath that in the forms of wind and water, visible and invisible, flowed through the universe. Among the concepts it gave rise to was *Feng-shui* – the siting of buildings and objects so that the harmonizing of Yin-Yang and other forces would protect them from malign influences, and this related to a keen appreciation, so apparent in Chinese painting, of landscape contours and topographical features.

Against that background, the compass came to be developed both to assist in the siting of buildings and for use on the divining board so important to the Han for prognostications, especially in war. The board consisted of a disc rotating on a square board, both marked with astrological and other divining signs, and with a lodestone in the middle. The lodestone was spoon-shaped with a ladle-like handle – following the configuration of the Great Bear or Northern Dipper – and it balanced on its bowl. The divining board and its magnetic spoon thus represent the progenitor of all dial-and-pointer instruments. Having learnt to magnetize iron by rubbing it with lodestone, the Chinese developed the lodestone spoon into a magnetized fish- or tadpole-shaped needle which they either floated on water or suspended by a silken thread. The device would take a thousand years to become known in Europe. However, although there is evidence of terrestrial direction-finding in Han times, its application to marine navigation awaited many centuries, perhaps because the Chinese were so little of a deep-seafaring nation, and their sailors began using it only about a century before their European and Arab counterparts did.

The invention of paper followed a similar evolutionary process. Paper consists of a sheet of plant fibres which are mixed, pounded, cooked, put in a mould, drenched by water through a sieve-like screen, and then dried to result in the finished product. Its origins probably lie in the pre-Christian era Chinese tradition of washing rags in water and allowing the fibres to form a felted sheet on a mat. The invention proper took place in 105 in the Imperial Workshops, as announced by its director, a eunuch named Ts'ai Lun who had previously been confidential secretary to the Emperor, Ho-ti. It was not expressly invented for writing, its first uses being for the decorative and fine arts, at ceremonies and festivals, for business and monetary credit transactions, sanitary and medical purposes, for personal attire and furnishings, for games and so forth; nor did it immediately replace bamboo and wooden slips for book-making. But as time passed its use for writing became very widespread, although the craft of papermaking took fifteen hundred years to become known to the greater part of the world (European manufacture started in the twelfth century). It was a necessary precursor to, and reached the summation of its potent role in human affairs through a further great Chinese invention, that of printing – which was still, however, some five or six centuries distant.

The Later Han produced other important inventions, such as the seismograph, the water mill, and the wheelbarrow. Astronomical science was advanced, and a beginning made in systematic botany and zoology as well as in glazes and proto-porcelain, while textile techniques were centuries ahead of those in Persia and Europe. The compilation of bibliographies was established, with one book-list naming seven hundred works by experts in magic, medicine, military science, history, philosophy, divination and astronomy.

These works and poetry constituted the literature of the time. Fiction existed only in the form of anecdotes, parables and jokes, many of immemorial vintage. The novel would not emerge for many centuries; likewise drama, so highly developed in the West, seems to have been as yet unknown in an age of dance and music. Thus what an educated person read was poetry and a wide range of specialist topics; the first dictionary, the *Shuo*

Wen, with about ten thousand characters, was completed in the second century AD.

But while so much redounds to the glory of the Han, one innovation seems bizarrely inhumane. This was the practice of female foot-binding. Beginning among the aristocracy towards the end of the dynasty, it later became widespread and lasted until the nineteenth century. At the age of about four a girl would have her toes broken and bent under the sole of her foot which was then bound with several metres of bandaging to stop the blood circulation. For some months she would not be able to walk and after a year could only get about by being carried in a sedan chair. When she could walk, the compression and atrophy of the toes were enhanced, and by about the fifteenth year the process was complete, leaving the foot only a few inches long. The bound foot was called the golden or perfumed lily and described by a modern Chinese writer as 'the highest sophistication of the Chinese sensual imagination'. Small feet, with the measured steps and gentle, swaying gait they caused, were desirable for a good marriage and associated with security and status. They were a woman's pride, the dominant form of erotic and aesthetic attraction.

In contrast with this cruel and primitive fashion stands the dynasty's superb achievement of beauty and lyricism in the arts and crafts. Each commandery maintained an agency for the production and embellishment of ritual vessels, robes, lacquer- and jade-ware, weapons, and the plated armour adopted by the army. The art of landscaping was highly developed, as evidenced by the park laid out behind the palace at Loyang, built up with artificial lakes and hills into a fairyland. Although little has survived of public architecture, because palaces, mansions and ancestral halls were largely built of timber (though with straight-tiled roofs), an idea of the magnificence of the palaces is given by a number of sources like this Han *fu* poem:

High halls and deep chambers, with railings
    and tiered balconies;

Stepped terraces, storeyed pavilions whose
    tops look on the high mountains;
Lattice doors with scarlet interstices; and
    carvings on the square lintels;
Draughtless rooms for winter: galleries
    cool in summer;
Crossing the hall into the apartments, the
    ceilings and floors are vermilion,
The chambers of polished stone with
    kingfisher hangings on jasper hooks;
Bedspreads of kingfisher seeded with pearls,
    all dazzling in brightness;
Arras of fine silk covers the walls, damask
    canopies stretch overhead,
Braids and ribbons, brocades and satins,
    fastened with rings of precious stone ...

What has survived, however, is tomb architecture, for the Han were China's greatest builders of tombs for monarchs and aristocrats. They used stone, brick and tile to fashion domes, barrel-vaulted ceilings, pillars, chambers and passages below ground, with shrines and towers above in front of the surmounting tumuli. The stone and brick lining of the tombs, which were up to seventy feet long, bore reliefs and engravings. These depicted scenes such as that of a large country house with two courtyards, double doors with mask-shaped handles, and flanking storage towers; or that of a two-storeyed house in whose kitchens on the ground floor a banquet is prepared for the host and his guests in the dining room above.

Sculpture in the round, particularly of the human form which was one of the glories of the Graeco-Roman world, had, except in miniatures, but a muted echo in China. Instead reliefs were the chosen form of modelling. Their subject-matter encompassed historical and legendary events, mythology and folklore, but also everyday scenes. Besides the above examples, there were those of men harvesting and threshing; there were salt mines set in a landscape of wooded hills, with hoist-towers and bamboo pipelines carrying the brine to the evaporation pans; and there were landscapes depicted in three dimensions by the application of aerial perspective.

Still more vivid were the great murals that adorned halls and palaces. A poet wrote:

Upon the great walls,
Flickering in a dim semblance glint and hover
The Spirits of the Dead.
And here all Heaven and Earth is painted, all living things
After their tribes, and all wild marryings
of sort with sort; strange spirits of the sea,
Gods of the hills. To all their thousand guises
Had the painter formed
His reds and blues, and all the wonders of life
Had he shaped truthfully and coloured after their kinds.

But of all Han painting the highest accomplishments were probably on rolls of silk, where pictures alternated with text. None has survived, students being left to imagine from all the available evidence what they must have been like. Figure subjects included illustrations of the Classics, while landscape themes included the *fu* rhapsodies of the royal palaces, hunting parks, and the wonders of the capitals. There were, besides, magnificent pictorial maps for military use or flood control.

A strong vein of art ran too through the decoration of lacquer objects, which were so popular that the author of the *Discourses on Salt and Iron* protested that the wealthy were spending millions annually on them. The work vividly exhibited the life and vitality of the subjects depicted, such as the ninety-four robed figures on a single box recovered from a tomb: filial sons, virtuous and wicked rulers, and ancient worthies, all seated and turning from one side or another, sometimes gesticulating, and everyone engaged in lively conversation. Other surviving objects like bowls and trays provide beautiful examples of the art: sweeping scrolls erupt into flame-like tongues which flying phoenixes turn into clouds; and these, set about with tigers, deer and hunters, are transformed into hills. In their sweep and movement they express the rhythms of Nature itself.

Han bronzes were generally much simpler than the magnificent products of the Shang but were nevertheless often beautiful, with inlays even on utilitarian objects like the trigger mechanism of the longbow. An exception to the simplicity was the complex design of bronze mirror-backs. These were often crowded with cosmological and other symbols, and sometimes had inscriptions explaining the design and conveying good wishes, as

> The Imperial mirror of the Imperial Workshops is truly without blemish ... to the left the Dragon and to the right the Tiger eliminate what is baleful; the Red Bird and the Black Warrior conform to the *Yin* and *Yang* forces. May your sons and grandsons be complete and in the centre; on it are the Immortals such as are customary. May you long preserve your two parents; may your joy and wealth be splendid may your longevity outstrip that of metal and stone; may you be like a prince or king.

The introduction of drills and cutting discs of iron wrought a big advance in jade carving. The scholar gentleman found in his three-dimensional figurines and animal subjects, his toilet boxes and small bowls, his pendants and garment hooks, his seals and playthings on his desk, a delight at the unity of aesthetic and moral beauty.

The combination of these two qualities expressed the dominance in Chinese art of Confucian and Taoist influences. The scholar gentleman class which filled the administration were at once practical civil servants and recluses who sat in their quiet gardens with their friends talking about or practising calligraphy, music, poetry and literature, and raised painting from a handicraft to art. Often under an emperor who himself composed poetry, their profound respect for cultivation of the intellect and spirit marked them, it has been said, as the largest single class of art patrons enjoyed by any civilization in the world.

The restraint in Chinese art, especially painting, owed much to the Confucian concept of *li*, which is to say good manners, discretion, and what is fit and proper in social and familial conduct. Hence violent emotions were seldom portrayed; and only in nature subjects like flowers and birds, never human life, was painting even sensuous; the obvious was avoided, the artist was always conservative. But Taoism, which in so many respects was incompatible with Confucianism, also had a strong influence. With its escape into reclusiveness and Nature, it was the well-spring of the great schools of landscape.

Another powerful influence, upon art as well as religion and much else besides, emerged in the Han Dynasty. Although merchants found a south-western way to India via Burma, the most important routes to and from the outside world lay along the silk roads extending across Central Asia westward to Persia and southward to India. Through them, Chinese artefacts found destinations far and wide from Siberia to Afghanistan, but silk travelled furthest through Crimea to the Mediterranean world of Egypt and of Rome, where there was a special market for Chinese silk. In the reverse direction, along one or other of these routes, came India's greatest export before the opium that would cause so much grief many centuries later. This was Buddhism.

Although Buddhist priests probably visited China a couple of centuries earlier, its real arrival during the first century AD was promoted by a surge of Taoist belief during the Later Han, for much in Buddhist practice found an echo in Taoism. A tale, possibly apocryphal, has it that the Emperor Ming-ti had a premonitory dream about a foreign god which prompted him to send a mission to Central Asia to enquire about Buddhism; it returned with two Indian monks who brought sacred Buddhist texts on the back of a white horse, a fact commemorated by the establishment of the Monastery of the White Horse. In the following century two Parthians translated a number of texts into Chinese, and a steady growth in the religion's following may be inferred from the Emperor Huan-ti's sacrifice at his Loyang palace to Lao-tzu, founder of Taoism, in association with the Buddha. This was followed by the formal introduction of the cult of Buddha to the court and the city. Towards the end of the dynasty a vast Buddhist temple was built in the east, near P'eng-ch'eng: several storeys high, with a spire adorned with nine discs and a bronze-gilt statue of the Buddha dressed in brocade, it held over three thousand people busy reading the Buddhist canon.

Increasingly Buddhism made its mark on Chinese architecture by way of monasteries, temples and pagodas. But its impact was felt also by Chinese philosophy, literature, language and art. It should be noted, however, that while the idea and practices of Buddhism and Taoism influenced each other, there was a basic contradiction. Buddhism conceived of a state of bliss in liberation from bodily existence, whereas much of Taoism was directed at prolonging bodily existence. As profound was the difference between Buddhism and Confucianism. The Buddhist believed that a man's improvement and salvation could be achieved without reference to his neighbours, but the Confucianist held that a person's significance lay in his relationships with his family and within the social order. And this was the concept so powerfully effective in the Han Dynasty that it would be perpetuated through almost the whole of China's subsequent history.

Indeed, with the ending of the Han Dynasty, the character of China – its culture, its political and spiritual beliefs, its customs, its level of civilization, its territorial bounds, its very nationhood – all may be said to have been so firmly established as to endure for the most part until the present. If, as Machiavelli said, history is always the same and never the same, the story of China henceforward is indeed a repetition of the past but with new elements obtruding.

CHAPTER FOURTEEN

Partition (220–589)

*U*pon the collapse of the Han Dynasty in 220, the sundering of China into the Three Kingdoms was largely determined by the pattern of water-supply and irrigation which made each Kingdom agriculturally, which is to say economically, self-sufficient. Thus Wei, occupying the north and north-west, was located to a great extent in the Yellow River valley; much of Wu, in the south and south-east, embraced the Yangtze valley; and the Shu, in the south-west, included the Szechwan basin.

The Kingdoms embarked on incessant warfare and intrigue against each other. The period, called San-kuo, bore some resemblance to that of the Warring States, but while the latter had at least the nominal central government of the Chou, each of the Three Kingdoms claimed full sovereignty. The most powerful claimant was Ts'ao P'i of Wei. Having received the imperial seals from the last Han emperor, he declared himself the recipient of the Mandate of Heaven over all China. He adopted the imperial name of Wen-ti and kept a magnificent court at Loyang. His was the richest of the Kingdoms, with a population, at about thirty million people, half as big again as the other two Kingdoms combined.

An interesting aspect of Wei history is that it saw Japan, then divided into numerous principalities, emerging from the Stone Age; and in consequence of missions between it and Wei in the 230s it imported many elements of Chinese civilization. These together with Chinese settlers helped transform Japan's ancient culture.

China's own horizons, however, were widening. Increased relations with the Middle East and southern Asia, together with a steady stream of Buddhist ideas, brought a realization that China was not perhaps the only civilized country in the world nor all foreign countries barbaric. Not that barbarians ceased besetting it in the north, which the nineteen tribes of the Hsiung-nu periodically harried, though some were moving west where they joined other tribes, eventually to appear in Asia and Europe as the dreaded Huns. Moreover, a comparatively new presence in China's history emerged from what became Manchuria, in whose southern part a tribal state called Yen threatened to link up with Wei's southern rival, Wu, in a pincer movement. Wei troops therefore attacked and annihilated Yen in 237.

In the south-western Kingdom of Shu, the wheatlands and a wealthy merchant class supplying grain to the surrounding mountain peoples, as well as trading in Tibetan products and exploiting the routes through present Yunnan to India, brought economic wellbeing, but the small population made defence difficult. Aggressive Tibetan tribes occupying the plateau in the west tried the state sorely, and finally in 263 the Kingdom of Wei swallowed it up.

In the south, the third Kingdom, Wu, was more populous than Shu but poorer. Its Thai people, who were displaced or subjugated by the migrating Chinese, cultivated rice in its marshy plains and narrow valleys and bred pigs and water buffaloes, which were practices the Chinese settlers had to learn in preference to their accustomed wheat cultivation and sheep- and cattle-breeding. To the Wu court established at its capital in the whereabouts of modern Nanking, near the mouth of the Yangtze, presently came reports of a massive Wei military build-up. This included prodigious ship-construction on the Yangtze in the Wei's conquered territory of Shu. The Wei preparations for attack were so thorough they took seven years and included the settlement of military farms to assure food supplies. Mammoth multi-decked war junks were built, six hundred feet long and able to carry two thousand troops plus horses. Alerted by pieces of scaffolding for boat-building drifting downstream, the Wu set up underwater obstacles and spanned narrow stretches of water with chains attached to rocks. The Wei general's riposte was to send huge rafts ahead to sweep away the obstacles; and with hundred-feet-long firewood torches doused in sesame oil he melted enough of the chains to make them fall to the river bed. Then he sailed his armada down the Yangtze and received the surrender of Wu in the spring of 280.

Before this, however, the Wei Dynasty founded by Ts'ao P'i had been overthrown. After years of internal dissension marked by assassinations and intrigue among the leading families, a scion of one of the latter, a certain Ssu-ma Yen, ascended the Wei throne in 265 as the first of a new dynasty called Chin. When both the other Kingdoms had been seized, the Chin Dynasty would thus seem to be ruling from Loyang a reunited China, but it was an illusionary impression. In the first place the central government had scant control even of the former Wei Kingdom. The Emperor ordered a general disarmament to help restore the economic situation brought low by all the fighting, and to use the metal in the surrendered weapons to increase the money in circulation; but few arms were handed in, even by the imperial forces – the shortage of money would in fact continue for almost six centuries during which exchange reverted to barter – and the many princes governing the regions would not enforce the order on their troops, who in large numbers traded their weapons to the Hsiung-nu for grants of land for themselves and their families. The Huns welcomed this influx of peasants who could provide them with produce, and eagerly accepted the arms.

Thus strengthened economically and militarily, the Huns were ready for a new era of conquest. Indeed, for over two hundred years the story of northern China is more about the northern frontier nomads than the Chinese. These so-called barbarians went about forming, unforming and re-forming tribal groups of diverse ethnic origin. In addition to the Hsiung-nu or

Huns, Mongolian, Turkic and Tibetan peoples appeared in varying confederations that ranged from northern China to Central Asia.

The Wei regional princes, often with barbarian allies, contended for power and rapidly brought about the disintegration of the Chin government. Between 300 and 306, six successive claimants to the throne were murdered. The struggles raging around the capital ignited a new explosion of migration. Some peasants fled north-west, to the present province of Kansu, where an able Chinese governor formed a sound administration and economy and asserted independence as the Earlier Liang Dynasty. Others and many gentry fled south across the Yangtze to the former kingdom of Wu: there a fugitive prince of the house of Chin, basing himself at Nanking in 317, founded the first dynasty of south China, calling it the Eastern Chin. A third wave of peasants and craftsmen made its way to the north, joined by gentry who had lost influence or suffered from the fighting.

These gentry were particularly welcomed by the Huns, whose leader, Liu Yüan, had like many Hun leaders a Chinese education. He introduced ceremonial on the Chinese model at his well-organized court in his capital to the south of present Shansi, and sought to make his nomadic followers participate in farming like the Chinese. The coincidence of his family name with that of the Han dynasty's rulers, and the many marriages between Hun leaders and Chinese princesses, emboldened him to claim legitimate descent from the Han and establish the Hun Han Dynasty, while he formed the ambition to be Emperor of all China.

He swept down on the foundering Chin state, and on his death his successor captured its capitals of Loyang and Changan and removed the Chin emperor. This was in 316, four years after the Roman Emperor Constantine converted to Christianity, with such profound consequences for the West. The Hun Han Dynasty was renamed the Earlier Chao Dynasty, ruling the western part of north China save for the Kansu enclave (Earlier Liang). The eastern part fell to a former follower of Liu Yüan, one Shih

Lo who had escaped from slavery in China. This man, leading detribalized Huns who adhered to their traditional warrior-nomad activities, had undertaken a great campaign southwards, slaughtering a hundred thousand Chinese, including forty-eight Chin princes. In 329 he annexed the whole of the Earlier Chao's territory, calling his own dynasty the Later Chao Dynasty and ruling all northern China except for the Chinese statelet of the Earlier Liang Dynasty in Kansu, which held on to its independence for another fifty years.

China now effectively consisted of a northern empire astride and north of the Yellow River ruled by the Huns' Later Chao Dynasty, and a southern Chinese empire astride and beyond the Yangtze ruled by the Eastern Chin Dynasty. In the northern empire Shih Lo's regime was unstable. He murdered the whole of the supplanted Liu family in an effort to tighten his grip, but his humble, ex-slave origins denied him the respect of the strongly hierarchical Huns and of the Turkic tribes allied to them. Many went off to a then small realm called Toba, of mainly Turkish but also Mongol migrants from the far north-east between present Mongolia and Manchuria. Toba was in the north of present Shansi province and much would be heard of it. Many others of Shih Lo's people followed a nomadic existence with their herds, well away from the court which under Shih Lo's successor, Shih Hu, was maintained with some magnificence. It abounded with foreigners, especially Buddhist monks who played a greater part than Chinese in running a sound administration. But it was weakened after his death as his sons engaged in mortal conflict, and in 352 the Later Chao Dynasty was eclipsed altogether by Mongols.

These had revived the state of Yen in southern Manchuria (defeated by Wei a century before) and conquered Korea, grown rich on trade with Japan. But their hold on the central and western areas of northern China was precarious. It was made increasingly so by the incursion of Tibetan tribes who eventually overcame the Mongols and established a dynasty called the Earlier Ch'in.

The Tibetan leader Fu Chien governed on a basis of military, not tribal, units. In addition to cavalry he organized a massive infantry army to which many Chinese, particularly effective in sieges on the plains, were recruited. He annexed the state of Yen, then Turkic Toba, and finally the western Chinese realm of the Earlier Liang, achieving control of all northern China from east to west, including the ancient capitals of Loyang and Changan. Himself Chinese-educated he attracted many Chinese to his court and strove to make the whole country culturally Chinese. Like the sinicized Hun emperor Liu Yüan over half a century before him he even aspired to make his Earlier Ch'in Dynasty master of all China, sending (383) an army of one million men to conquer the south. It was repulsed, and retreated in panic. When Fu Chien returned home he and most of his family were assassinated.

His empire of the north rapidly fragmented into a number of diminutive states, called by Chinese historians the Sixteen Kingdoms. With small exception they had no permanence or importance. Some, to the east, were warrior states; others, to the west, were traders with central Asia. Huns, Mongols, Turks, Tibetans marauded across plain and hill under various leaders and with various, often intermingling, tribal affiliations. One by one they fell away, the Tibetans as an ethnic group disappearing altogether and the Huns declining into unorganized herdsmen in the Ordos region. By contrast, as one of those strange tidal movements that shape history took charge, the small Turkish-Mongolian state of Toba in Shansi recovered from its defeat by the Tibetan Fu Chien and gradually began to expand.

While China was experiencing what has been termed its Dark Ages when its northern part lay prostrate under the heel of successive non-Chinese peoples, the Confucian gentry, together with poets, artists and craftsmen, were largely in eclipse. Although some served one or other of the alien administrations, most did not. Merchants, with their characteristic flexibility, contrived to cope with whatever difficulties afflicted them, and the peasantry – those who escaped slavery or enforced military service – went about their ancient, patient toil on the land. But if little can be said about the advance of Chinese culture and civilization in the northern empires during this period, much can be said about the advance of Buddhism.

To the upper-class Chinese, which is essentially to say Confucians, Buddhism had little appeal. It was anti-family in the sense that a true Buddhist was a monk who abjured his family to live in a monastery, a serious breach of filial piety. He had to give up sex, which was essential to preserving the family. His images of the Buddha, made to Indian standards of beauty as laid down in the sacred texts, were considered ugly and strange, and the dress, with one shoulder exposed, immodest. As to Buddhist ideas, like those about the world being the result of our imagination, and about sin and punishment – these seemed most peculiar.

For the common man, however, Buddhism had many attractions. For example, he was told that his superiors who treated him badly would upon being reincarnated occupy lowly rank and be punished, while he himself who had suffered injustice would in his next life be of high rank and enjoy a good time. Merchants, too, were well-inclined: being permitted to use Buddhist monasteries as banks and warehouses, they gave the monks money and land; and from them they learnt many Indian financial practices, such as loans on security, the gathering of capital by common stock, auction sales and, ultimately, lotteries.

At the ruler's courts, the reluctance of the gentry to serve meant a call on the only other educated people, the Buddhists from India and Central Asia. They used their influence for religious propaganda and did much translating of Buddhist texts into Chinese. The rendering of strange Indian terms was achieved by the use of familiar Taoist terminology, making the two beliefs similar to the unsophisticated, which helped give Buddhism readier acceptance. It is one of history's coincidences that Buddhism should have been penetrating almost all China while Christianity was doing likewise in Europe.

But to return to the state – more Turkish than Mongolian – of Toba as it continued its expansion from within the great elbow formed by the Yellow River flowing southward and then eastward. Many Hun and more Mongol tribal segments attached themselves to it, and by 409 it had met its need for produce by conquering the Later Yen state and so seizing the fertile plains of the east. In the following three decades it asserted its growing power by vanquishing states to the north and west of it, and even part of the south, incorporating the ancient and now ruined capital of Loyang. By 440 it ruled the whole of north China and was the most powerful state in the Far East. And so Toba, under the name of the Northern Wei, remained for almost a century, adumbrating the mighty Ottoman Empire which its remote descendants would establish many centuries hence, while that same century saw the disintegration of the Roman Empire as Attila the Hun, having driven the Germanic Visigoths before him into sacking Rome, swept into the Balkans, Gaul and Italy.

At first Buddhists were the predominant influence. Foreign monks at court regarded the Toba emperor as a reincarnation of Buddha, investing him with the prestige Chinese emperors had enjoyed as Sons of Heaven. He appointed a monk as 'pope' of the Buddhist state church to which he gave endowments on a large scale. He was also induced to give state slaves – criminals and their families – to work the temple and monastery lands, greatly strengthening the Buddhists' economic position.

All Turkish peoples had a myth about their ancestors coming into the world from a sacred grotto. Using money from the Emperor the Buddhists exploited this myth by beginning an amazing project – the burrowing-out of a vast complex of temples at three sites near the Toba capital of P'ing-ch'eng in northern Shansi. These sites are where the plains give way to the green river valley in which steep sandstone cliffs rise from the banks. Monks carved out cells for themselves and worshipped Buddha, represented in the course of time by tens of thousands of busts and reliefs sculpted in the stone and by paintings on the ceilings. Within the honeycomb of grottoes these images range in size from less than an inch to figures whose ears alone measure nine feet long.

For all this, Buddhism did not retain its hold on the Toba government. Gradually the state became sinicized. While fighting against the south rarely stopped, the ending of the military campaigns that brought Toba hegemony brought also an end to the loot which had produced great luxury. Furthermore, the Toba herds deteriorated for want of use – horses, for example, were little needed against the south. Many tribal leaders and families had been exterminated in the wars. And as the upper ranks of the Toba thinned or became impoverished, the Chinese gentry on their farming estates waxed in wealth and influence – at court, and even in military matters because they were specialists in fortifications and infantry warfare. Declining in numbers and means, and with many marrying into rich Chinese gentry families, Toba nobles lost further ground when the Chinese at court persuaded the Emperor to move his capital south to ancient Loyang, for whose greater protection a massive campaign against the southern empire of Eastern Chin pushed Toba's southern boundary to the Yangtze. The move rendered useless the Toba herds, now too distant from the market, and those nobles who went to Loyang found themselves superfluous since all important posts were held by Chinese.

Indeed, in the decade after 490 non-Chinese were not even allowed to speak their language in public life and were urged to adopt Chinese dress. Not only did Chinese become the official language, but the Emperor (Wen-ti, 467–499) deemed himself and his culture to be Chinese. He regarded himself as Emperor of all China, the southern Eastern Chin empire being therefore a rebel state – against which, however, his armies fought with little success.

The move to Loyang confirmed both the decline of the Toba nobility and the resurgence of the Chinese gentry together with Confucianism, which now dislodged Buddhism as the official credo. The revival of the city as a capital was an outstanding event in the Toba century. In nine years it rose magnificently from a ruin.

Across its fifty square miles was built a multitude of offices, hostels, monasteries, nunneries, granaries, markets and factories, and palaces, mansions and other accommodation for six hundred thousand people. Unprecedented town-planning resulted in a grid-pattern layout, both of the inner city within the ancient line of walls – now raised anew to heights of up to twenty feet and thicknesses of up to one hundred feet – and of the outer city, all divided into over two hundred walled wards. To many of the latter were allocated specific trades, such as craftsmen, butchers, traders, instrumentalists, singers, brewers, and coffin-makers/undertakers (who claimed that a ghost of good family had returned from the underworld with dire warnings about the fate of anyone buried in cheap wood). Drinking water came from wells, but the imperial gardens and lakes had channels laid to them, some stone-lined underground. Abundant food poured in from the lush surrounding countryside, grain being processed by water-mills and water-driven grinders. The prosperity of the place was phenomenal. Many of the palaces were extra-ordinarily luxuriant, occupied by extraordinarily rich men: one of the royal princes, for example, had six thousand slaves and five hundred women in his harem. The most spectacular structure was a pagoda – that form of building which Buddhism contributed to Chinese architecture – the Yung-ming pagoda, nearly four hundred feet high, topped by a ninety-foot mast. The widest street had a watercourse on either side of it and was called Bronze Ostrich Street because of the brazen ostriches and other beasts that lined it. By any standard, for a ruin to have been turned into a huge bustling city within a decade was a prodigious feat.

Two other developments during the century of Turkish rule over northern China merit notice. One was the introduction of a 'land equalization system': all land was nominally owned by the state, but every man and woman was given a right to a certain amount of it in their lifetime, after which it was to be redistributed; 'mulberry land', given for mulberry-growing for silk production, was, however, inheritable. This law lasted, perhaps more in the breach than the observance, for three hundred years and epitomizes the ceaseless struggle underlying most of China's history to give the peasantry an equitable land deal.

The second noteworthy development was the Toba's formal adoption of the informal tradition that society consisted broadly of two classes – free burgers (gentry and free farmers) and commoners. The latter consisted of, first, families rendering services which gave them their names such as tomb families, shepherd families, postal families, kiln families, soothsayer families, medical families, musician families, and so forth. Next were private bondsmen hereditarily attached to the gentry, then serfs who were usually the descendants of slaves and obliged to work three months a year for the state, and finally state and private slaves who were regarded as property and forced to marry in order to multiply. All these commoner categories had special laws of their own and could not intermarry or adopt. As to the upper class, each family was classified by rank, according to which its members could move into one of the nine ranks of the administration, for prolonged warfare had long ended the examination system, and the idea was that the higher the rank the higher the culture of its holder. Thus high-class families sedulously kept their genealogies to put their claim to positions beyond dispute, and they preferred marriage partners of at least equal rank. (This Toba rank system was subsequently borrowed by the Japanese.)

From about the 520s the Toba empire began to collapse. Grown impoverished, the remains of the tribes with their herds in the Ordos and Shansi regions were driven to formidable risings, in one of which they conquered the capital and massacred thousands of Chinese and pro-Chinese Toba before withdrawing. Tribal factions, military cliques, and warlords fought bloody battles; many emperors were murdered; and ruin overtook the magnificence of Loyang. Just before this last event, a thousand soldiers failed to prevent a fire destroying the towering Yung-ming pagoda, watched by the whole weeping population; two anguished monks rushed into the blaze to immolate themselves.

By about 550 the empire had split into two antagonistic states, one to the east and the other to the west, known respectively as the Northern Ch'i and Northern Chou. An Emperor of the latter suppressed both Buddhism and Taoism, closing down their places of worship. For nearly forty years they strove against each other and clashed with the Turkish, Mongolian and Hunnish peoples of the steppes who were in constant movement. Eventually the Chou not only overcame the Ch'i but by intriguing in the troubles then besetting the southern empire gained much of its territory. Although Chou was a remnant of the old Toba empire, in 581 it was the member of a Chinese family, one Yang Chien, who having massacred the imperial family, declared himself Emperor, the first of the Sui Dynasty. Then he turned his eyes on what remained of the south.

At this stage, more than two and half centuries had passed since the southward flight, in 317, of a prince of the dying Chin Dynasty which followed the Wei Dynasty's absorption of the Three Kingdoms subsequent to the Han. While these were centuries of alien – the Chinese would say barbarous – rule over northern China, the south was the inheritor of Han, and hence became the repository of Chinese, civilization. There in fact the highest refinement of culture in the Far East was attained.

The refugee prince declared himself Yüan-ti, first Emperor of the Eastern Chin Dynasty. The countless gentry and officials who followed him rapidly acquired much land and, like the immigrants before them, prospered from the fertility of the Yangtze valley southwards and the high level of trade at the capital, Nanking, soon frequented by merchants and missions from halfway across the world. Rice fields were developed and notable estates established, worked by immigrant Chinese peasants and indigenous peoples who became sinicized. There were great fruit plantations and luxurious buildings, often water-cooled for the gentry's occupation and surrounded by artificial ponds for pleasure and fish-breeding, artificial watercourses and mountains, bamboo groves, and parks thronged by parrots, ducks and large animals.

At these places and at the imperial princes' courts gathered scholars, artists and poets. Forming elite salons they elevated conversation on the arts to a fine art: it consisted of expressing the best thought – usually Taoistic – in the best language and tersest phraseology, and was called 'pure conversation'. Many gentry had splendid art collections, and much attention was given to garden design; but above all it was an era of aesthetics.

The way was led by calligraphy. The formal angularity of the script up until the end of the Han Dynasty had been transformed into a cursive style that bloomed with unmatched energy and grace, prompting techniques and standards that influenced painting for centuries. The movement was inspired by Taoism which offered an escape from the prevailing turbulence by its vision of the eternal. In art and literature, rigidly traditional Confucian views with their strong moral content gave way to a release of the aesthetic imagination. Books of criticism were written exploring the mysteries of poetic inspiration, and putting forth the non-moralistic principles by which alone paintings should be judged. One of the most famous works enunciated these principles, the 'Six Principles', as – a painting's expression of the cosmic energy that vitalizes all things, its fineness of brush-stroke, the fidelity of its rendering of form, likewise of colour, the placing of its constituent elements, and its respect for tradition. New heights were reached, particularly in landscape painting – the world's first – on scrolls and screens, and in portraiture. Almost all have been lost but the ideals behind them, especially the first of the Six Principles, have inspired Chinese painters to this day.

In literature, among many poets the one most praised by posterity was T'ao Yüan-ming. Of minor gentry stock, he held various official posts between resigning from them to tend his garden and fields, to which he finally decided to retire. This decision was repeatedly returned to in his poems, which sought to justify it, proclaiming the contentment it gave him, and praising past notables who had decided similarly. He glorified the individual's claim against the claims of public life with its inherent oppression. His work was a model of simplicity, as in 'Returning to Dwell in Gardens and Fields' where he described how

> For long time I was kept inside a coop,
> Now again I return to the natural way.

He is also credited with a collection of short stories about miraculous or curious events. Such collections became quite common. Many were tinged with Buddhism, whose monks imported animal tales from India, although in time those in which animals spoke to animals were eliminated, since animals cannot speak and children should not be told lies, except that an animal talking to a man was permissible since the animal was obviously a ghost or spirit, which as the Chinese believed could speak a human language.

Although the gentry were Confucian, they were fascinated by Buddhism, which became very widespread, especially the meditative schools ideologically close to Taoism and later called by the Japanese name of Zen. There was intense activity in translating texts from Indian and Central Asian sources, many brought back by Chinese monks on pilgrimage there since the beginning of the fifth century. Some also introduced to China the Indian systems of logic and philology, and works on mathematics, astrology, astronomy, and medicine.

Yet the glittering record of intellectual and artistic accomplishment in southern China during the fourth to sixth centuries stands in stark contrast to a political history made inglorious by a ceaseless struggle for power at the top. The protagonists were cliques of gentry families allied by marriage. These cliques sought to control the state, insinuating into government as many sons, cousins, nephews and in-laws as they could, and giving the Emperor a daughter – or, if they had none, giving him as concubine a girl from a lower-class family dependent on the clique. These women brought their servants to the palace where they acted as spies, and all tried to influence the Emperor. Lower-class members of a clique, consisting of its bondsmen, advisers and teachers, formed a network with people of the same status in other families of the clique and did secret work, like bribing officials or even killing the clique's enemies. The larger a clique the safer it was, for if a political move failed, the lives and property of most of its members could be saved. What mattered to people in politics then, and even to modern times, was not any ideology but who belonged to each clique and what his ties with his leader were.

Grim is the catalogue of intrigues, murders and military campaigns undertaken by and between the cliques, while the emperors they variously appointed, deposed, or assassinated were almost all nonentities. If not children, as they frequently were, these emperors were, with rare exceptions, given more to wine and women than statecraft. In the century after the Eastern Chin's founder, Yüan-ti, no less than ten men occupied the Nanking throne. This period encompassed the million-strong abortive offensive by the northern empire's Tibetan ruler and several severe risings, most notably in 400 when peasants on the south coast and inland of it revolted against oppression and exploitation, their movement being led by a secret society similar to that of the Yellow Turbans two hundred years earlier.

In 420 a general called Liu Yü killed the puppet emperor and, though he belonged to the imperial family, supplanted the Eastern Chin Dynasty by installing himself as first Emperor of the Sung Dynasty, usually called the Liu-Sung Dynasty to distinguish it from the later and greater Sung Dynasty. There was scarcely ever a time without fighting between the south and the north, most memorably in 450 when the Toba, to protect their move to Loyang, detached a large swathe of southern territory. Decades later, a rising of provincial princes led to the emergence of General Hsiao Tao-ch'eng as Emperor after he had killed first the reigning incumbent and then the latter's boy successor.

He replaced the Liu-Sung with another transient dynasty, the Southern Ch'i; and as happened after previous palace coups, many of the disaffected or ousted gentry fled north to provoke further attacks by the Toba. Dissolution of the Southern Ch'i started in 494 with a rising led by a prince who, having murdered the Emperor to become Emperor himself, proceeded to murder his own entire family lest any had a notion to emulate him. When he died, conflict between his remote relatives brought one of them, named Hsiao Yen, to the throne (502). He called himself Wu-ti and his dynasty the Liang.

Wu-ti, a lover of literature and Buddhism, lasted an exceptional forty-seven years until his death at the hands of a Toba tribal leader prominent in the uprisings that marked the Toba Empire's declining epoch. This man of Toba soon seated himself on the Nanking throne, but not for long: a Chinese army put an end to him and restored the Liang Dynasty. The new Emperor and his associates came from the upper Yangtze area and considered Nanking inconveniently distant from their estates. So Hankow, some three hundred miles westward, was made the capital, while army commanders held sway in Nanking, thus effectively dividing southern China between east and west.

In 555 an army of the Northern Chou, one of the states emerging from the Toba Empire's break-up, invaded with the help of a southern clique. Hankow was captured and a Chou prince installed as feudatory emperor, his dynasty being named the Later Liang. Eastward, a year or two later one of the Nanking warlords made himself Emperor, calling his dynasty Ch'en. However, neither the Later Liang nor Ch'en Dynasties were to last longer than a few decades. By 589 both had been swept aside by that same Yang Chien who conquered the north and established the Sui Dynasty. After three hundred and sixty years, the fragmentation of the country was over: the Sui ruled all China, and as far as Annam and Formosa in the south and Tashkent and Hami in Central Asia. The story of what followed is essentially that of a father and son.

CHAPTER FIFTEEN

The Sui (581–618)

Yang Chien, the master now of all China, came from a venerable aristocratic family in the area between Loyang and Changan. He made his way through a succession of successful military commands in the Northern Chou. Long-waisted, short-legged, reserved and harsh in manner, parsimonious, lacking warmth or magnetism, given to violent rages, his ascent to the top marked by much fighting and many murders, he emerged as a strong and exceptionally able leader under the imperial title of Wen-ti. He was fortunate in his wife, a sinicized Hun who shared his Buddhist faith, puritanism, and dedication to monogamy; to their unique partnership – governmental as well as marital – she brought a level-headed good sense, though also, on occasion, the supposed contrariness of her sex, for although she was said to weep every time she heard of an execution, when her husband wanted on her behalf to pardon a relative of hers who had committed a capital crime she said, 'This is purely a matter of State. Why should you consider personal factors?' And the man was duly executed.

Soon Wen-ti established a new capital. Chosen after due divination, a site south-east of old Changan was developed in the tradition of imperial magnificence by one of the most brilliant architect-engineers of the age. It was called Ta-hsing ('Great Revival') and occupied over thirty square miles, with the walled palace complex in the centre containing its great audience hall, Palace of the Cosmic Ultimate.

Wen-ti removed the old Northern Chou's proscription of Buddhism and Taoism. He founded many Buddhist temples and promoted a trained and disciplined clergy which did charitable work, performed sacred ceremonies for the state's welfare, and prayed for rain to come or to stop, for an end to epidemics, or for the spiritual felicity of imperial ancestors. Nevertheless, he did not discountenance Taoism, a crypto-Buddhist form of which had been taking shape for a century, in the process making Lao-tzu the chief divinity and producing temples, monastic orders, holy places and scriptures. But when it came to government, Wen-ti enforced a strictly Confucian ethos with its emphasis on obedience, which accorded well with Wen-ti's soldierly mind. It was hence Confucianism that powered the enormous political reform that distinguished the Sui Dynasty and which wrought reconciliation, unification and stability out of what had become a huge fissured empire incessantly at war and riven by regional rivalry, privilege, corruption and even differences in language.

The first need was to centralize government control. It was structured thus: at the top were three 'Preceptors' and the Three Dukes; beneath them were the real wielders of power, namely, the three ministries of State Affairs, Chancellery and Secretariat; while under the Department of State Affairs were boards of Civil Office, Finance, Rites, Army, Justice and Public Works; other important offices included the Censorate, Inspectorate General of Water Works, and nine 'courts' – Court of Imperial Sacrifices, Court of Imperial Banquets, Court of the Imperial Family, and so on. Each holder of office had, like every civil servant, a designated rank with its own code of dress, pay, and privilege. The core group was formed by tough, ruthless men of action, many of them non-Chinese from the remnants of the northern empires once ruled by the steppe people. Staffs in the upper echelons were recommended to the Emperor by a council of ranking ministers, while subordinate officials were chosen by the Board of Civil Office.

This Office revolutionized local government by directly appointing all its officials, hitherto in the gift of the local aristocracy; and civil administration was restored to areas that had fallen under military control. The officials were in nine grades (according to the population of their prefecture or county) which determined their salary – paid in bushels twice-yearly – and they defrayed their expenses from the income of official fields. Appointments were for terms of three years: they could not be made of someone previously appointed, and an official could not be accompanied by his close relative lest he became a conduit for undue influence. As well as the Censorate, an inspectorate sent from the capital kept a close check on local performance, acting as the eyes and ears of the Emperor, who was not above letting his undercover agents tempt officials with bribes and sentencing to death any who succumbed. He himself, declining to appoint a Chancellor and taking on a large part of that office, made many imperial progresses, during which he spent much time rooting out local malpractices. Moreover, thrice-yearly three representatives from each of the one hundred and ninety prefectures into which the country was divided had to assemble in the capital for an audit of local officials' performance, followed by the distribution of rewards and punishments. They also had an audience with the Emperor, who urged the necessity for integrity and other Confucian principles.

Wen-ti's indefatigable drive for reform was supported in two directions. One was a push for able public servants recruited from all the populace regardless of ethnic, regional or class distinction, excluding only artisans and merchants. Examinations based on the Classics for entry to the service were revived, and every encouragement given to people of moral worth rather than those with impressive genealogies. In another direction, a legal code was promulgated, the New Code, with 1,735 articles, about half a century after that seminal work for Western jurisprudence, the Byzantine Emperor Justinian's code. While it abolished such sentences as the public display of criminals' severed heads, dismemberment of the body, and the whip, it still gave expression to the Legalism which coloured the

Emperor's thinking: for example, a robber of a trifling sum could be executed, as could officials for quite minor derelictions or failing to denounce a crime or accepting the smallest gift. All the same, in promulgating the code, Wen-ti acknowledged the Confucian ideal of laws being superfluous if the virtue of the ruler prevailed: 'Perhaps the time is not far distant when, though they [the penal laws] have been promulgated, they are not used. Let the ten thousand regions and the myriad princes know these our intentions.' That time could of course never come and the essence of the Sui code continued for many centuries. Also promulgated was a codified body of statutes covering every rule on land, tax, and bureaucratic administration, so that no official had any doubt as to the law.

In military matters also Wen-ti introduced tight centralized control. All weaponry except the army's was banned and its private manufacture punished. Militarized zones were demilitarized, and the regional armies made subject to direct command from headquarters in the capital. Aristocratic privilege in martial careers gave way to merit, and the clear role was established of civil administration without army influence or interference. A sizable portion of the Sui's highly efficient military machine was needed to fend off incessant barbarian raids in the north, where agricultural colonies were set up beyond the Great Wall to feed the army, while the Great Wall itself was repaired and extended by the enforced labour of up to a million local barbarians. Punitive expeditions to as far east as modern Manchuria and as far south as Vietnam were not always successful, but generally throughout the empire tranquillity was ensured by a combination of military and diplomatic action which included a revival of the tribute system.

This helped the Sui Dynasty to become one of great abundance. A system of land allocation similar to the Toba's yielded plentiful supplies and taxes in the form of grain and textiles. A network of food reserves supplemented five major granaries in which the government's tax grain totalled up to ten million bushels.

As time passed, Wen-ti and his wife needlessly but increasingly subjected themselves to paranoia about plots against them. Their own sons were not exempt from suspicion, and cause was found to downgrade, execute or otherwise dispose of four of their five sons, the exception being the second-born, and the Emperor's favourite, Yang Kuang. It was he who on his father's death, following that of his mother two years earlier, became in 604 the second Emperor of the Sui, reigning under the title of Yang-ti.

In the position of Viceroy of the South given him by his father he had already done much to reduce the south's hostility to the north, which had been nurtured during the centuries of conflict and southern scorn for northern 'barbarians'. Tax concessions, the execution of notoriously oppressive officials, magnanimity towards defeated generals, and encouragement of both Buddhists and Taoists, had been among his means. Also, he married a southerner, an intelligent and sensitive princess with literary ability, whom he respected and loved all his life.

Not that this prevented his alleged increasing licentiousness – if later historians are to be believed – but since the Mandate of Heaven was presently to be withdrawn from him, earning him the inevitable malodorous sobriquet of Terminator of Dynasty, neither fabrication nor distortion was spared to vilify him. Whatever the truth about his lust, he was a fine poet and prose-stylist, a connoisseur of beautiful things and an adherent of the aesthetic movement which distinguished the old southern empire. The charge against him of financial profligacy, by contrast with his father's parsimony, did, however, have substance. He loved pomp and display. Having chosen the appropriate colours and costumes for his court, he ordered the rebuilding of Loyang, left in ruin again by the wars. This was done on a lavish scale and the city made one of three capitals – his father's Ta-hsing and his own Nanking being the other two. He constantly and flamboyantly processed between them, and to places all over the country, including a number of new palaces and several sacred sites where he made solemn sacrifices for national well-being.

The cost of this constant movement, clothed in splendour and with hundreds of officials and attendants, was huge. Together with his abhorrence of routine it had a disastrously unsettling effect on the stable central administrative structure established by his father, and after he had had three of the leading statesmen executed he tended to be surrounded by sycophants who insulated him from reality. Nevertheless, his reign is memorable for one solid achievement – the massive extension of the canal-building started by his father, which added immeasurably to the system of communication, transport and distribution in central China.

The new watercourse included linking rebuilt old canals and rivers, and it ran for several hundred miles north-west from present Hangchow to the Yangtze, continued for seven hundred miles or more to the Yellow River near Loyang, then stretched for over five hundred miles north-east to the vicinity of present Peking. For the construction in less than six years of this, the Grand Canal, over five million workers were mobilized and, where there were not enough men, women were conscripted for the first time; anyone who refused to labour was beheaded, and slackers suffered severe punishment. It is doubtful whether this feat, and that of the Great Wall have ever been matched in human history. Alongside much of the Grand Canal's banks roads were laid, fringed by elms and willows, and imperial pavilions were built between every two post stations – forty of them on the Yangtze/Yellow River leg. It was along this part that upon its completion Yang-ti sailed in a dazzling procession aboard a four-decked dragon-shaped junk two hundred and fifteen feet long and including two large audience halls, the countless accompanying vessels of every style stretching out stem-to-stern for sixty-five miles. All officials along the way had to provide provisions, about which an historian recorded: 'Those who made bountiful arrangements were given an additional office or title; those who fell short were given punishments up to the death penalty.

Relations with Japan, sustained after a fashion (mainly through Korea) ever since the Wei Kingdom four centuries before, culminated in the arrival of the first full Japanese embassy. Of more pressing concern were the Turks who had founded some time in the past a mighty empire stretching from the north of China to the gates of Byzantium, but subsequently split into the empires of the Eastern Turks and Western Turks. The latter occupied territory on China's north-western border, which only skilled diplomacy kept quiescent. More forbidding were the Eastern Turks who occupied modern Mongolia, and to contain them Yang-ti's father had extended the Great Wall. More, however, was needed, and this was done by the traditional recipe of judicious bribes, marriages, hostage-keeping, tribute-missions, shows of force and intrigue. There was an occasion when Yang-ti, making one of his showy ceremonial visits to the north, received at his sumptuous mobile palace the homage of the Eastern Turks' leader, their Great Khan: they exchanged gifts – three thousand horses from the Turks, thirteen thousand lengths of silk from the Emperor.

In one direction, however, neither diplomacy nor threat prevailed. Part of modern Manchuria and northern Korea formed the Kingdom of Koguryo. Yang-ti's father had once failed to conquer it, but undeterred and although he ruled an empire over three thousand miles east and west and five thousand miles north and south, Yang-ti coveted this small kingdom as once part of the Han empire, besides which he wanted to prevent a possible alliance with the Turks. When its King failed to make submission, Yang-ti ordered a massive attack by land and sea. Three times between 612 and 614 ruinously expensive campaigns were unleashed and three times failed. In his obsession Yang-ti ordered a fourth, but a spate of widespread rebellions intervened. The toll was being exacted of the human and financial cost of his canal-building and the onslaughts on Koguryo, his spendthrift lifestyle, and the disarray into which central government control had been brought by his ceaseless peregrinations. Within a few years the uprisings would total nearly two hundred; the gentry began to desert him and set up pretenders. His sycophantic circle contrived to keep the ever-worsening situation from him; one man who did try to speak out was beaten to death in the audience hall. When at last the gathering tide of disaster could no longer be gainsaid he fled to his southern capital.

Back in 615 a soothsayer had warned him that a man named Li would soon become emperor. A popular ballad echoed the prognostication. Yang-ti promptly had one of his most powerful generals who was called Li executed along with thirty-two members of his clan while remoter relatives were banished. One Li, however, was by his proven loyalty above suspicion. This was Li Yuan, Duke of T'ang, in whom the blood flowed of several royal houses of the old northern kingdoms. A brave and bold leader, a fierce adversary and cunning strategist, he had been given increasingly important commands and had distinguished himself in decisive action against rebels and bandits.

But in 617, observing the government to be in a state of collapse, and not uninfluenced by the ballad about the imminent ascendancy of a Li, he yielded to the pleas of his followers: he himself became the foremost rebel. With the Turkish Great Khan's help, which brought the strength of his army up to 200,000 men, he conquered the Sui capital of Ta-hsing. Thereupon he entitled Yang-ti, now profoundly melancholic in his southern capital, Retired Emperor, and put his six-year-old grandson on the throne. This doubtless bewildered child was, however, swiftly removed a few months later in 618 when Li Yuan attacked Loyang and proclaimed himself Emperor. With the death of Yang-ti, murdered in his bathhouse by one of his own generals, the Sui Dynasty was extinguished.

Yet, for all its brief tenure of less than forty years, this dynasty of father and son had not only made China whole again but through the cultural unity and political, military, legal and economic institutions it established, prepared the way for China's Middle Ages and perhaps the most illustrious of all its dynasties. Brief, but momentous: in three decades the Sui laid the foundations of a successor that lasted three centuries.

CHAPTER SIXTEEN

The T'ang (618-907) - I

A lmost as if dancing to a stately rhythm of the drums of time, Chinese history has much of it been repetitive. From a nation in ruin arises a gifted ruler who founds a dynasty that resurrects it; the State prospers; it decays; ruin ensues, and the drums beat on. So it was with the T'ang.

This was the name Li Yüan gave his dynasty at its foundation in 618. He assumed the title Wu-te, 'Military Virtue', but is remembered by his posthumous temple name, Kao-tsu. He was fifty-three years old, a fine horseman and bowman, much given to hunting and lavish musical entertainments. He is reputed to have won his beautiful wife at a shooting match in which the target was painted to resemble a peacock, each of whose eyes his arrows put out.

He declared Ta-hsing to be his capital, renaming it Changan after the nearby ancient capital, and set about the task of pacification. He took a decade to accomplish it. He did so by force of arms in half-a-dozen significant battles; but also, by giving rewards like prefectures to rebel leaders who surrendered voluntarily and an amnesty to their armies, by absorbing defeated armies into his own after executing their leaders, and by reappointing to their posts local officials who stayed loyal to Yang-ti, he persuaded many rebels to transfer their allegiance to himself. Progressively, with this protracted process, he ensured continuity of the Sui's strong centralized control of local administration and the military, the latter now being implemented by a system of local militia called up to serve for usually short periods.

He maintained the Toba – Sui system of land allocation, introduced a poll tax payable in two hundredweight of grain, a twenty-foot bolt of silk, and twenty workdays of labour, and, following the Sui revival of the use of currency, began minting a uniform coin. He strictly controlled trade, appointing a director of each market in the capital and provinces who had to keep order, register all shops, inspect weights and measures, and approve prices and quality. He continued the Sui revival of examinations, at first on a limited scale and with a bias in favour of the aristocracy. Finally, he appointed a commission to produce a new consolidated set of administrative laws and the T'ang Legal Code.

This famous Code reduced the 1,735 articles of the Sui New Code to 502. Such is the endurance of the beliefs that shaped the Chinese mind, the Code was clothed in a thousand years of attachment to the principles of Yin-Yang, as also to a compromise between the Confucian and Legalist philosophies. By complying with the Yin-Yang and Five Elements theories, it purported to achieve harmony with the natural world to which human society is holistically linked – a harmony jeopardized if human society is disrupted by crime, which if unpunished causes malign natural consequences like flood or drought. The Code was therefore inflexible in the punishments it specified, covering offences as diverse even as the inefficient checking of documents by an official, or warning the enemy of an impending attack or practising magic.

Though fines or loss of office could sometimes be substituted, it listed five punishments: ten to fifteen blows with a light stick; sixty to one hundred blows with a heavy one; penal servitude of up to three years; life exile; and death by decapitation or strangulation. Death was suffered for plotting rebellion or damaging ancestral temples, tombs or imperial palaces. Either of these two crimes also brought strangulation of the criminal's father and sons, the enslavement of several further generations of his family, and the confiscation of all his property. They headed a list called the Ten Abominations, which included lack of filial piety: if you hit your parent or paternal grandfather, or plotted to kill either of them, you were decapitated; if you did not go into mourning upon their death you were liable to exile for life. A woman who struck her husband got a year of penal servitude, while a concubine who did so got a year and a half. There were similar dire penalties for offences against superiors in the complicated hierarchy of personal status.

The severity of punishment increased as the hierarchy descended, except that those in higher positions were deemed to have a greater responsibility for obeying the law and therefore enjoyed less privilege than befitted their rank. The complexity of meting out punishment may be gauged from the number of rungs on the bureaucratic and social ladder, for each had a different penal consequence for any given crime. Society comprised, first, nobles and officials; second, commoners; third, inferiors such as bondsmen and slaves. The hereditary nobles were in five ranks; the officials in nine ranks divided in thirty grades but some had titular office at the same time, also carrying thirty grades. Besides the privilege of lesser punishments according to rank and grade, a similar advantage was granted to the young, the aged, women, the maimed, and the mentally handicapped. Voluntary confession of a crime before it came to the court's attention could earn a pardon, while a false accusation rendered the accuser liable to the same punishment as if he had committed the crime alleged. In sum, such was the comprehensiveness and precision of the Code that it lasted until the fourteenth century and became a model for Japan, Vietnam and Korea.

Externally, a constant threat from the north was posed by the Eastern Turks. The Emperor Kao-tsu's heavy bribes failed to stop repeated incursions, but a system of new fortifications helped to keep them substantially at bay. In this, as in his military successes during the pacification of the empire, much was owed to the able generalship of one of his sons, Li Shih-min. Not this son, however, but his oldest brother was appointed heir apparent, which led to an intense rivalry between them, with a third brother taking the heir apparent's side. After endless intrigue and manoeuvring, matters reached a pitch in 626 when Li Shih-min, aware of the increasing success of his two brothers in turning their father against him, was stung to action by a spy's report that they planned to murder him.

He thereupon baldly accused them of illicit relations with women in their father's harem. The two men, tipped off by a concubine, made for the palace to protest their innocence. They had to go through a gate watched over by imperial guards, but Li Shih-min bribed their commander so that with twelve trusted followers he had control of the gate. At the brothers' approach, Li Shih-min's arrow killed the heir apparent while his people did for the other brother.

One of Li Shih-min's generals then entered the palace in full armour and carrying a spear – normally a capital offence – to announce the deaths to the victims' aghast father. Three days later Li Shih-min was pronounced heir apparent and took charge of the government. Within a few weeks Kao-tsu, probably under duress, abdicated in favour of Li Shih-min and became Retired Emperor, to live indeed for the remaining nine years of his life in morose retirement in the countryside.

Thus Li Shih-min in 626 became at the age of twenty-six the second T'ang Emperor. He was to be known by his posthumous name of T'ai-tsung and revered as the shining paragon of all China's imperial masters. This was not a stature hinted at by his removal of any doubt about his accession by having all ten sons of his two slain brothers killed, which was not, however, consistent with the upper-class Confucian education that he had been given as a member of a partly alien but powerful Shensi clan. While he was a brave, dashing and brilliant commander, he was also well versed in classical and historical learning and a notable calligrapher.

From the arduous military campaigns fought in since his teens, he emerged an imposing imperial figure, magnificent to the point of intimidating in the royal court. Emotional and easily provoked, he went purple in the face when he raged – to the terror of those about him. Yet his reign, to which he presently gave the title Chen-kuan (True Vision), was in its early years marked by his deference to his ministers and officials.

He sincerely sought to improve his administration in the light of their frank criticism which he encouraged: all his officials, he decreed, should feel free to comment without fear. He forged a strong personal rapport with them, making them feel full participants in the running of the state. By strictly adhering to the Confucian principle of appointing scholar-officials about him, as well as by his frugality and his scorn of auguries and elixirs, he came close to realizing the sage-emperor ideals which the Master had enunciated a thousand years before.

His ministers were chosen from bureaucratic families across the regional spectrum that had a great deal of government experience. They were outstandingly able, all incorruptible and imbued with his concern for the welfare of his people. 'Oppressing the people to make them serve the ruler,' he adjured them, 'is like someone cutting off his own flesh to feed his stomach.' With these men he set about, in the admirable early years of his reign, honing the institutions of central and local government bequeathed him. He worked indefatigably, expecting the same from his senior officials who slept in shifts that they might be available to him at any time of the night as well as day. Memorials to him from high and low became so numerous that, in order to study them well into the night, he posted them on the walls of his bedchamber, where also he had screens listing details of provincial officials he wished to consider for promotion or demotion.

He continued the establishment, begun in his father's reign, of governor-generalships over groups of prefectures, and the rationalizing and improving of administrative structures; everywhere he most of all disavowed corruption. Twice he sent out commissions to investigate local officials, punishing thousands and executing seven for poor performance. In military affairs, likewise, he aimed at refining what was already there, particularly the maintenance of militia units: these, by providing their own rations and much of their equipment, relieved the Treasury of a substantial burden.

Intense frugality was indeed central to T'ai-tsung's economic policy. Combined with sustained internal peace, sound administration, the improved transport and distribution achieved by the Sui canals, and good harvests, it brought prosperity to the whole nation. The process was enhanced by vigorous trade: particularly as the T'ang dominions widened, as will be described below, merchants from Central Asia, Persia and Byzantium brought a flow of foreign goods, and with them foreign entertainments and customs. Tribute poured in from as far afield as Siberia and the Urals. Changan became an international metropolis. It housed minorities of people of many races, and educated the sons of many surrounding royal houses at its monasteries and schools. The formal schools at the capital, developed to prepare students for the examinations, included a School for Calligraphy and a School of Law. They catered for thousands, while thousands more young men from the provinces attended lectures all over the city on the Classics and history. At the same time the compilation of official dynastic histories – so singular a feature of Chinese culture – was put on a firm bureaucratic footing.

Among the most enthusiastic visitors were Japanese, who sometimes lived and studied in Changan for decades, returning to their country to help shape its institutions on T'ang principles and indelibly stamp Japanese culture with that of the Chinese. To the capital also came numerous embassies from foreign countries near and far. The death of Mohammed in 632 triggered the great era of Arab expansion which, reaching Persia, prompted the last of the Sassanid dynasty to send an appeal for help from T'ai-tsung; but he refused, and Persia fell. At his court he even received an embassy, thought to have been sent by the Eastern Roman Emperor Constans II, from the Byzantine province of Syria.

Foreign religions too made their appearance, notably the first gleam of Christianity in the form of a Nestorian monk. He arrived at the T'ang capital in 635, to be favourably received by T'ai-tsung who asked him to translate his Nestorian texts into Chinese; Buddhism was of course well established but it was invigorated by the return, after fifteen years in India, of the greatest of its pilgrim-travellers, Hsüan-tsang. For his part, T'ai-tsung was a Taoist, claiming descent from the sage Lao-tzu himself, and his attitude toward Buddhism was summed up by the observation towards the end of his life that it was vulgar and futile faith. He nevertheless admired Hsüan-tsang for his unique knowledge of Indian and Central Asian geography, customs, products and politics, and he vainly tried to persuade him to renounce his vows and become a court official.

It was to Central Asia that T'ai-tsung's martial mind in due course turned its attention. This happened after his army of 100,000 men utterly routed the Eastern Turks in a battle south of the Gobi (630). These Turks had already been racked by internal dissension and now they proclaimed T'ai-tsung their Heavenly Great Khan, while the Chinese settled multitudes of them in their own midst. The Western Turks too, after dominating the continent from the western end of the Great Wall to Persia and from Kashmir to the Altai mountains, were broken up by internal disaffection, and as faction contended with faction, T'ai-tsung fuelled the discord by recognizing and abetting now one, now another. While the Turkish menace was thus removed, the oasis kingdoms of the Tarim Basin where Indian, Afghan and Persian cultures intermingled, threatened the Silk Roads across which merchants journeyed from Central Asia, Persia and Byzantium. T'ai-tsung subjugated them one by one, his troops reaching an amazing distance of five thousand miles from his capital, and he set up a Chinese garrison in each under a Protector-General. Military and diplomatic action alike were also necessary to ensure peace with the Turkish Uighurs in the north-western modern province of Sinkiang, and with the Tibetans whose fierce and warlike tribes had at last achieved unity. But in 644 T'ai-tsung repeated the blunder of Yang-ti which instigated the fall of the Sui: he became obsessed with the ambition to conquer the Korean kingdom of Koguryo. Most of his ministers strove to dissuade him, but he was no longer the sage-emperor of the first decade of his reign. He had become haughty and self-willed and was determined to reclaim territory once ruled by the Han. How much of China's history is distinguished by a fanatical desire to recover lost territory previously grabbed from others! Twice the Emperor hurled vast armies – himself once taking the field – and armadas of up to five hundred ships against Koguryo, gaining some victories but an inconclusive result. In 648 he announced that he would the next year send an army of 300,000 men; but it never happened.

Instead, although not yet fifty he contracted an incapacitating disease that made him dizzy, impaired his vision, and exhausted him. In desperation he called in an Indian magician, to no avail: in the fifth month of 649 he died. He left a highly efficient administration, a buoyant economy, a mighty empire, and a tranquil nation full of self-confidence. More than that, to the generations that followed, T'ai-tsung shone out as the brilliant exemplar of a Confucian ruler – wise and conscientious, wielding firm authority based on empathy with and responsiveness to his well-chosen scholar-advisers, and profound concern for the welfare of his people.

His heir apparent for the past six years had been his ninth son who, ascending the throne in 649 – in front of his father's coffin, as was the custom – is known to history as Kao-tsung. He was well-meaning but as weak in character as in health (he suffered hypertension). Although his reign lasted for no less than thirty-four years, its story is mostly about his wife, the most extraordinary of all those extraordinary women who have periodically affrighted China.

Her name was Wu Chao. One account has her a chambermaid or low-ranking concubine of the then Emperor T'ai-tsung and entering a nunnery where Kao-tsung, now Emperor, on a visit was smitten by her beauty. At all events, brought back into the palace she deployed her high intelligence, acute assessment of men, and ruthless determination to intrigue remorselessly until she had supplanted Kao-tsung's wife as Empress. Within a month she caused the dethroned woman and a favoured concubine to be killed: they were deprived of their arms and legs and left to die in a wine vat.

Wu completely dominated her husband and the government. Leading ministers who had served T'ai-tsung were got rid of. Once, her attachment to religious and magical beliefs prompted a move to oust her on the grounds of participation in sorcery – one of the Ten Abominations – but the attempt ended in executions and her emergence unscathed. There was no limit to her pretensions. She had Loyang made a second capital to Changan, resulting in huge costs both in the upgrading of the buildings and the constant movement of the whole administration between the two cities. While the first two T'ang emperors had been content with a single reign-title, Kao-tsung had thirteen, and she insisted on the *feng* and *shan* sacrifices. These were performed on China's principal holy mountain, T'ai-shan, and were a pronouncement to Heaven and Earth that the Emperor had successfully accomplished his tasks. Because most emperors had feared that to make such a claim on an insufficient basis would cause serious disharmony in the natural order, only six in all history had dared – and none for the past six hundred years. Not only did Kao-tsung perform the sacrifices, starting on New Year's Day 666 but the Empress Wu defied all precedent by herself taking part. In 674 they took the grandiose appellation of Heavenly Emperor and Heavenly Empress.

Early in Kao-tsung's reign he gathered together scholars to work on dynastic histories, after which he sponsored a series of massive new literary anthologies; at the same time Buddhist scribes translated Sanskrit texts. The Empress then took a hand, forming a group of scholars who produced a variety of works including biographies of famous women. This group had, however, a sinister aspect, for it became a secret secretariat, known as Scholars of the Northern Gate, which usurped many of the policy-making and other functions of the six ministerial departments acting under the Council of State.

Wu stopped at nothing to preserve her dominance. When the Emperor's heir apparent died, she promptly had two other promising sons of the Emperor banished; and when another, having been made heir apparent, evinced signs of ability, she plotted his downfall too, causing his suicide; and she secured the appointment of her third son by the Emperor, the Prince of Ying, who at fourteen could pose no immediate threat. Then, three years later, in the twelfth month of 683, the Emperor's long endurance of ill-health was ended by his death.

In the meantime, the country was plunged in financial gloom: on top of the cost of Loyang came floods, poor harvests, droughts and locusts. Grain prices soared and vast numbers of peasants fled to undeveloped areas to avoid taxation. But the administrative systems were so sound that government operated smoothly in spite of these tribulations and Wu's manipulations. For example, the law code was regularly updated, and the examination system was reorganized to increase recruitment to the civil service, even if most of the new people were still sons of nobility and high-ranking officials since entry to the examinations was biased in their favour. A provision that the names of candidates were to be concealed to ensure that their identity and social status would not affect results proved to be short-lived. The basic curriculum continued to be Confucian, save for the addition of a Taoist classic. To the specialist schools of law and calligraphy was added one for mathematics.

On the frontiers, the vanquished Western Turks revived and re-took their lost territory until a Chinese expeditionary force, after campaigning for several years, decisively broke them. From about 660 the T'ang Empire stretched from the China Sea to the borders of Persia. It thus encompassed the greatest expanse of territory in China's history. But this spread its resources so thin that within a few years the Turks reasserted their independence.

About a decade after T'ai-tsung's death with Koguryo still unconquered, China again set its sights on that northern

Korean kingdom, accepting the proposal of an offensive alliance with the larger and more sinicized of the two southern Korean states. Eight years of fighting followed, ending in a complete victory at last: 200,000 Koguryoan prisoners were sent to China and a Chinese protectorate was set up. In the course of the war the smaller of the two southern Korean states became embroiled against the Chinese: a Japanese fleet sailed to its assistance and was defeated with the loss in battle of four hundred ships – one of the greatest naval disasters ever. But, as with Central Asia, the conquest of Koguryo was short-lived, for resistance so intensified that within eight years the protectorate had to be withdrawn and, while turbulence raged throughout the peninsula, China's military effort was distracted by Tibet.

A decade or two earlier, that newly united kingdom had, under its great King, Srong-btsan-sgam-po, begun an epoch of spectacular expansion. This extended in all directions, including the Tarim Basin, finally drawing the Chinese into violent clashes and throwing their western frontier into ferment. Also towards the end of Kao-tsung's life, the shattered remnants of the Eastern – now called Northern – Turks were united, and from beyond the Great Wall launched incursions that brought constant warfare to the northern frontier region.

All these frontier wars and the financial depression were the inheritance of Kao-tsung's successor, the Prince of Ying, known by his posthumous title of Chung-tsung. More ominously he also inherited his mother, Wu, who, reacting to the independence he began to exhibit, within six weeks had him dragged from his throne and banished from the capital. She proceeded to rule in the name of his more compliant brother, twenty-two-year-old Jui-tsung. The following year a revolt engineered in the great commercial centre where the Grand Canal joined the Yangtze was quickly quashed, but it fuelled her paranoia. She began an horrendous reign of terror.

Because it was mainly directed at senior officials, some historians have seen it as an attempt to sap the power of the aristocracy while Wu at the same time encouraged recruitment of commoners through the examination system. At all events, she had the Censorate and Board of Justice create a web of spies and informers, whose victims, accused of sedition, were put into a purpose-built prison to be tortured and tricked into 'confessions' before suffering execution and other cruel punishments including being thrown into a cauldron. A bronze urn was set up for people to put in anonymous, and often false, accusations. Many illiterate informers from every corner of the Empire arrived at public expense to make denunciations, receiving rewards such as high positions. Hundreds of aristocratic families were afflicted by the execution of their members, whose relatives were sent into exile or slavery and had their property confiscated. No minister dared cross the Empress for fear of the secret police arresting him. Unchecked by ministerial protest she could openly conduct scandalous sexual affairs, notably with a cosmetics pedlar: she had him ordained and installed as abbot of the most prestigious monastery.

But she was also a populist, seeking to ingratiate herself with the general public by proclaiming several so-called Acts of Grace which granted – despite the straitened economy – extensive tax exemptions and other favours, and clamped down on the ostentation of the unpopular merchant class; and she was a stickler for the fair administration of justice.

At the same time – for there was dawning in her a singular ambition – she cultivated an aura of majesty. She appeared frequently in public, leading magnificent ceremonies and adopting the rituals of the ancient Chou of golden memory – indeed, she claimed descent from the great Duke of Chou. In 688 a white stone 'discovered' in a river bore the inscription, 'A Sage Mother shall come to Rule Mankind, and her Imperium shall bring Eternal Prosperity'. If she did not know it for the fake it was, she certainly seized on it with ardour as an omen. She led her court to the Altar of Heaven to declare the river sacred and to prohibit fishing there, and she took the title, Sage Mother, Sovereign Divine. She then planned the most lavish ceremony China had ever known to venerate the find and change the reign-title to 'Eternal Prosperity'.

She announced that every eminent person in the Empire must without exception attend the ceremony in Loyang. Members of the imperial Li family and other princes suspected that they were being lured into a trap. Many rose in rebellion but were swiftly repressed. The consequent suicides, executions and other punishments wreaked havoc among the aristocracy, and the Li family was systematically almost totally destroyed.

Wu saw in this success a manifestation of Heaven's favour, and it fuelled her secret ambition. Her monk-lover unearthed a Buddhist text foretelling the imminent reincarnation of a female deity who would bring 'joy without limit' to the people, and he persuasively interpreted this to identify the Empress as that reincarnation. Wu ensured that the teaching was widely circulated and she advanced the Buddhist clergy to fresh heights, founding and funding Great Cloud Temples in every prefecture, raising some monks to dukedoms, and ordaining over a thousand monks.

Then, all being ready at last for the great ceremony, Wu gave vent to her ambition. After modestly rejecting three successive petitions for her to ascend the throne, she saw reports that her symbol, the phoenix, had been seen above the palace and a flock of vermilion birds fluttering about the throne room, as clear messages from Heaven. Jui-tsung abdicated and she declared herself Holy and Divine Emperor of the Chou Dynasty – first and only female Emperor of China.

CHAPTER SEVENTEEN

The T'ang (618–907) – II

China's propensity for moving multitudes of people from one area to another was once more demonstrated by the new lady Emperor who uprooted over one hundred thousand households in the vicinity of Changan and deposited them in Loyang, which having been made her capital she wanted appropriately populated (a small number compared with the four million people moved in 1999 to make way for a dam on the Yangtze). She quite wantonly had two favourite consorts of Jui-tsung – now entitled Emperor Expectant and for a time virtually imprisoned in the palace – executed on trumped-up charges. But she scaled down her reign of terror, contriving the murder of her secret police chief and initiating the trials and sentencing of eight hundred and fifty of his adherents.

More constructively, she opened up the examination system, thereby substantially increasing the number of lowly entrants to the civil service. If the economy was then strained by a huge expansion of the bureaucracy, the latter's upper echelons were tightly controlled by Wu through a constant switching and replacement of her ministers – eighty per cent of them suffered exile, execution, or demotion. They were, however, mostly highly able men who helped her to govern well.

She conducted foreign policy shrewdly. This was at first easy since internecine conflicts deprived the border tribes of any aggression. But skill and military action were needed to control renewed incursions by the Northern Turks and the Tibetans, while a newly emergent Mongol power, the Khitans, swept down from modern Manchuria's west to occupy territory around present-day Peking before being pushed back.

Wu's last years were filled with widespread corruption and patronage, which had previously been quite rare, but above all by her liaisons. Her cosmetic skills and sexual appetite concealed her age of seventy. After she tired of her monk-lover and had him lured to her palace and murdered, she took up with her Confucian physician. And then the Chang brothers entered the scene – two beautiful youths, 'painted and powdered, their robes of rich brocade'. She was so besotted with them that she made no effort to curb their descent into every kind of vice. When the court officials, desperate to dislodge the brothers' hold on her, brought charges against them she scotched the attempts. Often she was unwell and only the Changs had access to her, rudely sending away her ministers.

At length, early in 705, a group of leading officials coaxed the dismissed Emperor Chung-tsung from his residence to which he had been permitted to return from banishment, and with five hundred Palace Guards went to the palace courtyard. There they confronted the Changs and killed them. Wu suddenly appeared, dishevelled and angry: she addressed the plotters and her son in terms of withering contempt, then returned to her bed where she died some months later at the age of eighty-two. So ended the seventeen years of the so-called Chou Dynasty's incumbency of the throne, and fifty years of the remarkable Wu Chao's power. At her death she graciously forgave her enemies and renounced her title of Emperor. The official name given to her posthumously doubtless pleased her shade: Emulator of Heaven.

The state of the government she left behind her was more an emulation of Hell. Certainly it was a sink of corruption, nepotism and neglect. Ministers vied with relations of the returned Emperor Chung-tsung and of his Empress Wei in contending for power by every black deed possible. Once again a woman, in the person of the lewd and licentious Empress, assumed the ascendancy, and she was joined by her daughter, called the

An-lo Princess. The former enjoyed a succession of lovers while the latter amassed huge wealth through corruption. The bureaucracy was swollen by ever more numbers, including a thousand eunuchs and many people who had either bought office or graduated through a now degraded examination system. Economic hardship and disaffection were rife.

In 710 Chung-tsung died – believed poisoned by Empress Wei who forged a testamentary edict appointing a son aged fifteen to the throne. But a fortnight later a certain Li Lung-chi, the twenty-five-year-old son of ex-Emperor Jui-tsung by a concubine, sprang a coup. With some followers and the Palace Guards he one night beheaded the leaders of the Empress Wei's coterie, then burst into the palace to kill the Empress herself as she fled and the An-lo Princess in the act of applying her make-up. Presently Li Lung-chi's sister, the T'ai-p'ing Princess, dragged Wei's young appointee from the throne and installed Jui-tsung once again as Emperor.

Now it was the turn of this princess to hold sway, for Jui-tsung lacked energy and ambition. However, as the administration crumbled into increasing disorder and frontier troubles multiplied, he became uneasy. The portent of a blazing comet induced him to abdicate in favour of his son. So in 712 Li Lung-chi became Emperor, known to history as Hsüan-tsung. Relations between him and the thrusting T'ai-p'ing Princess rapidly deteriorated. She plotted to poison him and, failing, planned an armed coup, but Hsüan-tsung was forewarned. He had the ringleaders beheaded in front of the Audience Hall and allowed the Princess a dignified suicide, concluding a lurid era of female domination of China.

Hsüan-tsung was twenty-eight when he began the longest and most illustrious reign of the T'ang Dynasty. He had shared his family's incarceration in the palace by order of the Empress Wu, and his mother was one of the two royal women Wu wantonly murdered. These experiences and the three years of vicious infighting that brought him to the throne may have scarred him, but may also have helped shape his strength of character. He was distinguished by his warmth of manner, his affection for his brothers and relatives, his directness, his passion, his attachment to his advisers, and his firm and sensible exercise of power. He was what the West would come to call a Renaissance man, skilled in music, poetry and calligraphy, versed in Taoist philosophy, and a lover both of dramatic entertainment and of sport such as polo.

He cleared out the detritus of the previous administration and gathered about him three or four brilliant men of comparatively humble origins who had risen through Wu's examinations at their most stringent. These men enjoyed a permanence in office very different from Wu's constant changes. The foremost of their number agreed to take office only upon Hsüan-tsung's assent to a specific programme of reform. Forming the basis of imperial policy for many years to come, it included: humane government unreliant on harsh laws; no military adventures; application of the law equally to all, not omitting the Emperor's friends; exclusion of eunuchs from any political rôle; no excessive taxation; no central government posts for the Emperor's relatives; and ministerial advice given freely without fear. The driving force behind all the measures that followed was a desire for moral regeneration.

The best part of a decade was spent restoring the central government's morale and authority by streamlining it and bringing in scholars to draft edicts; by purging it of its many ill-made appointments; by posting able men to the provinces where all metropolitan appointees had to have had experience; by reviving touring commissions of inspection – whose work the Emperor's progresses supplemented – and by a revision of the legal codes to ensure uniform civil service rules and practices throughout the Empire. This last was important, not least for enabling a start to be made on the registration of taxpayers, the laxity of which sorely depressed revenue. The problem was the huge number of vagrants who had fled their homes to evade taxation and labour service or who had been uprooted by the establishment of vast estates by officials and aristocrats:

by offering six years of tax exemption for registering, the government brought eight hundred thousand householders back into the tax system.

So poor for so long, the economy badly needed revenue, particularly as a string of natural disasters from floods to droughts and earthquakes to locusts had beset the country, requiring an intensification of the granary system. The problem of the coinage, however – so acute that for a time even false currency was legal tender – proved to be intractable in the face of counterfeiting. Other moves were more successful, such as the systematic exploitation of new salt wells, and a reduction in frontier forces consequent on the putting down of a Turkish-Tibetan rising in the Ordos.

The Emperor sought to set an example of frugality: brocades, and the wearing of embroidered clothes, pearls and jade were prohibited at court, and the harem's numbers much reduced. Against this it must be noted that, although his Empress was barren, he fathered fifty-nine children, many of whom inherited his fertility – one son, for example, had fifty-five children, another fifty-eight, and a third thirty-six. All had to be given expensive households and fiefdoms, at a cost that would consume the taxes of a quarter of a million families. When the Emperor discovered an arrangement for a monk to perform magical ceremonies for the Empress and provide her with an amulet to make her fruitful he was enraged. In his dislike of sorcery he had banned fortune-tellers from visiting any official, and indeed had one official accused of consulting them flogged to death. He degraded his Empress to commoner status and never had another empress, contenting himself with favoured consorts.

Extensive reformation of the military organization was also undertaken. Conscription and the local militia were phased out as the frontier armies became increasingly professional. Soldiers were encouraged to take their families with them and to form agricultural colonies. The forces, totalling between four and six hundred thousand men, were grouped under military governors, often of barbarian extraction to make them, it was hoped, more manageable by the central government.

True to Hsüan-tsung's pledge to his first chief minister, the army's function was defence, not adventure. For the best part of four decades it enjoyed almost uninterrupted success in keeping at bay both the resurgent Tibetans and the Western Turkish Turgesh tribes in Central Asia where the long tentacles of Arab expansionism had begun to reach; there, among other places, the Chinese placed a powerful garrison in the Kashgar region north of Kashmir. The Khitans were a constant concern and were contained with difficulty. On the other hand, the Turkic-Mongol Uighurs finally eclipsed the Northern Turks and from their capital far to the north of the Ordos established friendly diplomatic and active commercial relations with China. A formidable Korean state called Parhae arose in eastern Manchuria and it too was friendly; indeed, as in the southern Korean state of Silla and in Japan, a strong attachment to Chinese culture obtained, and to a great extent these states made themselves copies of T'ang China.

From the north-east to the far west, numerous states and tribes were bound to China by military pact, marriage with the royal family, or the receipt of Chinese titles. Their emissaries sent to pay tributes and receive gifts in the traditional manner thronged Hsüan-tsung's capital. This, after periodic transfers to Loyang, was permanently Changan after 736, consequent on a greatly improved land and water transport system's assuring it of the regular supplies its poor environment had often failed to provide. As well as with the envoys, the place teemed with merchants and visitors from all over the Empire and far abroad. The Emperor's court was full of members of the learned academies he had founded: writers, poets, Buddhist and Taoist clergy, artists, painters, calligraphers, even masters of chess, and scholars of every kind were at his disposal. A comparison with Lorenzo de' Medici's Florence has been made: with the 740s the reign reached its apogee, a period called the High T'ang when the court at Changan was a scene of glittering magnificence.

It was sustained by a revived economy, which owed much to a very efficient bureaucracy whose members had only one day off in ten. After 736 the financial system, which embraced taxes, labour services, and prefectorial budgets, was overhauled, drastically reducing the half a million sheets of paper required to operate the previous system. As prosperity returned – despite further natural disasters – the age at which a man became liable to tax and the corvée was raised from twenty-one to twenty-three.

As time passed, however, the lengthening reign saw ministerial unity under strain. For example, antagonism between Confucian and Legalistic officials erupted when two brothers murdered a censor whom they believed responsible for the unjust execution of their father. Confucianists argued for the brothers' release because they had observed the canonical code of ritual filial behaviour, while the Legalists wanted them executed for breaking the law: the Emperor decreed execution. Growing ministerial intrigues and bitter factions prompted charges of treason to be flung about on real or invented evidence, resulting in a number of executions. Nepotism and corruption began to rear their heads again. Thus, the notoriously ill-educated son of one of the Chief Minister's friends was awarded the highest marks in the examination, but when the Emperor heard of this and personally re-examined the candidates the favoured son returned a blank paper.

The Chief Minister was too well-entrenched to feel any humiliation. He was Li Lin-fu, a man of aristocratic lineage who for many years presided over a government in which the old aristocratic clans came ever more to the fore. Genealogies of the most prominent families were officially published and regularly supplemented. These families, who seldom permitted marriage with outsiders, gained political influence through a web of relationships with the Emperor and his consorts. As they increasingly entered the ranks of the administration they supplanted examination graduates who had previously predominated.

The ascendancy of Li Lin-fu and his titled associates coincided with a growing tendency by Hsüan-tsung to withdraw from governing. This was not unconnected with his famous passion for his favourite concubine, Yang Yü-huan, entitled 'Prized Consort' or 'Her Preciousness the Imperial Consort Yang', of whom a poet was subsequently to write:

> She waited his pleasure at banquets,
>> with never a moment's peace;
> their Springs were spent in outings of Spring;
>> he was sole lord of her nights.
> In the harems there were beauties,
>> three thousand there were in all,
> but the love that was due to three thousand
>> was spent on one body alone.
> Her make-up completed in chambers of gold,
>> she attended upon his nights,
> when in marble mansions feasts were done,
>> their drunkenness matched the Spring.
> Her sisters and her brothers all
>> were ennobled and granted great fiefs;
> A glory that any would envy
>> rose from her house.

Whether the distraction of this lady or simple exhaustion after nearly four decades of vigorous exercise of his authority accounts for his declining interest in affairs of state (although almost to the end he continued to hold his dawn audiences), what is clear is that he became intensely enamoured of Eastern Buddhism with its Tantric practices. He had in his court a famous astronomer and equally famous mathematician who were devotees of the cult, which deployed magical spells, incantations and mystical techniques, and thus had much in common with Taoism. He had masters of both faiths compete in rain-making and suchlike. But it was to his old love of Taoism that he chiefly turned. He honoured it with a decree that every household had to have a copy of the primary Taoist text (on which he himself wrote a commentary); he set up special schools for Taoist studies, and made Taoist scriptures an important examination subject. He even took a new reign-title with a Taoist connotation, Heavenly Treasure.

Buddhism, however, was a different matter. When he came to power its church had grown inordinately influential and rich. He confiscated all its land and water-mills illegally acquired; put an end to church-building by rich people who thereby gained tax exemption; bore down on the abuse of ordination – another means of tax avoidance – by having more than thirty thousand monks return to secular life; and, by prohibiting public preaching, which had acquired much political content, confined monks' activities to their temples. As he embraced Taoism ever more ardently, the Emperor Hsüan-tsung clamped down further on the Buddhist church. He ordered every monk's status to be registered so as to prevent fraudulent ordination, reduced the number of village shrines, limited the amount of property held in perpetuity, and by vesting control of the church in his Foreign Affairs department pointedly defined it as a foreign faith.

Yet it was probably a Buddhist monk or monks who around this time (750s) or earlier gave China and the world one of man's greatest inventions, incalculably important to the preservation, spread and advancement of knowledge – printing. Its essential prerequisite, paper, had taken innumerable forms since first produced by the Han – kites, lanterns, playing cards, flowers, screens, wall-covering, even clothes, while paper images were burnt for ceremonial purposes, and variously coloured notepapers were used by painters and calligraphers. The idea of printing on plain sheets of paper seems to have been born of seal-making and the cutting of inscriptions into stone, both practised since at least the Shang.

The first phase of what the West would know as typography was block-printing: a smooth-surfaced piece of wood, usually from a fruit-tree, was carved out with figures in relief; it was carved in reverse – mirror image – then inked over, and pressed on paper. It would take another three centuries for movable type to evolve but block-printing reached the West even later, via Persia to Poland in the wake of the Mongols' thirteenth century invasion. By then playing cards and printed textiles and other matter were in wide circulation in Europe, and it is said that Gutenberg's Turkish wife saw Chinese printing-blocks in her native Venice and this gave her husband the inspiration for Europe's first printing press using movable type in 1458, seven hundred years or more after the Chinese invention.

No one could have foretold its vast ramifications. To the people of the time the chief glory of the High T'ang lay in its arts. To his orchestras and schools of drama and music Hsüan-tsung added a descendant of the 318 BC Academy of the Gate of Chi in the form of the Academy of Letters, predating by a millennium any comparable European institution and attended by his favourite scholars, poets and painters.

T'ang art is distinguished by its lavishness and delicacy. Its practitioners produced fine sculptures in stone, including marble; and wonderful frescoes and paintings, particularly Wu Tao-tzu whose 'grandeur of conception and fiery energy of execution,' a critic has written, 'make him one with Michelangelo.' His work was typical of the period in fusing Indian metaphysical with Chinese traditional. Portraiture and scenes such as court events were painted in glowing colours, while horses from the western regions – tough, stocky ponies – were vigorously represented. Two new schools of landscape-painting emerged, one using a precise line technique and the other a monochrome ink.

The arts of goldsmith and silversmith flowered. Furniture, musical instruments and gaming boards were painted, lacquered or inlaid with magnificent floral and animal patterns in mother-of-pearl, tortoiseshell or precious metal. Mirror-backs were now gilded and silvered with a profusion of ornaments in place of the old abstract and magical designs. Most notable of all, the art and craft of ceramics took a great leap forward with the first use of coloured glazes and the perfection of porcelain. Earthenware found extensive use in figurines placed in graves – toys, huge horses, Bactrian camels, officials, servants, dancing girls, musicians and, predominantly, women who were depicted on horseback and even playing polo.

But above all the arts soared poetry. It was not only promoted at court and on court occasions but given a peculiar impetus by the examination system. Graduates from the provincial examinations were required in the all-important metropolitan examinations to compose a poem, and the graceful composition of a poem became for the educated person as much a social as an artistic accomplishment. It was something done at parties, at banquets, on group excursions, upon visiting friends or not finding someone at home when called on. It was also a means of advancement: poems were presented to influential patrons or to gain entry into otherwise closed circles. Civil servants travelling on missions or to take up posts wrote poetry on the whitewashed walls of their overnight accommodation, and these poems might be responded to by other poems written on the pavilion walls by subsequent travellers. To disseminate their work, poets used scrolls but popular poems were spread by word of mouth or sung by entertainers (including at Changan circles of prostitutes much frequented by the gilded youth).

The poetic metre was based on the number of syllables in a line – five or seven syllables were the most common – together with correct tonal patterning and rhythms. Tense, pronouns, prepositions, singular or plural, and the definite or indefinite article are largely lacking in Chinese, these being imported by the sense. Thus the couplet

> Ancient tree is-no person path
> Deep mountain what place bell?

may be transcribed

> Ancient trees, trails with no one there,
> Deep in hills a bell from I know not where.

Poets composed lyrics about their feelings, adopted Taoist motifs, made historical or legendary events their themes, described nature, imagined scenes and places of times past, drew on the many encyclopaedias containing the literary lore of plants and animals, or produced character vignettes which presaged the drama to come. To the modern reader their work is still undeniably beautiful and full of vivid imagery:

> Perilous precipices where paths end,
> Snagging the stars on the high cliff's crags.

This is from a poem by Li Po: he and Wang Wei were two of the outstanding poets of the period, but the accolade belongs to Tu Fu, on whom generation after generation has conferred the status of a Shakespeare.

He was reaching maturity as a poet when he witnessed, and wrote many poems on, the abrupt shattering of the glittering success of Hsüan-tsung's reign. In 751 a Chinese army sent out to stem the Arab advance in the far west was routed at the Talas River, opening the region to the entry of Islam. (In that battle men skilled in paper-making were captured and taken to Samarkand to start production there, whence the craft passed to Baghdad, the religious and cultural capital of Islam, and eventually to Europe through the Arab conquest of Spain, a millennium after the Han invention.) The following year the powerful Chief Minister Li Lin-fu died after nineteen years of dominance. He was posthumously disgraced by his successor Yang Kuo-chung's allegation of treason, and deprived of all his ranks; fifty of his relations were banished or otherwise punished and his property was confiscated; the valuable grave goods were removed from his coffin and he was buried a commoner. His ability, however, was not shared by Yang Kuo-chung, a cousin of Prized Consort, and this, with the Emperor's withdrawal from government, cleared the way for catastrophe.

Following the Talas River débâcle, there were renewed troubles and repeated setbacks on the western frontier, but the greatest danger came from the Emperor's own troops on the north and north-eastern frontiers. These were controlled by an ambitious governor of mixed Soghdian and Turkish blood who, starting as a small-town interpreter, had rapidly risen in Chinese service. By name An Lu-shan – a tall, heavily built man, by tradition a witch's son at whose birth a halo around the house caused the beasts of the field to cry out loud – he and Chief Minister Yang Kuo-chung came into bitter conflict. When the latter saw (in a request from An to appoint non-Chinese in place of Chinese guards) a disposition to rebel, Hsüan-tsung followed his increasing policy of appointing eunuchs as his personal envoys by sending one of them to enquire of An's intentions. An Lu-shan bribed the man heavily to report back his unqualified loyalty. Still relations between Yang and An continued to deteriorate, especially after the eunuch's bribe-taking was discovered and the fellow executed. In December 755 An Lu-shan, fearful of recall and disgrace, openly rebelled. Over seven years of bloody fighting were to follow.

It started with An's striking southwards so fast that within a few weeks he was attacking a garrison on the Grand Canal a hundred and fifty miles east of Loyang, the second capital. When news reached him that the Emperor had executed his, An's, son and forced his wife to commit suicide, he massacred the entire garrison. Feebly opposed by hastily drummed-up levies, he went on to occupy Loyang. His advance to Changan, however, was blocked by an army at the impregnable T'ung-kuan Pass.

There was a pause here while rebel and loyalist fought each other over a wide expanse of the north and east. An Lu-shan proclaimed himself Emperor of a new dynasty of Greater Yen, and Hsüan-tsung called in his western garrisons and armies, leaving Eastern Turkestan vulnerable to the Tibetans and Uighurs and out of Chinese control for many centuries. He also appointed military governors all over the Empire, which effectively devolved power from the centre and thus gave a malign hostage to fortune to the future.

An Lu-shan went through a phase of widespread defeats, depleting his forces in front of the T'ung-kuan Pass guarding Changan. Yang Kuo-chung saw in this the moment to counter-attack. His insistence overcame the doubts of the Emperor

Hsüan-tsung who ordered his reluctant general at the Pass to launch an offensive. The result was that the army was ambushed in a defile between the Yellow River and the mountains, and butchered.

Upon tidings of this reaching Hsüan-tsung, he fled Changan in the middle of the night. Accompanied by his Prized Consort, Yang Kuo-chung, some of his eunuchs, and a small cavalry escort, he set off south-westward towards present-day Szechwan. A gruelling journey through the mountains turned into a nightmare when his escort became mutinous and first slew Yang Kuo-chung, whom they blamed for the T'ung-kuan Pass disaster, then demanded that the Emperor kill his Prized Consort, whom they detested for her influence: powerless, Hsüan-tsung ordered his chief eunuch to strangle her.

While he proceeded on his way to Szechwan, he left his heir apparent, the third of his thirty sons, within the great loop of the Yellow River to organize resistance. This he did to great effect, calling in aid from tributary tribes; but first he yielded to his officers' pleas and usurped the throne. This was in July 756. When the news reached Hsüan-tsung, old, exhausted and racked with remorse for the death of his love, he immediately despatched the imperial regalia to the new Emperor, posthumously known as Su-tsung. So ended the longest and most glorious reign of the T'ang.

By the following year Su-tsung's army, spearheaded by Uighur mercenaries, had recaptured Loyang and Changan. He sent for his father to return to live in the capital, where he died four years later at the age of seventy-seven. He outlived the rebel and upstart Emperor An Lu-shan who was assassinated in 757 to be succeeded by his son, the first of five successive rebel leaders to be assassinated by their successors. They maintained the rebellion until 763 when, having never enjoyed mass support, it was finally extinguished by the deep resources of the T'ang Empire. But the damage it did was deep and lasting.

CHAPTER EIGHTEEN

The T'ang (618-907) - III

*I*n the last year of the An Lu-shan rebellion serious risings occurred in Szechwan and along the Yangtze. Government forces sent to repress the latter in cities at the approach to modern Shanghai ran amok, looting and murdering thousands of foreign merchants. These events were, however, unconnected with An's rebellion whose most important effect was ultimately to destroy the dynasty. The military governors of the area where it began, Hopeh, asserted authority over the civilian population and thus made their provinces virtually autonomous, out of reach of T'ang control. Other governors, of provinces east and south-east of the capital, followed suit, even claiming hereditary succession.

In the same year, 762, that Su-tsung's father died, so did he. His Empress plotted to kill his heir, a son by another woman, and then install her own son, but she was foiled by a prominent eunuch and paid with her life. The heir apparent became Emperor, to be known as Tai-tsung.

His immediate concern was an onslaught from Tibet. Its tribesmen encroached ever more on China's western borders, on one occasion even entering Changan to loot and burn before being thrown back. A sporadic fifty-year war ensued as they raided and harried the T'ang empire. In the process the T'ang lost the lands they depended on for horses and pasture, so that henceforward they had to look to the Uighurs for horses at a cost of thousands of rolls of silk each year. Relations with the Uighur empire itself fluctuated – once its fighters temporarily took possession of Loyang.

The rebellions and frontier wars severely affected the economy. To make good the loss of revenue through neglect of the tax registers, the salt monopoly was rigorously enforced: providers had to be licensed and obliged to sell their products exclusively to officials who imposed a swingeing tax in passing it on to merchants. (Within the next decade a similar situation prevailed in the tea trade. For hundreds of years the Tibetan fashion of tea-drinking had spread through China, at first in the Tibetan way of mixing-in flour, salt and ginger, and then without additives. Szechwan and the south-east were the chief growers: traders bought from the peasants and accumulated stocks before selling. The government's attempt to monopolize cultivation failed, so a commission was set up to buy the tea from the producers and sell it to the traders, although a corrupt relationship between officials and the big wholesalers soon drove out the small traders.) Finances were also improved by a new specialist brand of financial administrators, with staffs of accountants and clerks, who cut across bureaucratic departments, incidentally opening a fresh career path into government.

But above all, the post-An Lu-shan era, often called the Late T'ang, was notable for the re-emergence of the eunuchs as a powerful influence on the state. For the most part recruited from prisoners of war and children from the far south earlier in the dynasty, they now numbered several thousand. Manipulative, corrupt, but often highly able, constituting the sole channel between the bureaucracy and the Emperor, they spread their authority from the Inner Palace to the government in the Outer Palace. As time passed they were rewarded with higher ranks, top military posts, and titles. Some adopted 'sons' and took nominal 'wives' to create 'families'. They were of course roundly resented and detested by the regular officials, including the financial administrators who had to cooperate with them because they controlled the Imperial Treasury which the troubles had caused to replace the State Treasury.

Towards the end of Tai-tsung's reign he increasingly turned, like Hsüan-tsung before him, to Buddhism which thereby once again enjoyed a resurgence in ordinations, new temples, and influence. This ceased, however, upon his death in 779 when Te-tsung, the first of his twenty sons, succeeded him and promptly stopped government support.

He was a reformer. He insisted on economies, the restoration of the State Treasury, and an end to the practice that had developed of provincial governors sending 'tributes' in lieu of regular tax payments. Under his regime, indeed, the whole system of taxation was overhauled. It would be eccentric to call the subject riveting, but revenue is the life-blood of any state. The system now (780) introduced replaced a diversity of often irregular taxes with two clearly defined imposts, giving rise to the name the Two-Tax System. One was on all households according to their size and property; the other, on all land under cultivation. These taxes, whose rates varied from province to province, were collected by the prefectures in one instalment in the summer and another in autumn. They were remitted in part to the central government and in part to the provincial administration, the balance being retained.

Before his great reform could take full effect, however, Te-tsung set about trying to end the separatist movement which had by now spread even to the south and made much of the country virtually independent of Changan: some of the governors actually styled themselves kings or even emperors. But his efforts, directed first at the Hopeh reign, came to nothing. At one stage when rebels cut off the canal bringing grain supplies to the capital, the consequent imposition of levies on Changan's citizens provoked a revolt which sent the Emperor fleeing. He could not return for nigh on a year, and as the 780s ended he had to accept living in a realm of highly complex decentralized regions.

He died in 805, ushering in the fateful ninth century with his eldest son becoming Emperor, known as Shun-tsung. Inauspiciously, this man had been rendered almost mute by a stroke the previous year, and after a few months' isolation with his favourite concubine and a eunuch he abdicated in favour of the eldest of his twenty-three sons, known as Hsien-tsung, who was to prove the strongest of all the Late T'ang emperors. For over a decade his armies fought to bring the recalcitrant provinces under control. They achieved almost complete success. For the present at least, China was a unitary state again. At the same time the Two-Tax System and vigorous economic measures helped restore financial and political confidence. In an Act of Grace promulgated a year after his accession, Hsien-tsung named his reign-title Fundamental Harmony, an aspiration he promoted by a widespread distribution of titles and rewards to officials and the military. He curbed the eunuchs and for some years the bureaucracy worked smoothly and efficiently.

It did not last. Rivalries rent officialdom and eunuch intrigue revived. In 820 Hsien-tsung suddenly died – murdered, some said, by a palace eunuch but more likely poisoned by the long-life elixirs he imbibed while dabbling in alchemy. A palace struggle for the succession ensued, with the eunuchs' machinations again putting their chosen man on the throne. He was Mu-tsung, a son of the late Emperor but devoid of his dynamism and ability, and he quickly lost control, so painfully gained, of the north-east provinces. He did not live long. A polo accident in 823 invalided him: many of his responsibilities were taken over by eunuchs until he died the following year.

Again eunuch activity secured the accession, by Mu-tsung's son, Ching-tsung. Aged only fifteen he turned out to be irresponsible and decadent. The political scene was set for an intensification of ministerial in-fighting. There were three categories of contenders: one was the eunuchs; another was the scholars, usually graduates of the highest examination and appointees by royal warrant to the principal literary institution, the Hanlin Academy; and the third was the factions consisting of pressure groups of individuals whose leaders were avid for power, the two foremost groups being known as the Niu and Li factions. While each category had its own agenda, in practice the factions incorporated almost everybody.

Their activities included influencing examination results which were so important to civil servants climbing the ladder of preferment. For these people ascending to the fifth and fourth ranks was crucial, not only for privileges such as attendance at certain court functions and financial and sumptuary advantages (of which the most prized was the right – the *yin* privilege – to appoint a son to the civil service without his sitting an examination), but above all because they would then be poised to rise to the third rank, from which chief ministers were chosen.

Having engineered Ching-tsung's elevation, the eunuchs within three years had had enough of him. They murdered him on his return from a drunken night-time excursion. Once more they contrived the succession, this time by a serious and studious half-brother, Wen-tsung.

He began by sending home many of the palace ladies, abjuring luxuries and reviving royal audiences which had not been held for many years. As eunuch power asserted itself ever more aggressively he determined to end it. An attempt in 830 failed when the eunuchs were forewarned, but in 835 more careful plans were laid. The imperial army guarding the capital was eunuch-dominated, so the Emperor's conspirators secretly assembled a force to the west of Changan. With the help of the leader of one of the two rival eunuch groups they had the leader of the other group cast into prison and assassinated. Then at a dawn audience it was announced that the auspicious portent of sweet dew on a pomegranate tree in the Outer Palace courtyard had occurred in the night, whereupon the Emperor sent out all the eunuchs present to investigate the miracle. The conspirators had a force waiting in a tent in the courtyard; but when the eunuchs arrived, a flap of the tent was blown open and they heard the clank of weaponry. Panic-stricken, most of them escaped to alert the imperial army which struck before the secret force outside the city could move. Rapidly rounding up the ministers involved, together with their families and many innocents, they tortured captives to extort confessions and proceeded to kill over a thousand people in government circles, including the chief ministers and their families who were executed in one of the market places.

The failure of this, the so-called Sweet Dew Plot, affected Wen-tsung deeply. He became withdrawn and morose and drank heavily. When the eunuchs intrigued over the question of succession they persuaded him to let his only son and heir be executed. Racked with remorse, he died the following year. His younger brother had been made heir apparent at the behest of one group of eunuchs, and when they secured his accession as Wu-tsung in 840 they arranged the executions of rival princes backed by other eunuch groups. For all their influence, however, it was not any eunuch but a chief minister who stands out as the dominant political figure of Wu-tsung's six-year reign. He was Li Te-yü, a member of the Hanlin Academy and a seasoned bureaucrat. His appointment meant victory for his, the Li, faction over the Niu faction. He was a charming, quick-tongued, knowledgeable, calculating, secretive and haughty man, a fine poet and essayist, who loved solitude on his large estate where he cultivated rare plants. Enjoying the confidence of his brash, fiery-tempered and stubborn Emperor, he much improved government efficiency and restrained the eunuchs.

Scarcely had he taken office than a great mass of Uighurs, in flight from southern Siberian Kirghiz tribes, pressed down from the Gobi. Li Te-yü instigated rigorous defensive measures, then the army he sent took the main Uighur camp by surprise and killed ten thousand men, with a similar number captured. This happened in 843 at a place in the Gobi to be called Kill-the-Huns Mountain (Sha-hu-shan). An important consequence was that the Uighur religion of Manichaeism – the creation of a third-century Persian seer who combined elements of Zoroaster, Buddha and Christ – which had spread as far west as Spain as well as east into China, was eliminated from the country.

Li Te-yü next put down a dangerous rebellion in the east of present Shansi, but the most important feature of his administration was the persecution of the Buddhists. Having recovered from past restrictions they had become so rich and powerful as to challenge the state. Their great temples were crammed with gold and silver objects, their vast estates rich in agriculture and forestry, their huge numbers of ordinands immune from tax. To an Emperor whose coffers were running low and whose predilection anyway was for Taoism, they were an irresistible target. In a programme of repression led by the minister Li Te-yü, thousands of temples and shrines were spoliated and with them much of the great Buddhist architecture, sculpture and painting that had been the chief preoccupation of artists during the past two centuries, while vast quantities of copper images, bells, chimes and fittings were melted down and cast into money to relieve the chronic shortage of cash due to insufficient mining, and a quarter of a million monks and nuns were forced back to secular life. Although Buddhism did not cease as an intellectual and artistic dynamic, by the time of the programme's completion during the following reign the church could never again rival the state.

It is probable that Wu-tsung was yet another royal victim of alchemical drugs when he died in 846. Eunuchs once again contrived the succession. Hsüan-tsung was an uncle of the brothers he succeeded. He had a fixation on the memory of the able Hsien-tsung whose thirteenth son he had been and whose death twenty-six years ago he believed to have been brought about by murder: he therefore ruthlessly hunted down anyone remotely connected with the matter. He was devoted also to his immediate family, once indulging his sister who, objecting to a suitor he proposed, broke her chopsticks and soup-spoon in the royal presence. His restraint on this occasion was the greater in view of his punctilious insistence on decorum in every minute detail. Determined to stamp his authority on his court, he relentlessly grilled his ministers, leaving one chief minister bathed in sweat after the ordeal. He sacked Li Te-yü, allowing the Niu faction something of a comeback; but in truth the long and bitter Li – Niu contest was at an end. At an end also was the Tibetan threat of these many decades past, as that state collapsed in a welter of factional, tribal and dynastic struggles. Nor did the

Uighurs any longer require constant conciliation – on one occasion horses could only be bought from them for half a million rolls of silk – after the Kirghiz tribes overwhelmed them and established friendly relations with China. Apart from some minor rebellions and some years' fighting to end the raids of a new power risen in the Ordos desert, the Tanguts, who were originally refugees from north-east Tibet, the country was largely at peace; and although a degree of separation persisted, the Emperor nominally at least enjoyed his Mandate of Heaven over the greater part of his Empire.

Art of course continued to hold its place in the national culture, however turbulent the times. Painters and sculptors throve and craftsmen produced exquisite objects in jade, gold and silver. While poetry maintained its popularity, the standard was below that achieved earlier in the dynasty; but literature benefited from a significant development of the short story. Curiously, the Changan ward system played a part in this. The division of the city into districts, the gates of whose walls were locked at sunset and opened at dawn to the beating of drums, meant that the visitor caught inside had to stay the night, and on this turned many romantic and erotic tales. Other subjects were faith plighted and broken, heroism, and affairs between humans and supernatural creatures. Some even glamourized the bandits who had increasingly plagued the country.

There had been river pirates against whom a special force had to be formed as long ago as the 830s. Gangsterism had, however, grown willy-nilly. Salt smugglers were associated with gangs sometimes numbering a hundred men. Officials journeying to the capital with tax cash, grain and cloth were vulnerable to attack; so were merchants, prosperous from their trade in tea and other commodities and the burgeoning international commerce through the southern ports. Some merchants avoided carrying cash by using promissory notes – forerunner of paper money – issued by gold- and silver-smiths acting as proto-banks; but the fraternity still provided rich pickings.

The gangs recruited peasants made poor by the increased burden of taxation or displaced by the establishment of ever-greater estates. By the late 850s the illicit movement was developing into serious rebellions, which included revolts by military garrisons along the Grand Canal and lower Yangtze, and one insurrection after another broke out in the hitherto stable south. A bandit leader called Ch'iu Fu, operating in the coastal province south of present-day Shanghai, assembled over thirty thousand men – 'bandits from the mountains and water, gangs of toughs and refugees from other provinces; they came from all directions, gathering like clouds'. He was only defeated with immense difficulty by very large forces that included a body of foreign horsemen.

A new threat arose, from the south-west. For some time the Tibetan-Burmese people there, occupying a state called Nan-chao situated on an almost impregnable plateau, had been bent on expansion. Having captured northern Burma they attacked Szechwan; repulsed, they made across the south towards the coast with its flourishing ports like Canton, and the fighting to pacify them lasted into the late 860s.

The cost in supplies for the military operations bore most heavily on the eastern and south-eastern areas, which were at the same time suffering severe natural disasters. Floods in the Great Plain which drowned tens of thousands of families were followed by drought and then a plague of locusts. Southward as far as the lower Yangtze there was widespread famine, and discontent grew over the persistent demands for foodstuffs for the armies.

More garrison mutinies broke out, the most serious starting in the far south. An officer named P'ang Hsüan led an initial force of eight hundred men northwards, first by land and then by sea, eventually crossing the Yangtze and arriving east of Loyang, by which time many bandit gangs and thousands of peasants had joined him. For a year he ravaged no fewer than ten prefectures before the government, again helped by foreign horsemen, defeated him.

In the midst of all this, in 859, Emperor Hsüan-tsung died. He had been ill for some time – yet another victim of poisoning by Taoist mineral elixirs. He had never named his heir apparent, which gave cliques of eunuchs the opportunity to intrigue over the succession as they had done for the past five reigns. One group of three claimed that the late Emperor had secretly communicated to them the nomination of his third son. They feared opposition from the officials and a famous eunuch general who favoured the eldest son, so, not divulging that the Emperor lay dead in the palace, they emerged from it with a purported imperial edict appointing the general to a distant command which would get him out of the way; but he was suspicious and secretly got into the palace, where he discovered the truth. The three eunuchs were executed and Hsuan-tsung's eldest son duly ascended the throne.

Known as I-tsung, he was extravagant, cruel and capricious. On one occasion he made his favourite musician a general. On another, when a minister warned him of a plot by the brother of his favourite consort, he executed the minister. In government he surrounded himself with eunuchs and minor aristocrats, arousing resentment among the leading factions and Hanlin scholars, who were only restrained by the looming menace of provincial unrest.

He ardently supported Buddhism, whose leading role in Chinese society his father had renewed. His chief minister was a devout Buddhist layman, neither drinking wine nor eating meat, and a writer of scholarly works on his religion. From his time dates the world's oldest extant book, the *Diamond Sutra*. Its date of 868 just precedes a great feast in I-tsung's palace to which he invited ten thousand monks. A couple of years later he decided to revive the ceremony of venerating Buddha's Bone, which was done with spectacular splendour. No doubt the chill wind of mortality had prompted him, for a few months later he died.

Yet again eunuchs procured the succession, this time of I-tsung's fifth son. Aged twelve, he ruled as Hsi-tsung from 873.

He had a boyish love of sports such as archery, riding and sword-play, and much pride in his prowess at the T'ang's favourite sport, football; he enjoyed mathematical calculations and music, but above all, gambling – on cock- and geese-fighting and especially with dice. As he grew older he took more interest in government but his cruel and arbitrary disposition ill-fitted him to rule the largest nation on earth with well over one hundred million people. In any event he was dominated by his chief eunuch, the greatly feared T'ien Ling-tz'u, who kept him occupied while himself busy gathering power in his own hands.

Yet the four chief ministers who replaced their mediocre predecessors in the Outer Court were of a higher calibre and lineage. They ended the corruption endemic in I-tsung's reign and improved government efficiency. But the situation they confronted was horrendous. Exacerbating the countrywide unrest another serious drought threatened mass starvation where people in the afflicted areas were having to eat berries and leaves; and the exigencies of the time permitted no forgoing of taxes, forcing peasants to vend the timber from their houses, sell their children into slavery, and hire out their wives as servants.

In this climate gangsterism flourished as never before. West and south of the Great Plain outlaws moved freely in the hills; across the salt-producing coastal districts an increased tax provoked extensive illicit trade; and brigands plundered merchants in the Yangtze valley. Some of the gangs grew as large as small armies, able even to attack walled cities: they did this by forming confederations of gangs under a dominant leader who often conferred his surname on his most prominent supporters, the more strongly to bind them to him.

For many years imperial armies fought to suppress them. The fact was that the central authority was everywhere breaking down. In several places the populace expelled or killed prefects they detested. There were numerous rural riots, although they usually ended with the peasants going back to their farming, and although it was peasants too who, goaded by poverty, joined the gangster gangs, other members were misfits, thugs, vagrants and people dislocated in the wake of the An Lu-shan rebellion. The gangster phenomenon was not, in short, a peasant movement but one of criminal intent, even if fuelled by a peasant discontent and on occasion assuming the mantle of rebellion against the state.

The first of the two most striking manifestations of gangsterism turning into rebellion started in 874. A confederate gang leader, Wang Hsien-chih, set out westward from Shantung and, growing stronger by the day, threatened Loyang before veering south. He ravaged the countryside and towns across thousands of square miles as far as the middle Yangtze. More Yellow River floods and another locust plague drove ever more peasants into his ranks. He entitled himself Supreme General and issued a denunciation of the government for injustice and corruption.

For four years the government strove to defeat him. It supplemented its military efforts with offers of a generous amnesty, even of government office, while at the same time it promoted the creation of local militia and promised a generalship and money to any commander capturing a bandit leader and three hundred of his men. Trying to solve the problem precipitated dispute and disharmony within the government, but at last it sufficiently asserted itself to launch vigorous attacks which culminated in Wang's defeat and death.

For a short while gangster activity was confined to small groups, but then Wang's one-time and more formidable partner, Huang Ch'ao, came to the fore. Once a salt merchant fallen into poverty, he now commanded all the major gangster forces and called himself Heaven-storming Generalissimo. At first the invigorated government kept him on the run. Deterred by a large force guarding Loyang he went south, crossed the Yangtze and raided across its delta. Next he marched several hundred miles across the wild and sparsely populated mountains of Fukien and sacked its coastal capital. With an imperial army so close behind that it snapped up some of his confederate leaders, he continued south and stopped outside Canton in mid-879. At first he tried to parley his surrender against appointment to a military governorship; when rejected, he violently attacked the city, which fell to him in a single day. He seized the governor and upon the latter's brave refusal to negotiate a settlement he killed him and proceeded to devastate the great port with merciless savagery. Out of a population of two hundred thousand only eighty thousand were left alive, the dead being mostly merchants from south-east Asia, India, Persia and the Arab world.

After this butchery Huang Ch'ao turned back northwards. Recruiting ever more robber bands he fought a number of battles against Hsi-tsung's armies, sometimes losing but without being decisively checked. His progress was the easier as commanders who should have opposed him were either treacherous, or cowardly or incompetent. Imperial authority was being utterly corroded as local leaders asserted their own ambitions in anticipation of an imminent end to the dynasty, while gangsterism flourished even in regions distant from Huang Ch'ao's operations.

He crossed the Yangtze with a vastly reinforced army and set Changan itself in his sights. As he advanced on it the forces guarding its protective passes panicked and fled. In the last month of 880 the capital fell to him. After a two-year march of over three thousand miles he entered the city seated in a golden sedan chair with several hundred thousand followers wearing brocade and red silk bandeaux. Thousands of harem women and officials came out to greet him, for their Emperor had vanished at dead of night with his eunuchs and a small retinue.

Wholesale destruction of the world's most prosperous city followed. To looting was added large-scale murder – eighty thousand are said to have perished – and the burning of the markets. The great metropolis was never to regain its splendour. Huang Ch'ao took it upon himself to ascend the throne and proclaim the Great Ch'i Dynasty (after the ancient name of his native Shantung). He replaced all the surviving top officials with men of little inclination or ability and embarked on a brief but appallingly harsh regime. Once when it was ridiculed in a poem written on the gate of one of the ministries, everyone in that ministry was killed, their eyes plucked out and their bodies publicly hung up; not only were the gate-guards executed but everyone else still in the city who could write poetry. All support from the educated elite and the provinces evaporated.

Meanwhile, young Emperor Hsi-tsung travelled hundreds of miles south-westward, crossing the nine-thousand-feet-high Ch'in-ling mountains and then a further four hundred miles over a second mountain chain into Szechwan. Here his court led an uneasy existence. He was effectively the prisoner of his chief eunuch, T'ien Ling-tz'u. Although strengthened by prominent officials who joined him in exile, his government was constantly at odds, with officials against eunuchs. Even in the provinces around him, rebellions and gangsterism prevailed. This activity was ubiquitous throughout China, leading to the establishment of substantial protective militia forces, often led by owners of great estates. Such people and the provincial governors were the de facto rulers of the country.

Yet all was not lost to the Emperor Hsi-tsung. A former chief minister in charge of a loyal force east of Changan wrote to him in his own blood vowing to recover the capital. When Huang Ch'ao sent an army against him it was routed. As the desertion of Huang's leading provincial supporters gathered momentum, loyalist forces gradually closed in on the capital. Cut off from all supplies the rebels sat in a deserted city; many were driven to cannibalism.

The government called in aid a frontier Turkic tribe, the Sha-t'o under the leadership of Li K'o-yung – his imperial family surname having been conferred on his father for similar help in an earlier rebellion. A number of government-administered setbacks resolved Huang Ch'ao on a climactic battle to destroy the Li K'o-yung menace, but the 150,000 men he despatched for the purpose were crushed. This and further reverses obliged him to abandon the capital in the first half of 883. After a year of battles and sieges, which he repeatedly lost, he fled east, remorselessly pursued by Li K'o-yung, until, reduced to a mere thousand men, he was cornered in the Valley of Wolves and Tigers in Shantung. Rather than surrender he slit his throat. His head was cut off and sent to the Emperor.

The ending of the great rebellions of the past decade brought neither peace nor unity to China. When the Emperor returned in 885 to his capital – a desolate place: 'thorns and brambles filled the city; foxes and hares ran everywhere' – this was the situation he faced: Sha-t'o Turks, Uighurs, Tanguts and other foreign tribes from beyond the Great Wall had poured in to occupy a wodge of the northern provinces, of which most of the remainder was in the hands of non-Chinese governors; in fact he only directly ruled the three provinces immediately surrounding Changan and, if he maintained a nominal suzerainty over nine regions strung along the south, all the remaining thirty provinces were controlled by independent governors – for the most part formerly either his generals or bandit leaders.

His position worsened when in desperate attempts to raise revenue he alienated Li K'o-yung, the Sha-t'o's leader, whose earlier help had been rewarded with the governorship of the far north-east. Li reacted by marching on Changan; all efforts to stop him failed and he entered and ransacked the city even more thoroughly than it had been before. Fleeing westward yet again, the Emperor crossed the precipitous Ch'in-ling mountains by the Linked Cloud Road. This was even more frightening than his previous route, since nearly fifty miles of it consisted of wooden trestles pounded into the sides of cliffs rising above roaring torrents. Some local military commanders rose against him, but others rallied to his side, especially after his hated chief eunuch T'ien Ling-tzu departed the court, and Li K'o-yung reverted to his allegiance. Thus Hsi-tsung was able to return to a ruined Changan after a two-year exile, but he was gravely ill and soon, in 888, his troubled life of twenty years ended.

Little remains to be related of the T'ang Dynasty. Hsi-tsung's younger brother, an able and intelligent man, ascended the throne at the age of twenty-one. Known as Chao-tsung, he had twice during his fourteen-year reign to flee his capital – once being rescued by Li K'o-yung who was rewarded with the most beautiful girl in the royal harem – and he was for a time a virtual prisoner with but the vestiges of power. Military commanders in the provinces intrigued and fought endlessly to assert an independent status and expand their territories. In court circles, suicides and executions were frequent and a vicious conflict raged between officials and eunuchs, until a brutal massacre in 903 wiped out the eunuchs. The following year Chao-tsung himself was murdered. His ninth son, aged twelve, who succeeded him as Ai-ti lasted only until 907, when he was deposed. After nearly three centuries – which in the West saw the rise of the Vikings, the inception of the Holy Roman Empire, and the accession of the caliphs – Heaven finally withdrew its Mandate from the T'ang.

Just before it did so, however, a development occurred, baleful and ominous for East and West alike: the invention, in a Taoist temple, of gunpowder. The consequence of this product of alchemical research, a blend of charcoal, sulphur and saltpetre, at first used for its smoke-producing and incendiary properties, was not immediately manifest; but time would give it a place with the magnetic compass, paper and printing among China's extraordinary contributions to the drama of world history.

CHAPTER NINETEEN

Five Dynasties, Ten Kingdoms and the Sung – I

The man responsible for the massacre of the eunuchs in 903 and for the assassination in the following year of the penultimate T'ang Emperor, was one Chu Wen. Descended from scholars and teachers, he had embraced soldiery and become a ruthless, brutal and devious general, said to have had incestuous relations with all eight of his daughters-in-law. He started his career in a gang of the bandit-rebel Huang Ch'ao and then opportunely went over to the government, in whose cause he fought before creating his own independent power base. By 907, having had the last T'ang Emperor deposed, and controlling a large part of the north and east, he declared himself the founder of a new dynasty. This was the start of an epoch called the Five Dynasties and Ten Kingdoms, the former in the north, the latter in the south. And thus was the Empire partitioned for the third time.

The Five Dynasties followed each other in rapid succession. The first, the Later Liang, which was the name given by its founder, Chu Wen (who was murdered by his son), gave way to the Turkic Sha-t'o's Later T'ang, subsequently the Later Chin. But then the resurgent Kitans who, led by a Mongolian tribe, had built an empire extending from Manchuria and Mongolia, founded a dynasty called Liao which dominated most of the north from its base near modern Peking, while two successive dynasties, one the Sha-t'o's Later Han and the other a Chinese general's Later Chou, occupied northern areas south of it. Details of these dynasties, which with the exception of the Liao came and went within half a century, and of the areas north of the Yangtze to beyond the Great Wall that they controlled, fought over, ceded or gained, need not detain us. Suffice it to say that for this period the north was in the hands largely of non-Chinese, and although Chinese soldiers and gentry, and Chinese culture, played a significant role, the turbulence of the times caused widespread impoverishment. The situation was very different in the south.

There the statelets of the Ten Kingdoms were for the most part ruled by former military governors of diverse origins – one started as a carpenter, another as a village thief – now calling themselves kings. Their territories were remarkably prosperous, principally from trade and mining. Szechwan was particularly well-off with its tea-growing and salt-production. Its ruler, the ex-thief, was of commanding appearance: since enlisting as a soldier he had risen high under the patronage of the infamous eunuch T'ien Ling-tz'u. He used the T'ang model for his regime, attracting many of the T'ang official class as well as artists and poets to his state. There the printing of Taoist books had been common for some years and presently a knowledge of book-printing moved eastward: in 932 the cutting of the Confucian classics on wood blocks had been started, to be completed twenty years later with the one hundred and thirtieth volume; the work was widely diffused, and book-printing proceeded apace.

One spring night in the year 960, a scion of a Chinese military family living south of present Peking who had risen to command the forces of the last of the Five Dynasties, the Later Chou, slept at his encampment near the dynastic capital Kaifeng, on the Grand Canal, close to the Yellow River about one hundred and fifty miles east of Loyang. He was awoken at dawn by his soldiers. They put a yellow robe on him, symbol of regal status, and overbore his conventional protests to acclaim him Emperor. A speedy *coup d'état* put an end to the Later Chou, and he named himself T'ai tsu. He called the dynasty Sung.

It was to last 319 years and be in many ways the most attractive as well as the most brilliant of all China's dynasties.

Before a description of its governance and achievements is ventured upon, however, the course of its sovereign life requires a brief outline.

In its first phase, to 1126, it is known as the Northern Sung with its capital at Kaifeng. Having consolidated his position locally, T'ai-tsu addressed himself to the problem of reuniting China. He considered trying to repel the aliens in the north, but the Khitan dynasty of Liao was so powerful and dominant that he turned to the south. Over a period of twenty years, operations were directed at subjugating the Ten Kingdoms, one after another. There still remained large areas of the north (the Liao), the north-west where the Tunguts were establishing the powerful Hsia Kingdom, and the south-west in present Yunnan where Burmese – Tibetan power prevailed; but in the main China was again unified.

In sporadic warfare with the 'barbarians' who ringed it north and west, its army had no great success so it kept them at bay with massive payments. From 1004 onwards, for example, it annually gave the Liao Khitans 100,000 ounces of silver and 200,000 bales of silk which, representing about two per cent of its total revenue, was a deal cheaper, and more effective, than military action.

Around 1110, during the reign of an Emperor called Hui-tsung, who was famous as a painter and art-collector, events moved in a direction that at first seemed favourable to the Sung. Tunguts, originally from Manchuria, formed a tribal alliance called the Jurchen who rejected the Khitans, to whom they had been subject, and attacked Liao. This proved to be in fact much against the Sung's interest, for the Jurchen not only defeated the Khitans, capturing their capital at present-day Peking in 1125, but the following year swept down on Kaifeng. The art-loving Emperor had lately retired and he and his son who succeeded him were captured. The new Emperor was transported north and at first treated with respect, being allowed to keep some of his concubines and servants; but step by step he was deprived of everything, including his dignity, before he died in a miserable hut. The Northern Sung totally collapsed as the Jurchen founded a powerful dynasty called Chin ('gold').

In the disaster of 1126, however, a brother of the captive Emperor escaped to the south. There he founded the second phase of the Sung Dynasty, the Southern Sung, with its capital at Hangchow. Although all the north from just south of the Yellow River was now in alien hands – even if the Chinese population grew to perhaps forty million in the Chin sphere, which in its many sinicized bureaucratic and cultural respects became 'the other China' – the truncated empire was not inconsiderable. With a starting population of fifty million it was economically supreme and contained the most influential families. The transition from the Northern to the Southern Sung was therefore almost seamless.

While unrest on the northern and western frontiers was endemic, battles against the Jurchen's Chin Empire gave way to peace treaties that made the Southern Sung nominally a vassal, paying an annual tribute. But in 1204 a military-supporting group in the Sung government, led by one Han T'o-wei, gained ascendancy and caused a campaign to be unleashed against Chin. It failed disastrously. The Sung sued for peace, cutting off Han T'o-wei's head and sending it, preserved in lacquer and packed in a box, to the Jurchen who displayed it in the imperial family's ancestral temple. A new peace treaty replaced the old.

It was in this period that over the steppes of the far north and north-east, a cloud at first no bigger than a man's hand was growing into the monstrous proportions that would deluge all the lands between the Sea of Japan and Europe. When during the Five Dynasties period the Turkic Sha-t'o quit China, they went back into Mongolia and became part of a Turkic-Mongol alliance which steadily burgeoned into what it called 'the Greater Mongol Empire'. In 1185 Genghis Khan became its leader. He swept across Central Asia as far as the Black Sea. Then he turned back and launched an invasion of the Tanguts' Hsia Empire on China's north-west frontier, his troops finally capturing its capital in 1227 to end a long siege. He himself died at this very time after a riding accident, with the result that a large part of the capital's population was massacred in order, it was said, to provide Genghis with a suitable escort in the after-life.

He had already set in train attacks on the Jurchen's Chin Empire and, under his successor as Khaghan ('Emperor'), one of his sons, Ögödei, the Mongols invaded in earnest. This culminated in 1232 with their investment of the Jurchen capital, Kaifeng. The year-long siege, in which many Chinese were among the defenders, was notable for the use of gunpowder by both parties. Grenades hurled by catapults wrought great losses of both men and horses, and Chinese artisans also made rocket-like flame-throwers called 'fire lances', which were tubes made of many layers of paper pasted together and packed with charcoal, iron filings, powdered porcelain, sulphur and saltpetre, then fastened to lances; when ignited they ejected a flame ten feet long, and could be reloaded. After the city finally fell the Chin Empire survived for only six more months.

Following Ögödei's death, two regencies and a short reign by his son brought to the fore as Khaghan one of Genghis's grandsons, Möngke (1251). He prepared to conquer the Sung. Proceeding with great care, he entrusted the task to his brother, Kublai Khan. First the Sung's western borders were secured and a navy built up. In 1268 Mongolian armies – they had Chinese, Persians and Uighurs as well as Turks and Mongols in their ranks – descended on the Southern Sung in a three-pronged thrust. Their first big point of attack was a city on the Han River, a tributary of the Yangtze. The Sung had built a massive castle and strong fortifications there and they stoutly withstood the onslaught. Kublai threw in a hundred thousand men and five thousand boats, and for siege machinery enlisted the help of Muslim engineers from Persia. Intensive use of projectiles and huge stones hurled from catapults enabled the Mongols to batter the city into submission after five years' resistance. They then pressed on, fighting battle after battle as the Sung army retreated south-eastward. For six years it resisted bravely and tenaciously, but in vain: the Mongols remorselessly pushed on and on, even through steamy disease-ridden jungles, until they reached the south-eastern extremity of the country. And there, near Canton in mid-1279, the last Sung Emperor, a child called Ping, drowned. The waters closed over him and his dynasty alike.

It had been a dynasty of magnificent accomplishment, meriting a retrospective review before we return to the victorious Mongols. It made the Chinese of the eleventh to the thirteenth centuries, along with Islam, the most civilized in the world, and it moved China out of the Medieval Age to the Modern.

In many respects its tone was established by its founding Emperor, T'ai-tsu. He was kind to fallen rivals and in every war he forbade slaughter and needless killing; nor could capital punishment be carried out without his consent. He loved study and with anxious care chose his officials from literary men. He set an example by his frugality. The warmth of his personal relationships was typified by his devotion to his brother: in obedience to his mother's wish, while nominating a son as his heir apparent he decreed that first this brother should succeed him (once, when the brother had to be cauterized for some affliction T'ai-tsu insisted on himself being cauterized also, in order to share the pain).

The success of his dynasty owed much to the stability of the throne. The Northern Sung, for instance, had only seven emperors, with an average reign of over twenty years before the last wretched incumbent was snatched by the Jurchen. No great scandals rocked the court, although one emperor did go mad and his Empress ruled until their son, Jen-tsung (1022–63), became perhaps the ablest and most humane Emperor of them all.

Beneath the throne the administration had a similar stability: its upper echelons were not blighted by the plethora of suicides and executions consequent on the intense factional antagonism of the past, and only towards the end of the dynasty did the cohesion of the government break down. The importance of civilian power, indeed its paramountcy in the state, was established very early in T'ai-tsu's reign. Little over a year after his accession he invited his top military commanders to a banquet. 'When,' according to a historical description, 'they had drunk deeply and were in a cheerful mood', he addressed them:

'I do not sleep peacefully at night.' 'For what reason?' enquired ... the generals. 'It is not hard to understand,' replied the Emperor. 'Which of you does not covet my throne?' The generals made deep bows and all protested, 'Why does Your Majesty speak thus? The Mandate of Heaven is now established. Who still has treacherous aims?' The Emperor replied, 'I do not doubt your loyalty, but if one day one of you is roused at dawn and forced to don a yellow robe, even if unwilling, how should he avoid being obliged to overthrow the Sung (just as I against my will was obliged to overthrow the Chu)?' All of them protested that none of them was sufficiently talented for such a thing to be thought of, and asked for his counsel. The Emperor said, 'The life of man is short. Happiness is to have the wealth and means to enjoy life, and then to be able to leave the same prosperity to one's descendants. If you, my officers, will renounce your military authority, retire to the provinces, and choose there the best lands and most delightful dwelling-places, and to pass the rest of your lives in pleasure and peace until you die of old age, would this not be better than to live a life of peril and uncertainty? So that no shadow of suspicion shall remain between prince and ministers, we will ally our families with marriages, and thus, ruler and subject linked in friendship and amity, we will enjoy tranquillity.' ... The following day the army commanders all offered their resignation on the pretext of imaginary maladies, and withdrew to the country districts, where the Emperor gave them splendid gifts and appointed them to high official positions.

Thenceforward administrative control of the country was everywhere vested in civilians, not in conjunction with the army as hitherto, even though the military, with its own school system and examinations, could be recruited to the bureaucracy.

The latter's ethos accorded with the Confucian ideal of government by the virtuous and able. A Council of State, consisting of five to nine members under the chairmanship of the Emperor, defined general policy and the Court of Academicians drafted official documents for it. Decisions were taken only after thorough discussion, and the Emperor saw his role as but to ratify them or exercise a casting vote. Great lengths were gone to in order that people everywhere and of every degree should be able to express their opinions and suggestions with impunity and have them heard. Implementation of the Council's decisions was up to one or other of the three great departments of state – economy and finance; armies; secretariat (responsible for, *inter alia*, justice and personnel – recruitment, appointments, promotions).

Beneath the central government, the three-hundred-odd prefectures into which the country was divided each had its administration, accountable to Kaifeng and later Hangchow. The prefectures again were divided into districts, each with usually three officials and about a hundred clerks and jailers. And finally, below them were the unpaid headmen of villages, each helped by a 'household chief' selected for three years to collect taxes and supervise three so-called elders who were responsible for law, order, the upkeep of roads and the building of bridges: the choice of all these functionaries was largely determined by the leading local families.

Successfully to maintain this apparatus of government and promote tranquillity through social progress and economic wellbeing, from the outset it was recognized that a highly educated class of officialdom was essential. In the result the Sung developed the examination system to an unprecedented extent. The fate of individuals, families and often entire communities hung on examination results. Status, power and wealth were linked to government service which could be entered principally either by people nominated by high-ranking officials and passing a placement examination (such entrants were called 'protected') or, above all and with the greatest prestige, through success in the examinations for degrees, pre-eminently the *chin-shih* degree.

The whole process was surrounded by ceremony, and being, as it was, so vital to a man's career (women being excluded) and often even to his acceptability in marriage, a huge amount of emotion was generated. Thus in 1002 when 14,500 candidates had converged on the capital to sit the examinations and the vast majority failed their preliminary, the disappointed candidates turned their shock and dismay on the director of the examination: he was excoriated in songs, and blood was daubed on effigies of him, while placards were hung by the roadside to be lashed by passers-by. Two centuries later, candidates in a southern prefectural examination rioted and burst through the gates of the examination hall where, armed with bamboo and wooden sticks, they badly beat the examination officials. Emotion ran high even when candidates tried to enter the examination hall and find a place, for the crush was sometimes so great that people were trampled to death.

The development of learning was greatly accelerated – indeed, rendered possible – by the development of printing. A lively book trade made books less expensive and far more available as printers multiplied: at one point the Southern Sung boasted 173 of them. Libraries proliferated – the biggest of them, established in the imperial palace as early as 978, had eighty thousand volumes, some in huge revolving bookcases. While Europe's discovery of printing four centuries later led through the vernacular Bible to the Reformation, in China it led through the Classics to the examinations. For these, the curriculum consisted of the six Classics – of Confucius, of history, of poetry, of rites, of the *Book of Changes* and the *Spring and Autumn Annals*. Final examination candidates had to write an abstract on political and philosophical principles and answer questions on complicated technical problems of government. They had to compose poems and poetic descriptions using precise, elaborate rules; and, besides questions on their chosen specialized classic, they had to answer questions on Confucius and Mencius. All needed an exact knowledge of the texts.

Education began early, at home or in small family and community schools. Elementary primers introduced a child to the written language's most commonly used characters, and gave a taste of moral and political philosophy, while exemplary stories attuned him to such decencies as correct deportment within the family. From eight to fifteen he might continue his education at home or attend either a privately run school or, more likely, one of the government schools in an empire-wide school system which by about 1100 had a combined enrolment of 200,000 students, including 3,800 at the august Imperial University. Entrance was competitive and progress determined by monthly and annual tests. The schoolboy had a hard road to travel: in his study of the Classics he had to learn texts totalling 431,386 characters by heart.

The conclusion of his formal schooling did not end his studying. To attain the highest, most desired degree, the *chin-shih*, he had to pass the Palace Examination, to sit which he had first to pass what was called the departmental examination, also held in the metropolis. But even before that he had to gain the essential preliminary of a *chü-jen* degree. While early in the Sung Dynasty a few tens of thousands at a time took this basic preliminary examination, which was held in the capital and all the prefectures, the number eventually rose to several hundred thousand. It was set every three years in the autumn and winter, and a candidate had to have a proven respectable lineage free of crime (notably any of the first four of the Ten Abominations) and himself a character vouched to be impeccable, untainted by crime or unfilial behaviour. He could not be an artisan, a merchant or a clerk, or ever have been a Buddhist or Taoist priest.

Waiting to write the preliminary examination, our student might attend one of the academies established, with the aid of benefactors, around distinguished scholars, or he might get a job teaching or tutoring in a wealthy household, working for a merchant, or helping with a family estate. If in due course he wrote his preliminary examination and attained his *chü-jen* degree he would be fêted by the local officials and then, often with government or community help, travel to the capital and after the welcoming ceremonies spend two or three nights in the examination compound. Presently, armed with an inkstone, brushes, ink, a water pitcher, an earthenware chamber pot, food, bedding and a curtain, he joined the thousands jostling to enter the examination cells. To answer the questions presented to him he had strictly to write only in black, first recording information such as his name and age. This, however, was covered up when he gave in his paper so that his calligraphy could not be recognized, and indeed only a clerk's copy of his answers was seen by the examiners.

These attempts to ensure impartiality in the marking did not always prevent collusion between examiner and candidate, who had presumably to devise a code to identify himself. There was also sometimes fraud, through the employment of someone to impersonate a candidate, or indeed through a candidate's copying of a vital text on his underclothes. And there was a flourishing trade then, as universally now, in sets of model answers for candidates to mug up before they sat.

Success in the examination at the capital cleared the way to the ultimate test, the Palace Examination, instituted by the study-loving founder of the dynasty. If our student failed it he might try again, and again, and again, each time having to go through the preliminary hoops anew. It is no wonder then that the average age of candidates attempting that supreme *chin-shih* degree was thirty-five. Men could spend their lives endeavouring, the while describing their occupation as *chin-shih*. Many gave up in despair and sank into drunken ruin or, freed from the straitjacket of the Confucian curriculum, became successful merchants, monks, or teachers. An elderly much-failed candidate might, however, take a special easier Palace Examination and gain a 'facilitated' degree.

There were in fact a number of special examinations – in law, for example, or for clerks with twenty years' service – which were sometimes available and sometimes not, but no trophy remotely matched the *chin-shih* in importance. The rise in status of the clutch of people who graduated – ranging from a handful to a few hundred at a time – was enormous. Besides their entrée into the civil service with an almost certain path to its highest grades (there were nine in all), they enjoyed innumerable rights and privileges. Their outward trappings included the wearing of distinctive insignia and occupation of houses distinguished from their less favoured neighbours by the type of roof tiles, the decoration of doors and gates, even the greater size of the reception room, and the display of a pennant to proclaim their *chin-shih*. The work they and their civil service colleagues undertook required their attendance for nine days out of ten, except for their annual holiday of over a month. They enjoyed numerous privileges, such as exemption from military service and taxes. They retired at seventy, on a pension increased under the Sung to more than half their pay (but their widows got no benefit).

CHAPTER TWENTY

The Sung – II (960–1279)

The Sung made striking progress in welfare reform. A bureau of housing and care was created in 1098 to provide houses for the old and destitute; so was one in 1102 to employ doctors to tend poor patients at home and in state hospitals, which were themselves extensively reorganized in 1143; from 1167 peasants could get low-interest state loans; state orphanages were established in 1247, and so were free pharmacies for the poor the following year. The system of state granaries hoarding grain in times of plenty to sell it cheap in bad times was fully maintained, though in some areas an enlightened exploitation of market forces resulted in prices at the granaries being increased instead of lowered at times of shortage, motivating merchants to import more grain, whereupon the granary prices were promptly lowered. Fire protection services were set up in the large cities, and starting in 1141 the government sought to quench fires of a different sort by opening twenty-three geisha houses in the capital for soldiers far from home. The public baths that had long existed were augmented by the provision of similar facilities in Buddhist temples. The state-wide establishment of schools and libraries has already been remarked upon, an enduring tribute to an enlightened administration.

Its work under the Council of State was spearheaded by a succession of able leading ministers. The most famous was one Wang An-shih who rose to prominence about a century after the founding Emperor. While the corridors of power were mainly bestridden by officials who were scholars, and gentry representing the great merchant and landlord families, Wang came from a modest family and championed the small landholders and dealers. Ranked by posterity as one of China's greatest reformers, he nevertheless cut an unprepossessing figure to his contemporaries, wearing, as he did, dirty clothes and never washing his face, besides being utterly convinced of his own rightness. But he used his position as the Emperor's confidential adviser with mandatory powers to introduce radical measures which he claimed to be based on a correct interpretation of the Classics – without whose authority (or that of historical precedent) no reform could, of course, be acceptable. The new decrees included a change in the system of handling local tax produce whereby, instead of being sent to the capital where it was often sold at below value, it would be redeemed on the spot for cash which would be forwarded instead; peasants would be given credit on the security of their standing crops; a substantial cut in the army would be balanced by the formation of a national militia for which every family had to provide one of its sons if it had more than two; and money payment could be substituted for forced labour. Wang also strengthened central control of the provinces and he intervened in the examination system, insisting on less style and more practical knowledge.

His reforms endured in the spirit rather than the letter but contributed to that change in tone marking China's transition from the medieval period. His reduction in the armed forces was particularly timely. The founding Emperor had demobilized the army of enforced conscription and replaced it with mercenaries. Their cost, however, mushroomed as their numbers increased through men grown too old for service remaining in the army; and ever-greater costly demands were made, like extra money for postings at a distance from home and the employment of porters to carry the baggage.

This was one of the causes of taxes falling short of expenditure. Recourse was therefore had to the coining of fresh money, made possible by a great increase in copper and iron production consequent on the use of coal instead of charcoal. Silver coins as well as iron and copper were in circulation, and variations in rates between them gave rise to much speculation which was fuelled by the state's issue of deposit certificates, opening the way to the use of paper money, first printed in 1024. Commerce also brought in negotiable instruments in the form of cheques, promissory notes, and bills of exchange.

China's economy had become a monetary one and the circulation of so much money resulted in inflation. This incidentally added to its tax revenue which, having been altered from dues on people to taxes on land-yield, moved its main source to commerce, with taxes on shops, products and trade. Besides these the state derived income from money payments in lieu of the corvée; profits from workshops and commercial enterprises it created for civil servants to run; its receipts from its salt, tea, alcohol and perfume monopolies; and the customs duties it imposed at ports and frontiers.

Merchants, however, were the greatest beneficiaries of inflation, despite the taxes on the commodities they dealt in. They invested their profits in land, accumulating the biggest estates China has ever known. Some of these had their own mills and textile factories and developed into villages. Some were owned by a whole clan which, operating under rules of mutual support and even maintaining schools, were regarded as welfare institutions and hence immune from tax. Agriculture itself added to the burgeoning prosperity of the time, as new tools and techniques of planting out seedlings and of seed selection gave an impetus to the expanding cultivation of rice in the Yangtze basin and south China: indeed, the obtaining of high yields from the paddy fields was crucial to the life and development of the whole of the Far East. For the Sung it meant abundant food as well as favouring inter-regional trade and the commercialization of agricultural produce.

China of the Sung, little disturbed by war, and only twice troubled by local rebellions of no lasting effect, moved under its stable and commerce-promoting administration from an agrarian to a mercantile state. Mining, for example, prospered as never before, based on technological improvements such as the substitution of pit coal for charcoal, as mentioned above, and the use both of hydraulic machinery for working the bellows and of explosives. Thus the production of iron, copper, lead and tin increased rapidly and many new mines were opened. Ceramics were produced in unprecedented profusion, not least porcelain which in its pure white variety and later in blue-and-white reached perfection. Almost all the regions were famous for some product – rice maybe, or paper, or cane sugar, or books, or whatever – and traders took full advantage of the country's, especially the Yangtze's, vast network of waterways and canals. It traversed ten thousand miles and bore a huge variety of ships which at some points on the Yangtze were so dense that they formed a floating village.

On the one hand, the growth of the great estates, augmenting the class of tenant farmers and labourers from the ranks of small independent farmers, who were many of them hard put to it to survive even when diversifying into fruit-culture or fish-breeding, and on the other hand the advanced techniques in agriculture released many people from the land. But the boom in commerce and industry created boundless new means of livelihood, especially in the cities, which attracted masses of shop assistants, employees of inns, taverns and teahouses, door-to-door salesmen and public entertainers, not to mention pickpockets, crooks, vagabonds and prostitutes of both sexes. In their private mansions the rich families and big merchants, especially in the capitals, employed armies of domestic servants.

The whole economic axis of the Empire was no longer along the Yellow River but from Kaifeng to the south-east along the Grand Canal and the lower Yangtze. Although big fairs and periodic markets became a feature of the countryside, the heart of the Sung's intensive commercial activity lay in the large towns, and especially the cities, along that axis. As in contemporary Europe, the growth of great cities was a feature of the age. Whereas such places had been primarily for the aristocrats and administrators who kept mercantile activity under tight control, they now, as the greatest consumers, became predominantly centres of money-making and amusement. The system of walled wards was abandoned so that shops, workshops, restaurants, teahouses and splendid theatres were set up everywhere (there are said to have been fifty theatres in Kaifeng). The withdrawal of the curfew meant that people could move freely about all through the night, and places of entertainment could remain open until dawn. The names of streets instead of districts enabled one to find one's way about, and indeed the street provided the throb and nexus of urban life.

Around as well as in these great cities hummed a whole complex of activity. On their outskirts an industrial quarter produced mainly silk; beyond were usually landlord-owned successive circles of, first, as a rule, mulberry trees for silk with vegetables grown beneath them, then staple crops like rice and wheat, and finally subsistence farmers. The traffic to and from them was unremitting, for society became greatly more mobile. Carriage was cheap and carts for hire were everywhere available; and commercial currents carried boatmen, carters, sailors and merchants along with them. By such means the urban attractions and opportunities brought an immense influx of impoverished peasants and people simply bent on advancement by whatever means. For the individual the daunting urban environment threatened isolation and a lack of mutual help, and so promoted the growth of associations of people from the same region, and merchants and craftsmen formed numerous 'guilds'.

One other aspect of the Sung's immense commercial ties requires noting. A huge volume of international merchandise passed through the ports on the country's south-eastern seaboard. At the most important of them, the government appointed maritime trade superintendents who employed interpreters and encouraged Asian and Middle Eastern merchants to trade with China; while Chinese merchants, now much raised in social importance, sailed far and wide – to the

Red Sea, to India and the whole of southern Asia, to Korea and Japan. The vessels they sailed in included treadmill-driven paddle-wheel ships and great high-seas junks, probably first built in the estuary of the Yangtze. These were four- or six-masted, with twelve big canvas or rigid matting sails and four decks, capable of carrying a thousand men. The invention of the stern-post rudder, seven hundred years before its appearance in Europe, was followed by watertight compartments, pivoting sails, capstans and other high-tech innovations, and of course mariners had the use of the compass. All these developments made China the world's greatest maritime power until well into the fifteenth century.

The material prosperity of the age owed much to a leap forward in the sciences, both pure and applied. As to the latter, besides the naval developments mentioned, and those in agriculture, mining and the use of explosive projectile weapons, others that may be noted include new surveying instruments, a device for measuring the distance travelled, the introduction of the caisson to bridge-building, and the devising of lock-gates and water-powered clocks. Codification of old systems of pharmaceutics and acupuncture aided the many famous physicians of the age; their knowledge of human organs was enlarged by autopsies; they had a code of ethics; they introduced variolation, precursor of vaccination; and twelve of them compiled the massive *Imperial Medical Encyclopaedia* (1111). Books of pharmaceutical botany reached unprecedented standards, while innumerable botanical and zoological mono-graphs explored a whole range of subjects – from citrus horticulture (the first in any language), bamboos, lychees, aromatic plants and flowering trees to crustaceans, birds and fishes.

A new class of scientific literature, that of miscellaneous notes and records, embodied numerous observations. They provided the discourse when scholars frequently met for discussion. The most famous is *Dream Pool Essays*, by Shen Kua, a contemporary of the great reformer Wang An-shih. In the course of his career as a scholar in the civil service he travelled much in the posts of ambassador, military commander, director of hydraulic works and Chancellor of the Hanlin Academy, all the time noting down everything he saw of scientific, humanistic or technical interest. In a short book he described how to make an inspection carriage comfortable, how to ensure that from the lacquered interior one could get a good view of everything passed, and what to take in one's travelling cases – a raincoat, medicine chest, 'mud boots', spare clothes and combs, tea and preserved food; a box of paper, ink, scissors, a rhyming dictionary and a lute; another for candles, knives, chessmen and a folding chessboard; and a container for any books bought en route, plus insecticide powder to keep worms away from them. Thus equipped he made the observations incorporated in the twenty-six chapters and four appendices of his *Dream Pool*. They concerned the magnetic compass, astronomy and meteorology, mathematics, fossils, metallurgical processes, the making of relief maps, physics, geology, anthropology, archaeology, philosophy, chemistry, a good deal of biology and much else.

His interest in mathematics reflected the work done by some of the greatest mathematicians of all time, especially algebraists, who made China pre-eminent in the world in this branch of mathematics. His encyclopaedic method found expression also in works by other hands, such as a chronological encyclopaedia in one thousand chapters of systematic quotations from ancient and medieval authors under subject-headings of every kind, and encyclopaedias of geography and of linguistics.

Alongside such monuments to scholarship were works on philosophy, expounding the Neo-Confucianism which constituted the core beliefs of the dynasty. Of the many great philosophers who avowed it, one of the most famous and for centuries the dominating figure in Chinese thought was Chu Hsi (1130–1200), known as Master Chu. His school of thought had a diversity of strands, one of the most interesting of which conveyed a concept called by that all-embracing word *li*.

It was understood as the mystical totality of the universe and the source of, as well as being immanent in, every thing therein. It is timeless, eternal and pure, and in its flawless ideal was called the Supreme Ultimate, which was perhaps the closest the Chinese came to the Western idea of God. Through a synthesizing principle or force called *ch'i*, *li* becomes incarnate – that is, the abstract becomes tangible in the form of all creatures, objects and relationships. Heaven and earth, man and his mind, a ship, a table, a blade of grass, the relationship of son to father and subject to sovereign, all have *li* in them, with *ch'i* determining the nature of each. When *ch'i* is defective the result may be evil. A man who succeeds in comprehending and realizing the *li* within him achieves Enlightenment. He does this by constantly striving to extend his knowledge and to practise the other Confucian virtues such as sincerity, propriety, good citizenship, and love of his fellow men. He strives, in short, to become a Sage. In doing so he is very much in and of this world, unlike the Buddhist or Taoist whose beliefs otherwise constituted elements of Neo-Confucianism but who respectively strove for non-being and ever-being. Not that the Neo-Confucianist was interested only in the world, for his concerns also embraced the problem of cosmic evolution and universal harmony, and the part of *Yin* and *Yang* in solving that problem.

Philosophizing was but one pursuit of the literati, who in no age have been more abounding – in officialdom and every educated class. Among the characteristics shared by many of them was a passion for collecting books and antiquities. They are exemplified by the twelfth century Chao Te-fu whose *Records on Metal and Stone* was a massive account of old inscriptions. His wife, Li Ch'ing-chao, wrote a vivid remembrance of his obsessive collecting. In part, and condensed, it reads as follows:

When I married, my husband was twenty-one and a student at the Imperial Academy. Our families were not well-to-do and we were always frugal. On the first and

fifteenth day of each month my husband would get a
short vacation from the Academy. He would pawn some
clothes and use the cash at the market to buy fruit and
rubbings of inscriptions. When he brought these home, we
would sit on our mats facing each other, rolling them out
before us, examining and munching. And we thought
ourselves persons of the mythical ancient Age of Perfect
Contentment. When some years later he took up a post, we
lived on rice and vegetables and dressed in common cloth;
but he would search out the most remote spots to fulfil his
interest in the world's most ancient writings and unusual
script. When various friends and relations held positions in
the Imperial Libraries where there were many ancient
poems omitted from the *Book of Odes*, unofficial histories,
and writings once hidden in walls [as, for example, at the
time of the Burning of the Books] and recovered from
tombs, my husband worked hard at copying such things.
Later, if he saw a work of painting or calligraphy or
unusual vessels of high antiquity, he would still pawn our
clothes to buy them. Subsequently, my husband governed
two prefectures in succession and used up all his salary on
scholarly work. Whenever he got a book, we would collate it
with other editions and make corrections together, repair
it, make title slips of rue leaves to keep out insects, and
with blue silk ribbons bind loose chapters into a volume,
labelled with a colophon. When he got hold of a piece of
calligraphy, a painting, a goblet, or a tripod, we would go
over it at our leisure, pointing out faults and flaws, setting
for our nightly limit the time it took for one candle to burn
down. I happen to have an excellent memory, and every
evening after we finished eating we would sit in our hall
we called 'Return Home' and make tea. Pointing to the
heaps of books and histories, we would guess on which
line of which page in which chapter a certain passage
could be found. Success in guessing determined who got
to drink his or her tea first. When the book collection was

complete we set up a library in our 'Return Home' hall, with huge bookcases where the books were catalogued in order. Nevertheless books lay ranged on tables and desks, scattered on top of one another on pillows and bedding. This is what took his fancy and occupied his mind, and his joy was greater than the pleasure others had in dancing girls, dogs, or horses.

Other literati were more creative and more diverse in their activities, which might include painting, poetry and prose, calligraphy, and music-making. Prose in particular flourished, lucid and complex and often employing the vernacular – as in memorials to the Emperor, letters, both informal and in diplomatic service, descriptions of places and visits, prefaces, miscellanies, funeral laments and addresses. Often the prose was mixed in with poetry and a writer who did this, considered the greatest of the age, was Su Shih, who wrote under the pen-name Su Tung-p'o, a contemporary and opponent of the reformer Wang An-shi. Poetry itself was produced in prodigious quantity – one famous poet, Lu Yu, had approximately ten thousand poems to his credit – and women as well as men wrote. Although their work did not reach the heights of T'ang poetry, one form of it represented a significant development. This was the song lyric, propelled by new melodies and performance traditions.

Such songs were often sung by women who were hired for parties and who sang at public entertainment establishments where, their services often being sexual as well as artistic, they might hope to find favour with a man of means who could buy them out for concubinage. In the song and dance quarters of the great cities there was also a rich offering of performance literature. Besides musical narratives combining verse with prose, professional storytellers treated their audiences to popularized and bowdlerized history, chivalric romances, love stories, stories of heroic bandits, and crime stories with a Confucian magistrate as detective. Their popularity prompted commercial printers to have these tales written down, and so began a tradition of written vernacular literature which culminated in novels.

The storyteller also told ballads and performed shadow plays and marionette plays. He did so in the open, behind screens; but the upper classes could watch real plays in the theatres. There too they could enjoy dancing, one style of which consisted of steps following the delicate patterns on the carpets being performed on.

While Sung sculptors, especially in wood and plaster, had what has been described as 'a suave and restless splendour' having much in common with European Baroque, the heights of artistic accomplishment were scaled by the dynasty's painters. Of their many schools, that of vivid figure-painting may be mentioned, if only because its chief exemplar, Li Kung-lin, was in his early life famous for his depictions of horses until a Taoist told him that if he continued he would become like a horse himself, whereupon he changed tack. More importantly, landscape painters covered large walls and screens with brilliant and monumental compositions.

In one respect the painters came close to the modern Surrealist, for instead of confining themselves to a view from a single position they asked themselves why if they could depict what they knew of the view they should restrict themselves only to what they could see of it from that one position. But unlike Europeans they did not think of their picture as defined by a composition within a frame. They thought of their experience as a moment of exaltation before the beauty of nature, a fragment of eternity. Hence the shape of a thing interested them less than its essential inwardness – painting a bird on a branch, they saw it as poised in limitless space, symbolizing the 'bird-on-bough' aspect of eternity. They avoided a complete statement, leaving areas of space because we cannot know everything, and they were but opening a door to the boundless universe. The most important of the patrons of painters – many of whom, if they were not leading civil servants, made their living from rich clients – was the court. The last emperor of the Northern Sung, Hui-tsung, was himself a gifted artist. He liked to set his painters themes: once, set the theme, 'A Tavern in a Bamboo Grove by a Bridge', the winner simply suggested the tavern by a sign-board set among bamboos. Hui-tsung was rigid in his standards and the penalty for independence was dismissal from the court. His insistence on a rigidly decorative, painstaking style governed palace painting for centuries.

However, while he gave a considerable impetus to the high art of flower-painting, the subjects chosen by painters were legion – portraits, buildings with their newly developed sweeping roof lines and curved eaves, fishes, domestic and wild animals (a whole school specialized in water-buffalo), vegetables and fruit. Dragons as dramatic cosmic manifestations were also much favoured: of the greatest practitioner of this genre, a high-ranking official, it was said that when he got drunk he gave a great shout, seized his cap, plunged it into ink and smeared on the design with it before finishing it with a brush – making him, it may be thought, kindred to many a twenty-first century exhibitor. But the greatest glory of the art produced by and for the most cultivated social and intellectual elite in Chinese history was achieved by the landscape painters, just as in the crafts the mastery of porcelain reached perfection.

This, then, was the society upon which the Mongols descended like wolves on the fold and wholly conquered by the year 1279.

CHAPTER TWENTY-ONE

The Mongols' Yüan Dynasty (1271 – 1368)

*I*t is said of Genghis Khan that once, when he was besieging an obstinate Hsia city, he promised to spare it if its commander handed over a thousand cats and ten thousand swallows. The commander duly had the cats caught and the swallows netted in those numbers; upon their being handed over, Genghis ordered his men to tie tufts of cotton wool to each of them, set the tufts alight, and turn the captives loose to return to their lairs and nests, and so quickly engulfed the city in flames.

Whether true or fanciful the episode exemplifies the ruthlessness that characterized the Mongols' devouring of Asia. Their empire was divided into Khanates, of which the Golden Horde consumed Persia and much of Russia before reaching its limit in Poland and Hungary. China, though the richest and most important constituent under its Great Khan, Kublai, thus became but part of an immense conglomerate, stretching north into Siberia and west to the Danube. The Tartars, as the fierce riders on their tough hairy ponies were called, created a legend of brutality and horror.* But also there arose a different legend, arising from the Tartars' conquest of Muslim peoples – 'Saracens' – as they swept west, that the Tartar leader might be Prester John, the mythical priest-king destined to succour

---

* The Russian revolutionary, Lenin, was part Mongol.

Christendom. For with the collapse of the Crusades the hope for such a saviour burnt bright.

Until this time, throughout the several thousand years of its history China was as familiar to the West as the other side of the moon, except that the moon was an established fact. The ancient Greeks and Romans had some intimation of a vague area to the east occupied by people called Seres because of the silk brought from them by middlemen. The Arabs, first through trade and then through the expansion of Islam, acquired some awareness of it, but only with the advent of the Mongols did Europe gain any real notion of a great and civilized country lying in the extreme east of the Asian continent.

The first bearer of such tidings was an elderly corpulent Franciscan friar called John of Plano Carpini. In April 1245 he set out from Lyon with a message to the Great Khan from Pope Clement IV. After fifteen months of gruelling travel he arrived at the Mongol capital, Karakorum, in the mountainous area north of the Gobi. The Khan returned a brief and haughty reply to the friar's address, but in the following decades there were other visitors to China, or Cathay as they called it. Notable among them were two Italian merchants, the brothers Polo. When they presented themselves to Kublai in about 1268, he received them warmly and questioned them closely on Christianity. It was a religion of which he knew something, because the Nestorians, who held an heretical belief in Christ being both a divine and a human person loosely united in one body, had long been establishing churches throughout Asia. He himself followed the traditional beliefs and practices of his shamans, but, like every Mongolian ruler, tolerated all religions, and he had a keenly curious mind. The Polos' replies stimulated him: not least with a view to attracting learned men to his administration he asked them to request of the Pope one hundred missionaries to teach their faith.

The request came to nothing; but in 1275, on the eve of Kublai's final conquest of the Sung the brothers were back at his court, this time with the son of one of them, twenty-one-year-old

Marco. He so endeared himself to the potentate that for the next twenty years he served him, he claimed, in various offices and travelled all over China as the Great Khan's eyes and ears. Upon his return home, within a year or two of his arrival in his native Venice, he joined the navy, and in a battle with the city's great trading rival, Genoa, he was captured. He shared his cell with one Rusticiano, victim of a war between his own Pisa and the Genoese. This man had some literary pretensions and upon hearing Marco recount his fabulous tales about Kublai's China he persuaded him to dictate them to him. Rusticiano wrote in coarse French which was soon translated into Italian, and the repeatedly copied manuscript was widely circulated, causing a sensation. It has been claimed to have promoted the Age of Discovery. However, fantastical passages, a lack of reference to such obvious subjects as the Great Wall, and Marco's ignorance of the Chinese language have created some doubts as to whether he ever was in China, and at all events his *Travels* were greeted in the main with incredulity. It would require nearly four centuries more before Europe became authoritatively informed about China.

Much of what he wrote does, however, resonate with knowledge of the Mongol regime. From him one may learn what the Great Khan Kublai looked like – well-built, of middle height and dark eyed. He had four wives, each with her own court and ten thousand people attached to it; they gave him seven sons. He also had carefully selected concubines, of whom six served him night and day for three days before giving way to another six who worked a similar shift, and so on; they gave him a further twenty-five sons.

Moving from the traditional Mongol capital of Karakorum, Kublai based himself for much of the year in a new capital near Kaifeng. In this city, which became known as Ta-tu and for centuries would be called Peking (Beijing), Kublai built a palace whose hall, says Marco, could dine six thousand people and 'it is quite a marvel to see how many rooms there are besides. The building is altogether so vast, so rich, and so beautiful that no man on earth could design anything superior to it.' Its walls were covered in gold and silver embossed with dragons and other subjects, likewise the ceilings, while 'the outside of the roof is all coloured with vermilion and yellow and green and blue and other hues, which are fixed with varnish so fine and exquisite that they shine like crystal.'

Other buildings were of a matching opulence, for Kublai wanted his capital to befit one who ruled not only China but the surrounding territories of Mongolia, Manchuria, Korea, Tibet and a great swathe of the north-west. It was, however, China that he wished to be identified with. He perpetuated its dynastic tradition by having himself declared Son of Heaven and dubbing his dynasty Yüan, his own temple title becoming the Emperor Shih-tsu. And, although, when in 1266 he ordered the construction of Ta-tu, he appointed a Muslim, Yeh-hei-tieh-erh, as architect, the design was essentially that of a typical Chinese capital – rectangular, with broad avenues extending geometrically from eleven gates set in the great, rammed earth outer walls. It differed substantially from his summer capital of Shang-tu, two hundred miles north in the steppes of Inner Mongolia – the Xanadu of Samuel Taylor Coleridge – where shamanistic and other Mongolian pursuits were maintained. Even in Ta-tu, however, the Mongolian hunting lifestyle was not entirely neglected, for Kublai's bedrooms were hung with curtains and screens of ermine skins; and in the parks, covered in grass from the Mongolian steppes, Mongolian-style tents were erected where Kublai's sons often lived, in preference to the palaces, and whither wives were moved in the last stage of pregnancy to give birth.

His most beloved wife was Chabi who, aspiring to be Empress of a powerful state and not simply wife of a tribal chieftain, strongly supported his efforts to govern China efficiently. He divided the country into provinces administered by prime ministers and subdivided into a hundred and eighty circuits. He and his successors headed their administrations with a Chancellor of the Right and a Chancellor of the Left. They were supported by numerous imperial agencies: one such was the Bureau of Imperial Etiquette whose duties included provisioning the imperial kitchens; another, subordinate to the imperial guards, was the Court of Imperial Attendants, under whose aegis the Agency of Men and Things Gone Astray had to find the owners of misplaced goods, animals and people (usually slaves, of whom the Mongols had a good many, mainly prisoners-of-war). To manage the education system an adjunct to the Hanlin Academy was set up: called the Academy of Scholarly Worthies it was later detached to supervise Taoist affairs, balancing the Bureau of Tibetan and Buddhist affairs.

Of more direct practical importance, a vast programme of roads' improvement was undertaken, and the postal relay system was extended far beyond its Han origins: 1,400 stations were established fifteen to forty miles apart, with 50,000 horses, 1,400 oxen, 6,200 mules, 4,000 carts, 6,000 boats and 200 dogs; and in an emergency rider messengers could carry news 250 miles in a day. And when the capital's population swelled, as visitors thronged the seat of government, the problem of feeding it was resolved by an extension to the Grand Canal so that abundant supplies could be brought from the south.

Despite Kublai's native harshness that could manifest itself in, for example, the flogging in his presence of errant officials, the penal laws he introduced halved the number of capital offences under Chinese law and were generally less severe. However, if the Mongol hand on the Chinese throat was but lightly pressed, the bitter fact of conquest could not be escaped. All households had to be registered and every artisan occupation made hereditary. This was part of a system of racial classification which relegated the Chinese to third position, after the Mongols – of whom about a million settled in the country – and foreigners, mainly Muslims. While the first two categories enjoyed numerous privileges, the Chinese were subject to many disabilities, such as having no right to bear arms, and Mongol was the official language. Although many of the Chinese governmental structures were adopted, the Chinese themselves played little part in a bureaucracy that became ever larger. All leading posts were given to non-Chinese who also acted as managers, tax-collectors, and intermediaries with the people. To put beyond doubt the denial of access to the civil service by most elite Chinese, the examination system was scrapped.

The large southern landowners were left little disturbed, as were the merchants, who went about their business with success, even if they resented the favouring of foreign merchants, called the ortogh and mainly Muslim, who had profitable partnerships with the imperial family and top officials, using imperial funds supplied under the supervising Money Bureau for moneylending and financing maritime trade and commerce across western Asia.

Of the comparatively small contributions to science made during the Yüan dynasty, the foremost was by geographers, of whom the most celebrated, Chu Ssu-pen, produced a famous great atlas. The arts were patronized but it was to craftsmen that the Mongols directed their main interest – a large contingent of them always accompanied the Mongols on their conquests. The Chinese literati and artists, even if some gained minor government appointments, tended to keep the Mongols at arm's length. They established private academies and largely withdrew into their own world. One of their number, a distinguished painter, asked why he had depicted a tree with no soil around its roots, replied, 'Because the Mongols have stolen the earth.' In truth, apart from their third-class status, they did not care for their masters – their cuisine, their table manners, their informality at court; and if some professed to see them as 'noble savages' in their simplicity, honesty and generosity, they never saw them as less than uncivilized.

In one respect the arts, or at least the entertainment industry, did flourish. What were called variety plays packed the theatres. These were plays interspersed with dances and songs selected from standard melodies – not quite opera nor quite drama. An odd by-product of the scrapping of the examination system was that many scholars being out of work turned to authorship.

Between them and the professional playwrights over six hundred plays were written and performed. The most renowned writer was a physician, Kuan Han-ch'ing (end of the thirteenth century), whose *Rescuing One of the Girls* was typical of his fifty-eight dramas. Concerning lost innocence in a corrupt world, its anti-hero is a courtesan who rescues her friend and fellow courtesan from a disastrous marriage. She does this by persuading her friend's villainous husband to sign divorce papers on the promise of herself marrying him, though she coyly confides in song to the audience that if she did marry him

> I'd pretend to act like an honest woman,
> to work at submission and be a good wife;
> but I can't help being what I am,
> just a no-good dance-hall girl
> fickle in heart and always
> meaning other than what I say.
> And how would the last act end?

So she reneges on her promise to marry, driving the duped and outraged husband to take the matter to court, but to the vast satisfaction of the audience he ends up being himself sentenced to sixty lashes and reduction to commoner status.

The Chinese who suffered most under the Mongols were the peasants, often tied to labour for the temples, frequently dispossessed as the Mongols conferred large estates on themselves, pressed to work on public projects and forcibly recruited to aid Kublai's military adventures. Those had been universally successful, except for his attempt to compel the Japanese Shogun to accept tributary status.

It happened in 1274, while his onslaught on the Southern Sung was in full swing. Following his conquest of Korea he launched a force of about 23,000 Mongolian, Chinese and Korean troops, guided by 7,000 Korean sailors, across the sea to Japan. They captured two islands and then landed on the coast of Kyushu where, while they were successfully engaged in battle with the Japanese, a fearsome gale struck; the troops took to the ships to ride out the storm, but the winds, waves and rocks shattered several hundred ships with the loss of 13,000 lives, effectively putting an end to the expedition. When Kublai sent an embassy the following year, the cock-a-hoop Japanese executed its members.

Seven years later he tried again. 100,000 troops with 15,000 Korean sailors in 900 vessels set forth on a two-pronged attack. But once more the elements prevailed: Kublai's army had been fighting in Kyushu for two months when a typhoon destroyed more than half of it. For the Japanese it was a 'divine wind' sent by the gods who would protect their country for ever – at any rate, as it turned out, for seven hundred years until a lethal wind of a different kind affrighted Hiroshima. For the Mongols the failure of this second assault severely dented their reputation of invincibility, and its enormous cost created an acute revenue problem for the Emperor.

In a succession of what the Chinese regarded as out and out crooks appointed by Kublai to superintend finances, the latest, a Tibetan called Sangha, raised their particular ire. They accused him of corruption, theft and disgusting carnality, but more to the purpose he gave active support to foreigners in preference to Chinese and reformed the currency whereby the Chinese had to exchange their old currency for the new at considerable loss. Moreover, the man under him who was put in charge of Buddhist affairs, a monk by the name of Yang, paid for the restoration and building of Buddhist temples in 1285 by looting the Sung's imperial tombs – 101 of them, from which he extracted 6,800 ounces of silver plus plentiful jade and pearls. Not unbiased Chinese historians accuse him of desecrating royal corpses in the process, even hanging the body of one of the last Sung emperors from a tree before burning it and burying the bones with those of horses and cows.

While the Mongol tolerance of religions was typified early in Kublai's reign when he presided over debates between Buddhists and Taoists, he gradually tended to favour the former. This was especially so after a Taoist temple was burnt down, allegedly by a Buddhist monk, but a court enquiry found that it had been a deliberate Taoist plot; in the result two Taoists were executed, one had his nose and ears chopped off, and six were exiled. Henceforth the Buddhists were allowed to acquire ever more wealth, to the chagrin of the upper-class Chinese.

Nor were they mollified by the Mongols' insatiable thirst for territory, for despite some effort to change to pastoralism, which was encouraged by a measure of inter-marriage, the most profound instinct of the Mongols remained that for the joy of conquest and pillage. Shortly after the first abortive expedition against Japan, Kublai decided to settle scores with a Burmese kingdom called Pagan, whose king had a few years earlier executed Kublai's envoys when they asked him to humble himself before the Great Khan. This king described himself as Supreme Commander of thirty-six million soldiers, swallower of three hundred dishes of curry every day, and sexual partner of three thousand concubines. When the Mongols engaged the Pagans the king despatched a horde of elephants against them, only for the animals to be stampeded by the Mongols' arrows. The battle was won but the country left unpacified until a further campaign in 1287 finally achieved its subservience.

Meanwhile, in the same year as the second attempted invasion of Japan, Kublai sent an army against the hostile kingdom of what is now South Vietnam. Heat, disease and a decisive defeat repelled the Mongols, but they returned a year later, fighting their way as far as Hanoi, until the whole of Vietnam sued for peace and vassaldom.

These operations did not satisfy the Mongol thirst nor arrest the drain on the Empire's financial resources, for Kublai next turned on Java, for all that it lay 2,500 miles to the south. He had sent an ambassador to demand the submission of its king who, alarmed by the threat he apprehended to his control of the south-east Asian spice trade, branded the man's face. The Great Khan therefore sent out a large seagoing force, and although it was at first successful after landing in Java in 1293, a big section of it was betrayed in an ambush and the men fled back to China.

This defeat deepened the gloom that had settled on Kublai. It had started with the death of his favourite wife, Chabi, and then that of their son and his designated successor. Rebellions in lands under his direct control were no balm – a rising in Tibet had scarcely been repressed than another occurred in Manchuria, whence he led his troops personally, borne into battle on a palanquin carried by four elephants. It was his last throw. Turning increasingly to food and drink for comfort he became obese and riven by gout. In February 1294, aged seventy-nine, he died in his palace.

His descendants who succeeded him inherited but few of his extraordinary abilities. The first was his grandson, Temür (Emperor Ch'eng-tsung, 1294–1307), a drunkard despite a Confucian upbringing. His administration was marked by a great increase in numbers, procrastination and corruption. The Empire was peaceful internally but had many years of conflict with the other khanates before peace was restored with the recognition of Yüan's suzerainty over the whole Mongolian world. These operations, the huge and corrupt administration, and lavish gifts to Mongol princes, bore heavily on the country's already straitened finances: the reserves were raided and the paper currency weakened, causing inflation.

Upon Temür's death, his nephew Khaishan succeeded him (Emperor Wu-tsung, 1307–1311) after a vicious fight between Mongol princes. He relied on retainers brought with him from Mongolia but also flooded the bureaucracy with yet more officials; and he was a lavish bestower of titles, even elevating artisans to dukedoms. As the financial crisis deepened, taxes were increased (salt licences were raised by thirty-five per cent) and more paper money was issued, increasing inflation.

He was followed by a younger brother, Ayurbarwada (Emperor Jen-tsung, 1311–1320), who had been tutored by a Confucian scholar. He restored the examination system to recruit more Confucians to government – not, however, without ensuring that the tests for Mongolian candidates were made easier. Indeed, the power and privileges of the Mongolian princes were little curtailed and they continued to get lavish gifts, which did not help the court's efforts to control expenditure, and an attempt to bring the land registers up to date caused the tax-threatened landowners to revolt. Meddling by his mother, the Dowager Empress Targi, caused such factional discord as to paralyse the last years of the reign.

A son, Shidebala, came to the throne at the age of eighteen (Emperor Ying-tsung, 1320–1323). His Chancellor of the Right, one Temüder, a protégé of the formidable Dowager Empress, turned on his political enemies who exposed his corruption and he had the lot executed, becoming virtually a dictator. Before long, however, both he and his patron died, whereupon the young Confucian-educated Emperor surrounded himself with Confucian scholar-officials, the infusion of Confucian ideas resulting in greater discipline in the bureaucracy and alleviation of the people's burden of the corvée. However, he also harboured a passion for Buddhism and had thousands of soldiers labour for three years to build a spectacular temple west of Ta-tu. His end came when he cancelled the annual lavish grants to the Mongol princes: some of them, together with the remnants of Temüder's faction, stormed the imperial quarters and killed him.

Envoys brought one of Temür's nephews, Yesün, from Mongolia, where he commanded a large army, to continue the Yüan dynasty (Emperor T'ai-ting, 1323–1328). He promptly executed or exiled all who had participated in the *coup d'état*. His government was led by his own Mongolian administration, for the most part Muslims who now gained unprecedented influence and did not cavil as using public funds for much mosque-building.

His death ignited a bloody struggle for the succession. One of Khaishan's sons, called Tugh, emerged victorious after the poisoning of his half-brother who was his rival contender. The new Emperor (Wen-tsung, 1328–1332) immediately visited death, exile or property-confiscation on the followers of the dead prince. Again Muslims were the leading ministers, but, despite continued lavish gifts to royal relatives, no fewer than eight aristocratic plots were hatched during the brief reign, adding to the political instability caused on the one hand by uprisings of ethnic minorities across the Empire's huge and disparate territories (from Kublai's time to the end of Tugh's reign there were more than 130 eruptions), and on the other by floods and droughts that rendered millions homeless. The Emperor sought to improve the consequently worse financial situation by reducing the aristocrats' grants, the number of costly Buddhist sacrifices in Shang-tu (down to 104 from 165), and, by ten thousand, the people serving the palaces. He was himself a Confucian enthusiast and he sought to create a sinicized image of his own court. An accomplished poet, calligrapher and collector of Chinese painting, he honoured Confucian scholars and each year praised men and women known for their filial piety and chastity. He founded the Academy of the Pavilion of the Star of Literature to promote Confucian high culture. It produced a vast compendium of Yüan documents and laws, called the *Grand Canon for Ruling the World*.

The dynasty was seen out by first the briefest-serving and then the longest-serving Yüan emperors. Tugh's son, Irinjibal, who succeeded him at the age of six, lived for only two months; he gave way to Toghon Temür (Emperor Shun-ti) son of Tugh's poisoned brother and aged only thirteen. He succeeded in 1333 and reigned for thirty-five troubled years.

Within a year or two the examination system was again scrapped but restored five years later. By 1336 the long-battered finances rendered paper money valueless. The crisis was little relieved by efforts to raise money – as much as thirty million ounces of silver were derived in a single year from the salt mines – since vast sums were needed in the following two decades to help the starving and uprooted victims of epidemics contemporaneous with the Black Death horrors in Europe, and of the exceptionally severe weather that marked almost every second winter, bringing droughts, floods and widespread famine to the Yellow River region. Besides all this, the constant migration of the government between the two capitals was costly, as was the court's disposition to provide office for ever more Mongolians and privileged foreigners, aggravating the bloated size and the corruption of the bureaucracy. Meanwhile the imperial family and their officials did very well out of the hundreds of commercial and manufacturing businesses they owned.

It was not a situation that could last. Small-scale risings in the provinces grew bigger through the 1350s. There was widespread gangsterism. All the signs were of a dynasty in terminal decline as gangsters and dissidents captured cities, pillaged stores, and killed officials. The Yüan troops, sapped by long inaction, had but partial success in coping with them. An able chancellor named Toghto did arise who sought to hold back the waves. To relieve the chronic revenue shortfall he issued new paper currency. To get free of the grip of a pirate who had gained control of all grain shipments to the capital he established large-scale rice cultivation nearby to meet the need. When the Yellow River again flooded and began shifting its course he put 120,000 soldiers and civilians to work re-channelling its course to south of the Shantung peninsula.

At the age of thirty-four Toghon Temür withdrew into semi-retirement. Oblivious to the ever-increasing disorder in the provinces where rebels, often antagonistic to each other, were setting up autonomous areas, he amused himself with his companions, with all-female dance ensembles and orchestras, and the sexual rituals of Tibetan Buddhism; he sailed the lake of the imperial palace in a huge pleasure boat, and he helped design and build a large water clock. But he made the grievous mistake of suddenly dismissing Toghto on the eve of defeating one of the biggest warlords. Thereafter power rapidly slipped from the hands of the Mongols as the state disintegrated.

One of the most successful dissident movements had germinated in southern Honan where the son of a wandering soothsayer and blind beggar-woman led a fundamentalist Confucian moral revolution. When he died in 1355 he was succeeded by a peasant made destitute by the death of his parents from plague. He was the remarkable Chu Yüan-chang. More will be said of him later, but for the present it suffices to say that rallying hundreds of thousands around his banner of the messianic cult of the Red Turbans (subsequently abandoned for pure Confucianism), he crusaded for over a decade to end the Yüan Dynasty.

Since he did not pillage or slaughter, the peasants came over to him in droves. Their economic hardships and the physical suffering of so many of them, like those compelled to toil in the Yellow River project, provided a powerful impulse to revolt. They were joined by the gentry, intent on shaking loose their long subordination to the Mongols. Thus the bulk of the Chinese population rose up behind Chu Yüan-chang, especially after he defeated most of the other rebel leaders. He captured Nanking and crossed the Yangtze, and finally, in 1368, his able generals, for the first time in the world using metal-barrelled cannon on a large scale, effortlessly captured Ta-tu as the Emperor fled on horseback to the ancient Mongolian capital of Karakorum.

So was the Mongols' occupation of China ended, although in truth it was never anything more than an attempted organ transplant ultimately rejected by the patient's immune system.

CHAPTER TWENTY-TWO

The Ming – I
(1368–1487)

The family of Chu Yüan-chang, conqueror of the Mongols, lived near modern Nanking. Under the Mongols' classification system it was registered as a 'gold-panning household' and as such had to present the government with a quantity of gold dust each year. But not finding any gold, it took to tenant farming so that it could exchange produce for gold in the market place where, however, merchants manipulated prices to exact the maximum profit. Before the plague finally wiped out Chu's parents the family had constantly to move about in search of a livelihood. He was born on 21st October 1328 and upon his parents' death when he was sixteen he was offered as a novice to do menial work in a Buddhist monastery. He was a tall sturdy youth whose rugged pock-marked face and jutting jaw gave him a strange and somewhat awe-inspiring appearance. He emerged from the fires of the insurrection against the Mongols as an autocratic tyrant, for all that the Confucian advisers with whom he surrounded himself imbued him with the idea of compassionate governance.

He reconstructed Nanking as his capital, with a surrounding wall thirty miles long; the former capital of Ta-tu (Peking) was renamed Peiping. The Hanlin Academy and National University were revived, and shrines to his ancestors built in proper relationship to the four gates of the city. Early in 1368, after sacrifices at the newly built Round Altar to Heaven and Square

Altar to Earth, after a proclamation of his impending accession had been delivered to the spirits, and after thrice ritually rejecting invitations to accept the Mandate of Heaven, he ascended the throne as Emperor Hung-wu and founder of a dynasty he called Ming (Bright or Radiant).

His thirty-year reign was marked by brutality and terror. These were sparked off by the slightest hint of disloyalty or corruption. The pre-stamped documents case is one in point. Local officials supervising revenue shipments to Nanking had to fill in forms which they were supposed to complete by noting the amounts being sent, but while stamping the forms as final they in fact left completion to the other end when the actual amounts received net of transit losses were known. The Emperor reacted with fury to what he regarded as bureaucratic abuse because of the corruption which the use of pre-stamped documents made possible: he had everyone whose name had appeared on the forms executed. This was in 1376. It was nothing, however, to his anger a few years later when a leading minister was suspected of treason: in a purge that lasted many years, over forty thousand people are believed to have been executed. On one occasion when a high official, charged with treason, committed suicide, his wife and relatives, together with over seventy members of his household, were all executed. In 1393 yet another purge followed the alleged treachery of a general: this time over twenty thousand people, including many nobles, were put to death.

Indeed his punishment for any transgression was harsh – he had a university instructor executed for allegedly slandering the head of the university, while a number of officials accused of abusing the examination system were dismembered – and he enjoined his princely sons to act likewise on their estates. But he kept faith with his origins, striving to protect the peasantry who suffered particularly from the arrogance and indiscipline of men ennobled for their help in founding the dynasty. Rules published in the form of iron placards made managers who used their power to take advantage of the people liable to be tattooed and have their noses cut off, their property confiscated, and their wives and sons banished to penal servitude; nobles unfairly acquiring the land, buildings or livestock of the common people were liable to be reduced to commoner status, and if they repeatedly appropriated valuable properties such as gold mines from their owners they could be executed.

He zealously paid respect to his forebears. In the Palace of Honouring the Ancestors which he built within the palace gate, he placed shrines to his four parental ancestors. There, incense was burned every day, and offerings to the ancestral spirits were made at every full and new moon and on his parental birth and death anniversaries. To remind himself always to fast on sacrificial occasions he had a copper statue made holding a bamboo tablet inscribed 'fast'.

Likewise he took his spiritual obligations as Son of Heaven very seriously. Once, in a severe drought he fasted and exposed himself to the elements for three days to persuade the rain spirits; not succeeding, on the fourth day before dawn he clad himself in a plain gown and straw sandals, then on a mat spread at the foot of the Altar to Mountains and Rivers outside the palace he sat down to subject himself to the day-long heat of the sun while his Empress – Ma, the adopted daughter of his old chief – and his consorts brought him farmers' coarse food they had cooked. After three days of this ritual he returned to his palace to fast. Six days later the rain fell in torrents.

He repeatedly changed the organization of his government, now adopting one form of cabinet rule, now another, sometimes none at all with himself acting as prime minister. Eunuchs, because of their function of handling all top paperwork, gained increasing influence even if they were prohibited from any political activity. The recruitment of scholars to the civil service nevertheless continued, especially after 1370 when the Emperor revived the traditional examination system; and to the curriculum of the Classics, discourse and political analysis he added tests on archery, horsemanship, calligraphy, arithmetic and knowledge of the law. The latter embraced the legal code promulgated in the century before and later frequently revised. However, within a few years he suspended the examination system for a decade and reverted to recruitment by recommendation, though the thousands of graduates from the National University provided a pool of capable talent.

A curious feature of his administration was his periodic issue of 'grand pronouncements'. These included a defence of the punishments he had meted out for treason; another, called 'Record of the Eternal Mirror', sought to guide the royal princes (he had twenty-six sons) with a salutary history of princes who had rebelled and in consequence brought ruin, and to them also was addressed his 'Ancestral Injunctions' setting out regulations for their conduct; yet another was a collection of the records of good and evil ministers, while his 'Study of Institutions' set forth detailed sumptuary regulations such as the dimensions of nobles' dwellings and the decoration of their sedan chairs. In his 'Placard of Instructions to the People' he dealt with the local administration of justice by village elders and directed that in every village a disabled, very old or blind person, led by a young boy should walk the streets, ringing a copper bell with a wooden clapper and chanting the 'six instructions' – maintain filial obligations, likewise harmonious relations with neighbours, instruct and discipline sons and grandsons, work peacefully for your own livelihood, and do not commit a wrongful deed.

To Emperor Hung-wu's iron grip may be ascribed the generally peaceful internal state of the nation during his reign. In 1369 he conferred titles on all the spirits of walls and moats, and magistrates had to offer regular sacrifices to them to help achieve prosperity. The spirits responded graciously, for the country enjoyed economic wellbeing. In return for shipments of grain, merchants received salt vouchers which could be redeemed for salt they could profitably sell, and this helped achieve stable prices throughout the reign. Although trade through the ports was discouraged, there was a substantial flow of tribute from all the surrounding countries. Copper currency replaced the use of silver, in which there was much speculation.

Military activity included a punitive expedition into Tibet, a strengthening of China's hold on Manchuria and the freeing of Szechwan and Yunnan from Mongol control. Against the expelled Mongols themselves there were almost continuous operations, extending far beyond the Great Wall and with varying degrees of success, including the burning down of Karakorum. But perhaps of greater concern was piracy, which brought the eastern seaboard under repeated attack by Japanese buccaneers, whom even a series of forts did not deter from forays inland.

Hung-wu died in 1398. Thereupon thirty-eight of his forty concubines took their lives – a Mongol practice, which was ironical since he had detested Mongol practices. In his last edict before he died he named a grandson, Chu Yün-wen, as his heir, and the enthronement took place within days, Chu adopting the reign-title Chien-wen.

He was a gentle and bookish man who surrounded himself with Confucian scholar-officials. He reduced taxation and restricted the wealth of Buddhist and Taoist clergy, grown rich under his father's patronage. But when he sought to clip the wings of the potentially rival ambitions of his uncles, the princes enfeoffed by his father, he ignited a civil war. An arrogant and power-hungry aristocrat, the Prince of Yen, after successful campaigns against the Mongols had a large army based on Peiping and in 1399 he attacked his neighbours. Three years of bloody fighting culminated in 1402 when the gates of Nanking were treacherously opened and the Prince's triumphant army set the imperial palace on fire. When the flames died down three charred bodies were identified as those of the Emperor, his Empress and his eldest son, though a persistent legend says that the Emperor escaped in the guise of a monk. The Emperor's second son, aged only two, and other surviving relatives were incarcerated – the little boy to grow to the age of fifty-seven before he would be released. The Prince of Yen with ruthless ferocity had tens of thousand of Chien-wen's officials and their relatives executed, imprisoned or banished.

Chien-wen did, however, live on as a tragic figure in stories and anecdotes for centuries to come.

The Prince of Yen ascended the throne as Emperor Yung-lo (Lasting Joy) in 1403. He had received a thorough classical education but his chief interest was the army: throughout his reign, conferring marquisates and earldoms on his leading generals, he created a hereditary military nobility. However, he also perpetuated the able civil administration he had inherited, appointing Hanlin scholars at its head. Examination graduates filled all the leading posts down to the level of county magistrates. But while the continuity and stability of his administration was a feature of the reign, eunuchs were still growing in influence. They carried out every kind of imperial service, notably spying on all and sundry, both civil and military. Given absolute authority to root out corruption they operated an agency called the Eastern Depot in the capital: it became infamous as the rumoured scene of torture and unexplained deaths. The Emperor gave his Imperial Bodyguard similar authority, but while he ruled he kept control of these instruments of power, which cannot be said of later reigns.

He went to enormous lengths to establish his legitimacy as Son of Heaven, ordering his scholars to rewrite dynastic histories for the purpose. He also cultivated the image of a sage Confucian ruler. In a didactic tract he set out the ethical standards for the conduct of an emperor and his subjects. On his instructions scholars compiled the *Great Compendium of the Philosophy of Human Nature*, containing selections from the Classics and interpretations of them. He sponsored an enormous compilation by more than two thousand scholars of extant classical literature, called *The Great Literary Repository of the Yung-lo Reign*, in over twenty-two thousand chapters which covered the classical texts, history, ritual, law codes, military affairs, medicine, zoology, botany, fiction and drama. These works shaped the intellectual and cultural outlook of the literati and, distributed abroad, helped promote Confucian orthodoxy in foreign lands.

Yung-lo's highest aim, however, was to extend the influence of China throughout the north and deep into Inner Asia. While he used diplomatic embassies and granted trading privileges under a tributary system – which included Korea among the participants and also, sporadically, Japan, until a new shogun declared in about 1417 that the gods of Japan forbade dealings with foreigners – he did not shrink from military action led by himself in person. The need for such action seemed inevitable as a mighty new power loomed up in the west.

During the reign of the founding Ming emperor this power had emerged under the leadership of the Mongol Timur (Tamerlane, the Tamburlaine of Marlowe): based in Samarkand, he established an empire embracing much of central Asia, present-day Iran, Iraq, Afghanistan, Azerbaijan, Georgia and Armenia, and he launched devastating invasions of Syria, Turkey, India and southern Russia. When envoys were sent to him, first by the Emperor Hung-wu and then Yung-lo, he executed them, and in 1404 he determined to conquer China and convert it to Islam; but having assembled an army of 200,000 men for the purpose, he died.

The removal of this threat did not, however, mean peace on China's northern frontiers, for the Mongol hordes were a constant menace. In five campaigns over a period of fifteen years Yung-lo led armies up to seven hundred miles north, north-west and north-east of Peking in an effort to destroy them, but, despite many successes in battle, he found it difficult to peg down the swiftly mobile tribesmen, and vast resources and energy were squandered. The Emperor also sought to incorporate Annam, the northern part of modern Vietnam and long a vassal state, directly into his empire. His army duly crushed resistance and he set up a Ming administration, but constant rebellion and guerrilla attacks could not be suppressed even by a massive commitment of troops, and eventually, after nearly thirty years' upheaval, the effort was to be abandoned.

It is not, however, for achievements on land but those by sea that Yung-lo's reign is chiefly remembered. In the Nanking shipyards great ocean-going vessels were built, ranging in size up to junks with nine masts, 444 feet long by 68 feet wide. Fleets of up to 300 such craft, manned by 27,000 men, were organized by the Emperor's eunuchs and led by a eunuch admiral, Cheng Ho. During six expeditions between 1405 and 1421 he ranged all around south-east Asia, Ceylon, India, the east African coast and up the Persian Gulf. In the process, many local kings were captured and brought to China, and no fewer than eighteen states sent envoys and tribute to the Ming court. Gifts to the Emperor included exotic animals, notably ostriches, zebras and giraffes, which had never been seen before. The enterprise vastly extended the influence of China and constituted the greatest maritime exploration in world history before the European voyages many decades later.

From early in his reign, Yung-lo determined that Peiping rather than Nanking should be his capital. Massive works of building and reconstruction were begun and, for fifteen years, hundreds of thousands of workers toiled to create a place of majestic splendour, much of which has survived to this day. Major repairs to the Grand Canal and the making of three thousand flat-bottomed barges to sail it ensured ample provisioning from the south. The Emperor enjoyed, however, only a few years' occupation of the Forbidden City – the imperial complex in the capital – before a series of strokes, for which he was treated with Taoist elixirs containing arsenic, lead and other metals, finally in 1424 killed him while he was returning from one of his Mongolian campaigns.

His eldest son succeeded him as Emperor Hung-hsi (Vast Splendour). Obese and with foot trouble, he was killed by a heart seizure within a year, whereupon the eldest of his four sons followed him as Emperor Hsüan-te. His incumbency started unpromisingly with a rebellion by his uncle; but it was quickly suppressed, the uncle reduced to commoner status before being gruesomely tortured to death; six hundred of his followers were executed and 2,200 banished to the frontier. After that the reign was conspicuously peaceful. Confucian-educated like his forebears, Hsüan-te put his government in the hands of Hanlin scholars, even though the influence of the eunuchs continued – indeed, a special school was set up in the harem to advance their education.

The administration sought to root out corruption among army officers who made excessive demands on the people, used their men as private servants, and robbed them of their wages. The Emperor provided relief for areas affected by natural disasters and lightened taxation. In his deep concern for justice he personally presided over many important trials, and he repeatedly ordered retrials of serious criminal cases, resulting in the acquittal of thousands of innocent people.

Tranquillity at home was matched abroad. The Mongol federation was split by a bitter division between the Eastern Mongol tribes and Oirat tribes in the west. The latter emerged victorious but maintained friendly relations with the Ming court. Diplomatic exchanges and trade with Japan were revived under a new shogun. A similar friendly intercourse was maintained with Korea, which was a provider of war horses but was also useful to the Emperor personally by responding to his requests for virgins and eunuchs for his harem and for cooks to serve the Korean delicacies he enjoyed; on one occasion he asked for a specific girl, one renowned for her beauty. He put an end to the long-drawn-out operation in Annam. Early in 1432 he ordered the eunuch admiral Cheng Ho to undertake the seventh and, as it turned out, last voyage: this was to reinvigorate the tributary relationships established by Yung-lo, and once again the fleet sailed as far as the Arabian peninsula and the north-east coast of Africa. After his death following a short illness in 1435, historians justifiably portrayed Hsüan-te as a Confucian monarch, excelling in the arts and dedicated to benevolent government.

Little of the lustre of his reign rubbed off on that of his successor, the elder of his two sons. As the Emperor Cheng-t'ung was only eight at the time, a regency council was formed which included three eunuchs, of whom one, Wang Chen, who had been educated in the harem school, became dominant. He had been the Emperor's tutor and had him totally in his grip. Clever and alert, with much personal charm, he intimidated the highest officials, not hesitating to jail or kill any who obstructed him. Though the government nevertheless functioned smoothly, there was unrest in the country at large as the corvée operated harshly, especially to provide for the continued building of Peking on a massive scale, and thousands fled their lands to avoid being forcibly rounded up. Moreover, droughts, floods and pestilence afflicted large areas every few years between 1435 and 1448, the last being the worst because the Yellow River once more burst its dykes and changed course, with consequent widespread damage and dispersal of population. From 1444 there were rumblings of rebellion and in 1448 two large-scale uprisings were put down with difficulty. At this time Wang Chen instigated a campaign against the Shan people of Burma adjoining Yunnan, which sucked in considerable resources in men and funds. But of more consequence was the Mongol situation. The Oirat leader, Esen, ruled a united horde that controlled all the north from modern Sinkiang to Manchuria, from which China's hegemony had been removed. For many years relations were maintained on a friendly trading basis, with the Chinese obtaining horses in exchange for tea, salt and textiles: a quota laid down that in every market one and a half million pounds of tea would be exchanged for four thousand horses. But Esen's ambitiousness led him to propose the marriage of his son into the Ming royal family, and when this was rebuffed he launched a three-pronged attack on northern China (1449).

Encouraged by Wan Chen, the totally inexperienced Emperor Cheng-t'ung, now twenty-two, determined personally to command an army to oppose the Mongols. He set out with perhaps half a million men, a formidable force but ill-prepared, ill-provided and incompetently led; and constant heavy rain mired them in mud. When the generals wanted to halt at a readily defensible position and send the Emperor back to the safety of Peking, Wang Chen furiously over-rode them; but when a large Chinese force just inside the Great Wall was slaughtered, he accepted the danger of trying to penetrate the steppe and agreed a retreat to Peking. The Mongols wiped out the Chinese rearguard, whereupon the main body camped at a post-station called T'u-mu near a river about seventy miles north of Peking. The incorrigibly arrogant Wang Chen rejected the generals' plea to move into a nearby walled country town. The army was without water for men or animals, and when it attempted to get access to the river the Mongols attacked. Panic spread through the Chinese army, which was destroyed with the loss of almost half its strength and immense amounts of arms and material; all the high-ranking generals and officials were killed (including Wang Chen, probably by his own officers), and the Emperor was captured. The despotic megalomania of a eunuch thus caused one of the greatest military disasters in Chinese history. Remarkably, Esen did not immediately advance on Peking, which lay open before him, but withdrew northwards, taking all his booty and the hostage Emperor.

At first, Cheng-t'ung's half-brother, Prince of Ch'eng, was appointed Regent, but then, since the Emperor was a captive and his son an infant, he himself ascended the throne as Emperor Ching-t'ai (Bright Exhalation) in 1450. Peking prepared for the inevitable assault by Esen. Morale was extraordinarily high and a spirit of determination animated both the populace and the able generals put in charge of 200,000 troops gathered from near and far. When Esen duly attacked, a series of battles was fought, some on a large scale and involving artillery. Though he briefly surrounded the capital, Esen became disheartened and withdrew to Mongolia.

With Peking saved, the government entered a period of sound administration, even if eunuchs still dominated it. The army was extensively reformed and huge works of repair, reservoir-building and lock-installation stabilized the Yellow River flood situation. But the period also saw extensive uprisings in the south, and many parts of the country suffered natural disasters by way of floods, droughts and excessive cold that froze innumerable people to death. State revenue was therefore much diminished, and at the same time vast sums had to be paid out for relief.

Meanwhile there was the issue of the captive Emperor Cheng-t'ung. The imperial incumbent, Ching-t'ai, was getting himself well ensconced on the throne and in no hurry to face the complication of his half-brother's return. After a year's half-hearted negotiating with Esen, the latter saw no advantage in holding onto his hostage and released him. He returned to Peking upon renouncing any claim to the throne and, denied all honours, was housed in a detached section of the palace. In 1457, however, when the new Emperor fell too ill to hold audience, a long-simmering conflict in court over the question of the imperial succession culminated in a group of leading ministers and generals seizing the chance to stage a *coup d'état*. They deposed Ching-t'ai, installing Cheng-t'ung once again as Emperor, this time under the reign-title T'ien-shun (Obedient to Heaven). Ching-t'ai was reduced to his princely status and died a few months later – strangled, one account says, by a palace eunuch.

The usual ruthless purge of high office-holders followed, together with the heaping of honours on the participants in the coup, many of whom, however, over-reached themselves and were extinguished. A remarkably stable administration took charge of affairs – no changes in the ministries occurred from 1458 to the Emperor's death in 1464.

His eldest surviving son was seventeen upon his enthronement as Emperor Ch'eng-hua. His reign was to be distinguished by over a decade's constant campaigning against the Mongols. The Great Wall was substantially rebuilt or added to in the form seen today: in particular 200,000 troops constructed a section across the Ordos, six hundred miles long and thirty feet high. It finally extended for about 4,500 miles, much of it thirty feet high, with watchtowers at frequent intervals from which smoke signals from burning wolf-dung were emitted. It was on a stone foundation, and made from compacted earth faced with incredibly strong bricks, as strong as concrete, with a mortar mix of rice flour, clay and lime. Eight million lives are said to have been lost in the construction of this, one of the greatest engineering feats on earth.

The wall and a series of successful battles largely stabilized the situation but Mongol raids never ceased to trouble the northern frontier. Within China, an area about two hundred miles south of the junction of the Wei and Yellow Rivers for a while posed an acute problem. It was a mountainous expanse of territory, well watered by rivers such as the Yangtze, and here had accumulated the survivors of centuries of invasion, refugees from drought and flood, and escapees from taxation and the corvée. This dislocated squatter population, hundreds of thousands in number, was ready fodder for bandit leaders. One such, a man named Liu who had reputedly lifted a stone lion weighing a thousand catties (a catty being 1.3 pounds) and hence known as Thousand-catty Liu, led a massive rebellion in the 1460s; not until 1466 was he defeated and his head chopped off. Seven years later there was a renewed uprising in the area but a considered policy of conciliation finally brought stability.

The Emperor Ch'eng-hua was stocky and stolid, and had a bad stutter. He was completely in thrall to his one-time nursemaid who was twice his age and, as the Lady Wan, became his chief consort. She loved dressing-up in military uniform and leading processions around the palace courtyard for his amusement. More sinisterly she exerted an unprincipled influence on the government, which in turn was dominated by what tradition calls 'the four evil eunuchs' and degraded by all kinds of corrupt doings: the Emperor's departure from practice in making appointments by direct decree, instead of through the usual bureaucratic procedures, was manipulated by the palace eunuchs virtually to sell offices, ranks and privileges; they creamed off special taxes; and they wheedled tax-free estates from the Emperor. He to an extent led the way by confiscating lands to create huge imperial estates.

Nor was his personal life exemplary. Through Lady Wan – and the supply to him at her instigation of pornographic literature and a Taoist sorcerer's aphrodisiacs – he became debauched. He soon put aside his childless Empress. And after his consort Lady Wan's only child died in infancy, she contrived through enforced abortions and even murder of concubines to ensure that no potential heir emerged. Or so she thought; but the Emperor's chance encounter with a girl – an aborigine from the Yao tribes in the south – in one of the palace store-rooms had in fact resulted in a son. This was only revealed to the Emperor when the child was five, by a eunuch who confessed to having withheld the potion Lady Wan had sent him to give the girl to induce an abortion. The delighted Emperor put the child under the protection of its grandmother, the Dowager Empress. Lady Wan, grown ill with anger, soon had the boy's mother poisoned. When consort and Emperor died within a few months of each other in 1487 the child, now a youth, succeeded to the throne with the title Hung-chih.

CHAPTER TWENTY-THREE

The Ming – II
(1487–1644)

*I*mmediately upon his accession the young Emperor Hung-chih made his intentions clear: finding a shocking sex manual in his father's quarters, he had its elderly donor, a sycophantic official, confronted with it in the presence of all the grand secretaries; the humiliated old man grovelled, speechless, until ordered out, to die within the year. Hung-chih proceeded to clean out the defiled court of the previous Emperor and Lady Wan by the execution, imprisonment or banishment of thousands of rapacious eunuchs, irregularly appointed officials and dishonest Buddhist and Taoist clerics.

Hung-chih proclaimed his wife, Lady Chang, Empress and was utterly devoted to her: indeed, he was probably the only monogamist in China's imperial history. A small, bright-eyed man with a drooping moustache and wispy beard, he was a dedicated Confucianist. He did his utmost to meet the demanding obligations this entailed: he performed all the prescribed rituals; he not only appointed exemplary Confucianist ministers but heeded their advice; and he showed himself to be deeply concerned about the people's welfare.

This paragon had, however, a weakness – Lady Chang, a foolish and demanding woman with expensive tastes – and he endlessly indulged her requests for her brothers, cousins, uncles and numerous hangers-on to be given titles, offices, land and opportunities for corruption. This clearly disturbed the cosmic order, for frequent and severe natural disasters beset his reign. The Yellow River again caused widespread floods until 120,000 men set to work blocking, channelling and dyking the water to change the course of the river to south of the Shantung peninsula, where it remained until the nineteenth century.

In government, Hung-chih followed the procedures of his predecessors. Ever since the founding Emperor abolished the position of prime minister, the Emperors had themselves fulfilled that function. All administrative action had to be authorized by their decrees, but instead of making these in conference with the Hanlin scholars who were generally the top ministers, rulers increasingly tended to base themselves on the advice tendered by ministers in the form of a rescript attached to memorials submitted to the throne. But this advice was often superseded or ignored by the recommendations of eunuchs having the Emperor's ear.

There had by now grown up a huge eunuch bureaucracy of well over ten thousand people. It became as numerous as, and operated in parallel with, the civil bureaucracy: each had its own hierarchy with career ladders and ranks with fixed incomes and rules. The leaders of the two sides fiercely competed in trying to control the Emperor, but most of the time they had to cooperate. The eunuchs had attained increasing responsibility in the military sphere by many of them achieving the rank of general and others supervising horse-purchase and weapon-production, while in civil matters they managed the great imperial silk, brocade and porcelain factories, controlled most foreign trade – which was conducted on the tribute system – procured all the products used by the court, managed all imperial building projects, and oversaw the nationwide police investigation and punishment system.

In the administration of the army, rewards and advancements for most of the troops were given on the basis of the number of enemies captured or killed, the latter being verified by the dead men's heads – a system which stimulated much indiscriminate head-hunting. Enemy heads taken in the north and north-east brought the highest rewards; those in the Tibetan and south-west sectors ranked second; and those of Chinese rebels or bandits last. For much of the fifteenth century, operations to repress uprisings in the far south by turbulent tribes like the Yao, the Miao and the Li – never assimilated by the Chinese – yielded a rich harvest of many thousands of heads. On occasion these included a woman's head, for many tribes had female leaders.

The Emperor Hung-chih was not yet forty when he died in 1505 – few Ming emperors reached that age – and his thirteen-year-old son succeeded him as the Emperor Cheng-te. He was very different from his father.

The youth soon stopped living with his consort the Empress and preferred the companionship of eunuchs. One of them, Liu Chin, was responsible for his entertainments and provided dancing, wrestling matches, a menagerie of exotic animals, and music. At Liu's suggestion he took to roaming the streets of Peking in disguise. These distractions and his propensity for getting drunk disinclined him to deal with affairs of state which he increasingly entrusted not to his civil officials but to his eunuchs, pre-eminently Liu Chin.

For three years this man conducted a reign of terror as he contrived to impose eunuchs as the instruments of government throughout the nation. Officials who dared speak out against him were beaten, tortured and dismissed; high officials who did not defer to him and committed a trivial offence, such as riding in a sedan chair without permission, were put into cangues – heavy wooden frames hung round the neck. He sought also to raise badly needed revenue. Salt was sold over the established quotas; ever greater quantities of silver were extracted from the mines; officials in charge of granaries and treasuries were fined for the slightest spillage or shortage in the count; and he raised the tax quota in many areas. In some of the latter, military households were affected, prompting unrest among the garrisons.

One such protest erupted into rebellion in central Shensi in 1510. It was quickly put down, but in the course of the campaign a senior eunuch officer became convinced that Liu Chin was plotting to assassinate the Emperor. When the officer pressed the charge during an imperial banquet, the Emperor, by now very drunk, refused to believe that his favourite would betray him. However, he became convinced next day when he inspected Liu's premises and saw the hoard of a quarter of a million bars of gold, nearly two million ounces of silver, great quantities of valuables, armour and weapons, including one allegedly to be used for the murder, namely a dagger, concealed in Liu's fans. Liu was sentenced to death by slicing. The slices must have been passing thin, since the process, vividly described throughout the land, took three days. Every one of Liu's measures was rescinded.

While the eunuchs' influence on affairs nevertheless continued, the Emperor now sought companionship in military officers. His first favourite was the commander of the Imperial Guard who lived in the royal quarters and often got drunk with his host, for whom he procured his favourite musicians, Muslim women for his harem, and Tibetan monks skilled in the magic of Tantric Buddhism. The commander was presently rivalled by another soldier, a warrior who caught Cheng-te's attention because of an incident in a battle with brigands: three arrows hit the man, one penetrating his face through to his ear; the man pulled it out and resumed fighting. These soldier friends stimulated the Emperor's desire for military adventures, which at first took the form of hunts and mock battles in the Imperial City. In 1514 during one of these hunts a tiger mauled him, but did not diminish his enthusiasm.

Soon afterwards a lantern festival was held, for he had a lifelong fondness for lanterns and he had been given a good number of beautiful new shapes for the festival. Placed in the courtyard of the residential palace they were lighted to spectacular effect, turning night into day. But it happened that yurts had been erected on the sides of the courtyard, a number for the storage of gunpowder needed for the Emperor's mock battles; somehow the gunpowder got ignited. The explosion caused a fire that raged all night and completely destroyed the palaces and audience halls. Thirty thousand troops and seven years were required to rebuild them.

Meanwhile the Emperor lived in an assembly of yurts he had set up in the Forbidden City, complete with gates, residences, courtyards, kitchens, stables and lavatories. When he travelled he took the whole complex with him. He increasingly ignored court protocols, attending rituals at his convenience, and for his rarely held audiences he turned up in the evening instead of at dawn, so that the entire court had to hang about all day. He brushed aside criticism from his officials and left everything to his eunuchs.

During his last years he travelled about restlessly, usually in a wide radius of Peking – once he got embroiled in a skirmish with the Mongols near the Great Wall – but even as far south as Nanking, the Emperor's second capital. (Over a hundred officials were beaten for opposing this journey.) Further south, a distant relation, the Prince of Ning, engineered a rebellion that started in Kiangsi; his forces included many of the brigands who had prospered under his protection, and some leading court eunuchs conspired with him. However, he was defeated in little over a month, captured, and after being moved about for upward of two years he was permitted to take his own life before his corpse was burnt; the conspirators suffered death by slicing – the penalty for high treason.

The Emperor was by now an addicted drunkard, charging an attendant to follow him about with a jug of hot wine and a ladle, so that he could imbibe wherever he happened to be. Once in a drunken moment he fell out of a boat and nearly drowned, whereafter his health steadily deteriorated. He delighted in getting his officials drunk too, and he issued ludicrous edicts such as perpetual banishment of anyone rearing and killing pigs, when pork was the main offering in most imperial sacrifices and the chief ingredient in almost all meat dishes. On his travels he seized women from private households, either for his harem or for ransom; but a singing girl he encountered became his favourite consort. If he gave anyone something, however trivial – a feather, a piece of meat – he expected in return a handsome gift of gold or silk. His court was as undisciplined as he was.

In 1516, one Tomé Pires, son of a Lisbon apothecary, had been appointed Ambassador to China by the King of Portugal. By judicious bribing of eunuchs Pires was able to proceed from Canton to Peking, which he reached late in 1520. But he never saw the Emperor, who was ill and indeed died in April 1521, at the age of only twenty-nine – the price, perhaps, of a misspent life. Pires and his party were then expelled, thus ending the first mission to China from a European kingdom.

Cheng-te died childless, and some months of uncertainty about the succession ended when his fifteen-year-old cousin came to the throne in 1522 as Emperor Chia-ching. Auspicious signs had marked his birth – the Yellow River was clear for five days and roseate clouds filled the sky. They misled. The court of the new Son of Heaven was soon plunged into controversy over the dynastic legitimacy of his parents, illustrating more than any other episode in Chinese history the importance attached to honouring one's ancestors: because his father had been the son of a concubine never raised to the rank of imperial consort, his descendants could not carry on the imperial line in their own right. The traditionalists argued that such a right could only be invested in the Emperor if in all matters of ritual he treated his uncle, the late Emperor Hung-chih, and aunt as his father and mother, and his real parents as his uncle and aunt. The issues involved in this fandangle included the Emperor's right to install his natural father's spirit tablet in the Ancestral Temple and his status to perform the customary imperial rituals and sacrifices. The controversy became incredibly complex, with a scouring of the precedents of hundreds of years and a bitter struggle between court factions. In the process hundreds of officials suffered punishment beatings, some unto death, and a number of grand secretaries rose and fell in power. Over twenty years passed before finally the Emperor could fulfil his desire and place his father's spirit tablet among those of his imperial forebears in a newly built Ancestral Temple. During these years the Emperor brought changes to many ritual ceremonies, including those for Heaven, Earth, the Sun, the Moon, and even the spirit of Confucius. He loved elaborate court ceremonial.

He also had a strong vindictive streak. Because he considered that his aunt, the Dowager Empress, had slighted his mother, he conducted a ceaseless vendetta against her, ensuring the death of one of her brothers by execution and of the other brother by starvation in prison. From about 1539 there were several occasions when his quarters were put on fire, in one of which he nearly died. They were not accidents. His short temper and heartlessness aroused the hatred of many around him, and even his concubines feared his visits.

One night in 1542 he fell asleep while with his favourite concubine. She and her attendants withdrew, leaving him in a wine-induced stupor. A servant girl in the concubine's entourage then entered with several palace women. Tearing off one of the silk cords holding the bed curtains, they knotted it and pulled it around the Emperor's neck while stabbing at his groin with their long hairpins. A eunuch watchman, alerted by the cry of one of the women who took fright on seeing that the Emperor was still alive, in turn alerted the Empress – the last of Chia-ching's three principal consorts – who rushed in and loosened the noose. Despite strong medication administered by his physician, the Emperor remained unconscious for eight hours before coming round, spitting blood and for long unable to speak. The Empress issued an order in his name for all the women implicated in the attempted assassination, including the favourite concubine, to be put to an immediate gruesome death. Chia-ching, however, could not forgive his Empress for his favourite's death, and some years later when the Empress's palace caught fire he refused to permit her rescue.

After the attempt on his life he retired into seclusion, moving with his consorts and concubines to the western park of the Imperial City, into the Palace of Everlasting Longevity. He had long stopped attending court audiences and now proceeded to rule through a small group of trusted advisers. For the next thirty years he was obsessed by the pursuit of immortality through drugs, rituals and esoteric Taoist regimes

Although he sacked most of the eunuchs who filled key positions in his late uncle's government, he appointed others in their place, and they dominated the administration. Few uprisings disturbed its even tenor. Rebellions by garrisons within the Great Wall west and east of Peking who felt hard done by were quickly put down. Of more moment was the constant raiding by Mongols. Peace with them might have been secured by the grant of trading rights, for they much wanted Chinese tea, metalware, fabrics and herbal medicines, but Chia-ching hated them and would not agree. The raids grew ever more frequent, penetrating deep into Shansi and Shensi and even to the outskirts of Peking itself. The cost of trying to contain them was enormous, and the financial situation was not improved by repeated floods and droughts and an earthquake which killed 800,000 people in the Wei valley alone.

The state's economic straits necessitated constant revenue-raising and cost-cutting measures. Among the latter was a reduction in the Nanking garrison's rations, provoking a riot in 1560 when the men dragged a vice-minister of Revenue from his office, killed him, and hung out his naked corpse for their comrades to shoot at with their arrows. Tax revenue suffered because so much land had disappeared from the registers and new land brought under cultivation went unregistered. One way and another, although the economy of the Empire flourished the government's did not. A bountiful source of tax, that of the maritime trade, was denied it by its own ban – first decreed by Hung-wu – on such trade. There had been some trade under the guise of the tributary system, but this had broken down. The fears that lay behind the ban were of foreign spies and of dangerous alliances being forged with foreign forces. The consequence was that for most of the reign the eastern coast for over a thousand miles south of Nanking was alive with smuggling and with piracy.

The eunuchs and other corrupt port officials largely disregarded the trade ban as wealthy families financed fleets of some hundreds of vessels, and from the 1540s a lively trade developed with Japan. From Japan too came warriors who attacked and pillaged numerous places along the coast, even north of Nanking. Chinese piratical activity was also intense, and merchant, pirate and smuggler often exchanged roles. Natural disasters in the area produced flocks of refugees who joined the pirate forces which sometimes occupied and fortified towns and looted their way deep inland. Imperial forces sent to dislodge them only sporadically succeeded, emerging from one such encounter with nineteen hundred heads. The situation was in fact totally out of control for many years until the late 1560s when a large government army gradually rooted out the pirates, and a few years later the coast was officially opened to maritime trade.

During his years of seclusion, following the abortive attempt by palace women to kill him, the Emperor, deep into his long-held Taoist beliefs and alchemy, based important decisions on divination. One of the methods consisted of two mediums holding the short arms of a T-shaped object from whose long arm a suspended awl traced out, on a platter of sand beneath it, the answers to supplications that had been written in gold ink on dark blue paper, addressed to a certain Taoist deity and then burnt, for the smoke to rise up to the deity. The Emperor's chief Taoist adviser, one T'ao Chung-wen, also prescribed aphrodisiac pills made largely of red lead and white arsenic, to which Chia-ching became addicted, gradually poisoning himself. For the attainment of immortality T'ao also recommended sexual intercourse with virgins, and in 1552 he collected eight hundred girls aged between eight and fourteen to serve the Emperor, adding one hundred and eighty more in 1555. None of this availed against the poisoning effect of the elixirs. Insomnia plagued him, and swings of mood from depression to rage. From 1564 his eunuch attendants put peaches – symbols of longevity – in his bed, saying they were gifts from the immortals, which much pleased him. His mental capacity shrank, and as his condition deteriorated he was moved from the Palace of Everlasting Longevity back to the Forbidden City, where he died at midday on 23rd January 1567, ending a forty-four-year reign of more oddity than achievement.

His eldest surviving son became the Emperor Lung-ch'ing at the age of twenty-nine. He may have been mentally retarded; certainly he was inarticulate, self-pitying and unassertive. He took little part in public affairs during his reign of a mere five-and-a-half years, but such was the strength of the bureaucracy under competent ministers that tranquillity and prosperity prevailed.

His son in turn ascended the throne as the Emperor Wan-li in 1573. He was only nine years old, an intelligent and precocious boy whose Buddhist mother's influence was manifest in his reluctance ever to sanction the death penalty. But his reign saw a deepening of the process long under way, that of estrangement between monarch and bureaucrat. The result was that Wan-li became ever more reclusive, a 'cloistered sovereign', and obese, and the government of his Empire was essentially conducted by whoever emerged from endless power struggles as his chief Grand Secretary.

The most notable of that ilk was Chang Chü-cheng. During the first decade of the reign he single-handedly brought about a vastly more efficient administration throughout the country and strong financial control, which combined frugality in expenditure with zealous revenue-collection. Thus, where the straitened economic circumstances of the past had left the State with no reserves at all, Chang's efforts produced enough grain in Peking's granaries to meet the needs of the next nine years and hundreds of thousands of pounds (weight) of silver in the treasury reserves; even the provincial treasuries were flush. He died in 1582. None of his successors had remotely his ability.

In 1596 eunuch commissioners were sent to local areas to supervise the gathering of tax from manufacture, trade and mining, causing widespread resentment among local officials, especially as the staffs they formed were often ruffians and adventurers. By this time both local and central government had become an ideological battleground in which the Hanlin academicians were arrayed against what was called the Tung-lin party. The latter was not in fact a party but a loose group of individuals noted for their adherence to strict Confucian principles.

It was in accordance with these principles that they opposed the Emperor's wish to nominate his favourite concubine's son, younger than his son by his Empress, as his heir apparent. Their will, not his, prevailed in this fiercely disputed matter, illustrating how limited an emperor's powers had become. Tung-lin followers – they founded an academy of that name in 1603 – also exerted a strong influence on the periodic evaluations of senior civil servants, who could suffer dismissal if an evaluation went against them. Antagonism between the Tung-lin adherents and their opponents resulted in an increasingly moribund bureaucracy which was yet, while trade was not respectable, the only vocational outlet for the upper classes.

Even the writers of the period were all civil servants. Those with no creative talent simply enjoyed a great deal of leisure, marked by their display of abundant wealth. Much of this was not invested but lavished on expensive curios like ivory and rhinoceros horns, or precious metals cast into utensils which they often buried underground. Country gentlemen surrounded their sedan chairs with retainers, and purchasers of rank erected flagpoles in front of their houses. Not achievement but status became the ambition.

As the reign advanced, the quality of government continued to deteriorate. The reclusive Emperor contributed to this by his non-cooperation with his officials. He constantly ignored, for instance, requests to confirm appointments and pensioned retirements: in 1604 the Ministry of Personnel reported that nearly half the magistracies of the realm were vacant, as were over half the ministries and vice-ministries in Peking and Nanking. He scarcely ever attended court meetings; sometimes officials knelt en masse in the palace courtyards unsuccessfully chanting and wailing to gain his attention; unanswered memorials to him simply piled up. The civil service became sceptical and demoralized. Only the departments of state engaged in raising revenue received his attention as he constantly devised means of diverting funds to his private treasury, gaining for himself the reputation of being the most avaricious emperor in Chinese history.

During these years domestic uprisings in several provinces and border wars with the Mongols and Burmese flared up but posed little threat. Far more significant for the future was the renewed arrival of the Europeans. In the late 1560s the Portuguese had been given the right to live and trade in Macao where a Chinese custom house collected duties, round which a wall was built to keep the foreigners inside. In 1578 the Portuguese were allowed to buy Chinese goods in Canton, whither in due course the custom house was moved. Foreigners in the city were strictly regulated, having to live in designated areas and only allowed a single trading session each year, on pain of services and supplies being withheld.

Meanwhile the Portuguese example prompted Spain to set its eyes on the Far East. In 1570 an expedition was sent to colonize Manila where some Chinese had long lived. The friction that in due course resulted caused Spain to consider invading China, but Philip II rejected the idea. A full-scale war did, however, eventuate in the Philippines, and in 1603 Spanish–Filipino forces drove out the Chinese; the best part of twenty thousand men died in the conflict.

The deep suspicion of the West engendered in the Chinese by these events was to a degree allayed by a remarkable European. This was the Italian Jesuit, Matteo Ricci, who first established a small Christian church some miles from Canton and then in 1602 based himself in Peking. By becoming sinicized and showing infinite patience he endeared himself to the Chinese upper class, not least – being himself an eminent mathematician and scientist – by his dissemination of Western scientific

298

knowledge, which he furthered by his translation of books by Euclid and others on hydraulics and astronomy. He did make a few converts of dignitaries, but his missionary efforts were uphill work: the upper classes sought personal enlightenment, the lower were superstitious and idolatrous, so neither were much interested in foreign religion; moreover, obtaining the ear of Heaven was the prerogative of the Emperor alone. Not long after Ricci's death in 1610 the newly established Christian church in China suffered its first – albeit mild – persecution.

A number of military campaigns marked the second half of Wan-li's reign. One was against a rebellion by the Miao people on the southern border of Szechwan, which lasted through the 1590s until it was put down by a Ming army that deployed psychological warfare by the use of bulletins and handbills. Another was in the far north, in the Ordos, where a short-lived rebellion was sparked by army pay arrears: the rebels holed up in a city which resisted the besiegers until a three-mile dyke was dug around the city and filled with nine feet of water into which the walls soon crumbled; the Mongol rebel leader burned himself alive.

Then there was an operation again the Japanese who in 1592 invaded Korea with the ultimate object of invading China: the Chinese counterattacked, with the ultimate object of invading Japan. The aspirations of neither side were realized by the seven-year war that followed on land and sea: fortune favoured now one party, now the other, until the whole affair ended with the Japanese departing, leaving only a small garrison in a Korean town. An interesting incident during one of the frequent truces during the war pointed up the Chinese belief that, as their Emperor was the Son of Heaven and therefore sovereign over all under Heaven, every foreign nation was his vassal: the Chinese undertook to invest the Japanese leader with the title King of Japan if he would withdraw his forces; but when the Chinese mission arrived with the imperial patent and silk robe for the investiture, the Japanese leader reacted with anger to the idea that he would be a tribute-paying vassal. Not for centuries would the Chinese abandon their belief in their possession of a universal empire with its dominant influence radiating from the celestial capital.

One further military adventure was to see the reign out and cast a deep shadow over the near future. The Mongolian-Tungusic people's alliance known as the Jürchen, who established the Chin Empire on the ruins of the Northern Sung in the twelfth century, before being driven out by a son of Genghis, retreated to the far north-east. There, reinforced by westward migrations from their native land north of Korea, they were to become known as the Manchus. Their armed forces were organized in units called 'banners'. Led by one, Nurhaci, then aged twenty-four, since 1583 they had been building an empire that soon embraced the whole of Manchuria and the Mongols in it. At first they were content simply to engage in commerce with the Chinese, with whom they enjoyed a monopoly in the trade of pearls, sable and ginseng, and they sent them tributary missions. But Nurhaci detested the Chinese and planned to cast off his people's vassalage. After launching a few successful skirmishes with Chinese troops he published a clutch of complaints – the so called Seven Grievances – against the Chinese, from whom he demanded a cession of territory and annual donations of gold, silver and silk.

This stung the Chinese into taking punitive action. An army of about 100,000, including a large contingent of Korean musketeers, invaded Manchuria in 1619. Its commander made the mistake of splitting it into four, whereas the Manchus, having but half the Chinese number, concentrated their whole force on each point of contact. The result was that within a week the Manchus won several brilliant victories, in one of which alone the Chinese force of 25,000 men was wiped out; and after one of the defeats, the responsible Chinese general committed suicide by igniting gunpowder under himself.

An immediate result of the rebuff was a huge number of desertions from the Chinese armed forces. Also, to bear the cost of the country's abortive effort, increased taxes were imposed, despite the Emperor's at last parting with some of the silver hoard which he had for long tenaciously hung on to. He was, in fact, in fast-failing health, and in the summer of 1620 he died. He had reigned for forty-seven years.

The population of his Empire now totalled over 150 million. Since the green light had been given to maritime trade in the late 1560s, Nagasaki and Manila had become the major trading centre for Chinese merchants. Their wares found their way across the world – silks worn in Kyoto and Lima, cottons sold in Filipino and Mexican markets, porcelain used in Sakai and London homes. China was paid in Japanese and Spanish silver, the huge inflow of which enabled the government to commute many taxes, strengthen the army and pacify the frontier, creating a sense of peace and prosperity.

It did not last. Severe price inflation, uncontrolled urban growth and business speculation increased the tensions endemic in a widening gap between rich and poor. The military campaigns such as those against the Japanese in Korea, and heavy expenditure on improving the canal network and the Great Wall, sorely strained resources. Nor was the situation improved by the Emperor Wan-li's extravagant spending on himself and his family, or by other factors, notably the fluctuating silver production in Peru, Mexico and Japan, intensified piracy, and persistent crop failures through adverse weather. A massive hike in taxes increased the rebellious mood which had begun to grip the country shortly before Wan-li's death.

His son became the T'ai-ch'ang Emperor but only survived for a month before dying from, it is said, faulty medication – the notorious so-called 'Red Pills'. Consequently, in September 1621, one of his sixteen children was enthroned at the age of fourteen as the Emperor T'ien-ch'i. A physically weak boy, poorly schooled, and of doubtful mental capacity, he eschewed any role in government affairs, preferring to pursue his hobbies such as furniture- and model-making deep in the imperial apartments.

His court seethed with infighting between factions, and imperial decisions were left to trusted servants. One of them, a eunuch named Wei Chung-hsien, acting in collaboration with a former imperial nurse called Madame K'o, became the dominant figure. He ruthlessly purged the court of its Tung-lin supporters and conducted a reign of terror which sapped the government of its dwindling authority. At the same time the Manchus were constantly pressing into Chinese territory; Dutch and Chinese privateers were severely hampering trade in the Taiwan Strait and the South China Sea; and major uprisings broke out among the peasantry.

T'ien-ch'i had reigned for less than seven years when he died childless in 1627. His seventeen-year-old brother succeeded him as the Emperor Ch'ung-chen (Lofty and Auspicious). Prompted by universal expressions of disgust at the behaviour of the eunuch Wei Chung-hsien, he ordered his arrest, which Wei thwarted by hanging himself: his corpse was dismembered and his head publicly displayed, while over twenty of his associates, including Madame K'o, were executed or committed suicide.

Tung-lin supporters again filled high posts in the administration but factional strife did not cease. The economy of the south-east gained a temporary improvement from the suppression of piracy along the coast, enabling trade with the Spanish in Manila to be resumed and with it the inflow of silver. But in the north-west an appalling winter following a bad drought resulted in many women and children being sold, and even cannibalism resorted to. Rebellion across central China spread, and in the midst of this the Manchus invaded again (1629–30). They broke through the Great Wall and advanced to the walls of Peking before withdrawing; they left thousands of corpses lining the approaches to the city. After being thrown back, when they attempted a few months later to exploit their gains south of the Wall, they were active again a year later, in the process besieging a Ming stronghold whose defenders were reduced to eating their horses and even their dead comrades.

More rebellions erupted: one that threatened northern Shantung took a year to suppress, but the fires in central China extended from the Wei valley to the Great Plain and as far south as the Yangtze, and government forces strove to suppress them with but sporadic success. The truth was that these uprisings, drought, ever-increasing taxation, a fall in the supply of silver (in which many taxes had to be paid), corruption, and constant ministerial changes consequent on faction-fighting in court, were all combining with the Manchu incursions to put the dynasty in dire peril.

In 1636 the Manchu leader proclaimed himself Emperor of a new dynasty he called the Ch'ing. After conquering Korea he turned his full attention to the conquest of China. By about this time two powerful rebel leaders had emerged, one in the north and central China, the other in the south, both conquering many cities and bent on the destruction of the dynasty. Even territory previously untainted by rebellion threatened trouble: along the south coast, tax increases followed by natural disasters – floods, droughts, locust-plagues – caused terrible suffering: here as elsewhere there was mass starvation, widespread beggary, infanticide, disease and even cannibalism. Taxes dried up as taxpayers abandoned their property, tenants attacked tax-collectors and landlords, servants rebelled against their masters, banditry proliferated, and peasants pillaged to survive.

In renewed attacks in 1642 the Manchus, with many Mongols and Chinese in their ranks, ranged north and east of Peking, taking ninety-four towns and cities, 360,000 prisoners and huge amounts of booty. For the present they then withdrew, but the outlook for the Ming Emperor was grim, with hordes of Manchus and rebels besetting him from every direction. Indeed, by April 1644 one section of the rebel movement stood at the very gates of his capital, moving his ministers to urge him to flee south to lead the resistance movement being organized there. He refused, then at the last moment attempted to escape dressed as a eunuch. When this failed, just after midnight on 24th April he climbed a small hill in the palace compound, entered the pavilion that housed the Imperial Hat and Girdle Department, and hanged himself – to ascend, tradition has it, to heaven on a dragon. The three-hundred-year Ming Empire had reached its end.

CHAPTER TWENTY-FOUR

The Ming Dynasty in perspective

*T*he flame of the Ming Dynasty was not yet, however, quite gone out. It flickered on for nearly two decades, during the period known as the Southern Ming. After the Ch'ing (Manchu) capture of Peking the whole of China south of the Yellow River became the stamping ground of armies, as a nation of one million people – albeit with Mongol help – set about the conquest of over a hundred and fifty million. At an early stage the invaders issued a decree unique in world history in that it imposed a single style of appearance on an entire country: to attest his allegiance to the Ch'ing every man had, on pain of death, to shave his pate, wear the rest of his hair on the back of his head, and don Manchu clothes.

The resentment this aroused stiffened resistance, but to little avail. Ming forces were beset not only by the Ch'ing but also by large armies of rebels, bandits and adventurers, who all fought each other and sometimes among themselves. It was a complex saga distinguished by the emergence of many heroes and villains, by massacres and pillaging, by some triumphs and more disasters, all the time the Ming being at a hopeless disadvantage as they lacked coordination between their commanders, suffered repeated desertions to the enemy, and were scarcely governed at all as the court, which was headed by a succession of imperial princes, disintegrated under the pressure of squabbles, bankruptcy and constant flight across the south from east to west.

During this peregrination a German Jesuit baptized as Christian several leading members of the imperial family; and another Jesuit, a Pole, was sent off with a plea to the Vatican, begging the Pope to pray for a Ming restoration: His Holiness responded with an uplifting message which, however, brought as little succour as repeated appeals for help from Japan. For a while, first one and then another maritime campaign along the south-east coast achieved more success than the inland campaign. The second, waged for a decade from 1649, was led by one Cheng Ch'eng-kung, son of a noted pirate leader and smuggler who had resisted the Manchus with distinction on land until deserting to them. Cheng scored victories which emboldened him to advance on Nanking with two thousand ships and 200,000 men, but he was utterly routed by the Manchu cavalry and infantry. Presently he moved his men to the largely barren island of Taiwan: there the Dutch East India Company had maintained a colony since 1624; after nine months of hostilities the Dutch were seen off, but soon afterwards Cheng died (although his family was to rule the place for another twenty years).

That was in 1662, the same year that the last Ming prince, called Yung-li, who had two years previously fled into Burma where he was racked by asthma and lived in wretched conditions, was captured by the Manchus and executed. Thus vanished the last vestige of the Mandate Heaven gave to the Ming.

The fact that that Mandate had held good for nearly three centuries owed much to the careful organization of government. A country so huge, a million and half square miles in extent, presented a singular administrative problem, lightened by the division of the Empire into metropolitan areas around Nanking (capital prior to 1421) and Peking (capital thereafter) and thirteen provinces. The latter were divided into prefectures, and the units of sub-prefectures and counties were in the charge of magistrates. Walled towns and cities provided the yamens or offices of the local bureaucracy, although only two such cities, the capitals – which were divided into five wards under a warden to supervise police patrols and fire watches – had an urban administration. A major section of the population lived in villages remote from government ('As Heaven is high, so is the Emperor far away') and these, under their elders, were the fundamental girders in the nation's governmental structure.

Towering over all in awesome splendour were the Sons of Heaven, before whom no one could have audience without first kowtowing – kneeling and bowing down to the floor nine times. There were sixteen Emperors in the 277 years before the Southern Ming era in the seventeenth century, with their deeds and misdeeds, their virtues and defects as summarized in the last two chapters. Their family name was Chu but the characters for an individual emperors' given name were tabooed in his lifetime. Upon ascending the throne each adopted an auspicious reign-title – Cheng-te, for example, Correct Virtue; Chia-ching, Admirable Tranquillity; and so forth. Being the Son of Heaven he could, however, only be addressed obliquely, as *pi-hsia* which meant 'at the bottom of the steps' (of the dais from which he gave audience). When mentioned in conversation he was 'Shang', the Superior. After his death, flowery titles were conferred on him such as Pure in Sincerity, Perfect in Virtue, Extensive in Culture, Thorough in Filial Piety, etc.

He could have as many consorts and concubines as he pleased, although only one at a time could be Empress, who very occasionally was demoted, especially if she did not bear a son. The secondary wife consorts, numbering six or more, were distinguished by titles ranging from Imperial Honoured Consort down to Consort for Reverent Service. Most of the harem's inmates came from commoner families, avoiding the threat posed by powerful noble clans in the past. They were either nominated at the age of puberty by local officials as virtuous, beautiful and well-mannered, or given as gifts by friendly foreign rulers. A girl's station on entering the palace was lowly but if she caught the Emperor's eye she might be promoted to secondary wife or even Empress, whereupon her close relatives received stipends and titles. Upon an Emperor's death, while a large number of bereaved imperial women followed the example of those who committed suicide when the founding Emperor died, the Emperor T'ien-shun's last testament in 1464 abolished the practice as uncivilized.

Among the harem's inhabitants were nearly a thousand women by the end of the dynasty, acting as maidservants and the like. Called female officials, they were all potential concubines and so were recruited on that basis. Also, there were a number of female clerks who, with the female officials, were divided into groups in General Palace Service, Ceremonial Service, Wardrobe Service and Workshop Service, with the office of Palace Surveillance maintaining discipline.

Seclusion of the harem was so tight that even communication with an outsider by letter invited the death penalty. If a woman fell ill, treatment was applied at the direction of a doctor but he was not allowed in. Inmates of the harem could be released or dismissed fairly readily: some were given as gifts to be a favoured dignitary's concubine; others after long service were sent home with a pension; others again could, after half a dozen years' meritorious service, return home free to marry.

The men originally engaged solely as custodians of the harem, the eunuchs, assumed as we have seen considerable political and military importance. This was so often malign that the founding Emperor had placards in the palace proclaiming that any eunuch involving himself in government affairs would be decapitated; but as our story so far has shown, this dynastic orthodoxy was repeatedly breached and the quantity and variety of public services many were called on to perform so increased their numbers that by the dynasty's end there were two thousand of them in the Peking palace alone and tens of thousands throughout the Empire.

When first presenting themselves for the Emperor's service they were carefully inspected to ensure that their genitals had been completely removed, and again every four years 'lest any thing should grow out again which hath not been well taken away'. They were characterized by insolence and organized in distinct agencies, the most important being the Directorate of Ceremonial. Its chief was effectively head of the imperial household, and it was through it that the eunuchs frequently gained dictatorial powers. Then there were the feared eunuch secret police, previously noted as being called the Eastern Depot, to which the Western Depot was added: their members worked with the Imperial Guard to root out and punish traitors, but were also the instruments for periodic reigns of terror.

The cost of the imperial institution always bore very heavily on the nation's finances, absorbing perhaps as much as a third of total revenue. Besides the magnificence of their palaces and all their appurtenances and the bloated staffing, including the army of attendants who accompanied their every outing (there were more people in palace service than in the civil service), the expense of their relatives was huge. All male and female descendants of the founding Emperor, that is, all bearing the surname Chu, were considered royal and entitled to stipends from the state, upon whose payroll there were many thousands of such people by the dynasty's end. The Emperors' fecundity had much to do with this, since half of them produced an average of thirty children each.

Males born to secondary wives were as legitimate as those born to an Empress, whom all called their mother. Usually an Emperor's first-born by his Empress was designated heir apparent and in due course was established with his own eunuchs and family in the Eastern Palace section of the imperial quarters, his administration staffed by respected scholar-officials.

All an emperor's sons were designated Imperial Princes and, in order to avoid any entanglement with the palace women or in state affairs, they were housed in palaces distant from the capital and could not leave their city without the Emperor's permission. Their generous state allowances were in part derived from the estates also settled on them. A staff of civil servants – the Princely Establishment – had the responsibility of running the household and was responsible too for a prince's conduct, so that if he misbehaved the head of the Establishment was punished as a scapegoat.

An intricate system of titles applied to successive generations of imperial clansmen. These included women, who all received allowances and whose husbands were ennobled. Descending titles and allowances were given to the daughters of imperial princes but none was accorded to the children of daughters because their mothers on being married lost their surname Chu. A jade register was kept by the Court of the Imperial Clan – which had to approve any proposed marriage by a member of the clan – and it recorded all marriages, births, deaths, and inheritance rights within the clan.

Outside the imperial clan, noble titles – duke, marquis, earl – were usually only awarded for military achievement. The recipients received a state allowance which was fixed at the time of their appointment, as was the heritability or otherwise of their status. Although prominent as adornments of the court and ceremonial, the nobility played little part in government beyond their military activities.

The real powerhouse of government was of course the civil service. 'At no time,' a leading authority has observed, 'was a government more dominated by civil servants recruited and promoted on merit than in Ming times.' That recruitment was pre-eminently through attainment of an examination degree.

This in turn was fed by the education system. There were the community elementary schools in villages and urban wards; specialist military and medical schools; private academies for mature students; and the National Universities in Nanking and Peking; but the backbone of the system was the nationwide institution of Confucian schools in every prefecture and county, where pupils spent about ten years after leaving their primary school (unless they went to university where they spent a like time). Some of these schools had upwards of two thousand pupils, and all were subject to rigorous inspection.

Inspection, indeed, was a prominent feature of Chinese life. No section or activity of the people was immune from some form of periodic inspection, be it the schools or the civil service in all its aspects, including the judiciary and the military. By constant monitoring and the handing out of rewards and punishments, the state sought to exact the highest standards of performance. Spearheaded by its department called the Censorate an army of investigators was constantly at work everywhere.

The examination system was very much as described for the Sung Dynasty: the provincial and metropolitan examinations for the *chü-jen* degree, holders of which could then sit for the *hui-shih* degree at the capital, followed for the graduate by the palace examination – for the purpose of ranking the graduates – consisting of a single essay on a policy problem. Success meant the crowning glory of a *chin-shih* degree, accompanied by great official and public acclaim akin to that lavished on a modern film or pop star. Indeed, the whole triennial examination period was marked at all the centres by much festivity: it was a major occasion in Chinese life, and examination success defined the country's elite.

The Ming examinations were open to an even wider spectrum of people than the Sung allowed: categories previously excluded, such as merchant families, were no longer so. The curriculum was still dominated by the Classics, but a departure was the requirement for a topic to be analysed, its pros and cons set out, and a step-by-step argument developed to a conclusion. These steps had to consist of eight contrasting statements, called 'legs', hence the description the 'eight-legged essay'.

The civil service, which the graduate entered under the jurisdiction of the Ministry of Personnel, had at its apex six ministries which ran the country in all its civilian and military aspects, at the direction of the Emperor. It had nine ranks (one being the highest) each divided into two grades, and to start with the graduate's position usually depended on his position in the pass list. Thereafter his career depended to a major extent on the periodic evaluations previously referred to. They took a variety of forms. One of the most important, called the great reckoning, involved monthly reports from the heads of all local agencies on their subordinates; these went to the prefectures who sent an annual consolidated report to the provincial head, who in turn sent a report every three years to the Ministry; and the evaluations in this report focused on eight kinds of fault – avarice, cruelty, frivolity or instability, senility, ill-health, weariness and inattention. Every three years a large number of officials from outside the capital appeared before the Emperor and were again judged according to whether they were superior, meriting promotion; inferior, meriting demotion; incompetent, meriting dismissal; or guilty of wrongdoing, involving a criminal trial. Officials inside the capital were reported on to the Ministry by their superior, but officials of the fourth rank and upwards sent self-evaluations direct to the Emperor, at whose pleasure they served. Another important addition to every official's dossier was the product of regional inspectors' thorough investigations, during which locals were encouraged to voice complaints; and if an inspector was apprised of misconduct he could submit a request for impeachment of the offender direct to the Emperor.

The vast majority of civil servants occupied the same post for most of their career, while the top people – almost always members of the Hanlin Academy – had a tenure of only about two years. All had special privileges depending upon their rank – exemption from taxes, miscellaneous corvées, assessments and corporal punishment; the right to wear special colours and style of clothing; absence of restrictions on the size and decor of their houses; entitlement to ride on horseback or in sedan chairs (forbidden to non-officials); and no action could be taken against higher officials except by an imperial order. There were, besides, two kinds of title bestowed on the holders of each rank. These were prestige titles, which ranged from Specially Promoted Grand Master of Splendid Happiness down to Secondary Gentleman for Ceremonial Service; and merit titles, ranging from Left Pillar of State to Governor Companion in Rectitude. Address thus became extremely cumbersome – a certain leading official, for example, could be called Supreme Chief Minister for

Administration, Grand Master for Assisting towards Goodness, Minister of Personnel.

But there were two serious downsides. First, a civil servant was very poorly paid; and second, throughout the dynasty he was liable to appalling punishment. The slightest failing or transgression was punishable – even a lowly official at a post-house would be beaten for reading a government document carried by a courier. Some of the purges to which he was subject have been recounted in the preceding chapter, and he was constantly at risk of impeachment on one allegation or another, so that nearly a third of all the highest officials ended their career in humiliation and disaster. Emperors did not hesitate to have their eunuchs or guardsmen flog officials on their bare buttocks in open court. Indeed, as we have seen, these eunuchs and the Imperial Guard often maintained a reign of terror, even if many officials bravely remonstrated against their Emperor's behaviour or policy.

To preserve impartiality, an official's relatives could not serve in the same agency as himself, nor, unless he were a school instructor, could he serve in his home province. He was expected out of filial piety to take a three-year leave to mourn a dead parent; and with permission he could take up to three months' sick-leave with pay. He could retire at fifty-five if he had a disability, otherwise at seventy, with a small pension. Upon his death, if he had a reputable record of service the Ministry of Rites could confer a flattering posthumous title such as Loyal and Incorruptible, although Giver of a Lifetime in Perilous Service might have been more appropriate.

Such, then, were the people, reared on the Confucian ethic, whose conduct and actions permeated every interstice of Ming national life. That many were as arrogant, corrupt, inept, greedy, cowardly, hypocritical or plain inefficient as popular fiction depicted is doubtless true, but so it is of the many who were honest, capable, sensible, brave and dedicated, and the fact is that their administration sustained a great dynasty for centuries and bore but lightly on the people, making it probably the most successful major government in the world of its time.

An interesting aspect is that the Mongol system of classifying families by occupation, which thereupon became hereditary, was continued by the Ming, but reduced to only three categories: the largest was called simply civilian families; the next, military families; the smallest, artisans or craft labourers. It was to the military families that the state mostly looked for army recruitment. The military system was elaborate and included both special schools and examinations. A soldier's basic pay was one bushel of grain per month, and to provide this, four Ming military farms were established. As these increasingly failed in their purpose, especially in the poor agricultural areas around the Great Wall, merchants were encouraged to deliver grain in exchange for vouchers with which they could profitably trade in salt. As the dynasty advanced, however, the central government had to give cash subsidies, for these only rapidly to dry up in the last stages of the Manchu invasion, when indeed the whole military organization was breaking down.

In Ming times the law was, as ever, whatever the Emperor declared it to be; but in the absence of a specific decree, custom and the Ming code held strong. The code represented a revision, conducted throughout the founding Emperor's reign, of the T'ang code. Like it, its function was to lay down punishments, not definitions of crimes, which for the most part were simply wrongs as generally understood. There was usually no penal imprisonment, although accused and accuser were detained until a trial was over. Instead, punishment ranged from ten to fifty strokes with a light stick, through sixty to a hundred strokes with a heavy stick, penal servitude, life exile (both these last always included heavy-stick strokes in addition), to death by strangulation, decapitation, or slicing. The judicial system, set out in numerous legal handbooks, was stern but thoroughgoing in its aims of fairness and impartiality; in its administration by dedicated officials, from magistrates to the Ministry of Justice;

in its appeals procedure, reaching right up to the throne; and in its concern for the proper treatment of prisoners. The wrongs for which punishment were prescribed included economic crimes, such as non-payment of tax on land transactions (all by written contract which had to be registered), not permitting redemption when a mortgage loan was paid up, charging interest in excess of three per cent per month on a private loan (up to a maximum of the amount of the loan), or for operating a cartel. All sentences were subject to review of one kind of another, and none of a capital nature could be carried out without the Emperor's approval. While the code maintained the traditional domination of men, women who offended were more lightly treated than they.

The arrival of the Portuguese in China, following Vasco da Gama's rounding of the Cape of Good Hope in 1486, only six years after Columbus's voyage in the opposite direction, had less dire consequences than the latter brought on the Americas. The waters around and south of China's south-eastern coast saw a good deal of naval action between Chinese, Portuguese, Dutch, Spanish and Japanese fleets in the sixteenth and early seventeenth centuries' trade war, but few places on the Chinese mainland were affected, except for Macao where the Portuguese repulsed both Dutch and Spanish attempts to replace their occupation. A settled pattern of trade developed with China, in return for silver, supplying the world with tea, silk, textiles, pepper and spices, sugar, lacquer, and a range of goods whose craftsmanship excited admiration everywhere. These were carried in European ships and their movement away from China symbolized the absence from China itself of any serious European impingement.

What European influence was felt in China may be attributed to the Jesuit missionaries who entered the country through Macao in the closing years of the sixteenth century. Subsequent to Ricci's efforts, missions were established in central and south China. They were, however, regarded with suspicion – the bellicosity shown by the Western powers and by Japan in Korea hardly gave cause for the foreigner to be loved – and in 1617 an imperial edict ordered all missionaries to return to their countries; but this was applied with little vigour and in 1629 a remarkable episode revived the evangelical cause. A solar eclipse was in the offing and the President of the Board of Ceremonies arranged for predictions of the day and time to be made by Muslim, traditional Chinese, and European methods. The latter proved to be the only accurate one. The Emperor thereupon approved a reform of the calendar on European lines, and a team of Jesuits and Chinese scholars was set to work making a range of scientific instruments and translations of scientific works. With their good standing thus established in Peking, the missionaries prospered elsewhere in China, reinforced as they were by Spanish Dominicans and Franciscans.

If the missionaries taught the Chinese something of Europe, it was through them that Europe began to gain a more solid knowledge of China than provided by Marco Polo's highly embroidered tales (for all that they fired Christopher Columbus's ambition). The process was, however, initiated by a Portuguese soldier and trader in the 1560s, Galeote Pereira. His description of the bloody punishment beatings meted out with cleft bamboo sticks began the tradition of Europe's belief in the cruelty of the Chinese, although in truth cruelty is no nation's monopoly. But for the rest he reported glowingly – the well-organized provincial bureaucracy; the government-supported rest homes and hospitals for the blind, sick and lame; the absence of beggars; the state granaries for use in droughts; and the fairness and flexibility of the legal system, with criminal trials held in public so that testimony could not be recorded falsely. He noted the fish farms, the artificial egg hatcheries, battery duck farming, and the tethering of ringed cormorants trained to catch fish. He was struck by the immense multitudes of people in the now highly commercialized cities, including pedlars and craftsmen who hawked huge quantities of wares door-to-door; by the meticulous collection of night-soil both human and animal; by the hygienic use of chopsticks for eating. But, as he added, 'The greatest fault we do find in them is sodomy, a vice very common in the meaner sort, and nothing strange among the best.'

Pereira's work was followed within a decade by the *Treatise* of Gaspar da Cruz. This Dominican friar may be said to have sewn the seeds for Europe's craze, before too many years, for all things Chinese. That people offered, he wrote, a glittering opportunity for conversion because they exceeded all other nations 'in populousness, in greatness of the realm, in excellence of polity and government, and in abundance of possessions and wealth'. Among the many picturesque details he related was the pleasure people had in keeping nightingales in separate but nearby cages so that they 'melt themselves in music'. He praised the 'very good harmony' of Chinese music, and plays on the public stage were 'very well acted and to the life'. Of the seamier side of Chinese life he noted how prostitutes, many of them blind or sold into prostitution by their mothers, had to be registered and were housed in special streets outside the city walls. Like Pereira he observed widespread homosexuality (which was due, he explained, to the lack of knowledge that it was a sin), but unlike him, and indeed Marco Polo, he did not let pass the social and aesthetic importance of female foot-binding, or the custom of tea-drinking as an essential feature of hospitality.

A Portuguese adventurer and novelist, Mendes Pinto, compiled a very long book called *Peregrinations*, published in 1640. Its account, although of doubtful accuracy, of the wonders of China, added impetus to European interest. Before that, however, it was really the publication in 1616 of the two manuscripts left by Matteo Ricci that raised the West's understanding of China to a new level.

He described the country as vast, unified and well-ordered by Confucianism. Introducing Confucius to Europe he wrote, 'if we critically examine his actions and sayings ... we shall be forced to admit that he was the equal of the pagan philosophers and superior to most of them'. He extolled the administration which, under a withdrawn Emperor, was run by a civil service selected on merit through examinations. Everyone in each class knew his place; marriages were arranged; rules of ritual and behaviour ensured harmonious social intercourse; and foot-binding kept women chastely at home. The introduction of Christianity, he wrote, was made difficult by the dominance of Buddhism, promoted by an often uneducated and immoral priesthood, and by the prevalence of astrology, which affected so many public and private decisions; above all, the Chinese could not embrace Christianity if they had to give up ancestor worship, but this practice, he considered, was a simple matter of homage and not a religious invocation, wherefore it could be tolerated without prejudice to Christianity. He was deeply critical of Chinese sexual mores, estimating that there were forty thousand prostitutes in Peking besides a great many male prostitutes, sometimes elaborately dressed.

But his most serious reservation about Chinese civilization was its falling behind in science. No longer did it lead the world in almost all branches of science, including astronomy and mathematics whose Western attainments Ricci reported to his hosts. Diverse explanations have been given of this stagnation. Perhaps the most cogent is the grip exerted by Confucianism. While its rigid rules helped bring about a tightly knit society, they formed a brick wall against which any questioning of orthodox knowledge foundered. And while science in the West was emerging from alchemy and astrology, Chinese thinkers concentrated on philosophy. Even Taoism, which vied with Buddhism as the most practised religion, concerned itself less with demons and magical mixtures than supporting Confucian morality. It was this morality – its source, its form, its purpose explored in endless discussions, lectures, and poring over the Classics and in particular the Four Books (*Analects of Confucius, Great Learning*, the *Mean*, the *Mencius*) – that dominated the intellectual concern of the age. Called Neo-Confucianism, it underlay all the thinking of scholars and the whole examination system which produced all the literati. Their's not to question the fall of an apple or be invited to investigate what laws might regulate the natural world, and when a glimpse of these laws was revealed, as for instance the Copernican system, the grudging acceptance of them contrasts with the avid acceptance of the novelty of the clock which Ricci introduced.

For all that, Ricci noted the abundance of printed books he saw everywhere on all sorts of topics, and indeed the degree of literacy was high (it has been estimated that ten per cent of the male population was highly educated), although the need to communicate with the illiterate was well appreciated by the administration – thus, if an illiterate wanted to file a lawsuit he recited it to an official in the county *yamen* who wrote it down in the 'oral accusation' register; and the Emperor distributed to magistrates any address he made to the nation so that their subordinates might publicly recite it – but the great number of literate people looked to the massive outpourings of the printing presses for information, knowledge and pleasure. These piled up in state, provincial and school libraries, while the private collector might boast of thousands of titles. They were printed mainly by the wood-block method, for although movable type had long been introduced, the convenience of not having to set-up anew for a repeated print-run was preferred. Wood-block illustrations in colour were widely introduced.

Publications included guides and manuals on almost every conceivable activity. Private letter-writing, for example, which was subject to conventional rules on structure and style and largely an exercise in literary elegance, was catered for by the *Complete Book of Pen and Ink*. (Letter-writers paid for unofficial use of the sophisticated state postal service, or entrusted their missives to travelling friends and merchants.) Route maps – not least nautical maps such as those compiled during Cheng Ho's expeditions – had long existed and, incorporating the grid system, were plentiful, and an innovation in 1570 was route books: they helped the merchant, the pilgrim, the migrant, the official, and the gentry tourist to find his way across the extensive network of roads – mostly well-kept – together with the post-stations along them, and the canals, on all of which the Ming lavished close attention. The commercial publisher, as distinct from the canonical such as Buddhist monasteries, throve as never before. He catered for the huge reading public with the route and how-to books, almanacs, primers, moral tracts, novels, plays, erotica, joke books, letter collections, and accounts of foreign customs. The obituary of a young student stated that he 'developed a love for unusual books. Ancient and modern history, books on geography and topography, maps, as well as books on Taoism and hermits were his favourite reading. These he would place under the Classics and read surreptitiously.' An incidental aspect of the boom in books was that it helped the wealthy merchant, excluded by immemorial tradition, break into the gentry class, membership of which required a knowledge of how to conduct rites, hold a refined conversation, compose poems, discuss the philosophers, and appreciate fine works of art, all of which could be learnt from books.

A new arrival on the book scene was the published diary. That of Yuan Chung-tao, for example, detailed in over six hundred pages his travels, small daily incidents, his pleasures and pains. And while the grand tradition of poetry continued, the subject became mired in controversy. A literary group called the Archaists promoted strict adherence to the models established by previous writers, as opposed to those literati who insisted on the poet's task as being to give direct expression to his feelings, even if the result could be informal, awkward, and concerned with everyday life. The reaction to the Archaists gave an impetus to prose fiction and drama, treating them on a par with classical poetry and the essay. It is therefore not surprising that an outstanding literary feature of the Ming Dynasty was the profusion of long romantic novels.

Written in the vernacular, sometimes mixed with the classical style, they were the product of story cycles evolved over centuries. The most famous examples were *The Romance of the Three Kingdoms*, on the wars following the end of the Han; *Water Margin*, on a band of righteous outlaws during the Sung; and *Monkey* or *Journey to the West*, on the mission of a T'ang monk to fetch Buddhist scriptures from India. Another was *Romance of the Gods*, a fantastical account of the overthrow of the wicked last ruler of the Shang, full of evil spirits in human guise, wizards, magical phenomena, immortals, and Buddhist imagery.

The most popular literary form, however, was what was called the Southern drama. The use of theatrical metaphors to comment on political or social life became commonplace, like 'All the World's a Stage'. The plays, mostly romantic, mixed speech with song; and many, intended to be read, were published in fine illustrated editions. They were immensely long – a tribute perhaps to the Chinese characteristic of patience – with many plot strands, and in upwards of fifty-five scenes.

As to the non-literary arts, the court painter and the gentleman-painter, the latter often a scholar living in the luxury of a country estate, built sedulously on the foundations of the pas – painting landscapes, birds and flowers, and with immaculate delicacy depicting bamboo. Much use was made of monochrome ink as well as colour. Nor was the subtle art of calligraphy neglected. Sculpture was practised with great vigour, large figures being cast in iron and smaller ones fashioned from ceramics, which also added gaiety and splendour to the roof-ridges of temples and palaces already glittering with yellow, blue and green tiles.

The Ming excelled in the decorative arts. Their marvellously wrought *cloisonné* enamel and lacquer objects have never been bettered, nor their richly woven textiles developed from earlier ages. These textiles were figured silks, embroideries and brocades worn by officials and the rich, while a form of tapestry woven from silk with the use of a needle as shuttle not only provided magnificent robes (often embellished with dragons) and decorative panels but interpreted paintings and calligraphy. It was so fine that whereas the finest Gobelin tapestry has eight to eleven warp threads per centimetre and twenty-two weft thread per centimetre of warp, the Chinese achieved twenty-four and a hundred and sixteen respectively.

But it was through their blue-and-white porcelain, turned out by numerous commercial kilns, that the Ming first made their mark on the West soon after 1600. The Dutch captured at sea two Portuguese vessels carrying a cargo of the exquisite ware, which caused a sensation when put on the market in Holland. Delft and other pottery centres strove to imitate it – in vain, until an alchemist in Dresden succeeded in making the first true porcelain in Europe. This was in 1708, a thousand years after its perfection in China.

Craft industry epitomized by porcelain manufacture enjoyed unprecedented prosperity during Ming times, as indeed did every form of commercial enterprise. Several factors may be noted as facilitating this. One was the development of an economy based on silver ingots and coins. Another was that, if science in many aspects languished, technological progress continued: silk looms with three or four shuttle-winders, improved cotton looms, the printing of wood blocks in up to five colours, methods for manufacturing white sugar and icing sugar, the invention of an alloy of copper and lead to make movable type, advances in ceramics, and so on. Many of the proliferating small businesses grew into large enterprises, often with an industrial character, like silk and cotton weaving, porcelain manufacture, iron and steel production, and paper-making (in the province of Kiangsi fifty thousand workers were employed in thirty factories). Techniques in agriculture similarly advanced: new machines were devised for working the soil, irrigation, sowing seed, and the treatment of products, all described in extensive published treatises; and many new plants were introduced, including groundnuts, sweet potatoes, sorghum and maize.

All this promoted great social change. A proletariat and urban middle class came into being; rural life was transformed by the agricultural progress and by the influence of the towns, so highly commercialized and constantly growing (the population at the end of the Mongol dynasty more than doubled by the end of the Ming); and a class arose of important merchants and businessmen such as bankers. The China of old went out with the Ming, and modern China came in with the Manchus.

Before leave of 'old China', which is to say to the end of the Ming Dynasty in the seventeenth century, is finally taken, however, it would be appropriate to reproduce an A – Z list in Joseph Needham's monumental *Science and Civilization in China* of the country's inventions and the lapse of time before these became known in the West.

		Centuries before known in West
(a)	Square-pallet chain-pump	15
(b)	Edge-runner mill	13
	plus application of water power	9
(c)	Metallurgical blowing-engines, water power	11
(d)	Rotary fan and rotary winnowing machine	14
(e)	Piston-bellows	c.14
(f)	Draw-loom	4
(g)	Flyer for laying thread evenly on reels in silk-handling, and application of water-power to spinning mills	3 – 13
(h)	Wheelbarrow	9 – 10
(i)	Sailing-carriage	11
(j)	Wagon-mill	12
(k)	Efficient harness for draught animals:	
	breast-strap (postilion)	8
	collar	6
(l)	Cross-bow (as individual arm)	13
(m)	Kite	c.12
(n)	Helicopter top (spun by cord)	14
	Zoetrope (moved by ascending hot-air current)	c.10
(o)	Deep drilling	11

(p)	Cast iron	10–11
(q)	'Cardan' Suspension	8–9
(r)	Segmental arch bridge	7
(s)	Iron-chain suspension-bridge	10–13
(t)	Canal lock-gates	7–17
(u)	Nautical construction principles (water-tight bulkheads, etc.)	10+
(v)	Stern-post rudder	c.4
(w)	Gun-powder	5–6
	Gun-powder used as a war technique	4
(x)	Magnetic compass – Lodestone Spoon	11
	– With needle	4
	– Used for navigation	2
(y)	Paper	10
	Printing – block	6
	– movable type	4
	– metal movable type	1
(z)	Porcelain	11–13

Contrariwise, Needham lists only four Western inventions of moment:

Screw – in China fourteen centuries later;

Force-pump for liquids – eighteen centuries;

Crankshaft – three centuries; and

Clockwork – three centuries.

CHAPTER TWENTY-FIVE

The Manchus' Ch'ing Dynasty (1644–1911) – I

*F*rom the time that the new Ch'ing Dynasty of the Manchus captured Peking in 1644, followed by the execution of the last Ming prince in 1661, until the extinction of the final remnants of resistance in the south-west in 1683, the conquerors sought to establish a stable government. Their first efforts met with limited success because the gentry despised them as aliens and loathed their enactments: a Manchu had to be alongside every Chinese in office; marriage between Manchu and Chinese was forbidden; Manchu soldiers garrisoned all the great cities; and Manchus as the master race did not have to sit examinations to gain appointment. Moreover, any literary work adjudged subversive brought upon everyone concerned in its publication the punishment of torture unto death – plus execution or enslavement of their family. And adoption of the Manchu hair and clothes style was rigorously enforced. In despair, many thousands of scholars, officials and landowners committed suicide.

But then the process steadily took hold that had characterized every conquest, namely, the absorption of the conqueror into the culture of the conquered. In short, the Manchu regime became increasingly sinicized. During the one hundred and fifty-odd years preceding the nineteenth century the Ch'ing Dynasty was maintained by only four emperors:

Shun-chih, 1644–61

K'ang-hsi, 1662–1722

Yung-chen, 1723-1735, and
Ch'ien-lung, 1736-1796.

Especially from K'ang-hsi onwards they became Chinese-speaking, established a reputable government on the Ming template, freed it of eunuchs, largely stamped out bribery, invited Chinese scholars to administrative posts, and immersed themselves in Chinese culture while encouraging their courts to do likewise. The result was that the literati streamed back into Peking and hostility died away; even the ban on intermarriage was much disregarded and Chinese concubines graced the harem.

It was a period of conspicuous tranquillity – the calm, it may be seen with hindsight, before the storm of the fateful next century. The government ruled through its bureaucracy, which extended far and wide through a network of local magistrates and their staffs, but essentially civil order was maintained by local gentry and the bonds of lineage. Population increased enormously, to three hundred million people by 1800 – the numbers in most provinces exceeded the combined population of Britain and the United States of America. The great cities' streets seethed with humanity about the shops, teahouses, theatres, temples and workshops, while outside them, among the scattered estates of the gentry, vast numbers of peasants – independent and tenant – toiled across the countryside, their lives centred on villages of about a hundred households each, although the population increase created more and more rootless migrants and as the dynasty advanced, there was growing agricultural poverty in the midst of which pawnbrokers thrived.

The population increase also, however, spurred commercial activity, marked by the development of banks and intensified internal trade. The latter often involved merchants' exploitation of minority tribes in the south whose economy and culture alike suffered the fate of so many colonized people: they became addicted to drink and then lost their money, their land, and their daughters. When a ban on foreign trade imposed in 1661 was lifted in 1684, the flow of silver into China in exchange principally for tea and silk was resumed, but towards the end of the eighteenth century much of it flowed out again as opium began to be imported.

The arts flourished. The Emperor K'ang-hsi promoted the compilation of giant encyclopaedias encapsulating the learning of ages, to be surpassed in the next reign but one of an encyclopaedia in 26,000 volumns. One or two exponents of science and technology began the long process of edging their country towards an acceptance of Western progress in these subjects. In painting, an Italian missionary introduced some European techniques, including perspective; but Chinese painter regarded the depiction of light, shade, shadows as unnatural. Dutch flower-painting gained adherents. In literature, while poetry – especially song-lyrics – and essays abounded, they were less remarkable than short stories, drama and novels. The writers of short stories, in which the supernatural figured prominently, inclined to the polished style of scholars; but novels were written in a partly colloquial style. One of these is rated the finest in Chinese literature, the eighteenth-century *Story of the Stone* or *The Dream of the Red Chamber*, a tale of a rich and powerful family's downfall and the decadent son's love of a high-born emotional lady: it broke new ground in openly expressing feelings, something the Chinese do not like doing. Written by Ts'ao Hsüeh-ch'in over the course of nearly twenty years, it has had the following in China of say Shakespeare or *Don Quixote* in the West. Many novels expressed social criticism, targeting the formalism of Confucianism, examinations and the social system; one even advanced that modish cult of the twentieth century, feminism, and inveighed against foot-binding, which before many years largely declined, being replaced by long fingernails as the mark of breeding. Playwrights added to the corpus of their Ming predecessors: a catalogue of 1781 has 1,013 titles. Some of the plays were inordinately lengthy: one of them embraced 240 acts and took two years to perform, although programmes usually consisted of acts from different plays.

The peacefulness of the age was little disturbed by quickly suppressed peasant revolts in the south, nor by the Manchus' military activity, which was considerable but all at a distance. They had already taken Korea before China and soon (1683) Formosa (Taiwan) fell to them. The Mongols had allied themselves to them but, as the Ch'ing Dynasty became sinicized, they turned hostile. Under their leader, Galdan, they waged war for six years until 1696 when the Emperor K'ang-hsi personally led an army of eighty thousand men with Western-designed artillery across the Gobi Desert into Outer Mongolia to south of Urga (Ulan Bator), nine hundred miles north-west of Peking. From the battle fought there the Chinese emerged victorious and Galdan killed himself. It was a decisive historical event, for the threat of the steppe peoples which had affrighted the north for thousands of years was substantially ended.

Two decades later a rising in western Mongolia led to the Chinese conquering the whole of Mongolia and Sinkiang. They followed with a campaign against Tibet, occupying Lhasa and installing a new Dalai Lama as leader of a Chinese protectorate. They extended suzerainty over Nepal, Burma, Vietnam and Siam. Thus by the eighteenth century the Chinese Empire reached its vast, maximum extent. While the southern conquests were in due course to be nullified, to this day Tibet, Sinkiang and Inner Mongolia have been ruled by China. Its penetration of Central Asia had, however, far-reaching consequences.

At that time Russia was expanding its own empire. Far to the north-east of Mongolia they established a fort by the River Amur. The Manchus regarded the area as part of their own territory and in 1685 they destroyed the Russian settlement. War was averted by negotiations in which Jesuit missionaries acted as interpreters. The result was the Treaty of Nerchinsk, but obscurities in the translation of the Chinese, Russian and Manchurian texts caused difficulties over the frontier line, so a revision was agreed at the town of Kyakhta in 1727. While to this day the Chinese dispute the fairness of the frontier provisions, they agreed to the Russians setting up a consulate, a trading mission and a church in Peking. This now seems the first of the 'capitulations' that caused such ferment in the next century, and led to misunderstandings of dire consequence. For the Chinese it was traditionally quite normal to grant tribute-bearing barbarians quarters for their legation and for envoys to be accompanied by a few merchants; similarly they were permitted to set up a temple of their own – all under the control of the Office for Regulation of Barbarians. For the European, however, a legation's purpose was to conduct continuous diplomatic relations as between equal sovereign states, and his merchants were not being favoured with the opportunity for an ad hoc business venture but entitled to trade fully and permanently throughout the country. This was quite contrary to how the Chinese viewed matters, and conduct which they regarded as perfectly correct was considered by the Europeans to be a breach of treaties. That Chinese superiority and Western arrogance would inevitably collide was now written in the stars.

In the seventeenth and eighteenth centuries the behaviour of Dutch and Portuguese embassies to the Emperor reinforced the Chinese conviction of their superiority, because these Westerners submitted to ceremonies of, in appearance, vassalage. First they brought a huge number of presents – in Chinese eyes, tribute – which could run into hundreds of objects. And second, they performed the kowtow in the presence of the Emperor – i.e. lying prostrate and knocking their head on the floor nine times, standing up to bow after every third time. In due course, when the relationship with Russia was being formed, the Russian ambassador refused to kowtow and had to leave. The British dealt with the problem differently.

In September 1792 a party of a hundred people including musicians set out from Portsmouth, England, for China. They were the company of Earl Macartney, appointed Ambassador Extraordinary and Plenipotentiary to the Emperor of China for whom he carried a letter from King George III of Great Britain. This letter, full of flowery tributes to the Emperor 'whom Providence had seated upon the throne for the good of all mankind', likewise puffed the achievements of his Britannic Majesty in gaining victories over his enemies 'in the four quarters of the world' but was now bent not on conquest but 'increasing the knowledge of the habitable globe'. Consequently he had 'an ardent wish to become acquainted with those celebrated institutions of [the Emperor's] populous and extensive empire'; he wrote of extending 'the bounds of friendship and benevolence,' and extolled 'the benefits which must result from an unreserved and amicable intercourse between such great and civilized nations as China and Great Britain'.

The Ambassador's secretary, Sir George Staunton, was subsequently to publish a detailed journal. On arrival in China, he quickly became aware of native suspicion and antipathy towards foreigners. The English in particular were suspect because of the supposed aid they had given the Rajah of Nepal whose incursions into Tibet had led to the Chinese takeover of that country. The Embassy had to leave behind on the coast an intended gift of guns and barrels of gunpowder. Its sixty-crate train of baggage and presents carried to Peking was adorned by the Chinese with banners reading, 'Ambassador bearing tribute from the country of England'. No opportunity was lost by senior Chinese officials – whom Westerners called mandarins, as they called the Manchus Tartars, and the Emperor the Great Cham – to be scornful of Western products and achievements.

To Sir George, however, the strange ways of the Chinese were matters of wonderment – female foot-binding, the universal currency of holed copper coins, the abacus, the pagodas, the style of the sedan chairs in which the mandarins were borne, the absence of any white clothing except on mourners, wheel-barrows equipped with sails, an ancestral tablet worshipped at in every house. He noted that it was an intensely patriarchal society where familial mutual help extended even to the remotest links, averting much of the need for public assistance; but if he rarely saw a beggar he learnt how impoverished people exposed their unwanted babies to die, especially girls since boys were essential to carry on ancestor worship. 'Almost every intercourse between superiors and inferiors,' he noted, was accompanied by an exchange of gifts (a practice which in transactions between Western traders and local mandarins readily descended into corruption).

Peking, approached by a broad granite-paved highway and marble bridges, was a revelation. From its base, twenty feet wide, the surrounding wall, tapered in steps to a height of forty feet, with a crenellated parapet wide enough for several horsemen to ride abreast and interspersed with many-storeyed watchtowers. The principal street was a hundred feet wide, unpaved since the Mongols tore up the slabs as unfriendly to their horses and was hence full of dust, which men sprinkling water strove to keep down. The roadside was jam-packed with houses, usually of a single storey, in front of which were busy shops. Notable features were the Temples to Heaven (round, copying the vault of the sky) and to Earth (square, which the ancients had thought the world to be). The magnificence of the place lay, however, in the walled-off area called the Tartar City. Here, within its fourteen square miles, was the Imperial Palace section – a complex of great buildings and courtyards amid trees and elegant and beautiful gardens, and all around were large parks and woods with pavilions and canals and artificial hills, valleys, and lakes with many boats a-sailing.

Hospitably received, the embassy was accommodated in a palace and Sir George could observe something of the court. Eunuchs were creeping back into favour and he was struck by their ugliness, with their hairless wrinkled faces, often painted, and their high girlish voices. The awesome majesty of the Emperor hung over all. Only he and his immediate family could wear yellow, upon which only he could have a five-taloned dragon embroidered; only he could wear a large pearl on his bonnet or use streets designed solely for him; and no one could approach him but on their knees.

The Emperors' monopoly of the pearl as an adornment contrasted with the sixteen kinds of button which mandarins wore on their caps, for the shape and colour of these objects betokened the wearer's rank – a six-sided, dark purple stone for the highest, a round silver button for the lowest. Purple stone wearers were to the forefront in the mandarins' curiosity about the British presents for the Emperor which were exhibited in a separate building. They included a Western carriage (from which the box the driver sat on had to be removed, otherwise the driver would be above the Emperor), Wedgwood vases, scientific instruments such as a telescope, a planetarium, various mechanical devices, and – whether greeted with delicate oriental mirth the record does not say – a volume of portraits of the nobility of Great Britain.

Before the Earl could be received by the Emperor, two awkward issues of protocol had to be resolved. The first was getting a Chinese translation of the King's letter, since Chinese translators feared severe punishment for the slightest error in etiquette or translation in something so intimately touching the Emperor (the usual punishment of an interpreter required the culprit to sit down on both knees with a long bamboo pole inserted behind them: two men – one on each side – pressed hard on his shoulders while standing on the pole, their movement towards or away from him increasing or easing the painful pressure on his legs; but error in relation to the Emperor invited death). When with help from missionaries the problem of the letter was overcome and the top mandarins with much parleying approved the final draft, the second difficulty proved more wearisome, namely, the kowtow. The Ambassador steadily maintained that to prostrate himself in front of the Emperor would be demeaning to his Britannic Majesty whom he represented. Weeks of wrangling with the insistent mandarins followed. At length the Earl came up with a brainwave: he would kowtow if a mandarin of a rank equal to his own kowtowed to a portrait of George III, which would be brought from the legation to a private room. The cold reception of this idea led to further lengthy negotiations until at last a procedure was agreed with the president of the tribunal of rites.

On the appointed day soon after dawn the Emperor Ch'ien-lung took his seat on a single throne on a dais in a great specially pitched tent. Before a brilliantly robed assembly the Ambassador, dressed in a long cloak over a richly embroidered velvet suit, on which he wore the diamond-encrusted Order of the Bath, advanced bearing his King's letter in a square box of gold adorned with jewels. He carried it with both hands held above his head and, amid a silence of almost religious awe, went up the steps to the foot of the throne where he knelt on one knee, bowed, and gave a short address. The Emperor, taking the box and placing it next to him – of course he well knew the contents of the letter in advance – responded in friendly tones. Indeed in the ensuing ceremonies, banquets, staging of brilliant acrobatic feats and other entertainments, the Son of Heaven who was in his eighties and would shortly voluntarily abdicate after an immensely successful reign of sixty-three years, was the soul of affability. He gave a bejewelled jade sceptre to the Ambassador who could account his goodwill mission soundly accomplished, even if he obtained no trade concessions, when in due course he departed for home. History, however, would all too soon conspire to account it all a piquant waste of time.

Sir George Staunton's journal, as that of an embassy of the Dutch East India Company a few years later, supplemented the many missionaries' reports of the seventeenth and eighteenth centuries, revealing the curiosities and wonder of China to avid Western readers. All things Chinese became fashionable, especially in France, and the European Enlightenment was to an extent fuelled by conceptions of Chinese civilization. Voltaire, Leibnitz – whose work on the binary system was indebted to the *I Ching*, the Book of Changes – and Montesquieu all wrote in praise of it; but sometimes they, and some non-Jesuit visitors, wrote in dispraise so that there began to develop an ambivalence in European attitudes which has continued to this day.

There was, however, no ambivalence in the important impact of many Chinese ideas, as distinct from inventions. For example, the modern science of demography owes much to the Chinese practice, since the Han, of census-taking – first carried out in French Canada in 1665 and then in Sweden in 1749. Likewise the system of examination for public service applicants was adopted by the French revolutionaries in 1791, the East India Company in India in 1800, and the British Government in 1855. Aesthetic standards were greatly affected by the beautiful Chinese blue-and-white porcelain, as was their design of gardens, furniture and knick-knacks; while their love of nature was one of the impulses behind the Romantic Movement. More subtle, and ironical in view of the stagnation of science in China in this period, was the influence of Chinese thought in releasing Western science from its concept of the universe as a machine with a Driver, and substituting a system of cooperative forces ordering the cosmos: Western scientists turned their attention to magnetism, fields of force such as gravity, propagation of many phenomena by waves, and the self-regulation of organisms in an organic totality.

The last years of the Emperor Ch'ien-lung's life were sorely tested by perturbations that convulsed the even tenor of the Ch'ing Dynasty. The worst of these was caused by a cult which battened on to the numberless landless peasants and rural poverty resulting from the massive population increase, which too led to the frustration of educated men as competition for official posts became intense and widespread corruption took root. The cult, originating in the eleventh century, was based on a mishmash of Buddhist, Taoist and Manichaean beliefs and was called the White Lotus Society. Its followers, in a network of devotional congregations, believed that a future Buddha would usher in peace and plenty, while a 'prince of light' would bring light to a world of ultimate cataclysm, although essentially the Society promised salvation for the soul and cures for bodily sickness.

As the sect spread through central China, in 1793 the government ordered an investigation of it. Predatory elements in local government used this enquiry to terrorize the villages, igniting resistance by the White Lotus armed militia, soon joined by gangsters from the forests. They attacked administrative posts in the villages and despoiled great swathes of the countryside. The government was simultaneously trying to suppress an uprising, begun in 1795, of the aboriginal Miao people in the far south against the flood of Chinese immigrants (another consequence of the population explosion) – a rising not finally put down until 1806. In the meanwhile the government at first sent forth armies to catch the White Lotus guerrilla leaders, but the Ch'ing military had lost its edge, and the misappropriation of funds to line the officers' pockets did not help. Eventually a system was established of organized local defences and village militia reinforced by mercenaries. The White Lotus began to crumble, and its largest force, over 100,000 strong, was crushed in 1805. But the dynasty had been dealt a damaging blow, its martial prowess brought into question in front of the looming Western powers and its treasury ruined by the cost of the war. Nor did the White Lotus go away: in the first half of the nineteenth century it bred numerous local rebel offshoots such as the Heavenly Principle Society and the Eight Diagrams Society. As if all this were not enough, coastal piracy flourished and the criminal brotherhood called Triads which, imported from Taiwan (Formosa) in 1786, was growing apace throughout southern China and has endured to this day.

The great and aged Emperor Ch'ien-lung whose final year had been so harrowing abdicated in 1796 because he considered it unfilial to occupy the throne longer than his illustrious grandfather. One of the unhappy legacies of his reign was the corruption which now controlled the bureaucracy, a culture introduced by the Emperor's favourite minister, Ho-shen. It continued through the reign of the next two Sons of Heaven – Chia-ch'ing (1796–1820) and Tao-kuang (1821–1850). Under the latter the Grand Secretariat was largely replaced by a Grand Council and generally a measure of integrity returned to government under the guidance of the chief minister, an uncompromising Confucianist Peking official called Ts'ao Chen-yung, although the downside of this was much inertia in the administration. For example, he advised the Emperor not to bother with the problems set out in the flood of memorials constantly reaching him but simply to scan the memorials for errors in calligraphy or composition, and punish any transgressors accordingly.

In such a climate it is not surprising that power increasingly ebbed from the central government. The process was hastened by the growth of commercialization and privatization. But the overriding element in Chinese history at this period was that spinner of dreams and harbinger of nightmares, opium.

CHAPTER TWENTY-SIX

Ch'ing: Opium Wars and the Taipings – II

*D*uring the decades which closed the eighteenth century and opened the nineteenth, China's chief ports for trading with the West were Macao, where the Portuguese had long held sway, and, more importantly, Canton, where a monopoly was asserted by the British East India Company, that cornerstone of the City of London and the agency for England's acquisition of India. Trade with Canton was a peculiar affair. The imperially appointed Superintendent of Maritime Customs, a mandarin called by Westerners the Hoppo, issued orders to licensed Chinese merchants, called Hongs individually and the Cohong collectively, with whom foreign traders exclusively dealt: they could not engage directly with the Hoppo. Since the latter was obliged to transmit to the Emperor a sizable chunk of custom duties, any discordancy was in no one's interest.

The Cohong made its money from selling tea and silk to the East India Company, which paid half in imports like woven cloth, and – since there were not enough imports – half in American silver currency. The Chinese merchants groaned under the exactions of the officials who corruptly neglected no opportunity to line their own pockets; indeed the Cohong established a fund called the Consoo Fund as a source of protection. While the deterioration in the central government continued apace, with bags of pearls being exchanged for high office and local taxes purloined, with the dire economic straits caused by the White Lotus rebellion, with Triad uprisings and coastal piracy, and with a major flood of the Yellow River for good measure, Peking looked for ever greater contributions from the Consoo Fund and individual merchants as trade with the West boomed, especially in tea.

But this boom – intensified by Americans, whose first ship arrived in Canton in 1785 – meant a severe imbalance in trade. The import neither of Indian cottons nor of articles such as music boxes (called singsongs and soon copied by the Cantonese) could right it. And then the answer was perceived; the import of opium. From 1819 trade in the drug flourished to such an extent that whereas in 1800–1810 China gained about twenty-six million dollars in her world balance of payments, in 1828–36 thirty-six million flowed *out*.

Opium had been used medically since the T'ang period, but following its introduction to the south-east coast by Formosans in 1620 it fell into such disfavour that in 1729 the Ch'ing government banned it. How despite this it became a countrywide addiction no one has been able to explain. Since trading in it was illegal, smuggling started on an ever-increasing scale. At first Macao was the channel until the government clamped down on the dealers, who then moved off-shore; but when in 1831 the East India Company agreed to carry the stuff to Canton from India, where the bulk of it was grown, imports flowed in. They became a flood when a few years later the British government withdrew the Canton trade monopoly enjoyed by the East India Company, and it was open season for all comers. Rivermen fought and bribed their way up the river system for their cargoes to be distributed by gangsters and Triads, while a leading figure in the India trade, Dr Jardine, sent heavily armed, sleek coastal clippers to sell opium up and down the south-eastern coast, and there were numerous other outlets.

By now the sale of opium was becoming important to Britain's economy: profitably sold in Canton and the proceeds invested with added profit in tea exports to the West, it financed much of the country's further colonization of India. The ban on the trade not only caused immense corruption as the inevitable concomitant of smuggling but highlighted for the British the many restrictions on legitimate trade as well, both in Canton and along the coast. These effectively closed the huge market of the interior to the manufacturers of Manchester and Liverpool whose voices were not the least heard in the battlecry of the age, Frcc Trade. Since the Macarthy Commission, and a later one led by Amhurst, had failed to gain trading concessions, thoughts turned to war, which, an English parliamentary select committee declared, could easily be won and so 'place our intercourse [with China] on a rational basis'.

The way to that war was marked by a number of 'incidents', starting in 1834 when Lord Palmerston as Britain's Foreign Secretary appointed Lord Napier, a Scottish naval officer and sheep-farmer, to be the first British superintendent of trade in Canton. Refused contact with the governor there, he led two warships up the Pearl River but, weakened by malaria, he turned back in the face of a river blockade by the Chinese. While the latter gained an impression of British helplessness, British traders were incensed by what they regarded as an insult to the flag and they agitated fiercely against the ban on trade with the interior and the extortions of local officials. James Matheson, whose company with Dr Jardine would be so prominent in Chinese commerce for more than a century, carried the agitation to England. In 1836, Lord Napier's successor, the rather more aggressive Captain Charles Elliot, was appointed. After a relatively fruitless show of naval force off Canton he awaited events.

In 1836 no less than eighteen million dollars' worth of opium was imported into China. The illegal trade turned numerous gentry and officials in both central and local government into addicts; there were open sales in Peking, and opium divans in many centres; and beside the degradation and criminal activity involved in opium usage, the value of silver rose with the metal's outflow, to the detriment of farmers who had to buy it with their everyday copper currency to pay their taxes. At the imperial court a debate raged, familiar enough in the contemporary West: should the ban be enforced, engendering corruption and lacking practical effect without a reign of terror, or should reality be grasped and the drug legalized, placing it under proper control to eliminate criminality and produce duties greatly boosting state revenue?

Advocates of enforcement won the debate. A fierce clamp-down on dealers brought two thousand arrests. A high official, Lin Tse-hsü, deeply imbued with Confucian rectitude, was in 1838 appointed Imperial Commissioner to end the Canton opium trade. He initiated a moral crusade at the same time as ordering the Hongs to hand over their opium stocks. A token response persuaded him that the president of the local British Chamber of Commerce was the key supplier, and ignoring the delicacy with which foreigners had always been treated, ordered the man's arrest to bring him under Chinese jurisdiction.

Captain Elliot sniffed war. Basing his available warships at the barren rocky island of Hong Kong, he took a small escort to Canton. There he found that the formidable Lin had placed thousands of troops around the foreign settlements – 'factories' – with their hundreds of occupants. To save their lives, Elliot ordered them to surrender their opium stocks at the expense of the British government. An exultant Commissioner Lin duly destroyed the stocks in sea-water ponds filled with lime, and believing that he had the barbarians 'trembling with awe' he demanded that the foreign traders sign a bond vowing never to handle the drug again. By decreeing that a breach of the bond would invoke the death penalty the effect would be to bring any English offender under Chinese, not British, jurisdiction and thus affright Britain's new-found colonialist principles. The conflict moved therefore from the issue of drug-dealing to that of 'territoriality', the Commissioner meeting Elliot's protests with the retort, 'How can you bring the laws of your nation to the Celestial Empire?'

Fearing arrest, the entire community of foreign traders, except the American tea-traders who signed the bond and remained to make windfall profits, moved out of Canton, eventually to the merchant ships anchored at Hong Kong. Convinced that Elliot alone protected crooked opium interests, Commissioner Lin wrote an open letter to Queen Victoria urging the immorality of the opium trade. Her government was in no mood to listen and soon the first shots of the Opium War may be said to have been fired: Lin believed that Elliot harboured the member of a gang of drunken seamen who had murdered a peasant, and he ordered his admiral to board any of the fifty-odd foreign merchant ships with Elliot and seize a foreigner at random as a hostage, whereupon Elliot, believing the admiral was about to attack his entire fleet, in November 1889 sailed up the Pearl River with two lines of warships and loosed a barrage against the admiral's ships, sinking some and dispersing the rest. When news of this reached London, together with Elliot's despatch urging 'immediate and vigorous means' to have the opium trade legalized, the two countries stood on the brink.

The Chinese Emperor decided that the time had come to expel the British for ever which, on the advice of Commissioner Lin, he thought would be easy. He overlooked the fearsome gun-power of the British navy's new iron steamers and the efficiency of their infantry's new percussion-lock, smooth-bore muskets, in contrast with China's antiquated matchlocks, equally antiquated artillery, and badly led, ill-trained forces – not to mention that among its proposed ferocious remedies for dealing with Western gunboats was to send down masters of the martial arts, who claimed the ability to stay underwater for ten hours, to bore holes through their hulls.

In Britain, Dr Jardine led a vigorous campaign supported by three hundred Midlands textile firms, depicting the 'siege of the factories' as another Black Hole of Calcutta and a deadly insult to the Queen. Palmerston despatched a large expedition to be at Elliot's disposal; but amid the clamour when the British parliament debated the issue, a resolution opposed to war was defeated by a mere five votes, Gladstone declaring, 'A war more unjust in its origin, a war more calculated to cover this country with permanent disgrace, I do not know and have not read of.' In truth the British public's unease over the opium trade was submerged in concern for establishing normal trading relations between two civilized countries. This concern Palmerston expressed in a note to the Chinese Emperor with a series of onerous demands.

The British expedition despatched by Palmerston – sixteen men of war, four armed steamers, and four thousand soldiers – entered Chinese waters in July 1840 and bore down on Chusan, south of Shanghai. Faced with a refusal to surrender, the British loosed a bombardment and then looted and occupied the island's town. Whereas the Chinese had previously regarded them as mere pirates they now viewed them as threatening to emulate previous barbarian invasions. The Emperor considered Commissioner Lin, plaintively advising that the British 'appetites are insatiable', a bungler; and he sacked him. His successor was Ch'i-shan, one of the richest men in China, a cultivated scholar and aristocrat of great bargaining skill. He persuaded Captain Elliot to lay off and conduct full negotiations in Canton. On an island in the Pearl River they agreed a peace convention in January 1841.

Although this met some British demands, it enraged both governments. The Emperor declared that the term in it ceding Hong Kong to Britain was a usurpation of power by Ch'i-shan: he had him removed from Canton in chains and confiscated his vast properties. Palmerston was equally furious at Elliot's giving up Chusan, from which he could have dictated much better terms, in exchange for a sterile Hong Kong. He was to be replaced by Sir Henry Pottinger, a stolid Irishman formerly a political agent in Sind.

Meanwhile the Emperor gave the governance of Canton to a triumvirate, which included a stone-deaf general, and he ordered up an Army of Extermination to reinforce the city, where redoubts were rebuilt, waterways dammed, and local militia recruited. Getting wind of this, Elliot moved his fleet up the Pearl, destroyed several forts and reached Canton. At first his threat to the city brought a temporary agreement with the deaf general to reopen trade, but the more bellicose of the ruling triumvirate insisted on aggression. Flaming rafts were launched on the river towards the British fleet which was simply stung into sinking seventy-one Chinese war junks, seizing sixty shore batteries, and decanting forces to occupy the heights above the city. The triumvirate quickly agreed to withdrawal of the Army of Extermination and payment of a six-million dollar 'ransom' within a week, whereupon Elliot lay off to await Pottinger.

The consequences for China were serious. Firstly, the assault caused much looting and disorder, emboldening the local robbers and pirates, who proceeded to create almost a decade of social turbulence in the surrounding provinces. Secondly, some of the British troops around Canton waiting for the ransom to be paid despoiled temples and raped women, inflaming twenty thousand local peasants to want to massacre them with hoes and knives. The Canton officials restored calm, but the belief lingered among the people that they would have triumphed; and thus was kindled an anti-foreigner and anti-official fervour alike, the latter foreshadowing an ominous later anti-Manchuism because the court was thought to be appeasing the foreigners to save its own skin.

Pottinger arrived at Hong Kong – now under British occupation – in August 1841 to command the new and bigger expeditionary force on the way: twenty-five ships of the line, fourteen steamers, nine support vessels, and troopships with ten thousand infantry. He took its advance section north to the important port of Amoy, south of Shanghai. It was guarded by fifty large junks, three forts said to be impregnable, and nine thousand troops, all of which the British swept aside before occupying the city. Pottinger then continued north to the island of Chusan, heavily reinforced but nevertheless occupied in three days; the nearby port of Ningpo soon followed, to become the expedition's winter base.

The plan was for a spring offensive up the Yangtze River to cut China into two. The Emperor welcomed the prospect of a land encounter since, fed on lies by his officials, he believed the British to be militarily incapable. He appointed a cousin, I-ching, commander in chief to destroy the foreigners. I-ching was an accomplished scholar whose sole qualification for the job was directorship of the Imperial Gardens and Hunting Parks.

In Soochow, about seventy miles west of Shanghai, he began assembling an army of over sixty thousand regular soldiers and militia. He encouraged the local gentry to offer their services and so gathered many young scholars, interrupting their study of the Classics and each demanding a personal bodyguard and other perquisites. The regular units came from several provinces and refused to take orders from each others' commanders, while in their huge encampment the scholar-officers made the rounds of tea parties, banquets and poetry contests. I-ching himself spent days devising a contest to decide which announcement of the coming victory was the best written. At last, moving down to Hangchow, a hundred miles west of Ningpo, he had oracles in a local temple consulted about the best day for battle. Inspired by the resultant divining slip's reference to tiger omens, he decided on 3 – 5 a.m. on 10th March 1842, being the tiger-hour on a tiger-day in a tiger-month during a tiger-year. It also happened to be at the height of the spring rainy season, so that the troops slogging through mud to reach their positions, which were out of reach of the mired provision wagons, were wet, exhausted and hungry as they prepared to attack the British.

Tiger-day brought calamity. Sixty per cent of the entire force was detached to guard the general staff. Indeed, only seven hundred aborigines from Szechwan, instead of the 36,000 soldiers planned, moved against Ningpo, and then because they scarcely understood Mandarin, the dialect of their superiors, they believed they were not to carry guns and armed only with knives advanced into the British mines and howitzers; when inexperienced Chinese troops eventually came up in support they were slaughtered in thousands and their blood ran through the streets. A second prong of the attack was doing rather better until critical reserves were not sent in because the commander, feverishly smoking opium, fell into a stupor. A third prong, of fifteen thousand marines, was planned to take Chusan but most became seasick as soon as they embarked and their commander was so afraid of the English that for weeks he simply sailed up and down the coast, periodically sending in false battle reports.

Pottinger's planned offensive up the Yangtze could now be started. Advancing into the most populous and prosperous region of the Empire, he first took the Manchu-garrisoned town of Chapu, found Shanghai undefended and abandoned, and then took Chinkiang, key to the whole river and cutting off that essential carrier of provisions to Peking, the Grand Canal. Chinkiang was defended with ferocity by Manchu bannermen who killed their own children, cut their wives' throats to save them from rape, and rather than surrender hanged themselves. Nanking, once the capital and still a symbol of the realm, lay open before the British.

The Ch'ing court was in ferment. For the Emperor the issue was a moral one – the wrongness of yielding to brute force – and many urged him to fight on. But there were other voices, which urged that the choice lay between danger and safety, not right and wrong. Why, they argued, risk the loss of an empire for mere trading rights? This was the opinion of the Emperor's clansman, the rich and highly polished Ch'i-ying, whom the Emperor therefore appointed imperial commissioner to negotiate a settlement. Ch'i-ying at once sent his emissaries with overtures of peace rushing into the British lines around Nanking just as an attack was imminent.

The negotiations over the following weeks culminated in the Treaty of Nanking, signed aboard Pottinger's flagship on 29th August 1842. In ending the First Opium War it provided that China pay an indemnity of twenty-one million dollars; open to trade by the British the five ports (the so-called 'treaty ports') of Canton, Amoy, Foochow, Ningpo and Shanghai; receive

British consuls at these ports; permit equal relations between officials of corresponding rank; abolish the Cohong monopoly at Canton; impose a uniform moderate tariff on imports and exports; and cede Hong Kong to Great Britain. No word was said about opium, to the continuing illegal trade in which Chinese officialdom turned something of a blind eye, as did the British navy while British, American, and other ships purveyed the stuff up and down the coast for distribution by Chinese dealers.

The Chinese now accepted that the British were not about territorial but trade expansion. Commissioner Ch'i-ying exerted his charm on Pottinger (even proposing to adopt his son as a gesture of friendship) to trim the scope of foreign rights, but with limited success. In 1843 the two men agreed a treaty supplementary to the Nanking Treaty permitting foreign residence in the five treaty ports and some travel outside them; the stationing of gunboats at each of them; jurisdiction by the British over their own nationals. And it included a 'most-favoured nation' clause whereby any benefits accorded to other powers in later treaties would be equally accorded to the British.

With the successive opening up of the treaty ports, legal trade poured through them while the illegal opium trade operated through twice that number of coastal stations, and as the legal trade – especially in tea and silk – flourished, so did the opium trade in order to fund it. The USA and France, and subsequently others, entered into similar treaty arrangements. The French, however, were less concerned with trade than the cause of Catholic evangelism. They obtained the partial revocation of a 1724 ban on Catholic missionaries who had ever since been forced to act almost as a secret society, and now Protestants – largely confined to the treaty ports – were equally tolerated. As for the Americans, their already-vigorous trading with China was stimulated by the repeal in 1849 of Britain's navigation laws, enabling them to trade directly with Britain and between her colonies; and so started the famous clipper ship tea races to London.

The treaty ports presented the curious phenomenon of fragments of Europe scattered along the coast of China. In these tiny quasi-colonies lived, by the 1850s, about five hundred foreigners watched over by their consulates. They dwelt outside the Chinese city, above the foreshore – 'bund' – where shipments and exports were brought to warehouses – 'godowns' – within the compounds – 'factories'. The greatest of the approximately two hundred foreign trading firms were Britain's Jardine, Matheson and Company, and the American Russell and Company of Boston. Such firms also developed ship-owning, banking and insurance services. While Canton remained of great importance, Shanghai took off meteorically, becoming the metropolis of China. The dynamism of these treaty ports was imparted by the relations between the Chinese officials, the Chinese merchants – 'compradors' – the consuls, and the 'taipans' – heads of Western firms. While life in the foreign settlements – 'concessions' – has often been romanticized, in truth much of it had a squalid side, with low Chinese cunning matching high European deceit, and 'squeeze' – bribes – a familiar element.

But trouble was brewing. The hundreds of people crammed in the foreign concessions on the Canton waterfront pressed for access to the city. At the same time local defence associations of villagers and gentry hostile to the British had been developing, leading to years of stone-throwing, beatings and riots, with ugly incidents in the countryside where the British went for relaxation. Exasperated by the denial of access to the city, the British in 1847 sent warships up the Pearl River and they spiked over eight hundred Ch'ing cannons: thereupon Ch'i-ying promised to open the gates within two years. When the British accordingly pressed again two years later; they held off in the face of a mobilized militia, Ch'i-ying having been withdrawn.

It was a dire period of local rebellion, piracy, Triad and associated secret society activity, while opium smuggling engulfed the south coast from Shanghai to Macao; and though the African slave trade had been abolished, the need for cheap labour in plantations from Malaya to Peru led to the opium-traders diversifying into trading in coolies. In 1854 the turbulence along the coast was mirrored in Canton where a movement called Red Turbans threatened the city until put down by the peasant militia and gentry-paid mercenaries, resulting in scores of thousands of executions.

This did not deflect the British, intent not only on access to Canton but on a wholesale revision of the Nanking Treaty. In 1857 Palmerston was returned to office and embarked on a fresh policy of coercing China, signalled by the despatch of a new expeditionary force. After a diversion caused by the Indian Mutiny, it reached Canton at the year-end by which time it had been joined by French forces out to avenge the murder of one of their country's missionaries.

The Anglo-French force of nearly six thousand men launched the Second Opium War by besetting Canton. After a bombardment they mounted the walls, marched round them and sent patrols through the city to capture the governor-general who was sent off to Calcutta where he died a year later. An allied commission was instituted with puppet Chinese administrations and it ruled the place for the next four years. The local militia maintained their hostility with an attack in 1858 which was beaten off, allied patrols penetrated deeply into the countryside, and when a militia headquarters fired on them it was seized and burnt. Gradually the militancy subsided and the Cantonese began to accept the mastery of the barbarians.

Lord Elgin, now in charge of British affairs in China, ordered the allied expeditionary force far northwards. Its capture of the sea portals to Peking and approach to Tientsin a mere seventy-five miles south-east of the capital brought plenipotentiaries hurrying from the Ch'ing government. The blandishment of Ch'i-ying and his colleagues availed little and under protest they signed new treaties with Britain, France, Russia and the United States. The aged Ch'i-ying lost so much face over this that, after putting him on trial, the Emperor, to be 'just and gracious', ordered him to commit suicide. The Tientsin Treaties were indeed burdensome: foreign ministers permitted to reside in Peking; a huge indemnity; a tripling in the number of treaty ports; foreign participation in the coastal and riverine carrying trade; opening of the Yangtze to trade as far as Hankow; modest uniform tariff duties; customs placed under foreign inspectorates; foreign travel in the interior under passports. Moreover, they legalized the opium trade: and so was evil sanctified. With the treaties signed, the allies withdrew, Lord Elgin presently sailed six hundred miles up the Yangtze to confirm the new trade opportunities.

But the war was not over. While Anglo-Chinese arrangements worked well at the treaty ports where, for example, both sides cooperated in trying to control the coolie trade, Peking was not happy. Most especially did the Tientsin Treaties' provision for the posting of permanent foreign resident ministers in the capital to conduct state-to-state relations stick in the traditionalists' craw. Their incorrigible belief was that barbarian delegates were only to visit, and that but once every three or five years, bearing tribute and kowtowing. In March 1859 the Emperor was prescribing that no envoy could have a retinue of more than ten persons, bear weapons or ride in sedan chairs in Peking. No foreign king could claim parity with him who enjoyed the Mandate of Heaven: such was the fundamental principle.

When a chance incident near Tientsin a few months later resulted in four hundred British casualties and their loss of four gunboats, the exultant hawks at court gained an abrogation of the Tientsin Treaties. Anglo-French reaction was sharp. In mid 1860 they despatched over two hundred and fifty ships with twenty thousand men, including a corps recruited from Hong Kong's underworld, to northern China. Soon they crushed the defences outside Tientsin. They had begun entering the town when Peking envoys arrived to propose that allied representatives repair to the capital to negotiate, but the allies insisted on an audience with the Emperor. As their forces moved closer to Peking the Emperor fled to beyond the Great Wall. During the advance the Chinese had seized as hostages some thirty-nine of the allied envoys' party, and when they released only a third of them and executed the rest, the allies looted and burnt the Emperor's Summer Palace north-west of Peking – a once magnificent assembly of pleasure pavilions designed in an extraordinary Sino-baroque style by an Italian Jesuit missionary, girt by elaborate fountains, and with furniture copied from French engravings, the walls hung with mirrors and Gobelin tapestries sent out by the French court in 1767.

The Emperor's young brother, the more conciliatory-minded Prince Kung, was left to come to terms with the barbarians upon their entry into the capital. By the Conventions of Peking, 1860, all the Tientsin Treaties' documents were confirmed except that the indemnity was increased and the Kowloon Peninsula added to the cession of Hong Kong to Great Britain. Leaving a garrison at Tientsin the allies then withdrew, and the Second Opium War was over.

The following year the Emperor died. After some upheaval his son, T'ung-chih, succeeded and the party of his uncle Prince Kung who advocated peace and compromise with the West held sway. A new order became well established: consular jurisdiction over treaty port powers' nationals; foreign administration of concession areas; foreign warships in Chinese waters and troops on Chinese soil; foreign shipping in the coastal trade and inland navigation; tariffs limited by treaty; and presently enlarged opportunities were accorded for trading up the Yangtze River. In the result, trade flourished. The relationship between mandarin, merchants and consuls deepened; foreigners bought up real estate at the trading centres, of which a number became major cities, and many Chinese received an English education.

In retrospect it can be seen that opium was but an element in the Opium Wars of 1840 to 1860 which were fought in the larger interest of trade generally. Their outcome was not the extinction of Chinese sovereignty but its overlaying by the treaty powers. These powers would progressively impinge on China's traditional society and culture, the more so as the increasing speed of steamships and the extension of cable and telegraphic communication propelled China into the Western orbit. Time would show whether the lesson that the Celestial Empire was not quite All under Heaven had been truly learnt.

Yet the perturbation caused by the Western onslaught did not threaten the Ch'ing Dynasty itself. That threat, of far greater moment to China at the time, was posed by the seismic insurrections which rocked the nation from 1851 to 1864, coincidentally with the second of the Opium Wars. It was in fact the ending of the first of those wars with the Treaty of Nanking in 1842 that started the trouble, for the opening up of the Shanghai treaty port diverted trade from Canton northwards, throwing thousands out of work. They added to the already boiling cauldron of disaffection throughout the province of Kwangtung which contained Canton, Macao and Hong Kong, together with its western neighbour of Kwangsi and much of Hunan north of them.

The bubbling brew included disbanded mercenaries no longer needed to fight the British, coastal pirates driven inland by the British navy, survivors of the White Lotus cult, ethnic communities at each other's throats – especially immigrant 'Han' Chinese called Hakkas – militia groups formed for defence by local gentry, and impoverished peasants, all united in the midst of their fighting and pillaging by loathing for the Manchus. It was a scene of utter powerlessness of officials to control the lawlessness, which produced rebellions in 1836 and 1847; and in these years came to be formed the Worshippers of God Society, soon to be known by the blood-soaked name of the Taipings.

The man responsible for the fiercest of all China's internal upheavals hitherto was a tall, bright-eyed man with a sonorous voice, Hamed Hung Hsiu-ch'üan. He was a peasant from just north of Canton; his studiousness was little rewarded by repeated failures in the degree examinations. While in Canton for his second attempt he met a missionary who gave him a work called *Good Words to Exhort the Age*. Whatever the achievements in their worldwide endeavour, Christian missionaries have rarely been harbingers of peace and tranquillity, although the donor of the tome to Hung could have had little notion of the consequences. It had been written by a poorly educated Cantonese under the influence of a British Presbyterian missionary and contained garbled passages from the Bible interspersed with scriptural sermons by the author: it conveyed a fundamentalist Protestant message of God's omnipotence, the vileness of sin and idolatry, and man's choice between damnation and salvation.

After a third failure in the examinations Hung took to his bed and suffered psychotic attacks; in his hallucinations he ranged the cosmos slaying evil spirits and being purified and reborn. Partially recovered he again attempted the examinations in 1843 and, failing, he was full of rage, especially against the Manchus – the contempt of whom for their weakness against the Western barbarians he fully shared with his countrymen. Turning again to *Good Words* he now read it as a call from God: he, Hung, was the younger brother of Jesus Christ, with a sacred mission to bring the world back to the worship of God through Christianity. He wrote a number of tracts and poems aimed at reconciling Christianity with Confucianism, as a result lost his job as a schoolteacher, and set about converting the Hakka in southern Kwangsi. He gained able lieutenants who exploited the countryside's intense inter-communal strife by imparting Hung's vision that united people in religious ecstasy. Hung, under the tutelage of an American Baptist missionary in Canton in 1847, recharged his zeal and in the next few years his association called the God Worshipping Society gained ever-increasing momentum and a growing militancy.

In 1851 the Society's network of congregations came together at a village on the West River: twenty thousand peasants, rural workers, and even Triad members, who had burnt their houses, and let their hair grow without pigtails to demonstrate their anti-Manchu feelings, placed their possessions and themselves at the disposal of what had become a military camp. They affirmed their adherence to the Taipings' rigid discipline and puritanism, and on Hung Hsiu-ch'üan's thirty-eighth birthday proclaimed the Heavenly Kingdom of Great Peace, interpreting Hung's messianic vision as a claim to dominion over the whole Empire of China.

Then they launched a crusade northwards. Inaugurating a new calendar – traditional mark of a regime's legitimacy and, calling on their countrymen to rise against the wicked, evil, and oppressive alien Manchus, they declared their intention to establish a heavenly kingdom on earth. As they penetrated the rich region of the lower Yangtze they fought many battles with the uncoordinated forces of the Ch'ing, losing some, winning some, but fanatically pushing on and on while gathering legions of new followers. By the time they captured Nanking in 1853 their number totalled over two million.

They named Nanking the Heavenly Capital and set about creating a fundamentalist Christian state, symbolized by the instigation of a Western-style Sunday, whose citizens had the righteous knowledge that they were the saved in the battle against the damned. Wine, opium, tobacco, gambling and adultery were banned, along with concubinage and foot-binding since women were treated as equals, with their own armies. All land was God's property, to be allocated by the state to every man and woman in equal lots in furtherance of the Taipings' anti-landlord and anti-wealth doctrines. Hung claimed the title of Sovereign, and his subordinate leaders were dubbed Kings, the most prominent of whom fell into trances the better to transmit divine commands. To help recruiting for the bureaucracy, examinations were instituted, based on Christian themes and Taiping virtues. When the gentry, who did not care for the anti-tradition, anti-establishment and peasant ethos of the Taipings, showed reluctance to enter, they were forced by the threat of decapitation.

It was the gentry class, however, which was finally to mount a proper response to the Taipings as the movement spread north and west, controlling three hundred miles of the Yangtze and bringing over 100,000 square miles under their administration; they even sent an expedition far northwards, where it was only stopped by cold and hunger when almost in sight of Peking. It was a time of mortal danger to the Manchu throne. Not only were its armies in disarray against the Taipings killing their way up from central China and the Western forces thrusting in from the eastern seaboard, but it had simultaneously a substantial second rebellion to deal with. It was by a movement called the Nien. For years remnants of the White Lotus cult had been active in the bandit gangs pillaging the countryside north-west of Nanking, and when in 1855 the Yellow River catastrophically changed its outflow from south to north of the Shantung Peninsula passions were intensified by the inter-community strife of people struggling to survive. An illiterate landlord and salt-smuggler became head of the Nien movement which brought together all the lawless groups into armies, sometimes cooperating with the Triads. It took a decade's striving by the Ch'ing forces for the rising to be put down, success in the end coming from a change in the traditional Manchu cavalry charges to methodical encirclement. The tactician responsible for this defeat of the Nien was a one-time teacher in Peking who had risen high in the administration, Tseng Kuo-fan, fresh from campaigning against the Taipings.

Tseng was the brilliant representative of a new kind of men developed in the countryside by the Taiping uprising. They were the local elite, the gentry and landlords who, compelled by the threat to their lives, property and traditions, militarized themselves and formed rural cadres of militia. Tseng and his colleagues organized this armed resistance to the Taipings on the basis of quality not quantity, in the first place gathering together men bound by lineage. Well-trained and well-led, they were consolidated into what came to be called the Hunan Army, financed with Peking's help by the sale of ranks and titles and a mercantile tax kept out of government control. When augmented by regular Ch'ing troops it proceeded to confront the God Worshippers.

The latter were busy establishing a state within a state from their Heavenly Capital. They redistributed land and lowered rents and taxes. But while the people had to conform to the severely puritanical code demanded by their religion, their leaders – the 'kings' – arrogated privileged rights to themselves, living in luxury and not eschewing concubinage. Before long they descended to a ferocious power struggle marked by assassinations and massacres (in one instance, following the murder of a particularly prominent 'king' who claimed to be the reincarnation of the Holy Ghost, twenty thousand people were slaughtered).

During this period of disorganization (1856–58) the Taipings lost important towns in the mid-Yangtze valley, but there was a resurgence wrought by able new leaders under Hung – 'Sovereign' but increasingly mad and remote – who gained victory in two big battles. They then turned eastward to secure the Yangtze delta as an economic base for an assault up-river. Hung hoped for assistance from the Westerners as fellow-Christians, but the West saw the God Worshippers as immoral, blasphemously superstitious and – more to the point – a threat to trade. Thus not only were appeals to Hong Kong for steamships for the projected advance up the Yangtze rejected, but, when the Taipings threatened Shanghai, the British and French intervened with forces and the provision of the latest artillery and repeater rifles to the Ch'ing. A number of American officers were involved on the West's side, while an outstanding British commander was Major Charles George Gordon, later to be the general who gave his life for his Queen at Khartoum. Skirmishes over several years cleared the approaches to Shanghai while higher up the river Tseng Kuo-fan's armies gradually broke the Taipings: in 1864 they advanced on Nanking.

The walls were breached, the city burnt, and its inhabitants slaughtered. To the end the Taipings fought fanatically, refusing to surrender: in consequence 100,000 of them were added to the death-roll of millions in the far-flung lands once conquered by the God Worshippers. Sovereign Hung, rejecting pleas for him to quit his Heavenly Capital as the enemy closed in, poisoned himself, his body being later found under his palace, wrapped in a yellow satin robe with dragon embroidering. Although some of his followers who escaped and joined the Nien survived until 1868, the destruction of Nanking effectively finished off the Taiping kingdom.

These were not all the dramas played out in the theatre of Ch'ing history during the first seven decades of the nineteenth century. In the vast semicircle of territory stretching for the best part of four thousand miles from Manchuria in the north-east, through Mongolia in the north and Sinkiang in the north-west to Tibet in the west, tranquillity seldom prevailed. Mountain, desert and steppe were occupied by peoples of confused and confusing ethnicity: Chinese, Manchus, Mongols, diverse Turkic-speaking Muslim tribes of Central Asia, and Tibetans. Trade, or rather attempts to obtain opportunities for trade, drove events, for Chinese policy – as the West had painfully learned – was consistently to restrict trade across its frontiers and to tax it when it was allowed.

The British conquest of Nepal in 1816 placed the Union Jack on the border of Tibet, which had been incorporated in the Chinese Empire since 1792, and in succeeding years Britain tried vainly to open up trade with the Kingdom of Snows. The Russians pressed down from the north and so began the Great Game as Britain sought to keep them away from India, but they fared better by advancing along the Amur River in north-west Manchuria, of which country they obtained a large chunk of the north-east by a treaty in 1864 which also gave them trading rights to facilitate the exchange of their furs for tea, consumed with the same enthusiasm in Moscow as in London.

The three Chinese dependencies in the region, namely, Tibet, Mongolia and Sinkiang (Chinese Turkestan conquered in the 1750s), fared variously. Tibet was effectively autonomous and mostly went its own Dalai Lama-led way. The once mighty people of Mongolia were sadly reduced as nomadism gave way to agriculture, the peasantry impoverished by debt inflicted by the intensive intrusion of Chinese merchants, and much of the population was riddled with syphilis. And in Sinkiang, girt about by a frequently rebellious Kansu, by Tibet, Kashmir and Russia, the warriors of East Turkestan waged *jihads* deep into the territory to gain trading rights for their merchants.

By and large, however, despite concessions to the Russians and the Muslims, the Ch'ing government by a mixture of diplomacy, Chinese migration, and the occasional use of force, maintained control. And thus did the Empire enter the fateful final years of the century with its integrity substantially intact.

CHAPTER TWENTY-SEVEN

Into the twentieth century

The Emperor – Hsien-feng – died in 1861 before he could return to his capital after his flight when the Anglo-French troops took Tientsin. His only son, a boy of five, was his heir, enthroned as the Emperor T'ung-chih. The dying Emperor had appointed eight officials to assist the lad but in a *coup d'état* which Prince Kung helped engineer they were disposed of by execution or disgrace, and two Dowager Empresses became the effective rulers of China. One was the late monarch's widow, the other his concubine who was the mother of the new Ch'ing incumbent. The dominant woman in this team was the mother and former concubine: as the Dowager Empress Tz'u-hsi she would bestride the imperial government for the next forty-seven years. The dynasty which she had henceforward to preserve, and which was bruised but unbowed by the events so far in the nineteenth century, confronted two hard facts of life.

One, in the words of a leading minister, was 'the demonic new world of expanding national power'. This meant that while the Chinese departed not a jot from their belief in the superiority of their civilization and culture, there were aspects of the West that needed to be taken serious note of – most especially its advanced technology in general and its armoury in particular. If the West's aim to acquire profit rather than territory was accepted, nevertheless the ever-present risk that it might choose to assert its strengths and be recalcitrant or overbearing called for preparedness. Hence modernization, called 'self-strengthening', became the watchword. Tapping into Western knowledge was an expression of this; indeed, already a score of books had been written on Western production of guns, cannon, mines, bombs and explosives.

There was the relevance also of the second fact of life. This was the deterioration, remarked upon earlier, in the quality of government, notably local government. The ancient values of Confucianism had mouldered into disuse and cried out for revival. 'Government,' wrote a prominent scholar-official, 'depends on human talent, while human talent depends on scholarship.' His Neo-Confucian fellows loudly advocated a renewed application of moral principles, and the classical examination system was reinvigorated. This too was part of the self-strengthening drive, for as a minister wrote in his diary, 'In order to obtain self-strengthening, an improvement in administrative affairs and the search for virtuous talent are after all the urgent tasks; but one concrete effort should be to learn the casting of cannon and the construction of steamships and equipment.'

In support of some reform of the armed forces a few shipyards and arsenals were created, the most important being near Shanghai and down the coast at Foochow – that at Shanghai becoming by 1870 one of the largest industrial enterprises in the world. British and French experts assisted, their governments having already provided the Ch'ing with some of the artillery that helped defeat the Taipings. Attached to these establishments were schools which, staffed with British and French as well as Chinese, combined the teaching of the Classics with that of Western sciences.

The drive for self-strengthening took a further turn in 1872 when thirty Chinese students, mostly Cantonese, arrived at Hartford, Connecticut, USA. The first Chinese to be educated in the United States had graduated from Yale in 1854 and, upon his return, he advocated a scheme for sending Chinese youngsters to be schooled in America. After much debate, fuelled by the knowledge that Japan was sending its sons to Europe to learn gunmaking and shipbuilding, eventually the throne agreed that a hundred and twenty boys should go, aged between twelve and sixteen (the latter instead of the age twenty first proposed, in order to lessen the risk of a parent dying while their offspring was unable to carry out the mourning rites), and that target was reached in 1875. Dispersed among private families and taught with the help of the Connecticut Board of Education, the youngsters soon acquired an enjoyment of baseball with their pigtails tucked under large caps, but they were kept close to their roots by attending lectures on the Sacred Edicts of the Manchu Emperor and making periodic obeisance in the direction of Peking.

Only a sprinkling of their countrymen had visited the West until the American Gold Rush and subsequent railway expansion attracted tens of thousands of immigrant labourers, brought on crowded cargo ships known as 'floating hells'. As the century advanced, 'Chinatowns' grew up in many American cities, and the Chinese ran fruit farms, fished, worked abandoned mines for leavings, toiled in shoe and cigar factories, and set up laundries and restaurants. At first tolerated, they became the objects of trade union hostility, harassment and even lynch mobs: once, over twenty of them were killed in Los Angeles riots, and nearly thirty in Wyoming.

Parallel with the American education scheme, another was initiated, for Europe. This was for more mature students. From 1877, in which year the first Chinese legation in London was opened, Chinese trainees arrived to study at the Royal Naval College in Greenwich, the schools of naval construction at Cherbourg and Toulon, and the school of mines in Paris, while chemistry, law and politics were taught them at King's College in London and also in Paris. Further groups went to Europe between 1882 and 1897.

The self-strengthening movement, both industrially and educationally, was largely financed by customs receipts, especially from the thriving treaty ports. An English employee of the Ch'ing, Robert Hart, organized a highly efficient customs service which netted twenty per cent of the government's total revenue. But in truth the movement produced only a trickle of products and qualified personnel to cope with the advancing forces of modernization and industrialization. A school of languages established in Peking turned out some polished diplomats, but mostly in vain did Western diplomats and well-wishers advocate technical colleges, railway and telegraph systems, and machine-working of mines. There was no matching of contemporaneous Japan's single-minded absorption of Western knowledge and skills, a process greatly helped by its merchants – a class always of but ambivalent status in Chinese society.

The problem was the conservative, not to say reactionary, elements in the Ch'ing government. Appealing to that most powerful imperative in Chinese political thinking, tradition, they believed that to exalt the barbarian by learning from him, copying him, was a heresy and a humiliation. It would lead to a loss of the popular support which was the nation's fundamental need. Confucian principles were squarely against utilitarianism, just as a Confucian cosmological myth blamed the accumulation of flood, drought, and earthquake disasters during these years on Western innovations disturbing the geomantic spirits of wind and water. More rationally, they argued that, whatever its merits, Western technology consumed natural resources which were limited; and it would produce social injustice because the rich by using machines would be richer while the poor becoming jobless would be poorer. Above all, undertakings motivated solely by profit must inevitably end unprofitably. And thus it was that, despite the sustained efforts of highly able reformist ministers and thinkers, progress towards catching up with the West was cautious and slow.

Nowhere was the encroachment of the West more apparent than in the missionary movement unleashed by the Opium Wars' treaties which enjoined toleration of Christianity. For some years France, eager to offset the influence of Britain, had championed Catholic missions; protected by the treaties, they throve, and by the century-end had nine hundred priests. Protestant missionaries from many denominations like Baptists, Methodists and Presbyterians, were supported by numerous societies spawned by the late-eighteenth-century's Evangelical

Revival in Great Britain and the Great Awakening in the USA – the London Missionary Society, the Church Missionary Society, the British and Foreign Bible Society, and the American Board of Commissioners for Foreign Missions – so that by the century's end there were over three thousand Protestant missionaries in China, ninety per cent British or American, and half of them women.

The influence of these people, for the most part brave and dedicated souls, was both good and bad, but in either case significant. As proselytizers of the Christian faith they were a failure: half a century of endeavour produced little more than three-quarters of a million converts – a drop in a potential ocean. But their secular deeds were impressive. They established thousands of schools, orphanages, and centres for teaching the deaf and blind, rehabilitating opium addicts, and providing famine relief. They set up hundreds of hospitals and dispensaries, with medical schools that turned out hundreds of Chinese doctors, and they advised officials on public health, housing sanitation, water-supply, government hospitals and medical education. They vigorously sought to improve the status of women, who traditionally had to be submissive to parent and husband and were denied education and entry to the civil service. They introduced the first girls' schools, and their crusade against the lingering practice of foot-binding was rewarded with a total ban on it soon after the turn of the century. Their own and Chinese presses turned out numerous text books and studies of Western science and mathematics, besides works on British, American and indeed world history and international law. They therefore played an important part in the modernization movement. Missionaries and some of the leading Chinese reformers befriended each other, and when in the 1890s a renewed thrust for reform occurred, it was largely led by Chinese Christian converts from the treaty ports where, of course, Western influence was strongest.

Against these achievements, however, must be set the enormous hostility the missionaries engendered. To begin with, certain courses of conduct vexed, such as the taking of children into Catholic orphanages where they were willy-nilly baptized and brought up, chiefly by nuns, in a Christian environment; sometimes, indeed, money was paid to parents to give up their infants. Missionaries used their position, privileged by extraterritoriality, to interfere in local affairs to obtain converts from the least law-abiding who thereby got protection. Churches were built in disregard of geomancy (*feng-shui*) and the missionaries set themselves in firm opposition to many other cherished beliefs and values like ancestor worship, concubinage, and attendance at festivals, including the theatre, while Confucius was largely scorned.

When peasant outrage welled over into riots, the missionaries used their treaty rights to demand indemnities for any damage done and this was exacted by a local tax; pockets were also hit by the need for extra contributions to the cost of festivals because of the ban on converts' participation. Converts themselves caused irritation by many of them behaving arrogantly under the missionaries' protection. Passions were further inflamed by a stream of scurrilous anti-Christian publications which demonized the missionaries who were said to be committing the foulest sexual and sadistic crimes; and since the West had throughout the century given the Chinese little cause to love it, the strange-looking white men with their big noses, beards and tight clothes – not to mention their supposed addiction to tea and rhubarb, without which they would go blind – became the objects of a hate in which missionaries merged with Europeans generally, all becoming 'foreign devils'. The result was thousands of riotous anti-missionary incidents all over the country.

While what little success the evangelical enterprise enjoyed was among the lower orders of the populace, the scholar-gentry had scant time for it. This was in stark contrast with Japan where thirty per cent of Christian converts were from the samurai, and educated Christians played a prominent part in the intellectual life of the nation. The Christian element in the Taiping's uprising, to which was added suspicions of Christian influence on the earlier dreaded White Lotus cult, seemed for the upper classes of Chinese to confirm the danger of Christianity to the Empire's social and political life. Besides, that religion's very validity had long been questioned. As far back as 1640 Buddhist and Confucian scholars were writing, 'If God is really as good and powerful as Christians claim, how could He permit Adam and Eve to commit a sin so contaminating that it was transmitted to all subsequent generations?'

In one area, however, the missionaries had undoubtedly a positive influence. This was through the reformist books and periodicals produced by Protestant writers from the 1880s and reaching a peak in the 1890s. They were in effect a wake-up call, inspiring many Chinese with a belief in reform – the ideas of progress, of the benefit of scientific advances, and of a new world order of harmony and peace. Even if the Chinese discovered that they could reject God and yet have progress, their debt to the missionaries was still considerable.

The China of this period, as the twentieth century hove into view, presented its immemorial panorama of a vast and superstitious peasant community, about four hundred million strong, mostly spread outside the great cities across the land parcelled for the greater part into small lots clustered around villages, with here and there the estates of scholar-officials, aristocrats, and successful merchants. The latter invested in land under managers from the local elite, called bursary owners, who actually lived as a rule in nearby towns and used local officials to enforce payment of rents.

The peasants mostly farmed wheat and rice, but many supplemented their income by hand-spinning and weaving cotton. They sold it, at one of the 63,000 local markets, for making clothes which all but the upper classes wore. Imports and machine mills had not yet made the impact they would in the next century, and so the industry flourished. Tea-processing too was an important handicraft industry until the 1880s when Indian and Ceylon (Sri Lanka) teas began severely affecting exports, but silk-weaving on handlooms in central and southern China brought steadily increasing trade. At the same time urban handicraft factories produced soy-bean oil for Europe and Japan, besides fireworks, fans, bamboo furniture and Chinese medicines.

As the century closed, the Empire moved, ever so slowly in the teeth of conservative opposition, towards industrialization and rather less slowly into debt. The first railways were built and telegraph systems established, but they were financed by foreign loans; an attempt at floating a domestic loan failed. It was therefore in a deteriorating financial climate that foreign relations problems had to be faced.

In 1866 Thomas Wade, who became the British minister in Peking, had memorialized the government on the advantages not only of technical training and industrial modernization but of establishing diplomatic representatives abroad to foster 'a warm feeling between governments'. In consequence, with Prince Kung's authority an official investigative committee was sent forth. It was well received in the half-dozen European capitals it visited, and returned with detailed descriptions of Western social customs, tall buildings, gaslights, elevators and machines, but little of political institutions. Another mission went overseas in 1868, under the retiring American minister in Peking whom Prince Kung wanted to dissuade the USA and Europe from trying to force the pace of change, and indeed a strong measure of cordiality was achieved.

But that, alas, was the last chance of East and West coming together in friendship, for it was swept aside, first by a wave of anti-Christian feeling in the 1870s. At the town of Tientsin near Peking the Catholic orphanage's practice of paying for orphans brought into it encouraged villains, called 'child brokers', to kidnap children for the money, and this plus the high mortality rate arising from the nuns' keenness on having sick children to baptize, enraged the locals who were further inflamed by rumours that the orphanage children were being bewitched, their bodies mutilated, and their hearts and eyes torn out for medicines. When an official went to investigate he found nothing wrong, but a mob had gathered and the French consul who was attending fired a shot, killing the official's servant. The mob promptly killed the consul and his assistant and burnt down the orphanage and church. The strain this incident imposed on international relations was intense, but the French were distracted by their war with Germany and closed the affair by accepting the proposals of a leading mandarin: compensation of half a million dollars, the execution of eighteen of the rioters, and a letter of apology from the Chinese Emperor.

The mandarin's name was Li Hung-chang; he along with Prince Kung may be accounted the most important of nineteenth century Chinese statesmen. Following a distinguished part in suppressing the Taiping and Nien rebellions he became a leading exponent of self-strengthening. A public career of fifty years would culminate in 1896 with a triumphant trip across the world when he was received by the Kaiser and Bismarck, Queen Victoria and President Cleveland.

The foreign diplomats who, in fulfilment of the Opium Wars' treaties, had taken up residence in Peking in 1861 were for years denied audience of the Emperor. There was some excuse while he was a boy but after he came of age and in 1873 assumed personal rule – albeit entirely under the thumb of the Dowager Empress – the diplomats' claim became irresistible. Protracted negotiations about the rituals to be observed finally brought agreement that the resident ministers upon admittance to the royal presence could simply bow and not kowtow. They were convened to meet at the Pavilion of Purple Light (a sly thrust by the traditionalists, since this was the venue for the reception of tributary envoys) at 5.30 a.m. on a certain summers day, but the Son of Heaven did not appear until 9 a.m., when the exasperated British, American, Japanese, Russian, French and Dutch ministers presented their credentials. The episode augured ill.

In 1874 Lord Salisbury, head of the India Office in Disraeli's ministry, espoused the idea of a mission to investigate whether a back door to China might be opened by way of a proposed railway from Burma to Yunnan. When China agreed, a young British vice-consul called Margary went up the Yangtze to the Burmese border to await the mission. He disregarded warnings that the area was infested with Burmese anti-foreign guerrilla bands, one of which in fact killed him. With no justification under international law Britain demanded redress from China. When China did not respond as he wished, Wade the British minister in Peking withdrew his legation to Shanghai amid rumours of war. To avoid a breach, China agreed to compensate the bereaved family, to open more treaty ports, and other concessions including the sending of a letter of apology from the Emperor to Queen Victoria. It was the diplomat entrusted with this letter who stayed on to set up the country's first foreign legation, noted above as established in London in 1877. It was followed by legations in Paris, Berlin, Spain, Washington, Tokyo and St Petersburg. China joined the world.

The country's scholars and conservative gentry, however, did not see matters that way. They insisted that historically barbarians were transformed by Chinese civilization, not the other way about; that westernization and foreign association were disgraceful; that appointments abroad were akin to banishment; and that no man of rectitude would wish to engage in foreign affairs. But wished or not, foreign affairs were to become of mortal concern.

The Great Powers emerged from the Industrial Revolution with a lust, fed by nationalism and evangelism, for empire – for converts and markets, and all not without a little avarice. Events such as the end of the American Civil War, the Meiji Restoration in Japan, the unification of Italy and of Germany, and the opening of the Suez Canal (1869), released energies and opportunities for expansion which mighty armaments made possible. China, with its ruling Ch'ing Dynasty under the Dowager Empress Tz'u-hsi in decline as corruption spread ever deeper, with its lack of any real progress in self-strengthening, and alike sinking into debt and lacking a substantial military organization, seemed like a great ripe plum waiting to be plucked. Only rivalry between the powers precluded such plucking: instead, they whittled away frontier areas and tributary states.

Thus Japan laid claim to the Ryukyu islands north of Taiwan (Formosa), reinforcing the claim with a threat to invade the latter, a Chinese possession. When the Chinese found that defence would be ineffective – their guns, cast by one of their arsenals, proved to be capable only of firing salutes and burst if real shells were used – they initiated negotiations which ended with Japan's formal acquisition of the Ryukyus.

After Japan, Russia. During the Muslim rebellion in Sinkiang – Chinese Turkestan – the Russians had seized a north-western area called Ili from the river that ran through it. Once the rebellion had finally been put down in 1877, four years of negotiation followed as China sought the return of the Ili territory. They were tense years as Russia threatened war, sending twenty-three warships to demonstrate off the Chinese coast and contemplating a thrust from Siberia through Manchuria to Peking. The Chinese called in Charles ('Chinese') Gordon to help them and he urged parleying instead of the war wanted by a faction at court. His arguments prevailed and in 1881 the Treaty of St Petersburg restored most of Ili to China. But Russian expansionism was not abated.

Next, France. The fervently Confucian state of Vietnam, known to the Chinese as Annam, was a tributary of China, but the French had long been involved there through Jesuit missionaries. An armed invasion by France forced the Vietnamese into a treaty (1874) making their country a French protectorate and its southern end, called Cochin China, a French possession. China refused to accept the treaty. The bellicose faction at court pressed for war, but on the advice of Li Hung-chang no less than a decade of negotiations ensued, punctuated by military Sino-French clashes with varied fortunes on each side, until ultimately in 1885 Li concluded a treaty with France confirming the 1874 treaty.

The following year Burma, another tributary of China, was reduced to a British protectorate, the Burmese being permitted a tribute payment to China but once in every ten years. And now Japan, not content with the Ryukyus, really began to assert itself.

Having hurtled into dynamic modernization under the stimulus of the West, it was developing its ambition to establish a protective cordon of acquired territory – a policy whose extremes of expression would many decades hence bring upon itself the hell of Hiroshima. It turned its attention to China's leading tributary state, Korea. That strongly sinicized kingdom had already caught the eye of France and the USA – the former seen off by a force sent to inflict punishment for a Korean massacre of Catholic priests, and the Americans withdrawing after a bombardment in retribution for the burning of a merchantman sent in vain to demand trade. The Japanese were more insistent. With a massive show of force, including a naval bombardment, it exacted a number of concessions, among them Korea's acknowledgement that it was an independent state, no longer under the suzerainty of China. The Ch'ing court tamely acquiesced in this by the Japan – Korea Treaty of Kanghwa, 1876.

However, internecine struggles in Korea between pro-Chinese and pro-Japanese factions culminated in the assassination in China of the pro-Japanese leader, his body being sent to Korea for mutilation and a warning to traitors. Japan deemed this an affront and sent an army. Li Hung-chang's efforts to get Russian and then Britain to intervene were as fruitless as American pleas for peace. When the Japanese sank a ship with Chinese reinforcements, drowning 950 soldiers, China and Japan declared war on 1st August 1894. Within seven months the Japanese drove across Korea from south to north and into Manchuria, then into Shantung, routing Chinese land and sea forces. The Japanese military machine, assisted by English and German advisers, had become simply too well-trained, well-led and well-equipped for the shaky Celestial Empire.

With the suicide of China's naval commander and Japan poised to attack Peking, Li Hung-chang was empowered to make peace. At Shimonoseki on the Japanese island of Kyushu he signed a treaty whereby China recognized Korea as independent with no liability to render tribute, agreed to pay a huge indemnity, opened itself to Japanese commerce, and ceded Taiwan to Japan. It also ceded the Liaotung peninsula, that southern segment of Manchuria just across the bay from Tientsin, hard by Peking, despite which the Ch'ing court duly ratified the treaty.

As matters turned out, under pressure from Russia, France and Germany, Japan agreed to disgorge the Liaotung peninsula. However, only a year or two later Russia occupied Port Arthur at the tip of the peninsula and obliged China to grant a twenty-five-year lease of the place as well as the right to build railways in Manchuria. This Russian move was made on the pretext of protecting China from the Germans who, reacting to the murder of two of their missionaries, had seized the port of Kiaochow in the north of Shantung and extracted a ninety-nine-year lease of it, together with the right to build railways in the peninsula.

Not to be outdone, Britain added to its hold on Hong Kong, Canton and Shanghai, plus a wide arc of territory above the latter two, by obtaining a twenty-five-year lease of the port at the northern tip of Shantung and a ninety-nine-year lease of the New Territories opposite Hong Kong. Furthermore, Japan gained rights round the southern port of Amoy, and France got a ninety-nine-year lease of Kwangchow Bay south of Macao as well as rights in the far-flung adjoining territory. It was as if China lay like a prostrate dragon while circling vultures tore off strips of its flesh, although the appetite of the Foreign Powers was less for territory than for commercial concessions within 'spheres of influence'.

The United States held off, being preoccupied by the Spanish war and the Philippine Revolution, but when these were over it accepted British proposals for a so-called Open Door policy. This sought to preserve the treaty port system but to respect China's territorial integrity and sovereignty. More or less acquiesced in by the other Powers, the Open Door served, together with rivalry during the heyday of imperialism, to dampen down the scramble for concessions (often referred to as the partitioning of China).

Thus preserved, the Ch'ing Dynasty tottered on. There had been no lack of belligerent voices in the government urging a vigorous stand against the West and Japan, but they had been overridden by that latest in the line of remarkable women who have played a conspicuous and disastrous rôle in Chinese history – the Dowager Empress Tz'u-hsi. She had been the effective ruler for over thirty years and was now in her sixties. Having been Co-Regent during her infant son T'ung-chih's brief life as Emperor and again after appointing as his successor her young nephew Kuang-hsü, she had become sole Regent when her partner in office died in 1881; and although ostensibly retired when Kuang-hsü assumed the throne at the age of eighteen in 1889, she still directed affairs.

Daughter of a Manchu noble and only about five feet high, she retained the beauty which had originally gained her entry to the harem of the Ch'ing court. She retained also her immense charm and exquisite manners, although she could be forceful and imperious. A foreigner found her character 'the more complex, intricate, baffling, inscrutable and exasperating each time, and the longer one confronts it'. Portraits reveal her seated in some magnificence on her throne dressed in a richly brocaded gown with a great web of pearls draped about her shoulders and breast, with her nine-inch fingernails brightly painted, and wearing a lavishly jewelled bonnet adorned with the large imperial pearl.

Within the Tartar City (the northward adjunct of the Chinese City) of Peking, lay the Yellow or Imperial City, and within it the Purple or Forbidden City where the Dowager Empress dwelt. Here behind great gates were gilded palaces, pavilions, temples and towers, with names like Palace of Accumulated Elegance, Rain Flower Pavilion, Precious Moonlight Tower, Hall of Protecting Harmony, Studio of Eternal Spring. They were interspersed with vermilion columned courtyards, marble-staired porches with eaves carved in the shape of dragons, lacquer-screened verandahs overlooking lotus pools and flower gardens, and spacious galleries leading to chambers fragrant with incense. No drone here of the West's dark satanic mills, no thunder of naval salvo, no sigh of toiling peasant – no murmur at all of the world beyond the thirty-foot-high walls of the city could penetrate Her Majesty's seclusion which she shared with her nephew the nominal incumbent of the Dragon Throne, his wife and concubines, and diverse princesses, all attended by eunuchs who had to be Chinese and slave girls who had to be Manchu. Thus, hidden and mysterious – only in the past few years had any Westerner been permitted to set eyes on her – and so sacred that to criticize her was to invite death, she ruled the vast Empire in the name of her subservient nephew.

Surrounded by corrupt eunuchs, whose revived prominence testifies that there had actually been a further deterioration in government, and by advisers who swayed her this way and that; unsupported by any national unity of will as many in the upper classes became increasingly anti-Manchu; and with her armies under-organized, under-equipped and so ill-trained that the military examinations still focused on archery and swordsmanship, she was untouched by reality. Thus, despite the state's precarious finances which compelled it to borrow heavily from the Russians, the British and the French, she lavished millions on building and laying-out a gorgeous Summit Palace some hours' drive from Peking.

Small wonder then that for a long time she little heeded the intellectual convulsion that seized China in the 1890s. The self-strengthening movement was given new impetus by the humiliation of defeat at the hands of Japan, traditionally despised as inferior. A group of young Cantonese scholars sparked the process. Their leader was one K'ang Yu-wei. Having intensively studied literature as well as Confucius and Mahayana Buddhism, he addressed a series of memorials to the throne urging modernization – Westernization – in every sphere; a nationwide system of Confucian churches, together with the replacement of the traditional measurement of time, that is, by dynasty and reign, by the years elapsed since the date of Confucius' birth; and the introduction of Western knowledge into the examination system. Above all, by advocating a constitutional and parliamentary method of government, he introduced for the first time the concept of democracy. Behind his proposals, however, was the Confucius-inspired moral quest for an ideal human community from which the misery which pervaded the world would be banished, although at their core was a nationalist belief in the state's necessity, if the Western threat to its integrity and Confucian ethos were to be fended off, to be wealthy and powerful. K'ang's ideas, expressed in lectures he gave to an academy he established and in numerous publications, spread widely and influentially through the scholar-gentry class.

The defeat by Japan persuaded K'ang that to attain constitutional government, reform at the top was insufficient: there had to be 'development from below'. He and his fellow reformers set up 'study societies', first in Peking and then elsewhere, to educate and mobilize the gentry; and they deployed that invaluable instrument of propaganda, newspapers, of which no fewer than sixty were ultimately launched. One of them, for example, published in Shanghai, contained vivid contributions by a K'ang student, who argued that technological progress could only be made effective by political reform releasing the collective dynamism of the nation, the foremost need to achieve this being the removal of the ancient monarchy, orientated as it was towards maintaining by repression the power of the dynastic regime. A fellow reformer went so far as to attack the whole traditional social order underpinned by the basic Confucian doctrine of the Three Bonds – the obedience owed by subject to ruler, wife to husband, son to father – which he vigorously asserted were perverse, corrupting and repressive.

Such radical ideas were too much for the many moderate adherents the reform movement had by now produced. Even in centres where liberal principles had begun to flower, both moderates and conservatives united in what they perceived to be an assault on the sacred values and institutions of the nation, in no particular more evident than in the proposed use of Confucius' birth to measure time – clearly a treasonous threat to the dynasty. The consequent backlash caused a clamping-down on the radicals, and extensive if incomplete suppression of 'study societies' and newspapers alike. But then, in June 1898, officials were pitched into a state of high alarm: the Emperor summoned K'ang Yu-wei to expound his views at a personal audience.

Since 1889 when the eighteen-year-old Emperor Kuang-hsü had formally assumed power, the Dowager Express had forgone her regency but continued to keep a tight rein on affairs. This, however, was less the cause of an increasing rift between them than her nephew's interest in Western knowledge. In 1894 after three years of studying foreign languages under foreign teachers, he began reading the works of the reformers, and when in the following year the Dowager Empress learnt that he was reading translations of Western writers she put a stop to all his tutorial studies save traditional Chinese learning. His growing addiction to Western thought disturbed her the more because by now factions were emerging in court with moderate reformers fiercely at odds with radicals.

The latter were encouraged by K'ang Yu-wei's arrival in Peking in 1897 to renew his reformist campaign. In memorials to the Emperor he proposed the drafting of a constitution and calling up a national assembly, as well as measures to concentrate authority in the hands of the Emperor and his radical advisers, which would strip the court and bureaucracy of their power. As soon as the first memorial reached him Kuang-hsü had K'ang's writings brought to him, prompting his June 1898 summons.

The audience lasted for hours. In urging wholesale institutional changes K'ang assured the Emperor, 'After three years of reform China could stand on its own. From then on, China would daily make progress and outstrip all other countries in terms of wealth and power.' The young Emperor was so fired up that he immediately initiated the explosive period called the Hundred

Days. Imperial edict after edict was issued to energize reform in every aspect of the nation's commercial, educational and institutional life. Almost every one of K'ang's ideas was adopted except those for a constitution and national assembly, but even here the Emperor announced his readiness to discuss fundamental reform.

Officialdom was in ferment. Not only did the decrees represent an ideology abhorrent to traditionalists but they also undermined both traditionalists' and moderates' vested interests: a revamped examination system with a Western bias threatened the career prospects of vast numbers of literati; and a streamlining of government departments, a bypassing of bureaucratic channels, a reform of the military, and the appointment of young radicals to office – all corroded the position of countless officials. Moreover the programme defied the Dowager Empress as well as threatening her leading eunuchs.

She did not stand idly by. With her strong palace faction she quietly consolidated her power, notably by putting a trusted protégé in command of all armies in north China. When, in September of 1898, the Emperor appointed young reformist scholars to the Grand Council itself, she struck. On the 21st of the month she staged a *coup d'état*, stripping the Emperor of power and placing him under house arrest. Then she dismissed and arrested many of the people in K'ang Yu-wei's movement, executing six of them; one prominent reformer escaped on a Japanese gunboat, while British officials helped K'ang himself to flee to Hong Kong, and thence Japan. The Dowager Empress embarked on her third regency 'to give instruction on administration' and revoked every important edict promulgated during the One Hundred Days.

She had apparently dealt the reform movement a deadly blow, but she could not hold back its consequences – the widespread demands for change expressed by a new phenomenon, public opinion, and the emergence of a class of intelligentsia distinct from the class of scholar-gentry who had traditionally sustained the imperial dynasty. For the moment, however, the stage was taken by new and fearsome characters.

The setting was the widespread rural misery and disaffection caused first by the inundation in 1898 of hundreds of villages by the Yellow River bursting its banks, and severe floods elsewhere, followed the next year by a serious drought. The belief took hold that these calamities were caused by the foreigners, whose propagation of their religion offended the spirits and whose commercial activities, such as railway-building and mining into mountains, disturbed the harmony between man and nature. The resultant loathing and fear of missionaries, and indeed of all foreigners, were vigorously exploited by a secret society descended from the formidable White Lotus cult and developed throughout the 1890s in the provinces north of the Yangtze. Its name, derived from the callisthenics practised by its members, was Righteous and Harmonious Fists, and since the Chinese word for fists could be translated as boxer, Europeans called the society the Boxers.

Its pantheon of legendary and historical figures reflected its nationalistic character, and it was based squarely on superstition: by magic arts – charms, incantations and rituals – its members believed themselves endowed with supernatural powers that gave them immunity from bullets, enabled them to fly, and invoked the aid of the spirits in battle. Being fanatically anti-foreign they scorned guns, preferring swords and lances. These were tipped with red, which was the colour of their turbans and sashes and of the cloth used to bind their sleeves and ankles. With their wild loose hair and movement in prescribed steps they presented a terrifying spectacle, reinforced by their barbaric conduct in the widespread riots they whipped up against missionaries and Chinese converts, promoting a contagion of massacre and mutilation. They also destroyed railways and telegraph lines as symbols of the hated foreigners.

A group of them was called the Big Sword Society and, when news of their trumpeted spiritual powers reached the Dowager Empress, she sent for their leaders. They completely won her over. From then on she gave the Boxers the full support of her government and army. The ageing moderate statesman Li

Hung-chang, having been shunted off as governor-general of Canton, opposed her attitude and together with the leaders of the southern and south-eastern provinces begged her to change it. When their appeal failed, their areas of China abstained from any part in the ensuing events.

By now the foreign diplomats had become so alarmed by the advancing Boxer threat that they called up some hundreds of guards from the foreign navies anchored off Taku, the port for Tientsin and so Peking. On 3rd June 1900 the Boxers cut the railway line between Tientsin and Peking, whereupon the British minister, fearful for the lives of all the foreigners in Peking, appealed for help from Admiral Seymour, commander of the British ships off Taku. Within a week he set out with over two thousand marines and sailors, but they were blocked midway by Boxer assaults and had to fight hard to get back to Tientsin.

The Boxers burst into Peking to burn down churches and foreign homes, kill Chinese converts, assassinate first the chancellor of the Japanese legation and then the German minister, exhume the bodies of long-dead missionaries for mutilation, and attack the grounds of the foreign legations. The frenzy seems to have infected the Dowager Empress for, relying on unreliable news of Boxer successes against the foreign forces at Tientsin, she determined that the moment had arrived for all foreigners to be got rid of: on 21st June war was declared on the foreign powers. Bands of Boxers, armed now with guns by the government forces that joined them, hurled themselves in thousands against the capital's foreign legations.

There were upwards of a dozen of these in an area of about a square mile within the Tartar City, close to the gate – named (of all names) Gate of Heavenly Peace – of the Imperial City. By far the largest compound, adjoining the Hanlin Academy, was the British: within its walls were the minister's house; the chancery and offices; living quarters for staff, students and servants; a theatre, chapel, bell tower, armoury, stables, bowling alley, fives court and, all-importantly, water wells. Cheek by jowl with it and each other were the Russian, American, Spanish, Japanese, French and German compounds, with the Austrian, Italian and Belgian a little way off. Inside the legations were 450 guards, 475 men, women and children (including diplomats and missionaries with their families), and 2,300 Chinese Christians. They put up a doughty resistance as the attacks, starting at 4 p.m. on 20th June, intensified by day and night – rifle and artillery fire, surrounding buildings set ablaze, efforts to mine under the legation walls.

The news of the Siege of the Legations reached an England in the throes of the Boer War and just getting over the Siege of Mafeking which had been lifted scarcely a month since. The government acted promptly in concert with the other interested Powers to despatch troops to the Chinese coast at Taku. By the end of July a force of twenty thousand Britons, Americans, Japanese, French, Austrians and Italians was assembled. On 4th August it set out for Peking. It scored three decisive victories over the Chinese, to march into the capital ten days later. The legations were found to be largely in ruin, hundreds of the defenders dead or wounded: the defence had been conducted under an almost continuous hail of bullets and shells, the air heavy with smoke from burning buildings. While the men had manned the walls and barricades against wave after wave of attacks, the women had spent the long, terror-filled days sewing sandbags, tending the sick and wounded, and preparing meals, which came to include dogs and mules.

The day after the allies entered the city the Dowager Empress fled it. She had with her the protesting Emperor, whose favourite concubine she had thrown into a well, and a small retinue. An arduous two-month journey south-west of Peking took the party through country swarming with refugees, mutinous soldiers, and renegade Boxers, and across mountains to the ancient T'ang capital city of Sian which now became the seat of the court. In half-ruined Peking, whose streets were littered with human and animal corpses, the foreign troops indulged in an orgy of looting. For the Boxers, once active in forty-five cities where they killed thirty thousand Chinese converts and over two hundred missionaries, it was the end. Bullets *did* kill after all, magic or no magic.

The allies had never formally responded to the Chinese declaration of war but now they haggled long and hard over the terms of peace. These were addressed on China's behalf by old Li Hung-chang who, white-headed and half paralysed, was recalled for the purpose and signed the articles of what was called the Collective Note or Boxer Protocols finally agreed in September 1901, only months before his death. The Germans had wanted draconian terms, including the destruction of Peking – so that, the Kaiser declared, 'no Chinese will ever dare to look askance at a German'. If the agreed terms did not go as far, they were severe enough: over a hundred Boxer leaders and pro-Boxer ministers and officials executed or imprisoned for life; an indemnity of over sixty-seven million pounds* payable over thirty-nine years at four per cent interest, secured on customs duties and tariffs; an apology mission to Japan and Germany; a two-year ban on arms imports; and the stationing of foreign troops from Peking to the sea. At the same time two hundred thousand Russian troops were pouring in to occupy Manchuria on the pretext of restoring order.

With what little promise, then, did the new century seem to herald the Celestial Kingdom. Yet promise remained in the ideas which had illumined the reform movement and which now, in these frowning years, continued to ferment.

* In the event, most of this was forgiven by the Powers.

TWENTY-EIGHT

Epilogue:
the twentieth century

*I*n 1902, after a year and a half's absence, the Dowager Empress Tz'u-hsi was carried into Peking in a chair trimmed with peacock feathers. She was a chastened woman: the discomforts of her self-imposed exile. and the experience at first hand of the poverty, squalor and misery of so many of her subjects, forced her out of her cocoon and into the glare of reality. She was galvanized into pronouncing a programme of reform. It included streamlining the bloated and corrupt bureaucracy, encouragement of commerce, reorganization of the army, and a wholesale change to the educational system which was to be equally available to girls. The state, however, was almost bankrupt, and despite the imposition of taxes that increased the widespread disaffection, there was not enough money to realize most of the reform programme.

Most importantly, after a commission returned from studying constitutional government in Europe, America and Japan, the Emperor with his aunt's blessing announced that preparation would be made for the establishment of such a government in nine years time. And in a start to revising the penal code, an end was decreed to the punishment of slow slicing, public exhibition of heads, beheading of corpses, and tattooing; likewise collective responsibility and torture; and flogging with the bamboo was replaced by fines.

In the meanwhile, Russian attempts to occupy Manchuria affrighted Japan; and the two countries went to war (1904).

Japan emerged decisively triumphant and so took its place among the Great Powers. The event hastened the influx of Chinese students to Japan. Soon their community numbered perhaps thirty thousand for, rather than sending students further abroad, it was cheaper and easier for them to acquire Western learning through teachers in Japan and the many Japanese translations of Western books available there. In 1906 China took the momentous step of scrapping the 1,300-year-old examination system, whereafter it sought its civil service and army officer recruits among graduates from its newly established state schools and from foreign schools, notably those in Japan.

Japan, indeed, at this time and for years to come played a forceful role in Chinese politics. Its own rush to Westernization owed much to what it had seen happen under Western pressure in consequence of China's technological backwardness, and it credited the constitutional reforms of the Meiji restoration with providing the framework for its own advancement. It therefore actively sympathized with the Chinese reform movement, not least because a strong China would be a counterweight to the West's aggressiveness in the Far East. Influencing the students too were those radicals who had escaped the *coup* after the One Hundred Days: they worked up anti-Manchu sentiments together with support for the reform movement generally and constitutional reform in particular; and many Japanese liberals gave encouragement to the young men who, additionally, caught the nationalism and patriotism so strongly evinced by their hosts. And, in due course, as the Russian revolutionary movement gathered momentum, its propaganda filtered through too.

The Chinese government was aware of potential trouble from the students in Japan and took some measures to apply a brake, but these availed as little as attempts to extinguish either the small flames of revolution which had been ignited among little groups of people all over China or the greater conflagration threatened by one outstanding individual, a Chinese Christian and doctor named Sun Yat-sen. Born near Macao in 1866, he was educated in Hanoi and Hong Kong, and in his twenties when foreign life and the reformist movement alike had influenced him, his thoughts turned to revolution. Having tried in vain to gain the ear of Li Hung-chang, at the end of 1894 in Hanoi he founded China's first modern revolutionary association, the Society to Restore China's Prosperity. It had loose ties with the numerous secret societies in China, and was composed mostly of lower-class people until Japan's victory over Russia brought in many gentry and merchants. Christian missionaries and their converts also supported him, but he had a constant struggle to drum up recruits and funds.

A rising he plotted in Canton in 1895 quickly collapsed and he fled abroad to promote his revolution. A bizarre incident marked his visit to London in 1896. For reasons unknown he visited the Chinese legation, where he was seized and arrangements put in hand to ship him to China and doubtless death. Two Englishmen who had been his teachers successfully intervened and after twelve days' confinement he was released amid a blaze of publicity, becoming an international celebrity. He at once wrote to the newspapers to thank the British, praising 'the generous public spirit which pervades Great Britain, and the love of justice which distinguishes its people'. And he continued, 'Knowing and feeling more keenly than ever what a constitutional Government and enlightened people mean, I am prompted still more actively to pursue the cause of advancement, education, and civilization in my own well-beloved but oppressed country.' After some months' study in the British Museum he made his way to Japan via Canada where he raised money among the overseas Chinese. His highly successful book, *Kidnapped in London*, could not be published in China for many years.

In Tokyo he was active among the Chinese radicals and their Japanese sympathizers and in 1900 thought the time ripe for another attempted rising in Canton, but it fared no better than in 1895. Again taking refuge in Japan, in 1905 he set up the Revolutionary Alliance to try to draw together the many small revolutionary groups, mostly students, scattered across China, all taking an oath to drive out the Manchus and establish a republic; and they assiduously spread ideas for reform. The early years of the century saw numerous risings, all abortive but unmistakably marking the twilight of the Ch'ing Dynasty, whose prospects were not improved by the infection of many soldiers with the reformist zeal.

In 1907 the Dowager Empress suffered a stroke which caused the right side of her face, particularly her mouth, to drop. She continued nevertheless to make the life of the Emperor, effectively a prisoner, wretched, surrounding him with insolent eunuchs and omitting his apartment when she had electric light installed in the palace. In 1908, after decade of maladies, he took to what soon proved to be his deathbed. He refused to wear the Robes of Longevity tradition prescribed for a Son of Heaven in these straits and is said to have scribbled a curse on Tz'u-hsi. Although suffering severely from dysentery she was nevertheless present, together with his Empress and his concubine called Lustrous, when he died at the Hour of the Cock (5–7 p.m.) on 14th November 1908. The very next afternoon, at the Hour of the Goat (1–3 p.m.), the Dowager Empress herself died.

The court astrologer she had always consulted determined the time, nearly a year thence, when she should be buried. Then a resplendent funeral procession wound its way out of the capital to the Eastern Tombs: officials in mourning robes of white, Buddhist priests and lamas in saffron and with crested hair-cuts, thousands of eunuchs and musicians playing dolefully, the Dalai Lama and other dignitaries garlanded with flowers and walking under state umbrellas, and with camels and banner-flying cavalry in attendance. As the procession passed through the countryside, people burnt paper images of servants, money, food and clothes to conjure up guardian spirits and riches to accompany her into the magnificent mausoleum constructed at her orders in accordance with geomantic oracles. To all intents and purposes, though not quite yet nominally, the Ch'ing Dynasty was at an end. (Two decades later bandits dynamited the tomb and crawled through the dark vaults to rob the coffin. They stripped the corpse to the waist, half pulled down its ribboned pantaloons, and flung it on one side. So was all the majesty of the Dowager Empress Tz'u-hsi ignominiously undone – symbolic of the dynasty of whose glories she had been the final repository.)

Of more concern than the state funeral, the first steps towards constitutional government were taken by elections in every province for a Provincial Assembly. The qualified electorate was predominantly from the gentry. The assemblies were essentially advisory bodies for the provincial governors. Elections started in the same year for a National Assembly which met the following year, its members imperial nominees from the Provincial Assemblies, its purpose too being only consultative. A system of local assemblies, all advisory, was also instituted. Although none of these bodies had muscle or teeth, they could have presaged the democracy and parliamentary government which, had other events not intervened, time may well have delivered. But other events did intervene.

Before her death, the day after the Emperor's, the Dowager Empress nominated his nephew P'u-i as the new Emperor Hsüan-t'ung. As he was only three his father, a somewhat weak man, became Regent and the late Emperor's widow became the new Dowager Empress. The Ch'ing court was composed largely of the Manchu clan while the government tried to cope with an empire in a state of collapse. Nervous of the assemblies it brought into existence, whose wings it assiduously kept clipped, it was unable to stem the rising power of the provincial governors – strengthening them indeed because of the need to raise ever more revenue. Many began to talk of independence.

As 1909 gave way to 1910 the reform movement – now more accurately to be described as the revolutionary movement – gathered impetus. It proceeded in parallel with sporadic uprisings on local issues: together with the activities of diverse revolutionaries and the restlessness of many provincial and county leaders, they created a climate of turbulence throughout the country. The revolutionaries themselves were divided between those who wanted to be rid of the Manchus and the Emperor alike, and those who wanted constitutional change on the lines of Japan's emperor-and-parliament system. The many leading activists at local and national level either vied with or supported Sun Yat-sen and his Revolutionary Alliance in advocacy of the former view, while an exponent of the latter view was a powerful general in the north. He was Yüan Shih-k'ai, soon to be notorious, who commanded China's only modern army and was therefore crucial to either the defence or the overthrow of the Manchu Dynasty. His representatives met those of Sun in negotiations in Shanghai to seek a common policy.

Late in the year matters began to come to the boil, first in Szechwan, when the government announced plans for foreign loans and to nationalize railways owned by private companies. The loan proposals were seen as over-favourable to the ever-greedy West, while the compensation terms for the railways outraged the shareholders – mainly students, gentry, and merchants. Peking did not consult either the National or the Provincial Assemblies on these matters, and brusquely rejected the outpourings of protest. When the railway investors refused to pay tax and the Szechwan Assembly demanded a voice in legislation, the governor-general, who was loyal to the throne, arrested leading protesters, whereupon the whole province erupted. The various revolutionary groups, with the Revolutionary Alliance in support, sprang into action, but they were sidetracked by angry peasants, secret society members, and even bandits, who destroyed police and tax offices, opened jails, looted warehouses and cut telegraph wires. Government troops, weakened by the multiple defections to the revolutionary cause, were overwhelmed by as many as a hundred thousand militant citizenry.

Szechwan had been aflame for some weeks before what is regarded as the real beginning of the Chinese Revolution occurred in the neighbouring province of Hupei. There on 10/11th October 1911 a small rebel band of soldiers intent on revolution was joined by thousands of their comrades in a night's fighting that broke Ch'ing authority in the city of Wuchang. The revolutionaries then formed a military government of Hupei and proclaimed a republic. Over the next seven weeks the greater part of the Manchu garrisons in no fewer than fifteen provinces was murdered, and under the leadership of the army and the Revolutionary Alliance these provinces declared their independence.

Soon after the Wuchang uprising, the court, in dread and desperation at the turn of events, entrusted itself to the general, Yüan Shih-k'ai, who accepted the office of prime minister. His belief in constitutional reform was put in question by his continuing negotiations with the revolutionaries who were adamantly for a republic, which the intently watching Great Powers, led by Great Britain, also favoured.

China was now in the grip of a political crisis as great as any in its history. The Revolution was in full flood across the country as cities and counties were proclaiming their autonomy even before their provincial authorities did likewise: local and provincial regimes rose and fell as army officers, assembly leaders, former Ch'ing officials, gentry, merchants, secret society leaders, and members of the Revolutionary Alliance and other revolutionary groups grappled with the problem of establishing stability. Most of the provinces set up a regime headed by a military governor in cooperation with the Provincial Assembly and representatives of these interests. Unlike the Russian Revolution, which was then only a handful of years in the future, no great ideology was involved, only a desire – which had now become preponderant – to be rid of the Manchus and to decide on what precise form a republic should take, even if there was some support still for a constitutional monarchy. As almost every aspect of the old order was swept away, Young China emerged.

About ten weeks after the Wuchang uprising, in December 1911, Dr Sun Yat-sen was at last in sight of his goal. For twenty years he had endured much travail as he sailed the world to drum up money and support; he had promoted ten uprisings, all failures; his Revolutionary Alliance had enjoyed only fitful influence; but now with the revolutionaries in Nanking he set up a provisional government of the Republic of China, with himself as President on the understanding that, upon the demise of the Ch'ing, he would give way to Yüan Shih-k'ai. In Peking the latter informed the court that the dynasty's position was no longer tenable and his army could not be relied upon.

Tense negotiations were ended by a pronouncement from the Dragon Throne on 12th February 1912 that 'the will of providence is clear and the people's wishes are plain': the monarchy was renounced and a republic decreed. In Nanking, Sun Yat-sen resigned and recommended Yuan Shih-k'ai as President, to which position he was duly elected in October 1912, and the foreign powers recognized the new state.

Heaven's Mandate that it had bestowed for the greater part of two millennia was now withered and an awesome dynasty of almost three centuries duration sank suddenly and quietly into extinction. The child Emperor and his family were permitted continued residence in the Forbidden City; in a bizarre incident in 1917 he was actually reinstated as Emperor for a whole eight days, but at the age of eighteen in 1924 he was driven out, and while he later became puppet-emperor of a Japanese-occupied Manchuria, he would end his days as a humble worker in the People's Republic of China, dying in 1967.

But to return to the heady days of 1912 in Peking. General Yüan Shih-k'ai, President of the new republic, was an able but perfidious animal. At the time of the Emperor Kuang-hsü's One Hundred Days reforms, realizing that he was raising dangerous opposition from the Dowager Empress the Emperor had consulted Yüan about pre-empting any move by his aunt; while pretending to help, Yüan in fact informed the Dowager Empress of the young Emperor's plans, prompting the formidable lady to spring her *coup d'état*. After her death the royal family vented their anger on the traitor by exiling him to the north 'to nurse a bad leg', but in the panic in court as the revolution loomed closer with the Wuchang uprising the family – as noted above – in desperation called him back. At first coolly announcing that his 'leg was not quite healed' he presently returned to Peking, now as prime minister. But instead of using his position and his powerful army to protect the dynasty, he craftily contrived its demise, clearing his way to become President. This still did not slake his ambition, for after pulling off what was effectively a *coup d'état* he had an even loftier aim which would presently emerge.

His election as President was not without opposition: there were constant risings and his armies had to suppress Canton's effort to break away from the Empire. He also had external problems. Tibet agitated against its status as a Chinese dependency and was supported by Britain, which then suffered a severe boycott of its goods. (The matter was left largely undecided until the Chinese Communists conquered the country in 1950. Efforts to pattern its society on that of China caused an uprising in 1959; it was quashed and the Dalai Lama fled to India, since when Tibet has continued to be considered by the Chinese to be part of their country.) Russia too presented a problem, with demands on Outer Mongolia, which by a treaty – secret, to avoid the wrath of the people – Yüan agreed should enter the Russian orbit, while Inner Mongolia remained part of China. It was Japan, however, that threatened most. It increased its penetration of Manchuria, and when in 1914 the First World War broke out it occupied German-leased territory in the province, of Shantung. This was followed the following year by its infamous 'Twenty-one Demands' on China for a string of concessions and rights, including making the whole of mineral-rich Shantung a protectorate.

Yüan's government cravenly conceded most of the demands. Peking's students were infuriated, but Yüan's mind was on other things. He wanted to become Emperor and found a new dynasty, and he cowed the National Assembly into agreeing. Before he could ascend the throne, however, Heaven intervened: he suddenly died (June 1916).

The structure of government was fast disintegrating. Provinces continued proclaiming independence. The Western

Allies, engaged in the struggle against Germany, forced Peking to declare war on Germany, with but little practical consequence. The collapse of government proceeded apace: an attempt was made to restore the last Ch'ing Emperor but army generals sent a plane that dropped two bombs on Peking and ended an episode of precisely eight days. North China was roamed about by generals – the 'warlords' – intent on gaining what power they could, while in the south Sun Yat-sen followers again set up an opposition government. All the time Japan gained an increasing financial grip by financing many of the warlords and rebels.

So matters stood when the Peace Conference was convened in Paris in 1919. The decision was taken to confirm the rights given in secret by the Allies and by Yüan to the Japanese following their expulsion of the Germans from the leased areas of Shantung in 1914. Chinese loathing of the Japanese had already been raised by the Twenty-one Demands and, when the Conference's decision, and Yüan's complicity, became known in Peking, there was an explosion of rage. On the afternoon of 4th May, three thousand students gathered to protest at the Gate of Heavenly Peace (that is, at today's T'ien-an-men Square). Peaceableness gave way to violence as a pro-Japanese official was beaten up and a government minister's house burnt down. The government rounded up hundreds of students for imprisonment, inflaming passions across the country: student disturbances occurred in two hundred locations; Shanghai merchants shut their shops for a week; workers in forty factories went on strike. Facing the birth of a great student movement, with female participation and the broad support of the public – in all an entirely new expression of nationalism – the Peking authorities backed off and 1,150 students marched victoriously out of jail. 'May 4' became a legend. While not of itself a seismic event, it gave its name to a whole era of Chinese intellectual, cultural and political development heading away from the habits, ideas and beliefs of the past.

Sun Yat-sen's rôle as leader of the south now went under the title of generalissimo, and his revolutionary party changed its name yet again, and finally, to the Kuomintang, the Citizen's Party, often referred to as the KMT or Nationalists. Coincidentally in 1921, on 1st July, under stimulation by Soviet Russia, about a dozen Chinese and two Comintern agents met in a school in the French Concession of Shanghai to found the Communist Party. It was divided on the issue of whether a Communist revolution should be a proletarian or peasant movement, but since the only proletariat were in Shanghai the latter view would prevail. At this time the KMT accepted cooperation with the Communists who in fact had a strong presence in the party since two Russian Communists had advised Sun on the framing of his party's constitution and forty other Russians helped re-organize the armies of southern China, now led by Sun's trusted aide and brother-in-law, the charismatic and highly capable General Chiang Kai-shek.

Sun himself, 'Father of the Revolution', died in 1925 in Peking, where he had gone in a vain attempt to seek an accommodation between the Citizens' Party and the northern generals. This was a period of much anti-British feeling in south China and when British soldiers shot at a mob demonstrating in Shanghai a boycott of British goods caused serious loss to British trade and allowed Japan to establish an iron grip on the east coast shipping – an ominously deepened penetration of China's economy.

At the 1926 Second Congress of the Citizens' Party in Canton, Chiang Kai-shek emerged as its undisputed leader. He faced up to the task of trying to reunite a nation of four hundred million people, of whom ninety-five per cent were peasants and fewer than twenty million literate, with Peking but a shadow government and every part of the country at odds with each other. He launched his army, modernized and trained near Canton with German technical and material aid, northwards. As much by diplomacy as arms he defeated leader after leader who opposed him. Reaching the Yangtze he removed his capital to Hankow. Behind him masses of people were rising to support him or the Communists who were exciting the peasants with promises of land grants, reduction of the big estates, lower taxes and humiliating landlords by forcing them to wear tall conical hats of mockery.

The KMT was essentially middle-class but with a strong tincture of socialism, not communism, of which Chiang Kai-shek was profoundly mistrustful. When his army captured Shanghai he turned on the comrades. He executed or dismissed the Russian advisers, had thousands of Communists killed and set his face to exterminating them, firmly planting the seeds of the civil war to come, for the surviving Communist leaders dispersed, especially to the province of Kiangsi where they gathered a growing following. For his part Chiang, having at his disposal the resources of the great Shanghai banking families allied to his wife, and with access to foreign capital, could pay his troops and run an efficient government, now based in Nanking and supported by his small but well-trained army.

In the years that followed, years of disruption across the country and with it the endurance by millions of misery, displacement, lawlessness, and loss, Chiang pursued his dream of unification. He fought, plotted, manoeuvred and bribed to bring the warlords to heal. At the same time his Nationalist forces hunted the Communists who, in the face of repeated attacks, made a dramatic decision in October 1934. They quit Kiangsi and about ninety thousand of them set off on what history has called the Long March northwards through Western China. After two years' privation, during which they struggled across swampland and mountain, constantly damp and sick without medical supplies, sometimes bombed, often attacked by hostile tribes, freezing by night and all the time so famished they had to eat poisonous weeds and berries. They lost fifty thousand of their number before settling in Yenan in Shensi province. There, one Mao Tse-tung emerged as their leader – to prove to be the third of the triumvirate, with Sun Yat-sen and Chiang Kai-shek, who comprised China's men of destiny in the twentieth century.

Mao Tse-tung was born in 1893 near Changsha, capital of Hunan Province. The eldest of the three survivors of his mother's seven children, he worked on his father's three-acre farm from the age of six, continuing in his spare time when he went to the village school. His father encouraged him to master the abacus that he might help with the accounts; he also married him off at eighteen, but his wife died when she was twenty-one. Sporadically he attended a variety of schools, at one period studying privately in a library where he stopped only to eat two rice cakes for lunch; when he was seventeen he walked thirty miles to join a new school. He read voraciously, starting with historical novels and moving to the Classics, and then Western learning; he wrote poetry. A famine in Hunan prompted peasants to seize stores of rice, including his father's, and this started his political consciousness. His reading introduced him to great names – Napoleon, Catherine the Great, Wellington, Gladstone, Rousseau and Montesquieu, but especially Washington, of whom he read, 'After eight years of difficult war he won victory and built up his nation.' He became an ardent hiker and swimmer. When his radical newspaper brought news of the 1911 Revolution and Sun Yat-sen's rising in Canton, he converted to the revolutionary cause, cutting off his pigtail as so many people were doing in rejection of the Manchus. He spent a brief spell in the republican army and finally at the age of twenty-four he graduated. For a short time, living off a narrow lane in a poor district of Peking, he shared three rooms with three other students while he worked as a clerk in the university library. He began reading Marxism. On his return to Changsha he first taught history in a school there and then founded and successfully ran a bookshop. He attended the first Congress of the Communist Party and became a busy activist, whipping up recruits and organizing strikes. He was with the Nationalists in Chiang Kai-shek's campaign northwards against the militarists but, being absent from the Shanghai shambles when Chiang turned on his comrades, he began organizing a peasant army, moving his base northwards to the mountainous area between Hunan and Kiangsi. It was from there that he joined the Long March, and at its conclusion took up residence in a cave while yet another child was born to him – the fourth to survive of the ten children borne by three women.

For Chiang Kai-shek, efforts at reunification and the repression of the Communists were totally overshadowed by the cataclysmic events starting in 1937. Japan, as we have seen, had long been a menacing and acquisitive presence; in 1928 its troops had bloodied the nose of Chiang's doughty but young Nanking army, and over the next few years got its grips on Manchuria, forming it into its puppet state of Manchukuo; and its forces moved closer to Peking.

The 1930s was a period of fateful decision for the world as the shadow of Hitler fell across Europe. Western policy had been to play off China and Japan against each other, and Japan sought to break out of the isolation this imposed by joining the 'axis powers' of Germany and Italy (1936); and it determined to bring into being a 'Greater East Asia' to provide raw materials and markets, to fend off the Great Depression then throttling the world and, lest the Western powers became hostile, to obtain space for its burgeoning population, and to establish a security girdle to keep Russia at bay. It would begin by conquering China. Only a small pretext was needed to ignite the powder keg and this was provided by the Marco Polo Bridge Incident of July 1939. Close to midnight on the seventh of that month, Japanese troops stationed between Tientsin and Peking (then called Peiping) in accordance with the Boxer Protocol were on manoeuvre near the bridge, which was about ten miles south of Peiping, when they were allegedly fired upon by Chinese soldiers and had one of their men seized (he had not been and soon returned). A month's intense sabre-rattling culminated in the Japanese Prime Minister's declared intention to reach 'a fundamental solution of Sino-Japanese relations' while Chiang Kai-shek vowed to fight an all-out war of resistance.

In a massive three-month onslaught on Shanghai the Japanese wiped out a quarter of a million of the Nationalist troops. Even worse was to follow, in the 'Rape of Nanking'. When the Chinese army in that city surrendered, the Japanese launched themselves into an unspeakable orgy of brutal destruction. They killed all the soldiers and in the course of six weeks bayoneted, covered in kerosene and set on fire, buried alive and mutilated two hundred thousand civilians; and they raped eighty thousand women before disembowelling them or cutting off their breasts. (At the later Tokyo War Crime Trials a few Japanese were indicted and executed; but Japan has consistently tried to cover up this whole episode of martial insanity.)

The Japanese moved on to control large areas of the country. After the fall of Nanking, Chiang fled far west to Chungking on the Yangtze in Szechwan. It was an agricultural area devoid of industry and so the Nationalists carried to it everything they could dismantle of the eastern seaboard factories; students and professors followed with the contents of their universities. From this remote city, presently supplied from the air by the Allies led by the USA, Chiang conducted China's resistance, reinforced by Mao's Communist guerrillas. It was brave and staunch but in vain. In eight terrible years of war, fifteen million Chinese soldiers and civilians perished, and incalculable property was devastated. It ended only when Japan's dream of a Great East Asia was shattered by the atom bomb on Hiroshima in 1945. China at last was free.

But not quite. There was an unbridgeable gulf between Nationalist and Communist. All the Allied efforts to persuade them to form a united front had failed, even after Chiang Kai-shek had given his half-hearted encouragement when he was briefly kidnapped by a northern warlord. Now battle between them was seriously joined. From his lair in Yenan, Mao Tse-tung had devoted the past nine years to organizing and refining the tactics of peasant guerrillas. He himself reverted to his peasant roots, vaunting the simple life in scorn of intellectuals and becoming coarse: he would open his belt to search his groin for lice as he talked, or take off his trousers to cool himself while lying on a bed being interviewed. But his bond with the peasant masses was intense as by spoken and written word he hammered out a programme and gospel of revolutionary Communist rule.

In the resumed hostilities against Mao, Chiang Kai-shek was at first successful, his forces entering Yenan and moving on to Manchuria; but there the local Communist leader, well equipped with surrendered Japanese arms, as well as Russian, inflicted a severe defeat. Demoralization bit deep and far into the Nationalists. They yielded to the Communists in Shantung and after a decisive battle in 1948 soon gave up Peiping, and then Nanking, and then city after city. Chiang Kai-shek fled to Taiwan, restored to China after Japan's surrender, taking with him about two million supporters and three hundred million dollars of his country's reserves; and he founded a successful capitalist society under United States protection. The victorious Communist Party meeting in Peiping made it once more the capital, renaming it again Peking (Beijing). There, on 1st October 1949 Mao Tse-tung proclaimed the founding of the People's Republic of China. As his words sounded out in the square below the Gate of Heavenly Peace, he stood ruler of a nation that numbered 1,000,000,000 people. No ruler on earth has ever known power of such magnitude.

A new dynasty was born, based not on genealogy but on ideology, not on a family but on the Communist Party. If the Han, the T'ang, the Sung, the Yüan (Mongol), the Ming and the Ch'ing (Manchu) are added in, the seventh Empire of China came into existence. It watches the West as warily as the West watches it. All may be well if the noblest beliefs that exalt the soul of either are to assert themselves: the West's Christian ethos of goodwill, of turning the other cheek, and the Chinese deeply buried intuition of our universe – man and Nature together – being in constant search of balance and harmony, so that if bad upsets the balance good is needed to right it: *Yin* repairs *Yang*; and *Yang*, *Yin*. This is the gossamer thread that runs through the vast history of a vast land with its vast population and vast edifice of civilization which these pages have but falteringly chronicled.

Bibliography

Alexander, W., *Picturesque Representations of the Dress and Manners of the ... Chinese* (John Murray, 1814)

Allom, T. and Wright, G. N., *The Chinese Empire Illustrated* – 2 vols. (London Printing and Publishing Co., c.1845)

Anderson, A., *A Narrative of the British Embassy to China 1792–4* (J. Debrett, London, 1795)

Andersson, J. G., *Children of the Yellow Earth* (The MIT Press, Mass., 1934)

Anon., *Along the Yellow River* (Foreign Languages Press, Peking, 1975)

Anon., Chinese *Painting and Calligraphy from the Collection of John M. Crawford Jnr.* (Pierpont Morgan Library, N.Y. 1965)

Anon., *Historical Records Unearthed in New China* (Foreign Languages Press, Peking, 1972)

Anon., *Marco Polo's Adventures in China* (Cassell, 1965)

Anon., *New Archeological Finds in China* (Foreign Languages Press, Peking, 1973)

Anon., *A Selection of Ancient Chinese Bronzes* (Wen Wu Press, Peking, 1976)

Balazs, E., *Chinese Civilization and Bureaucracy* (Yale U. Press, 1964)

Baynes, C. F., *The I-Ching* (Routledge & Kegan Paul, 1951)

Beattie, H. J., *Land and Lineage in China* (Cambridge U. Press, 1979)

Beeching, J., *The Chinese Opium Wars* (Hutchinson, 1975)

Bennett, A. A., *John Fryer the Introduction of Western Science ... China* – 2 vols. (Harvard U. Press, 1967)

Birch, C. (ed.), *Anthology of Chinese Literature* (Grove Press, N.Y., 1965)

Bielenstein, H., *The Bureaucracy of Han Times* (Cambridge U. Press, 1980)

Birrell, A. (tr.), *New Songs from a Jade Terrace* (George Allen & Unwin, 1982)

Bishop, J. F., *Chinese Pictures* (Cassell & Co., 1900)

Bishop, J. F., *The Yangtze Valley and Beyond* (John Murray, 1899)

Blake, C., *Charles Elliot R.N. 1801–75* (Cleaver-Hulme Press, London, 1960)

Bloodworth, C. P. & D., *The Chinese Machiavelli* (Secker & Warburg, 1976)

Bodde, D., *Festivals in Classical China* (Princeton U. Press, 1975)

Boulnois, L., *The Silk Road* (George Allen & Unwin, 1966)

Braam, A. E. Van, *Embassy of the Dutch East-India Co. to ... China* – 2 vols. (R. Phillips, London, 1798)

Brent, P., *The Mongol Empire* (Book Club Assoc., London, 1976)

Budge, E. A. W. (tr.), *The Monks of Kublai Khan* (AMS Press, N.Y., 1928)

Cambridge History of China (various eds) (Cambridge U. Press – Vol. 1, 1986 and ten subsequent vols. by 2000)

Cameron, N., *Barbarians and Mandarins* (John Weatherhill, N.Y., 1970)

ALL UNDER HEAVEN

Carl, K. A., *With the Empress Dowager of China* (KPI, London, 1906)
Carter, T. F., *The Invention of Printing in China* (Ronald Press Co., N.Y., 1925)
Catalogue of Important Archaic Chinese Bronzes (Sothebys, London, 1967)
Chaffee, J. W., *The Thorny Gates of Learning in Sung China* (Cambridge U. Press, 1975)
Chan W. K. K., *Merchants, Mandarins, and Modern Enterprise in Late Ch'ing China* (Harvard U. Press, 1977)
Chang, K. C., *The Archeology of Ancient China* (Yale U. Press, 1977)
Chang, K. C., *Early Chinese Civilization* (Harvard U. Press, 1977)
Chang, Chung-li, *The Chinese Gentry* (Washington U. Press, 1955)
Chaves, J. (tr.), *Pilgrim of the Clouds* (John Weatherhill, N.Y., 1978)
Chen Chi-yun, *Hsün Yüeh* (Cambridge U. Press, 1975)
Chen Chi-yun, *Hsün Yüeh and the Mind of Late Han China* (Princeton U. Press, 1980)
Ch'en, J., *China and the West* (Hutchinson, 1979)
Ch'en, P. H., *Chinese Legal Tradition under the Mongols* (Princeton U. Press, 1979)
Chesneaux, J. and others, *China from the Opium Wars to the 1911 Revolution* (Harvester Press, Sussex, 1977)
Hsiao Ch'i-ch'ing, *Military Establishment of the Yüan Dynasty* (Harvard U. Press, 1977)
Ch'u T'ung-tsu, *Han Social Structure* (Washington U. Press, 1972)
Clark, G., *Impatient Giant: Red China Today* (Ronald Press Co., N.Y., 1925)
Cotterell, A., *The First Emperor of China* (Macmillan, 1981)
Cotterell, Y. Y. & A., *Chinese Civilization, Ming to Mao* (Book Club Assoc., London, 1977)
Cotterell, Y. Y. & A., *The Early Civilization of China* (Book Club Assoc., London, 1975)
Cranmer-Byng, L., *A Vision of Asia* (Readers Union, London, 1932)
Creel, C. G., *The Birth of China* (Frederick Ungar, 1937)
Creel, C. G., *The Origins of Statecraft in China* (Chicago U. Press, 1970)
Creel, C. G., *Shen Pu-hai* (Chicago U. Press, 1974)
Danton, G. H., *The Culture Contacts of the U.S. and China* (Columbia U. Press)
Dardess, J. W., *Conquerers and Confucians* (Columbia U. Press, 1973)
Davidson B. and others, *Fossil Man in China* (Geological Survey of China, Peiping, 1933)
Davis, J. F., *The Chinese* (Charles Knight & Co., London, 1840)
Dawson, R., *The Chinese Chameleon* (Oxford U. Press, 1867)
Dawson, R., *Imperial China* (Hutchinson, 1972)
Dawson, R., *The Chinese Experience* (Weidenfeld & Nicolson, 1978)
De Bary, T. (ed.), *Sources of Chinese Tradition* – 2 vols. (Columbia U. Press, 1964)
DeFrancis, J., *Beginning Chinese* (Yale U. Press, 1963)
Dillon, M., *Dictionary of Chinese History* (Frank Cass & Co., London, 1979)
Dolby, W., *A History of Chinese Drama* (Elek Books, London, 1976)
Drake, F. W., *China Charts the World* (Harvard U. Press, 1975)

Dudbridge, G., *The Legend of Miao-shan* (Ithaca Press, London, 1978)

Eamer, J. B., *The English in China* (Curzon Press, London, 1909)

Eberhard, W., *A History of China* (Routledge & Kegan Paul, 1950)

Eberhard, W., *Social Mobility in Traditional China* (E. J. Brill, Leiden, 1962)

Eberhard, W., *Conquerers and Rulers* (E. J. Brill, Leiden, 1970)

Ebrey, P. B., *The Aristocratic Families of Early Imperial China* (Cambridge U. Press, 1978)

Elisseeff, D. and V., *New Discoveries in China* (Chartwell Books, N. Jersey, 1983)

Ellis, H., *Journal of the Proceedings of the late* [Amherst] *Embassy to China* (John Murray, 1817)

Fairbank, J. K., *Trade and Diplomacy on the China Coast* (Stanford U. Press, 1964)

Fan Hong, *Footbinding, Feminism and Freedom* (Frank Cass, London, 1997)

Fesslev, L. and others, *China* (Time-Life International, 1963)

Fitzgerald, P., *Ancient China* (Elsevier Phaidon, London, 1978)

Franck, I. M. and Brownstone, D. M., *The Silk Road* (Facts on File, N.Y., 1986)

Franke, W., *A Century of Chinese Revolution, 1851–1949* (Basil Blackwell, Oxford, 1970)

Franzblau, A. (ed.), *Erotic Art of China* (Crown Publishers, N.Y., 1977)

Freehill, N., *China: All About It!* (Seven Seas Publishers, Berlin, 1959)

Frodsham, J. D. (tr.), *The First Chinese Embassy to the West* (Clarendon Press, Oxford, 1974)

Fry, R. and others, *Chinese Art* (B. T. Batsford, London, 1925)

Fryer, J., *The Great Wall of China* (New English Library, London, 1975)

Fullard, H. (ed.), *China in Maps* (George Philip & Son, London, 1968)

Fung Yu-lan, *A Short History of Chinese Philosophy* (Macmillan, 1948)

Gascoigne, B., *The Treasures and Dynasties of China* (Jonathan Cape, 1973)

Gernet, J., *Daily Life in China, 1250–76* (Stanford U. Press, 1962)

Gernet, J., *A History of Chinese Civilization* (Cambridge U. Press, 1982)

Gerson, J. J., *Horatio Nelson Lay and Sino-British Relations* (Harvard U. Press, 1972)

Giles, H. A., *A Chinese Biographical Dictionary* (Ch'eng Wen Publishing, Taipei, 1975)

Giles, H. A., *A History of Chinese Literature* (Charles E. Tuttle Co., Inc., 1973)

Giles, L. (tr.), *A Gallery of Chinese Immortals* (John Murray, 1979)

Glover, A. E., *A Thousand Miles of Miracle in China* (Pickering & Inglis, London, 1904)

Goldstein, J., *Philadelphia and the China Trade 1682–1846* (Pennsylvania U. Press, 1978

Goodall, J. A., *Heaven and Earth* [Ming encyclopedia extracts] (Lund Humphries, London, 1979)

Goodrich, L. C. and Cameron, N., *The Face of China, 1860–1912* (Gordon Fraser Gallery, London, 1978)

Graham, A. C. (tr.), *Poems of the Late T'ang* (Penguin Books, 1965)

Graham, W. (tr.), *The Lament of the South* (Cambridge U. Press, 1980)

Gray, J. H., *China* [laws, manners, customs] – 2 vols. (Macmillan, 1878)

Greene, F., *Peking* (Jonathan Cape, 1978)

Greene, R. A., *Hsiang-ya Journal* (Shoe String Press, Conn., 1977)

Grosier, J. B., *A General Description of China* – 2 vols. (G. G. J. and J. Robinson, London, 1788)

Grosier, J. B., *The World of Ancient China* (Editions Minerva, Geneva, 1972)

Guisso, R. W. L. and others, *The First Emperor of China* (Stoddart Publishing Co., 1989)

Gulick, E. V., *Peter Parker and the Opening of China* (Harvard U. Press, 1973)

Gulick, R. H. van, *Sexual Life in Ancient China* (E. J. Brill, Leiden, 1974)

Hall, W. H., *Narrative of the Voyages and Services of The Nemesis* (Henry Colburn, London, 1845)

Han Suyin, *The Crippled Tree* (Jonathan Cape, 1965)

Harrington, L., *The Grand Canal of China* (Bailey Bros. & Swinfen, 1974)

Hart, H. (tr.), *Seven Hundred Chinese Proverbs* (Stanford U. Press, 1937)

Hart, H., (tr.), *The Hundred Names* (California U. Press, 1933)

Hayden, G. A. (tr.), *Three Judge Pao Plays* (Harvard U. Press, 1978)

Hirth F., *The Ancient History of China* (Columbia U. Press, 1923)

Ho Ping-ti, *The Cradle of the East* (Chinese U. of Hong Kong, 1975)

Hong Ying, *Summer of Betrayal* (Bloomsbury, 1997)

Hopkirk, P., *Foreign Devils on the Silk Road* (John Murray, 1980)

Hosie, D., *Portrait of a Chinese Lady* (Hodder & Stoughton, 1929)

Hsiao Ch'ien, *A Harp with a Thousand Strings* (Pilot Press, London, 1944)

Hsü Chin-hsiung, *Menzies Collection of Shang Dynasty Oracle Bones* – 2 vols. (Royal Ontario Museum, 1977)

Hsu, Cho-yun, *Han Agriculture* (Washington U. Press, 1980)

Huang, R., *Taxation and Governmental Finance in Sixteenth Century Ming China* (Cambridge U. Press, 1974)

Huang R., *China a Macro History* (M. E. Sharpe, N.Y., 1997)

Hucker, C. O., *China's Imperial Past* (Duckworth, 1975)

Huc, E., *The Chinese Empire* (Longman, Brown, Green & Longman, 1855)

Hughes, E.R., *Two Chinese Poets* (Greenwood Press, Conn., 1960)

Hummel, A. (ed.), *Eminent Chinese of the Ch'ing Period* (Ch'eng Wen Publishing, Taipei, 1970)

Ides, E. Y., *Three Years Travels from Moscow Over-land to China* (W. Freeman, 1706)

Jenner, W. J., *Memories of Loyang* (Clarendon Press, Oxford, 1981)

Johnson, W. (tr.), *The T'ang Code* (Princeton U. Press, 1979)

Johnston, R. F., *Twilight in the Forbidden City* (Victor Gollancz, 1934)

Kao, G. (ed.), *Chinese Wit and Humour* (Coward-McCann, N.Y., 1946)

Keswick, M., *The Chinese Garden* (Academy Editions, London, 1978)

Kuan Han-ching, *Selected Plays* (New Art and Literature Publishing, Shanghai, 1958)

Lai, T. C., *The Eight Immortals* (Swindon Book Co., 1972)

Lai, T. C., *Imperial China* (George Allen & Unwin, 1966)

Lai,T. C.,*Ways to Paradise* (George Allen & Unwin, 1979)

Lai,T. C., *A Scholar in Imperial China* (Kelly & Walsh, Hong Kong, 1970)

Langlois, J. D. (ed.), *China under Mongol Rule* (Princeton U. Press, 1981)

Latham, R. (tr.),*TheTravels of Marco Polo* (Penguin Books, 1958)

Laufer, B., *Sino-Iranica* (Ch'eng Wen Publishing Co.,Taipei, 1973)

Le Compte, L., *Memoirs and Observations ... Journey through ... China* (Benj. Tooke, London, 1697)

Legge, J. (tr.),*The Chinese Classics*,Vols. I – V (Hong Kong U. Press, 1960)

Legge, J. (tr.),*TheTexts ofTaoism* (The Julian Press, 1959)

Legge, J. (tr.), *I Ching – Book of Changes* (Bantam, 1969)

Levenson, C. (tr.),*The Golden Casket* (Harcourt, Brace & World, N.Y., 1964)

Levenson, J.R. and another, *China: An Interpretive History* (California U. Press, 1969)

Li Yu-ning, *ShangYang's Reforms* (M. E. Sharpe Inc., 1977)

Lindqvist, C., *China Empire of theWritten Symbol* (Harper Collins, 1991)

Lin Yutang, *From Pagan to Christian* (World Publishing Co., Ohio, 1959)

Lo Hui-min,*The Correspondence of G. E. Morrison* – 2 vols. (Cambridge U. Press, 1976)

Loewe, M., *Crisis and Conflict in Han China* (George Allen & Unwin, 1974)

Loewe, M., *Imperial China* (George Allen & Unwin, 1966)

Lou Tsu-k'uang (ed.), *Asian Folklore and Social Life* – 2 vols. (Orient Cultural Service,Taiwan, 1975)

Lowe, H.Y.,*The Adventures ofWu* (Princeton U. Press, 1983)

Lum, Peter, *FairyTales of China* (Cassell, London, 1959)

MacGregor, D. R.,*TheTea Clippers* (Percival Marshall, London, 1952)

MacKerras, C. P.,*The Rise of the Peking Opera* (Clarendon Press, Oxford, 1972)

Magaillans, G., *A New History of China* (Thomas Newborough, 1688)

Mao Tun (ed.), *Chinese Literature, monthly No. 2* (Foreign Language Press, Peking, 1964)

Mao Yi-sheng, *Bridges in China, Old and New* (Foreign Languages Press, Peking, 1978)

Martin, R. M., *China; Political, Commercial and Social* (James Madden, London, 1847)

Mason, G. H.,*The Costume of China* and *The Punishments of China. Illustrated* (W. Miller, London, 1800)

Maspero, H., *China in Antiquity* (Dawson, 1978)

Maxim, H. S., *Li Chang's Scrapbook* (Watts & Co., London, 1913)

Melchers, B., *Chinesische Schattenschnitte* (Friedr. Lomesch, Kassel, 1956)

Meng,WuWu, *Houses of Joy* (The Olympia Press, 1958)

Meyer, C. and Allen J., *Source Materials in Chinese History* (Frederick Warne, 1970)

Mirsky, J.,*The Great ChineseTravellers* (George Allen & Unwin, 1965)

Moss, H. M. (ed.), *Chinese Snuff Bottles, No. 3* (Chinese Snuff Boxes, London)

Munro, D. J.,*The Concept of Man in Early China* (Stanford U. Press, 1969)

Murals from the Han to the Tang Dynasty (Foreign Language Press, Peking, 1974)

Myerdal, J., *Report from a Chinese Village* (William Heinemann, 1965)

Nagel's Encyclopedia Guide: *China* (Nagel Publishers, Geneva, 1968)

Nancarrow, P., *Early China and the Wall* (Cambridge U. Press, 1978)

National Geographic Magazine, *China's Incredible Find* (National Geographic Society, April 1978)

Needham, J., *Science & Civilization in China* – Vol. 1 1954 and 19 Subsequent Vols to 2000 (Cambridge U. Press)

Newnham, R., *About Chinese* (Penguin Books, 1971)

Nowak, M. and Durrant, S., *The Tale of the Nisan Shamaness* (Washington U. Press, 1977)

Ogilby, J. (tr.), *Embassy from the East-India Company ... to ... China* (John Macock, London, 1699)

Oliphant, L., *Narrative of the Earl Elgin's Mission to China ...* – 2 vols. (Blackwood, 1859)

Onan, U. (tr.), *The Golden Chinggis* (Folio Society, London, 1993)

Overmyer, D. L., *Folk Buddhist Religion* (Harvard U. Press, 1976)

Owen, S., *An Anthology of Chinese Literature* (W. W. Norton & Co., 1996)

Ping-ti Ho, *The Ladder of Success in Imperial China* (Columbia U. Press, 1962)

Pirazzoli-t'Serstevens, M., *The Han Dynasty* (Rizzoli International, 1982)

Pratt, J. T., *China and Britain* (Collins, 1944)

Prawdin, M., *The Mongol Empire* (George Allen & Unwin, 1940)

Qian Hao and others, *Out of China's Earth* (Frederick Muller, London, 1981)

Rawson, J., *Mysteries of Ancient China* (British Museum Press, 1996)

Reischauer, E.O., *Ennin's Diary* (Ronald Press Co., N.Y., 1955)

Ross, J., *The Original Religion of China* (Oliphant Anderson & Ferrer, 1909)

Salisbury H., *To Peking – and Beyond* (Hutchinson, 1973)

Schafer, E. H., *Pacing the Void* (California U. Press, 1977)

Schurmann, F. and Schell, O. (eds), *Republican China* (Random House, 1967)

Science Press, *Atlas of Primitive Man in China* (Science Press, Beijing, 1980)

Scott, A. C., *The Classical Theatre of China* (George Allen & Unwin, 1957)

Shabad, T., *China's Changing Map* (Methuen & Co., 1956)

Schirokauer, C., (tr.), *China's Examination Hell* (Yale U. Press, 1976)

Shapiro, H. L., *Peking Man* (Book Club Associates, London, 1976)

Sharf, F. A. and Harrington, P., *China 1900: The Eyewitnesses Speak* (Greenhill Books, London, 2000)

Shih Chung-wen, *The Golden Age of Chinese Drama* (Princeton U. Press, 1976)

Sickman, L. and Soper, A., *The Art and Architecture of China* (Penguin Books, 1956)

Siren, O., *A History of Later Chinese Painting* – 2 vols. (Medici Society, London, 1937)

Smith, R. J., *China's Cultural Heritage, The Ch'ing Dynasty* (Westview Press, Colorado, 1983)

Sotheby Parke Burnet (Hong Kong), *Five Chinese School* (4.12.78)

Spence, J. D., *Emperor of China* (Jonathan Cape, 1974)

Spence, J. D., *The Death of WomanWang* (Wiedenfeld & Nicolson, 1978)

Spence, J. D., *The Memory Palace of Matteo Ricci* (Faber & Faber, 1985)

Spence, J. D., *The Chan's Great Continent* (Allen Lane, 1998)

Spence, J. D., *Mao* (Wiedenfeld & Nicolson, 1999)

Spender, S. and Hockney, D., *China Diary* (Thames & Hudson, 1982)

Staunton, G., *An Authentic Account of an* [i.e. the Macartney] *Embassy ... China* – 2 vols. (G. Nicol, London, 1798)

Sullivan, M., *A Short History of Chinese Art* (Faber & Faber, 1967)

Sun E-tu Zen and DeFrancis, J. (tr.), *Chinese Social History* (Octagon Books, N.Y., 1966)

Taylor, R.L., *The Cultivation of Sagehood* (American Academy of Religion, 1978)

Theroux, P., *Sailing through China* (Michael Russell, 1983)

Thubron, C., *The Silk Road to China* (Hamlyn, 1989)

Torbert, P. M., *The Ch'ing Imperial Household Department* (Harvard U. Press, 1977)

Treistman, J. M., *The Pre-History of China* (David & Charles, 1972)

Trevor-Roper, H., *A Hidden Life* (Macmillan, 1976)

Tsai Kuo Ying Paul Tsai (tr.), *The Last Manchu* (Arthur Barker, 1967)

Tsao Hsueh-chin and Kao Ngo, *A Dream of Red Mansions* – 3 vols. (Foreign Langauges Press, Peking, 1978)

Tuchman, B. W., *Stilwell and the American Experience in China, 1911–45* (Macmillan, 1971)

Twitchett, D., *Financial Administration under the T'ang Dynasty* (Cambridge U. Press, 1970)

Twitchett, D., *The Birth of the Chinese Meritocracy* (China Society, London, 1974)

Waddell, H., *Lyrics from the Chinese* (Constable and Co., 1945)

Waley, A. *The Opium War through Chinese Eyes* (George Allen & Unwin, 1958)

Warner, M., *The Dragon Empress* (Wiedenfeld & Nicolson, 1972)

Watson, B. (tr.), *Courtier and Commoner in Ancient China* (Columbia U. Press, 1974)

Watson, W., *The Arts of China to AD 1900* (Yale U. Press, 1995)

Webb, J., *An Historical Essay Endeavouring a Probability That the Language of China etc.* (Nath. Brook, 1669)

Wechsler, H. S., *A Mirror to the Son of Heaven* (Yale U. Press, 1974)

Welch, H. and Seidel, A., *Facets of Taoism* (Yale U. Press, 1979)

Wellcome Historical Medical Museum and Library, *Chinese Medicine* (1966)

Wheatley, Paul, *The Pivot of the Four Quarters* (Edinburgh U. Press, 1971)

Williams, S.W., *The Middle Kingdom* – 2 vols. (W. H. Allen & Co., London, 1883)

Wolseley, G. J., *Narrative of the War with China in 1860* (Longman, Green, Longman & Roberts, 1862)

Wu Chêng-ên, *Monkey* (George Allen & Unwin, 1942)

Wu Ching-tzu, *The Scholars* (Foreign Languages Press, Peking, 1957)

Yang, C. K., *Religion in Chinese Society* (California U. Press, 1970)

Yule, H. (tr.), *The Book of Ser Marco Polo* – 2 vols. (John Murray, 1903)

Yule, H. (tr.), *Cathay and the Way Thither* — 2 vols. (Ch'eng Wen Publishing, Taipei, 1972)

Zheng Shifeng and others, *China* (Frederick Muller, London, 1980)

Zürcher, E., *The Buddhist Conquest of China* (E. J. Brill, Leiden, 1972)

Index

INDEX

405

ALL UNDER HEAVEN

Grand Dowager Empress 136–9
Grand Pronouncements, Ming dynasty 276
Grand Unity 124
Great Britain 328–33, 336–50, 354–61,
365–71, 374, 376–7, 381, 385, 389
Great Ch'i Dynasty 231–2
Great City Shang 12–16, 23
*Great Compendium of the Philosophy of Human
Nature* 278
Great Khan 190–1, 198, 259–70
Great Learning 317
*The Great Literary Repository of the Yung-lo
Reign* 278
Great Mongol Empire 238–40, 258–73
Great Proscription 152
Great Wall 92, 104, 116, 153, 187, 189–90, 202,
261, 284–5, 302
Greece 8, 16, 23, 25, 112, 116–17, 260
Guan Hanqing *see* Kuan Han-ch'ing
Guan Zhong *see* Kuan Chung
Guangdong province *see* Kwangtung province
Guangwudi (Liu Xiu) *see* Kuang-wu-ti (Liu
Hsiu)
Guangxi *see* Kwangsi
Guangxu *see* Kuang-hsü
Guangzhou *see* Canton
gunpowder
invention 234, 239, 323
military uses 239, 290–1, 323
mock battles 290–1
guns 21, 234, 239, 290–1, 323, 340–50
Guomindang *see* Kuomintang
Gutenberg 214

Hakkas 350–2
Han dynasties 100–67, 178, 333, 394
demise 155, 158–67
Former Han 100–39
interregnum 137–49
inventions 159–61, 213, 216, 333
Later Han 145–67
Han Feizi *see* Han Fei-tzu
Han Fei-tzu 85
Han state 90
Han T'o-wei 238
Han Tuowei *see* Han T'o-wei
Hangchow 238, 242, 343
Hangzhou *see* Hangchow
Hankou *see* Hankow
Hankow 182, 348
harems 146, 150–1, 247, 306–7
Later Han 146, 150–1
Ming dynasty 247, 306–7
harnesses 322
Hart, Robert 359–60
He Jin *see* Ho Chin
head-hunting practices, Ming armies 288–9
'Heaven'
concepts 27, 123–4, 130–1
Western Chou 27
Heavenly Principle Society 334
Hedi *see* Ho-ti

Hegemons
Chung-kuo 36
Duke of Ch'in 58
helicopters 322
Heshen *see* Ho-shen
High T'ang period 210–14
Hiroshima 393
historical documents 1–2, 94–5, 121–2,
126–7, 133–4, 138–40, 197, 200–1, 248,
278
see also writing
Historical Records 121–2
Hitler 392
Ho Chin 155–6
Ho-shen 334–5
Ho-ti 147, 150
Holy Roman Empire 234
Home sapiens 3
Homo erectus 2
Homo sapiens 3–11
homosexuals 115, 136, 316
Hong Kong 341–2, 345, 348–50, 369, 374
Hong Xiuquan *see* Hung Hsiu-ch'üan
Hongs 336–7, 339
Hongwu (Zhu Yuanzhang) *see* Hung-wu (Chu
Yüan-chang)
Hongxi *see* Hung-hsi
Hongzhi *see* Hung-chih
the Hoppo 336–7
horses 22, 32, 86, 175, 219, 226–7, 259, 275,
282
housing
early development 5–7
Great City Shang 12–13
Sung dynasty (960–1279) 247–8
Hsi-tsung 228–34
Hsia dynasty 8–11, 28, 34
Hsia Kingdom 237–9
Hsiao Tao-ch'eng, General 182
Hsiao Yen 182
Hsien-feng 357
Hsien-tsung 222, 225
Hsin dynasty 137–8
Hsiung-nu 103–5, 115–17, 121, 127, 153,
168–70
see also Huns
Hsüan-te 280–1
Hsüan-ti 128–31, 138
Hsüan-tsang 198
Hsüan-tsung 207–12, 216–18, 225–8
Hsüan-t'ung (P'u-i) 383–4, 386
Hu barbarians 96
Hu-hai (Second Emperor) 98–9
Huan-ti 148–51, 166
Huandi *see* Huan-ti
Huang Ch'ao 230–5
Huangdi (Yellow Emperor) *see* Huang-ti
(Yellow Emperor)
Huang-ti (Yellow Emperor) 10, 65, 83, 137, 140
Hubei *see* Hupei
Huidi *see* Hui-ti
Hui-ti 104–5

410

Poland 214, 259
political issues *see* governmental issues
Polo brothers 260
Polo, Marco 260–1, 315–16, 392
polygamy, Eastern Chou 38
Popes 260, 305
porcelain 301, 320–1, 323, 333
Portugal 292, 298, 314–21, 328, 336
postal system, Yüan dynasty 263
postmasters 102–3
pottery 4–6, 7, 14, 301, 320–1, 323, 333
Pottinger, Sir Henry 341–5
Prince Kung 349, 357, 364–5
Prince of Ning 291
Prince of Yen (Yung-lo) 277–80
Prince of Ying (Chung-tsung) 201–7
printing, invention 160, 213–14, 234, 236,
    243, 323
productivity issues 107, 249, 252, 321, 363–4
promissory notes, merchants 226, 249
propaganda 372
prose 226, 256–7, 278, 318–20
see also writing
psychological warfare 299
P'u-i (Hsüan-t'ung) 383–4, 386
Puyi (Xuantong) *see* P'u-i (Hsüan-t'ung)

qi concepts *see* ch'i concepts
Qi state *see* Ch'i state
Qiang *see* Ch'iang
Qianlong *see* Ch'ien-lung
Qin soldiers, terracotta figures *see* Ch'in
    soldiers, terracotta figures
Qin state *see* Ch'in state
Qing dynasty *see* Ch'ing dynasty
Qinling mountains *see* Ch'in-ling mountains
Qishan *see* Ch'i-shan
Qiu Fu *see* Ch'iu Fu
Qiying *see* Ch'i-ying

racial groupings 2–3
railways 366, 375–6, 384
Ran Qiu *see* Jan Ch'iu
'Rape of Nanking' 392–3
Records on Metal and Stone (Chao Te-fu) 254
Red Eyebrows 143–5
Red Turbans 272, 347
reformists 381–94
    Ch'ing dynasty 381–9
    Former Han 126–8, 131–2
    Hsin dynasty 140–2
relativity, Logicians 80
religious issues 7, 54–5
    see also rituals
    Buddhism 165–6, 171–6, 180, 198, 204,
        212–13, 220–8, 266–71, 290, 317
    Chou aristocracy 52–5
    Christianity 170, 173, 198, 224, 259–60,
        298–9, 305, 314–16, 327, 345, 347,
        351–5, 360–7, 375–6, 394
    Former Han 124–5, 131–2
    gods personified 54–5

Lungshan Culture 7
Mongols 262–70
    scepticism 62
    serfs 45
    Shang dynasty 16–18, 29
    Taoism 80–1
    Western Chou 27, 29
    world religious founders 60–1
Renzong (Ayurbarwada) *see* Jen-tsung
    (Ayurbarwada)
Republic of China 386–94
revolutionary movements 381–94
Ricci, Matteo 298–9, 314–18
rice fields 168, 178–9, 249
Righteous and Harmonious Fists *see* Boxers
The Ritual 49, 57
rituals
    see also ceremonies; religious issues
    ancestral temples 29, 54, 124–5, 132
    Eastern Chou 54–5
    Former Han 124–5
    li 67–9
    Lungshan Culture 7
    Ming dynasty 287–8, 293
    Western Chou 30
river systems, geographical details 1–11, 167,
    285
roads
    Former Han 107–8, 114, 120, 139
    Later Han 145
    Ming dynasty 318–19
    Shih-huang-ti 92
    Sui dynasty 189
    Sung dynasty (960–1279) 250–1
    unification 92
    Yüan dynasty 263
Romance of the Gods 320
The Romance of the Three Kingdoms 319
Romans 16, 112, 116, 119, 127, 142, 158–9, 165,
    170, 174, 186, 197, 260
Romantic Movement 333
route books 318–19
royal burials, Shang dynasty 15–16
royal-family protocols, Ming dynasty 308–9
Ruizong *see* Jui-tsung
Russell and Company 346
Russia 259, 327–8, 347, 355–6, 367–71,
    377–8, 385, 387, 389
    Ch'ing dynasty 327–8, 347, 355–6,
        367–71, 377–80
    Ili territory 367
    Japan 379–80
    Republic of China 387, 389
    revolutionary movements 385, 389
Rusticiano 261

sacrifices 110, 200
    Chou dynasty 27, 29
    food 17
    Former Han 131–2
    humans 16, 27, 87
    Ming dynasty 273–5

INDEX

INDEX